SCHAUM'S OUTLINE OF

THEORY AND PROBLEMS

of

PRINCIPLES OF ECONOMICS

•

by

DOMINICK SALVATORE, Ph.D.

Professor of Economics
Fordham University

and

EUGENE A. DIULIO, Ph.D.

Associate Professor of Economics
Fordham University

SCHAUM'S OUTLINE SERIES

McGRAW-HILL BOOK COMPANY

New York   St. Louis   San Francisco   Auckland   Bogotá   Düsseldorf   Johannesburg
London   Madrid   Mexico   Montreal   New Delhi   Panama   Paris
São Paulo   Singapore   Sydney   Tokyo   Toronto

DOMINICK SALVATORE received his Ph.D. in 1971 and is currently Professor of Economics at Fordham University. He is the author of the Schaum's Outlines of *Microeconomic Theory* and *International Economics,* and is the coauthor of *Development Economics.* His research has been published in numerous scholarly journals and presented at national and international conferences.

EUGENE A. DIULIO, currently Associate Professor of Economics at Fordham University, received his Ph.D. from Columbia University in 1966. He has also authored the Schaum's Outline of *Macroeconomic Theory*. His research has been in the area of financial markets and financial market rates.

Schaum's Outline of Theory and Problems of
PRINCIPLES OF ECONOMICS

6 7 8 9 10 11 12 13 14 15 16 17 18 19 20 SH SH 8 7 6

Sponsoring Editor, Harriet Malkin
Editing Supervisor, Denise Schanck
Production Manager, Nick Monti

Library of Congress Cataloging in Publication Data

Salvatore, Dominick, date.
   Schaum's outline of principles of economics.

   (Schaum's outline series)
   Includes index.
   1. Economics—Outlines, syllabi, etc. I. Diulio,
Eugene A., joint author. II. Title.
HB171.5.S245   330'.02'02   79-22713
ISBN 0-07-054487-5

Preface

The purpose of this book is to present in a clear and systematic way the analytical core of a one-semester and a one-year course in introductory economics. Students are often overwhelmed by the encyclopedic nature of introductory texts and need a clear and concise statement of the essentials. While primarily intended as a supplement to all introductory economics textbooks, the statements of theory and principles are sufficiently complete to enable its use as an independent text as well.

Each chapter begins with a statement of theory, principles and background information, fully illustrated with examples. This is followed by a set of multiple-choice review questions with answers. Numerous theoretical and practical problems are then presented with detailed, step-by-step solutions. These solved problems illustrate and amplify the theory, bring into sharp focus those fine points which the student often feels unsure of, and provide the application and reinforcement so vital to effective learning. There are also sample midterm and final examinations with answers.

The topics are arranged in the order in which they are usually covered in all basic economics textbooks and introductory courses. A one-semester course in economics usually covers Chapters 1–6, 8, 10, 15–16 and 19–20. In a one-year course, Chapters 1–13 are usually covered in the first semester stressing macroeconomics, and Chapters 1–2 and 14–23 in the second semester covering microeconomics. This sequence can be reversed, however, without loss of continuity.

The methodology of this book and its content have been tested in both small and large classes in introductory economics courses at Fordham University. The students were enthusiastic and made many valuable suggestions for improvements. To all of them, we are deeply grateful. We also would like to thank George Carovanos, Francis Hilton, Julie Ross and Kevin Wynne of our graduate school for their helpful comments.

In addition to *Principles of Economics*, the Schaum's Outline Series in Economics includes the following titles: *Microeconomic Theory, Macroeconomic Theory, International Economics, Development Economics* and *Mathematics for Economists*.

DOMINICK SALVATORE
EUGENE A. DIULIO

Contents

CONTENTS

CONTENTS

Chapter 1

Introduction to Economics

1.1 THE SUBJECT MATTER OF ECONOMICS

Economics is a social science which studies individuals and organizations engaged in the production, exchange and consumption of goods and services.

Economics seeks to develop principles, theories or models that isolate a few of the most important determinants or causes of economic events.   The goal is to develop policies that might prevent or correct such problems as unemployment, inflation and waste in the economy.

Economics is subdivided into *macroeconomics* and *microeconomics*.   Macroeconomics studies the *aggregate* level of economic activity, such as the total level of output, the level of national income, the total level of employment and the general price level for the economy viewed as a whole.   Microeconomics studies the economic behavior of *individual* decision-making units such as consumers, resource owners and business firms in a free-enterprise economy.

EXAMPLE 1. Economic conditions greatly affect all of us throughout our lives.   They affect where we live, what we eat, what school we attend, whether we go to work or to college, what job we get, and how much we earn.   Economic conditions affect the peace and stability in our cities and in the world.   Problems of unemployment and inflation fill the front pages of our newspapers and news programs.   It is practically impossible in today's complex world to be a responsible citizen without some grasp of economic issues and principles.   Economics seeks to give us a better understanding of how our economy operates and what can be done to avoid, correct or alleviate unemployment, inflation and waste.

1.2 THE PROBLEM OF SCARCITY

Economic resources of labor, capital and land are scarce or in limited supply in every society. Since resources are scarce, the amounts of goods and services that can be produced are also limited. As a result, society must use its scarce resources as efficiently as possible to produce the goods and services most wanted by society.

Scarcity is the fundamental or central problem of every society.   Without scarcity, there would be no need to study economics.   It is because economic resources and goods and services are scarce that they are not free but command a price.

EXAMPLE 2. Scarcity affects each individual.   Time is scarce for the individual.   In a given day, if a person spends 8 hours sleeping, 4 hours in class and another 2 hours traveling and eating, the person has only 10 hours left to study, play or watch TV.   The more hours spent playing or watching TV, the fewer left to study. Money may also be scarce for an individual.   If a person buys a new car, he or she may have to forego a vacation.

Scarcity is also the crucial economic problem for society as a whole.   The greater the number of people trained to provide medical services, the fewer available to be lawyers, teachers or accountants.   As more of society's capital equipment is used to produce cars, less is available to produce washing machines, motorboats or bicycles.   If more land is used to produce wheat, less is available to produce corn or for buildings.   Thus, in economics, we deal with *economic resources* and *economic goods* and *services* to stress the crucial fact that they are scarce and therefore command a price rather than being free.

1.3 PRODUCTION POSSIBILITIES

A production possibility schedule or table shows the different combinations of two commodities that society can produce by fully employing all of its resources with the best technology available.

It also indicates how much of one commodity must be given up in order to release enough resources to produce more of a second commodity.   When a production possibilities schedule is graphed, we get the *production possibilities curve* or *transformation curve*.

Since resources are not equally efficient in the production of both commodities, for each additional unit of a commodity we produce, the more we must give up of the second commodity.   Thus, we generally face increasing costs of production.

EXAMPLE 3.   Table 1 presents a production possibilities schedule which illustrates the rising costs of producing food.

Table 1

Alternative or Point	Units of Food	Units of Cloth	Cost of Additional Units of Food
A	0	10	1
B	1	9	2
C	2	7	3
D	3	4	4
E	4	0	

Table 1 shows that this society can either produce no food and 10 units of cloth (point *A*), 1 unit of food and 9 units of cloth (point *B*), 2 food and 7 cloth (point *C*), 3 food and 4 cloth (point *D*), or 4 food and no cloth (point *E*).   Moving from *A* to *B* in Table 1 shows that by reducing the units of cloth produced from 10 to 9, just enough resources or factors of production are released to produce the first unit of food.   Thus, the cost to produce this first unit of food is equal to the 1 unit of cloth that had to be given up.   A movement from *B* to *C* shows that we have to give up 2 units of cloth (from 9 to 7 units) to produce the second unit of food. Thus, the cost of this second unit of food equals the 2 units of cloth that had to be given up.   To get the third unit of food, 3 units of cloth must be given up (a movement from *C* to *D*).   Finally, the cost of getting the fourth unit of food is 4 in terms of the amount of cloth that must be given up.   Thus, as we produce more food, we incur higher and higher costs in terms of cloth foregone.   This is so because we must use resources which are less efficient in the production of food.

EXAMPLE 4.   In Fig. 1-1, the data of Table 1 is represented graphically as the production possibilities curve.   Note that the production possibilities curve is concave to the origin or bulges outward.   As we move down from point *A* to point *E* we incur rising costs in food production.   This is indicated by the downward arrows of increasing length along the vertical cloth axis.   A point inside the production possibilities curve such as *U* implies that the economy is not utilizing all of its available resources and/or not using the best technology available to it.   A point outside (such as *F*) cannot be reached with the resources and technology available.

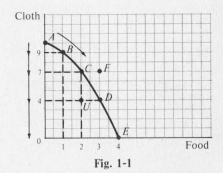

Fig. 1-1

1.4 FUNDAMENTAL ECONOMIC QUESTIONS

Every society, regardless of its political organization, must answer three fundamental economic questions.   These are: "what to produce," "how to produce" and "for whom to produce."   What to produce refers to the kinds and quantities of goods and services to be produced.   How to produce refers to the combination of various resources and the techniques to use in production.   For whom to produce refers to how to divide up what has been produced among the consumers in the economy.   These questions arise only because resources (and, therefore, commodities) are scarce.

EXAMPLE 5.   Every society must somehow decide how many luxurious mansions and how many low-cost apartments to construct, how many full-size and compact cars to build, how many schools to erect and teachers to train, how much food and medical services to provide, and how many civilian and defense goods and services to produce.   Since goods such as houses and cars, and services such as education and medical treatments can usually be produced with many different techniques and combinations of labor, capital and land, it is crucial to determine which of the many techniques and factor combinations available are to be used.   Finally, the distribution of high and low incomes among the population will determine the quantity of mansions, full-size cars, private schools and exotic and expensive foods produced as well as the availability of low-cost apartments, compact cars and basic education, food and clothing.

1.5   CAPITALISM AND THE CIRCULAR FLOW OF ECONOMIC ACTIVITY

In a capitalistic or free-enterprise economy, the three fundamental economic questions of what, how and for whom to produce are answered by the price-mechanism.   Only those commodities for which consumers are willing to pay a price per unit sufficient to cover the cost of producing them are normally produced or supplied.   Since resources are scarce, goods and services are to be produced with the technique and resource combinations which minimize costs of production.   Finally, the economy will produce the goods and services that satisfy the wants of those people who have the money to pay for them.   All these questions are answered in the process of the circular flow of economic activity as described in Example 6.

EXAMPLE 6.   During the course of business activity, firms purchase or hire economic resources supplied by individuals and households in order to produce the goods and services demanded by individuals and households.   Individuals and households then use the income received from the sale of resources (or their services) to business firms to purchase the goods and services produced by business firms.   In this circular flow of economic activity, commodity and resource prices are determined (see Chapter 2); what goods are to be produced, how they are to be produced, and for whom they are to be produced are also determined.   The economy also provides for its own maintenance and growth [see Problem 1.17(c)].

In a mixed economy such as in the U.S. today, this process is often modified by government action.   In a planned or centralized economy such as that of the U.S.S.R., the fundamental questions of what, how and for whom to produce are determined for the most part by a planning committee.

Important Economic Terms

Circular flow of economic activity.   The flow of resources (or factors of production) from households to business firms and of goods and services from business firms to households.

Economic principle, theory or model.   A generalization and abstraction of reality that seeks to isolate a few of the most important determinants or causes of an economic event in order to develop policies that might prevent, correct or alleviate economic problems.

Economic resources or factors of production.   Labor of various types and skills, equipment such as machinery, factories and transportation networks, and agricultural, mining and construction land that are available to society to produce goods and services.

Economics.   A social science that studies how individuals and organizations in society engage in the production, exchange and consumption of goods and services.   Or, the study of the allocation of scarce resources to satisfy human wants.

Fallacy of composition.   An invalid or incorrect generalization from the individual to society.

Macroeconomics.   The study of the *aggregate* level of economic activity, such as the total level of output, the level of national income, the total level of employment and the general price level for the economy viewed as a whole.

Microeconomics.   The study of the economic behavior of *individual* decision-making units such as consumers, resource owners and business firms in a free-enterprise economy.

Mixed free-enterprise system.   One in which the operation of the price mechanism is modified in various degrees by the government in order to solve the basic economic questions of what, how and for whom to produce.

Production possibilities or transformation curve.   The graphic representation of the various alternative combinations of two commodities that society can produce by utilizing fully all of its economic resources and the best available technology.

Scarcity.   The limited availability of economic resources and goods and services.

Review Questions

1. Economics studies individuals and organizations in society engaged in the (a) production of goods and services, (b) exchange of goods and services, (c) consumption of goods and services, (d) all of the above.
    Ans.   (d)

2. Economic principles, theories or models seek to
    (a) explain and predict economic events in the hope of developing policies to correct economic problems,
    (b) identify all the numerous detailed causes of an economic event,
    (c) develop rules of individual economic behavior in order to generalize and predict society's economic behavior,
    (d) all of the above.
    Ans.   (a)

3. Which of the following does *not* refer to macroeconomics?
    (a) The study of the aggregate level of economic activity.
    (b) The study of the economic behavior of individual decision-making units such as consumers, resource owners and business firms.
    (c) The studies of the causes and the policies to reduce the level of unemployment.
    (d) The study of the causes and possible causes for inflation.
    Ans.   (b)

4. The central economic problem of every society is (a) to maintain peace in the world, (b) to prevent riots in our cities, (c) the scarcity of economic resources, (d) to preserve democracy.
    Ans.   (c)

5. The word "economic" refers to (a) scarce, (b) limited, (c) commanding a price, (d) all of the above.
    Ans.   (d)

6. A production possibilities curve shows
    (a) how much of the resources of society are used to produce a particular commodity,
    (b) the various alternative combinations of two commodities that can be produced,
    (c) the rate of unemployment in the economy,
    (d) the rate of inflation.
    Ans.   (b)

7. Which of the following statements is *not* true?
    (a) In the real world, we generally face increasing costs of production.
    (b) Increasing costs of production mean that we must give up increasing amounts of a commodity to release enough resources to produce each additional unit of a second commodity.
    (c) Increasing costs of production arise because resources are homogeneous or equally efficient in the production of all commodities.
    (d) Increasing costs of production are reflected in a concave production possibilities curve.
    Ans.   (c)

8. The fundamental or central economic problem of every society is (a) what to produce, (b) how to produce, (c) for whom to produce, (d) all of the above.

    Ans. (d)

9. "What to produce" refers to
    (a) which goods and services and how much of each is to be produced,
    (b) how many of the wants of various people are to be satisfied,
    (c) which goods and services to produce to maximize the rate of economic growth,
    (d) the combination of resources and techniques of production to be used.

    Ans. (a)

10. "How to produce" refers to
    (a) which goods and services and how much of each are to be produced,
    (b) how many of the wants of various people are to be satisfied,
    (c) how to maintain the economic system by replacing capital goods used up in the production process,
    (d) the combination of resources and techniques of production to be used.

    Ans. (d)

11. "For whom to produce" refers to
    (a) who should receive the goods and services produced,
    (b) how many of the wants of various people are to be satisfied,
    (c) how much of current production should go toward economic growth,
    (d) those who can save to provide for the maintenance of the system.

    Ans. (b)

12. In a free-enterprise economy, the questions of what, how and for whom to produce are solved by (a) a planning committee, (b) the elected representatives of the people, (c) the price-mechanism, (d) none of the above.

    Ans. (c)

Solved Problems

THE SUBJECT MATTER OF ECONOMICS

1.1.   (a) Explain the statement "Economics is a social science."   (b) Why is the study of economics important?

   (a)   The social sciences study how society is organized and functions.   Economics, sociology, anthropology, psychology and political science are all social sciences.   Each studies the organization and functioning of society from a particular point of view.   Economics studies how individuals and organizations in society engage in the production, exchange and consumption of goods and services.

   (b)   An understanding of basic economic issues and principles is essential to be a well-informed and responsible citizen.   Our newspapers and news programs are filled with information about unemployment, inflation, price controls, taxes, energy, imports, the monopoly power of large corporations and other problems.   Without some knowledge of economics, it is practically impossible to understand the issues involved and form sensible opinions on these important matters. Economics can also help individuals to operate their businesses and control their personal finances by providing a basis for understanding how to protect or reduce the impact of inflation, how tax reforms and energy conservation programs affect them, etc.

1.2.   (a) How are economic principles, theories or laws developed?   What is their function?
        (b) What are some of the difficulties in studying economics?

   (a)   Economic principles, theories or laws are abstractions and generalizations of reality.   They seek to cut through the many details surrounding an economic event to arrive at and isolate a few of its most important causes or determinants.   For example, inflation or rising prices is the result of many causes, but if we can isolate a few of its most important determinants we may learn to control them and so prevent or reduce inflation.   Thus, the function of economic principles is that they may enable us to predict and explain recession, inflation and other economic problems.   This is the essential first step in the attempt to develop policies that might correct economic problems or reduce their most harmful effects.

(b)   Some of the difficulties in studying economics are:

(1)   Our preconceived notions about the cause and cure of economic problems are often either completely wrong or partially wrong and misleading.

(2)   Generalizing from individual experiences often leads to wrong conclusions (this is called *the fallacy of composition*).   For example, when an individual increases his savings he becomes richer, but when society as a whole saves more by demanding fewer goods and services it may become poorer by putting people out of work.

(3)   The fact that one economic event precedes another does not necessarily imply cause and effect.   For example, the collapse of the stock market did not cause the subsequent Great Depression; both were caused by other factors.

(4)   Since economics is a social science and laboratory experiments cannot be conducted, economic laws can only describe average behavior.   Thus, they are not as precise or reliable as natural laws, such as the law of gravity.

1.3.   (a) Distinguish between macroeconomics and microeconomics.   (b) Which of these two areas is generally more appealing?

(a)   *Macroeconomics* studies the economy as a whole or in major components such as households, business and government.   It deals with the *aggregate* (or total) level of output and employment, the level of national income and the general price level.   It deals with total private expenditures, total investments, total government expenditures and total imports and exports of goods and services.   It seeks the causes and cures for unemployment, inflation and balance of payments deficits.

   Microeconomics, on the other hand, studies the economic behavior of *individual* decision-making units such as consumers, resource owners and business firms in a free-enterprise system (i.e. one in which the government does not directly control economic activity).   It deals with how an individual consumer spends his income to maximize satisfaction, how a business firm combines resources or factors of production to maximize profits and how the price of each commodity and each type of resource is determined by demand and supply.   It studies how these individual decisions are affected by different forms of market organization.

(b)   Experience shows that students are generally more interested and identify more closely with the macroeconomic problems of unemployment and inflation than with microeconomic problems of the individual's and the firm's allocations of income and resources.   Because of this, macroeconomics is usually presented first.   However, both are important and should be studied.   After an overview of demand and supply (Chapter 2), this book follows most other texts in presenting macroeconomics first (Chapters 3–13) and then microeconomics (Chapters 14–23).

THE PROBLEM OF SCARCITY

1.4.   (a) Distinguish between economic resources and noneconomic resources.   (b) In terms of economics, discuss the meaning of labor, (c) capital, (d) land.

(a)   Economic resources (factors of production or inputs) are the various types of labor, capital equipment, and land required to produce goods and services.   Since in every society these resources are not unlimited in supply but are limited or scarce, they command a price (i.e. they are *economic* resources).   Economic resources can be contrasted with noneconomic resources such as air, which (in the absence of pollution) is practically unlimited in supply and, therefore, free.   In economics, our interest lies with economic resources rather than with noneconomic resources.

(b)   Labor refers to the various types of skills which the people of a nation possess and which can be used to produce goods and services.   These range from the rudimentary skills of the ditchdigger at one extreme to the specialized skills of the surgeon at the other.   Some of these skills are much more productive than others, require a great deal more effort in acquiring and cost much more to hire.   Entrepreneurial ability is a very special type of skill.   The entrepreneur is a person who sets up a firm by combining labor, capital and land to supply a good or service that he or she thinks society wants.   Thus, while labor in general receives wages, entrepreneurs hope to make profits.

(c)   Capital refers to all manmade tools, equipment, machinery, buildings and transportation networks which are used in and facilitate the production of consumer goods and services.   A man with a shovel produces very little compared to a man with a tractor.   But some present consumption must be sacrificed to release the resources to produce the tractor.   Those who make the sacrifice and save are induced and rewarded with interest income.   Note that the purchase of a stock, which in everyday language is referred to as an investment, is simply a financial transaction from an economic point of view.   An investment in economics refers to the actual use of resources to create a piece of machinery, a factory or a road to facilitate future production.

(d)   Land refers to the agricultural, mineral and construction areas or sites available to society.   To some extent, these "gifts of nature" are given and fixed.   Agricultural land, however, can be destroyed by erosion or increased by reclamation projects.   The owners of land receive rental income from the users of this resource.

1.5.   (a) How did the petroleum crisis bring the problem of scarcity to public attention?   What is the relationship between scarcity and economics?   (b) Discuss the statement "Economics studies the allocation of scarce means among competing ends."

(a)   The more than quadrupling of petroleum prices since 1972 greatly affected each and every one of us.   We now drive smaller cars, use less heat in our homes, and spend more of our income for gasoline, oil bills, and petroleum imports.   Other nations with less petroleum and coal resources were affected even more adversely.   More important than these personal sacrifices, the petroleum crisis forcefully reminded us of the limitation of all our resources and the need to economize or use them as efficiently as possible.   If resources were not scarce or limited, there would be no need to economize or use them efficiently and so there would be no need to study economics.

(b)   A more sophisticated definition of economics than that given in Section 1.1 is to say that economics studies the allocation (use) of scarce (limited) means (resources or factors of production) among competing (conflicting) ends (aims).   That is, the economic aim of society is the production of goods and services for consumption.   Since the resources to produce goods and services are scarce, we cannot produce all the goods and services and as much of each as we want.   Thus, we have competing or conflicting uses for our scarce resources.   The more we use them to produce some goods and services (or waste them), the less are available to produce others.

PRODUCTION-POSSIBILITIES

1.6.   Explain the production-possibilities schedule given in Table 2, citing the assumptions on which it is based.

Table 2

Alternative or Point	Units of Food	Units of Cloth
A	0	8.0
B	1	7.5
C	2	6.5
D	3	5.0
E	4	3.0
G	5	0.0

A production-possibilities schedule shows the various alternative combinations of two commodities that society can produce on the assumption that all of its resources and the best technology available are used.   Table 2 shows that this economy can produce either 0 units of food and 8 units of cloth, 1 unit of food and 7.5 units of cloth, 2 food and 6.5 cloth, 3 food and 5 cloth, 4 food and 3 cloth, *or* 5 food and 0 cloth.   Note that since we start with the assumption that society is utilizing all of its resources and the best technology available, the only way it can produce more units of food is by giving up some of its cloth production so as to release resources to produce more food.   Thus, we say that the cost of each additional unit of food produced equals the opportunities foregone or the amount of cloth that had to be given up.   What we are measuring, then, is the *opportunity cost* of food.

1.7.   (*a*) Starting from zero food production in Table 2, find the cost of producing each additional unit of food in terms of the amount of cloth that must be given up.   (*b*) Why are food costs rising?

(*a*)   Looking at Table 2, we see that in order to produce the first unit of food we must give up 0.5 units of cloth (from 8.0 to 7.5).   Thus, the opportunity cost of the first unit of food is 0.5 (units of cloth given up).   To produce the second unit of food, 1 unit of cloth has to be given up (from 7.5 to 6.5), and the (opportunity) cost of the second unit of food is 1.   Similarly, the cost of obtaining the third unit of food is 1.5; for the fourth it is 2 and for the fifth it is 3.   This is summarized in the fourth column of Table 2A.   Notice that the cost of each additional unit is rising.   This is referred to as *the law of increasing costs*.

Table 2A

Alternative or Point	Units of Food	Units of Cloth	Cost of Additional Units of Food
A	0	8.0	0.5
B	1	7.5	1.0
C	2	6.5	1.5
D	3	5.0	2.0
E	4	3.0	3.0
G	5	0.0	

(*b*)   The cost of producing each additional unit of food rises because resources are not homogeneous.   That is, the resources of a nation are not all equally efficient in the production of food and cloth.   As a result, to produce the first unit of food, the nation uses those resources which are most efficient in food production and least efficient in cloth production.   Thus, the amount of cloth that must be given up to produce the first unit of food is very little.   But as we want more and more food, resources must be utilized which are less and less efficient in food production and more and more efficient in cloth production.   As a result the cost of each additional unit of food increases in terms of the amount of cloth that must be given up.

1.8.   Draw a production-possibilities curve from the data in Table 2.   On the same figure, plot point *U* referring to 3 units of food and 3 units of cloth and point *H* referring to 3.5 units of food and 6 units of cloth.   What do points *U* and *H* indicate?

By plotting on a set of axes each of the alternative combinations of food and cloth production shown in Table 2, we get the corresponding production-possibilities curve.   The curve, and points *U* and *H*, are shown in Figure 1-2.

Point *U* inside the production-possibilities curve implies that resources are not fully employed and/or that this economy is not utilizing the best technology available to it.   That is, there are unemployed and/or underemployed resources.   By fully employing all of its resources and using the best technology available, this society can move from point *U* inside to a point on the production-possibilities curve and produce either the same units of food but more cloth (point *D*), the same cloth and more food (point *E*), or more food and cloth (a point between *D* and *E* on the curve).   A point such as *H*, outside (or above) the transformation curve, involves a combination of food and cloth which this society cannot produce with its presently available resources and technology.

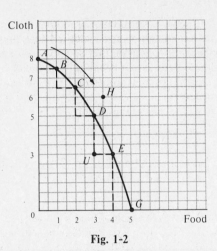

Fig. 1-2

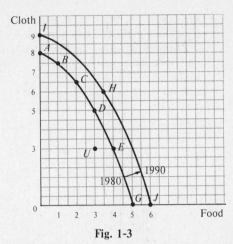

Fig. 1-3

1.9. (a) How does the slope of the transformation curve in Fig. 1-2 imply increasing food costs? Increasing cloth costs? (b) How can growth be represented for this economy?

(a) Increasing food and cloth costs are reflected in a concave or bulging out transformation curve. Moving down the transformation curve from point A to points B,C,D,E and G shows that to produce each additional unit of food (the one-unit length horizontal dashed lines in Fig. 1-2), we must give up more and more units of cloth (the vertical dashed lines of increasing length). Moving up the transformation curve from point G to points E,D,C,B and A shows increasing costs in cloth production. By giving up the last or fifth unit of food, resources are released to produce the first 3 units of cloth (a movement from point G to point E). Thus, the average cost of producing the first 3 units of cloth is 1/3 (unit of food that must be given up). By giving up the fourth unit of food, 2 more units of cloth can be produced (a movement from point E to point D) at an average cost of 1/2 (up from 1/3). The student should continue this process up to point A.

(b) A particular production-possibilities curve is a picture at one point in time. Through time, the resources of the nation grow (except for those depleted) and technology improves. As this occurs, the nation's transformation curve shifts up or outward, indicating that it can produce both more food and cloth. In Fig. 1-3, transformation curve ABCDEG (the same as in Fig. 1-2) indicates the choices open to society, say in 1980, while transformation curve IHJ shows what is possible after growth, say in 1990. Note that if the resources and technology that grow through time are more appropriate for food than for cloth production, the transformation curve will shift more along the horizontal than along the vertical axis and vice versa.

1.10. Refer to the production possibilities schedule in Table 3. (a) Find the (opportunity) cost of food (in terms of cloth). How is this cost condition different from that discussed in Problem 1.7? To what is the difference due? Is this new cost situation realistic? Why? (b) Plot the production possibilities curve. How is it different from that of Problem 1.7? What is the marginal cost of food and cloth on this new transformation curve? How are they different from the marginal cost of food and cloth examined in Problem 1.7?

Table 3

Alternative or Point	Units of Food	Units of Cloth
A	0	8
B	1	6
C	2	4
D	3	2
E	4	0

(a) Table 3A is the same as Table 3, except for the addition of the fourth column giving the cost of food.   From the last column in Table 3A, we see that to produce each additional unit of food, 2 units of cloth must be given up.   The (opportunity) cost of food (in terms of cloth) equals 2 and is constant in this case, while it rose in the earlier case.   Constant cost would occur only if all resources are equally efficient in the production of food and cloth.   This is unrealistic and so in the real world we usually have increasing costs.

Table 3A

Alternative or Point	Units of Food	Units of Cloth	Cost of Food
A	0	8	
B	1	6	2
C	2	4	2
D	3	2	2
E	4	0	2

(b) Plotting the food and cloth alternatives shown in Table 3, we get the production possibilities curve in Fig. 1-4.   While the transformation curves seen earlier were concave or bulging out, the one in Fig. 1-4 is a straight line.   The slope of this new type of transformation curve is constant and equals 2, the cost of food.   The slope of the transformation curves seen earlier increased or became steeper as we moved down, indicating rising food costs.   The slope of the transformation curve here remains constant and indicates constant food (and cloth) costs.

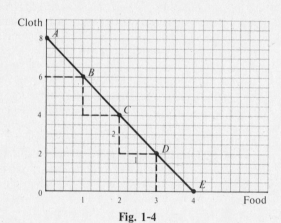

Fig. 1-4

FUNDAMENTAL ECONOMIC QUESTIONS

1.11.   (a) Why is "what to produce" a problem in every economy?   (b) Why is "how to produce" a problem?   (c) "For whom to produce"?   (d) What other general economic problems do societies face?

(a) "What to produce" refers to those goods and services and the quantity of each that the economy should produce.   Since resources are scarce or limited, no economy can produce as much of every good or service as desired by all members of society.   More of one good or service usually means less of others.   Therefore, every society must choose exactly which goods and services to produce and how much of each to produce.

(b) "How to produce" refers to the choice of the combination of resources and the particular technique to use in producing a good or service.   Since a good or service can normally be produced with different resource combinations and different techniques, the problem is which of these to use. Since resources are limited in every economy, when more of them are used to produce some goods and services, less are available to produce others.   Therefore, society faces the problem of choosing the technique which results in the least possible cost (in terms of resources used) for each unit of the goods and services it decides to produce.

(c) "For whom to produce" refers to how much of the wants of each consumer are to be satisfied. Since resources and thus goods and services are scarce in every economy, no society can satisfy all of the wants of all of its people.   Thus, a problem of choice arises.

(d) Besides answering the what, how and for whom questions, society must also ensure that all of its resources are fully employed, that the best technology available is used, and that there is no inflation.   In addition, society must provide for the maintenance and growth of the economic system.   The maintenance of the economic system is accomplished by providing for the replacement of the skills, machinery, buildings etc. that are used up in the course of producing the current outputs.   Economic growth depends on the growth of resources and technological improvements.   In order to provide more and better skills, equipment and technology so as to ensure future growth, resources must be released from the production of goods and services for present consumption.   Sacrifices must be made in the present in order to be able to produce more in the future.

CAPITALISM AND THE CIRCULAR FLOW OF ECONOMIC ACTIVITY

1.12.   What are the distinguishing characteristics of a capitalistic economic system?

The distinguishing characteristics are as follows:

(1)   In a capitalistic (also referred to as a free-enterprise or *laissez-faire*) system, most of the means of production are owned privately by individuals and organizations rather than by the government.

(2)   Individuals are free to sell their resources (or the use of their resources) in amounts as they see fit and for the highest price they can obtain.   Individuals are also free to spend their income to buy the goods and services that maximize their satisfactions.   Entrepreneurs have the freedom to set up new business enterprises, to run them by combining resources and using the technology which minimize costs of production, and to sell their output in markets where profits can be maximized.

(3)   Competition, or the existence in the marketplace of many sellers and buyers, each too small to affect the price of goods and services.

(4)   The functions of government are strictly limited to providing for defense and a few basic services, and to enforcing general rules for protecting economic and political freedoms.   This reflects the capitalistic belief that individuals are the best judges of their own welfare and that as individuals seek to maximize their welfare, the welfare of society in general is also promoted.   As an extreme form of economic and political organization stressing personal freedoms, a pure capitalistic society does not, and probably never did, exist.   In the U.S. and other western democracies, we have a mixed-enterprise system in which the government often modifies and sometimes *replaces* the operation of the market as a method of allocating scarce resources.   See Section 2.6.

1.13.   What aspects of all developed economies are responsible for their superior ability to produce goods and services?

One important aspect of all modern economies, regardless of their form of organization, is the use of skilled labor, a great deal of capital equipment and advanced technology to produce goods and services.   With minimal training and education, no capital equipment and primitive technology, very little can be produced.   Training, education and sophisticated equipment embodying advanced technology increase productivity substantially.

A *second* important characteristic of all modern societies is division of labor and specialization in production.   This means that the population within a given geographic region, instead of being self-sufficient and producing the full range of goods and services demanded, expends most of its time and resources in the production of only one or a few goods and services in which its efficiency is greatest. Thus, specialization and division of labor allows large increases in productivity.   By then exchanging part of the goods and services so produced for other wanted goods and services, the nation as a whole ends up consuming many more kinds of goods and services, in greater quantities, than would be possible by attempting self-sufficiency.

A *third* important characteristic of modern societies is the use of money as a means of facilitating exchange.   In a *barter* economy (i.e. one where there is no money), each individual would have to seek others who both want what he wants to sell and have exactly what he wants to purchase. This is extremely difficult and time consuming.

1.14. (*a*) Draw a diagram showing the direction of the flows of goods, services, resources and money between business firms and households. (*b*) Explain why a cost to households represents income for business firms, and vice versa.

(*a*) Figure 1-5 is a simple schematic model of the economy.

(*b*) The top loop in Fig. 1-5 shows that households purchase goods and services from business firms. Thus, what is a cost or a consumption expenditure from the point of view of households represents the income or the money receipts of business firms. On the other hand, the bottom loop shows that business firms purchase the services of economic resources from households. Thus, a cost of production for business firms represents money income for households.

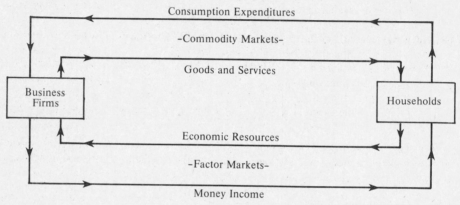

Fig. 1-5

1.15. (*a*) How does the price-mechanism solve the problem of what to produce in a capitalistic economy? (*b*) In a mixed economy? (*c*) In a centralized economy?

(*a*) In a free-enterprise economy, only those commodities for which consumers are willing to pay a price per unit sufficiently high to cover at least the full cost of production will be supplied by producers in the long run. By paying a higher price, consumers can normally induce producers to increase the quantity of a commodity supplied in any time period. On the other hand, a reduction in price will normally result in a reduction in the quantity supplied.

(*b*) In a mixed economy such as ours, government (through taxes, subsidies, its own expenditures, etc.) modifies and, in some instances (by imposing direct controls), replaces the operation of the price-mechanism as a means of determining what to produce.

(*c*) In a completely centralized economy, the dictator, or more likely a planning committee appointed by the dictator or the party, determines exactly what to produce. We in the West believe that this is inefficient. Our feeling seems to be confirmed by the fact that the Soviet Union, never a completely centralized economy, has been moving recently toward even more decentralized control and toward greater reliance on the price-mechanism as the determinant of what to produce.

1.16. (*a*) How does the price-mechanism solve the problem of how to produce in a capitalistic economy? (*b*) In a mixed economy? (*c*) In a centralized economy?

(*a*) In a free-enterprise economy, the price-mechanism freely solves the "how to produce" problem. Because the price of a resource normally represents its relative scarcity, the best technique to use in producing a good or service is the one that results in the least dollar cost of production. If the price of a factor rises in relation to the price of others used in the production of the good or service, producers will switch to a technique which uses less of the more expensive factor in order to minimize their costs of production. The opposite occurs when the price of a resource falls in relation to the price of others.

(*b*) In a mixed economy, the operation of the price-mechanism in solving the "how to produce" problem is modified and sometimes replaced by government action.

(c) In a centralized economy, this problem is solved by a planning committee, and not by the price-mechanism.

1.17.   (a) How does the price-mechanism solve the problem of for whom to produce in a capitalistic society?   (b) In a mixed economy?   (c) How are the maintenance and growth of the system provided for in a capitalistic society?

(a) In the absence of government regulation or control of the economy, the problem of "for whom to produce" is also solved by the price-mechanism.   The economy will produce those commodities satisfying the wants of those people who have the money to pay for them.   The higher the income of an individual, the more the economy will be geared to produce the commodities he wants (if he is also willing to pay for them).

(b) In the name of equity and fairness, governments usually modify the workings of the price-mechanism by taking from the rich (through taxation) and redistributing to the poor (through subsidies and welfare payments).   They also raise taxes in order to provide for certain "public" goods, such as education, law and order, and defense.

(c) The maintenance of the system in a free-enterprise economy is assured by output prices which are usually sufficiently high to allow producers to cover not only their day-to-day production expenditures but also to allow for the depreciation of capital goods.   Similarly, in a free-enterprise economy, the price-mechanism also determines, to a large extent, the rate of economic growth. For example, the prospect of higher wages motivates labor to acquire more skills.   Capital accumulation and technological improvements also respond to expectations of profits.

1.18.   (a) What are the major economic goals of most western democracies?   (b) How do governments seek to achieve these goals?   (c) What are the major shortcomings of economics today?

(a) The major goals of western democracies are the achievement and maintenance of full employment without inflation, an "adequate" rate of growth, and an equitable distribution of income.   This list is neither complete nor is the order of importance of these goals generally agreed upon.   Full employment is attained when all those seeking work are able to find work, except for 3 or 4 percent of the labor force temporarily out of work because they are in the process of changing jobs (frictional unemployment).   No inflation means stable prices, or prices which rise very slowly, at say, 1 or 2 percent per year.   Economic growth refers to more and better goods and services, or a rising standard of living.   An equitable distribution of income is one which avoids "very poor" and "very rich" and reduces income inequalities throughout the economy. More precise goals may not be specified and the ones stated here may be open to controversy.

(b) Governments usually attempt to achieve full employment without inflation with fiscal and monetary policies.   When they fail they may rely on direct government job-creating programs and direct price controls.   Economic growth can be stimulated with tax incentives, subsidies, sponsored basic research, etc.   Only recently, and primarily as the result of the petroleum crisis and shortage, has serious concern about conservation and the environment come to the fore.

An equitable distribution of income is sought through progressive taxation (i.e. high-income people paying a higher percentage of their income in taxes than lower-income people) and welfare programs for the poor.   Sometimes the pursuit of some of these goals facilitates the achievement of others.   For example, eliminating unemployment also results in greater economic growth. At other times, the pursuit of some goals (such as the elimination of unemployment) may make the achievement of others (such as price stability) more difficult.

(c) The major shortcoming of economics in recent years has been its inability to specify consistent and effective policies to reduce the rate of unemployment and inflation to less than 6 percent annually.   On a more general level, economics may have become too abstract and too mathematical and divorced from real world problems and their solutions.   It has also frequently failed to incorporate the contribution that other social sciences might have made to shed light and help provide solutions to many social problems.   These shortcomings should not, however, detract from the great importance and many achievements of economics.   After all, medicine, perhaps the most esteemed of the sciences, still does not know the cause and cure of many diseases. It is in recognition of its generally superior achievements that economics is the only social science in which Nobel Prizes are given.

Chapter 2

Demand, Supply and Equilibrium

2.1 DEMAND

An individual's *demand schedule* shows the amounts of a commodity that the individual is willing and able to purchase in a given time period at various alternative commodity prices. The graphic representation of the individual's demand schedule is his *demand curve*. The demand curve slopes downward (from left to right) because the individual will buy more of a commodity at lower prices. This is known as the *law of demand*. It results because as the price of a commodity falls, the individual substitutes this commodity for others in consumption. For example, when the price of coffee falls, the individual consumes more coffee and less tea. Also, when the price of a commodity falls, the person is able to buy more of it with the same money income.

The sum of the demand curves of *all* individuals in the market for a commodity gives the *market demand curve* for the commodity.

EXAMPLE 1. Table 1 gives an individual's demand schedule and the market demand schedule for wheat. Assume that there are 1000 identical individuals in the market. The table shows that at the high price of $5 per bushel, 3.5 bushels of wheat per month will be bought by one individual and 3500 bushels will be bought by the 1000 individuals in the market (point *A*). If the price were lower, say $3 per bushel, each individual would buy 6 bushels per month; 6000 would be bought by the market as a whole (point *E*). At the low price of $1 per bushel, the individual will purchase 11 bushels per month, while the market purchases 11,000 (point *G*). Note that the lower the price, the greater the quantity demanded by the individual and the market.

Table 1

Price ($ per bu.)	Quantity Demanded by One Individual (bu. per mo.)	Quantity Demanded in the Market (bu. per mo.)	Alternative or Point
5	3.5	3,500	A
4	4.5	4,500	B
3	6.0	6,000	E
2	8.0	8,000	F
1	11.0	11,000	G

EXAMPLE 2. Plotting each pair of price-quantity values in Table 1 as a point on a graph and joining the points, we get the individual's demand curve and the market demand curve for wheat shown in Fig. 2-1. This shows

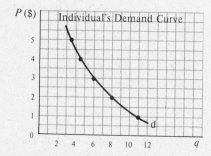
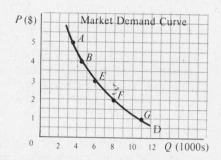

Fig. 2-1

14

that if the price of wheat is $5 per bushel (measured along the vertical axis), the individual will purchase 3.5 bushels of wheat per month (measured along the horizontal axis, in the left panel of Fig. 2-1) and the market will purchase 3500 bushels (point *A* in the right panel), etc.   Note that both demand curves are negatively sloped (i.e. slope downward to the right) indicating that at lower prices, the quantities demanded are greater.

2.2 SUPPLY

An individual producer's *supply schedule* shows the amounts of a commodity that the producer is willing to supply over a given period of time at various alternative prices.   The graphic representation of the individual producer's supply schedule gives the *supply curve*.   This usually slopes up (from left to right) because higher prices must be paid to induce the producer to supply more of the commodity.   It results because the producer usually faces increasing costs of production.   The sum of *all* the individual producers' supply curves for a commodity gives the *market supply curve* of the commodity.

EXAMPLE 3.   Table 2 gives an individual producer's supply schedule and the market supply schedule for wheat.   Assume that there are 100 identical producers in the market.   The values of Table 2 are plotted in Fig. 2-2.   They show that at the low price of $1 per bushel, each producer will supply only 10 bushels of wheat per month, for a total of 1000 bushels by the 100 producers in the market (point *R*).   If the price were higher, say $3 per bushel, each producer would supply 60 bushels per month for a market total of 6000 bushels (point *E*).   At the high price of $5 per bushel, each producer would supply 75 bushels for a market total of 7500 (point *H*).   Note that to induce producers to supply greater quantities, a higher price must be paid.   Thus, the supply curves are positively sloped (i.e. they slope upward to the right).

Table 2

Price ($ per bu.)	Quantity Supplied by One Producer (bu. per mo.)	Quantity Supplied in the Market (bu. per mo.)	Alternative or Point
5	75	7500	H
4	70	7000	J
3	60	6000	E
2	40	4000	N
1	10	1000	R

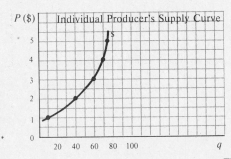
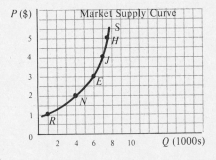

Fig. 2-2

2.3 DEMAND, SUPPLY AND EQUILIBRIUM

The *equilibrium price* and the equilibrium quantity of a commodity are determined by the market demand and supply of the commodity in a free-enterprise system.   The equilibrium price is the price at which the quantity of the commodity that consumers are *willing* to purchase over a given period of time exactly equals the quantity producers are *willing* to supply.   At higher prices, the quantity demanded falls short of the quantity supplied and the resulting *surplus* will push the price down toward its equilibrium level. At prices below the equilibrium price, the quantity demanded exceeds the quantity supplied and the resulting *shortage* will drive the price up toward the equilibrium level. Thus, the equilibrium price, once achieved, tends to persist.

EXAMPLE 4. Table 3 combines the market demand and supply schedules of Tables 1 and 2 and shows the pressure on the price of wheat toward its equilibrium level. At the high price of $5 per bushel, the quantity demanded of 3500 bushels of wheat per month falls short of the quantity supplied of 7500 bushels, leading to a surplus of 4000 bushels. This surplus of unsold wheat pushes the price down toward the equilibrium level. At the opposite extreme, a price of $1 per bushel leads to a quantity demanded of 11,000 bushels, a quantity supplied of only 1000 bushels and a shortage of 10,000 bushels, which drives the price up toward the equilibrium level. Only at the price of $3 does the quantity demanded (6000 bushels) exactly equal the quantity supplied (6000 bushels) and there is no pressure on price to change.

Table 3

Price ($ per bu.)	Quantity Demanded in the Market (bu. per mo.)	Quantity Supplied in the Market (bu. per mo.)	Surplus (+) or Shortage (−)	Pressure on Price
5	3,500	7,500	+ 4,000	downward
4	4,500	7,000	+ 2,500	downward
3	6,000	6,000	0	equilibrium
2	8,000	4,000	− 4,000	upward
1	11,000	1,000	−10,000	upward

EXAMPLE 5. Figure 2-3 combines the market demand and supply curves of Figs. 2-1 and 2-2 and shows how equilibrium is determined at the intersection of the two curves. The figure shows that at the high price of $5, there is a surplus of *AH*, which pushes the price down. As the price falls, the quantity demanded rises (a movement down the market demand curve) and the quantity supplied falls (a movement down the market supply curve) until the equilibrium point is reached. On the other hand, at the price of $1, there is a shortage of *GR* which drives the price up to its equilibrium level. Thus, the equilibrium price is $3 per bushel and the equilibrium quantity is 6000 bushels of wheat per month.

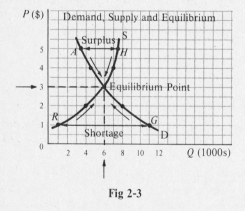

Fig 2-3

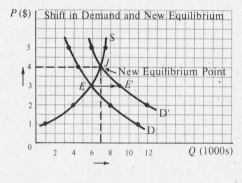

Fig. 2-4

2.4 SHIFTS IN DEMAND AND EQUILIBRIUM

In defining the market demand curve for a commodity, it is implicitly assumed that all other things that affect demand remain unchanged. These other things are the number of consumers in the market, their tastes, money incomes and the prices of other (related) commodities. If one or more of these things changes, the entire demand curve shifts. The market demand curve will *shift up* if the number of consumers increases, if their tastes for this commodity increase, if their money incomes rise, if the prices of substitute commodities rise and if the prices of complementary commodities (i.e. those used together, such as coffee and sugar) fall.   Opposite changes will cause a downward shift in demand.   A commodity's equilibrium price and quantity will both rise when its demand curve shifts up; both will fall when it shifts down.

EXAMPLE 6.   In Fig. 2-4, D and S are the same as in Fig. 2-3.   Suppose that D shifts up to D'.   This means that at the original equilibrium price of $3 per bushel, 9000 bushels of wheat per month (point E') rather than 6000 (point E) are demanded in the market.   However, to induce producers to satisfy this higher demand, a higher price must be paid.   Thus, we move from original equilibrium point E to new equilibrium point J (where D' intersects S) giving the new equilibrium price of $4 per bushel and the new equilibrium quantity of 7000 bushels per month.   · The student can pencil in the effect on the equilibrium price and quantity of a downward shift in demand.   With regard to Fig. 2-4, it is extremely important to distinguish between a *change in demand* (i.e. a shift in the entire demand curve as a result of a change in tastes, income, etc.) and a *change in quantity demanded* (i.e. a movement along a given demand curve as a result of a change in the commodity price only).

2.5   SHIFTS IN SUPPLY AND EQUILIBRIUM

In defining the market supply curve of a commodity, it is implicitly assumed that the number and size of producers of the commodity, technology, factor prices and the prices of other commodities (such as corn, which is related to wheat in production) all remain unchanged.   If the number and size of producers of the commodity increase, technology improves, or the price of factors and other (related) commodities fall, then the entire market supply curve of the commodity will increase (i.e. shift down and to the right) leading to a lower equilibrium price and a higher equilibrium quantity. A rise in the price of factors and related commodities will have the opposite effect.

EXAMPLE 7.   Figure 2-5 is the same as Fig. 2-3 except that S has now increased (i.e. it has shifted down and to the right) to S'.   At the original equilibrium price of $3, producers are now willing to supply 9000 (point E' on S') rather than 6000 bushels of wheat per month (point E on S) because their costs of production have fallen.   However, to sell a larger output, the price of wheat must fall.   Thus, the new equilibrium price of $2 and the new equilibrium quantity of 8000 bushels are defined at point N where D intersects S'.   The student can pencil in the effect of a *decrease* or *upward* shift in supply and distinguish it from a change in the quantity supplied.   (For the effect of simultaneous shifts in both D and S, see Problem 2.16.)

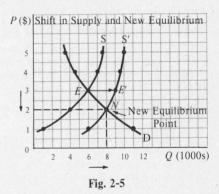

Fig. 2-5

2.6   THE PRICE-MECHANISM AND ITS FUNCTIONING

Thus far, we have seen that in a free-enterprise economy, the equilbrium price and quantity of a commodity are determined at the intersection of the market demand and supply curves of the commodity.   This helps determine "what" commodities and how much of each are produced. Similarly, the equilibrium price and quantity of each factor of production are determined at the intersection of the market demand and supply curves of the factor.   These factor prices help determine "how" businessmen should combine factors of production to minimize production costs. In addition, factor prices, together with inheritance, luck, etc., determine the distribution of income in society, which in turn determines "for whom" goods and services are produced.   In a mixed-enterprise system such as ours, this operation of the price-mechanism is modified by government regulation (see Problem 2.20).

Important Economic Terms

Change in (market) demand.   A shift in the entire demand curve for a commodity that results from a change in the number of consumers in the market, their tastes, their money incomes, or prices of substitute and complementary commodities.

Change in (market) supply.   A shift in the entire supply curve of a commodity resulting from a change in the number and size of producers of the commodity, a change in technology, a change in the price of the factors of production, or prices of other commodities related in production.

Change in the quantity demanded.   A movement along a given demand curve for a commodity as a result of a change in its price.

Change in the quantity supplied.   A movement along a given supply curve of a commodity resulting from a change in its price only.

Distribution of income.   The allocation of purchasing power among the various members of society. This depends on the quantity of factors owned and their prices and is affected by inheritance, luck and taxation.

Equilibrium.   The market condition where the quantity of a commodity that consumers are *willing* to purchase exactly equals the quantity producers are *willing* to supply.   Geometrically, equilibrium occurs at the intersection of the market demand and supply curves of the commodity.   The price and quantity at which equilibrium exists are known, respectively, as the equilibrium price and equilibrium quantity.

Factor price.   The amount of wage, interest and rent required to hire one unit of labor, capital or land, respectively.

Income effect.   The increase in the quantity purchased of a commodity with a given money income when the commodity price falls, or the increased purchasing power of a given money income.

Market demand curve.   A graphic representation showing the total quantities of a commodity that consumers are willing and able to purchase over a given period of time at various alternative prices, while holding constant everything else that affects demand.   The market demand curve of a commodity is negatively sloped, indicating that more of the commodity will be purchased at lower commodity prices.

Market supply curve.   A graphic representation of the total quantities of a commodity that producers are willing to produce or sell over a given period of time at various alternative commodity prices, while holding constant everything else that affects supply.   The market supply curve for a commodity is usually positively sloped, indicating that a higher price must be paid to induce producers to supply more of the commodity.

Price-mechanism.   The forces of market demand and supply which determine commodity and factor prices in a free-enterprise economy.

Shortage.   An excess in the quantity demanded over the quantity supplied of a commodity (or factor) over a given period of time which leads to an upward pressure on the commodity (or factor) price.

Substitution effect.   The increase in the quantity purchased of a commodity (or factor) when its price falls which results from switching from the purchase of other similar commodities (or factors) whose prices have not fallen.

Surplus.   An excess in the quantity supplied over the quantity demanded of a commodity (or factor) over a given period of time which leads to a downward pressure on the commodity (or factor) price.

Review Questions

1.   A demand schedule shows the relationship between the quantity demanded of a commodity over a given period of time and (*a*) the price of the commodity, (*b*) the tastes of consumers, (*c*) the money income of consumers, (*c*) the price of related commodities.

     Ans. (*a*)

2. At lower commodity prices more of the commodity will be purchased in the market because
   (a) consumers substitute this (now relatively cheaper) commodity for others in consumption,
   (b) at lower prices, consumers can purchase more of the commodity with given money incomes,
   (c) more consumers buy the commodity at lower prices than at higher prices,
   (d) all of the above.

   Ans. (*d*)

3. A supply schedule shows the relationship between the quantity supplied of a commodity over a given period of time and (a) factor prices, (b) the price of the commodity, (c) technology, (d) the prices of other commodities related in production.

   Ans. (*b*)

4. In order to induce producers to supply more of a commodity, a higher commodity price must be paid because producers usually face (a) decreasing production costs, (b) economies of scale, (c) increasing production costs, (d) specialization and division of labor in production.

   Ans. (*c*)

5. The intersection of the market demand and supply curves for a commodity determines (a) the equilibrium price of the commodity, (b) the equilibrium quantity, (c) the point of neither surplus nor shortage for the commodity, (d) all of the above.

   Ans. (*d*)

6. Which of the following statements is *not* true with regard to a price above the equilibrium price?
   (a) There is a shortage of the commodity.
   (b) The quantity supplied exceeds the quantity demanded of the commodity.
   (c) The pressure on the commodity price is downward.
   (d) There is a surplus of the commodity.

   Ans. (*a*)

7. An upward shift in the market demand curve for a commodity results in which of the following changes in its equilibrium price and quantity?   (a) The price rises and the quantity falls.   (b) The price falls and the quantity rises.   (c) Price and quantity both rise.   (d) Price and quantity both fall.

   Ans. (*c*)

8. Which of the following does *not* cause an increase (i.e. an upward shift) in demand?   (a) An increase in consumers' incomes, (b) An increase in consumers' tastes or desires for the commodity, (c) A reduction in the commodity price, (d) A reduction in the price of a complementary good.

   Ans. (*c*)

9. A downward shift in the market supply of a commodity results in which of the following changes in its equilibrium price and quantity?   (a) The price rises and the quantity falls.   (b) The price falls and the quantity rises.   (c) Price and quantity both rise.   (d) Price and quantity both fall.

   Ans. (*b*)

10. Which of the following does *not* cause an increase (i.e. a downward shift) in supply?   (a) An increase in the commodity price, (b) An improvement in technology, (c) A reduction in factor prices, (d) A reduction in the price of other commodities related in production.

    Ans. (*a*)

11. Which of the fundamental questions facing every society is primarily answered in the *commodity* markets of a free-enterprise economy?   (a) What to produce, (b) How to produce, (c) For whom to produce, (d) All of the above.

    Ans. (*a*)

12. The distribution of income in our mixed-enterprise economy is determined by (a) factor prices, (b) inheritance, (c) tax laws, (d) all of the above.

    Ans. (*d*)

Solved Problems

DEMAND

2.1. (*a*) Distinguish between a need (or want) and demand.   (*b*) What do a demand schedule and demand curve show?   Why are these concepts important?   (*c*) What does the negative slope of the demand curve show?   Why is the demand curve negatively sloped?

(*a*)   Demand refers to the willingness *and the ability* to buy a commodity.   The existence of a need or a want is a necessary but insufficient condition for the existence of demand.   The need or want must be backed by the ability (i.e. money) to transform it into *effective* demand for the commodity.   Our needs or wants may be infinite but our demand for any commodity is limited by our purchasing power or ability to pay for it.

(*b*)   A demand schedule shows the quantities of a commodity demanded per unit of time at various alternative prices, holding constant eveything else that affects demand.   A demand curve is nothing more than the graphic representation of a demand schedule.   The concept of demand is important because, together with supply, it determines the equilibrium price and quantity of commodities in a free-enterprise economy.

(*c*)   The negative slope of the demand curve shows that price and quantity are inversely related. That is, the lower the commodity price, the greater the quantity of the commodity demanded per unit of time.   This conforms to our everyday experience as consumers and is the result of the substitution and income effects.   The *substitution effect* says that as the price of a commodity falls, we substitute this for similar commodities in consumption.   For example, if the price of tea falls but the price of coffee remains unchanged, consumers buy more tea and less coffee. The *income effect* refers to the fact that as the price of a commodity falls, a given money income will allow the consumer to buy more of this and other commodities (i.e. the consumer's purchasing power is greater).

2.2. Suppose that the wheat market is composed of individuals 1, 2 and 3, whose demand schedules are given in Table 4.   (*a*) Derive the market demand schedule and (*b*) plot the individual and market demand curves.

Table 4

Price ($ per bu.)	Quantity Demanded by Individual 1, q_1 (bu. per mo.)	Quantity Demanded by Individual 2, q_2 (bu. per mo.)	Quantity Demanded by Individual 3, q_3 (bu. per mo.)
5	2.25	0.75	0.25
4	2.50	1.00	0.50
3	3.00	1.50	1.00
2	4.00	2.25	1.75
1	5.50	3.50	2.75

(*a*)   The market demand schedule is obtained by adding the quantities demanded by all individuals at each price (see Column (5) in Table 5).

Table 5

(1) Price ($ per bu.)	(2) q_1 (bu. per mo.)	(3) q_2 (bu. per mo.)	(4) q_3 (bu. per mo.)	(5) $Q = q_1 + q_2 + q_3$ (bu. per mo.)	(6) Alternative or Point
5	2.25	0.75	0.25	3.25	A
4	2.50	1.00	0.50	4.00	B
3	3.00	1.50	1.00	5.50	E
2	4.00	2.25	1.75	8.00	F
1	5.50	3.50	2.75	11.75	G

(b) Plotting each pair of price-quantity values in Table 5 as a point on the graph and joining these points, we get the demand curve for individual 1 (d_1), for individual 2 (d_2), for individual 3 (d_3) and for all three individuals in the market together (D).   See Fig 2-6.   Note that the market demand curve for wheat can be found graphically by summing horizontally the three individuals' demand curves.

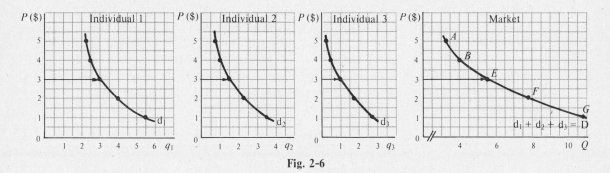

Fig. 2-6

2.3. Suppose that instead of three different individuals in the wheat market, there are one million individuals with demand curves for wheat identical to that of individual 1 in Problem 2.2. Derive the market demand schedule and plot the demand curve.

Since there are one million individuals in the market for wheat with demand schedules identical to that of individual 1 in Problem 2.2, the market demand schedule for wheat is obtained by multiplying q_1 in Table 5 by one million.   This is given by Q in Table 6.   The market demand curve for wheat is plotted in Fig 2-7.

Table 6

Price ($ per bu.)	q_1 (bu. per mo.)	Q (bu. per mo.)
5	2.25	2,250,000
4	2.50	2,500,000
3	3.00	3,000,000
2	4.00	4,000,000
1	5.50	5,500,000

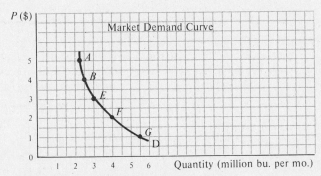

Fig. 2-7

SUPPLY

2.4. (a) What do a supply schedule and supply curve show?   (b) What is the usual shape of the supply curve? Why?

(a) A supply schedule shows the amounts of a commodity that a producer is willing to supply over a given period of time at various alternative prices.   The supply curve is nothing more than the graphic representation of the producer's supply schedule.

(b) The supply curve is usually positively sloped (ie. it slopes upward and to the right) indicating that a producer will supply more of a commodity only at higher prices.   This results because producers usually face increasing production costs.   However, while the demand curve is always negatively sloped (with only a rare and unimportant exception) so that we have the so-called *law of demand*, the supply curve can also be vertical, even though it usually slopes upward and to the right. A vertical supply curve means that the same quantity of a commodity will be supplied regardless of its price.   This happens if the period of the analysis is so short that more of the commodity cannot be produced or if, as in the case of original Rembrandts, the quantity supplied is given and fixed forever.

2.5. Suppose that there are three producers of wheat with hypothetical supply schedules given in Table 7.   (a) Find the market supply schedule and (b) plot the individual producer and market supply curves.

Table 7

Price ($ per bu.)	Quantity supplied by producer 1, q_1 (bu. per mo.)	Quantity supplied by producer 2, q_2 (bu. per mo.)	Quantity supplied by producer 3, q_3 (bu. per mo.)
5	37.5	22.5	17.5
4	35.0	20.0	15.0
3	30.0	15.0	10.0
2	20.0	10.0	5.0
1	5.0	2.5	0.0

(a) The market supply schedule is obtained by adding the quantities supplied by all producers at each price (see Column (5) in Table 8).

Table 8

(1) Price ($ per bu.)	(2) q_1 (bu. per mo.)	(3) q_2 (bu. per mo.)	(4) q_3 (bu. per mo.)	(5) $Q = q_1 + q_2 + q_3$ (bu. per mo.)	(6) Alternative or Point
5	37.5	22.5	17.5	77.5	H
4	35.0	20.0	15.0	70.0	J
3	30.0	15.0	10.0	55.0	E
2	20.0	10.0	5.0	35.0	N
1	5.0	2.5	0.0	7.5	R

(b) Plotting each pair of price-quantity values in Table 8 as a point on a graph and joining these points, we get the supply schedule for the first producer (s_1), for the second (s_2), for the third (s_3) and for all three producers in the market together (S).   See Fig. 2-8.   Note that the market supply curve for wheat can be found graphically by summing horizontally the three producers' supply curve.

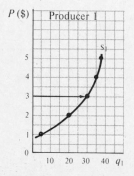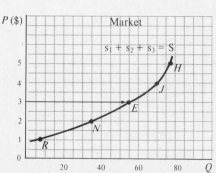

Fig. 2-8

2.6. Suppose that instead of three different producers of wheat, there are 100,000 wheat producers identical to producer 1 in Problem 2.5.   Derive the market supply schedule for wheat and plot it as a supply curve.

Since there are 100,000 wheat producers with supply schedules identical to that of producer 1 in Problem 2.5, the market supply schedule for wheat is obtained by multiplying q_1 in Table 8 by 100,000.   This is given by Q in Table 9.   The market supply curve is plotted in Fig. 2-9.

Table 9

Price ($ per bu.)	q_1 (bu. per mo.)	Q (bu. per mo.)
5	37.5	3,750,000
4	35.0	3,500,000
3	30.0	3,000,000
2	20.0	2,000,000
1	5.0	500,000

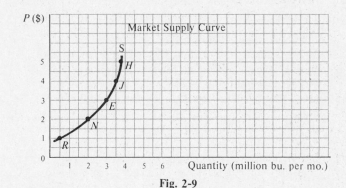

Fig. 2-9

DEMAND, SUPPLY AND EQUILIBRIUM

2.7. (a) Combine the market demand schedule of Table 6 and the market supply schedule of Table 9, and use it to show the surplus or shortage and the pressure on prices toward the equilibrium level.   (b) Plot the market demand schedule and the market supply schedule from part (a), showing graphically the equilibrium price and the equilibrium quantity.

(a)   See Table 10.

Table 10

Price ($ per bu.)	Quantity Demanded of Wheat in the Market (million bu. per mo.)	Quantity Supplied of Wheat in the Market (million bu. per mo.)	Surplus (+) or Shortage (−)	Pressure on Price
5	2.25	3.75	+1.50	downward
4	2.50	3.50	+1.00	downward
3	3.00	3.00	0.00	equilibrium
2	4.00	2.00	−2.00	upward
1	5.50	0.50	−5.00	upward

(b)   The equilibrium price of $3 per bushel of wheat and the equilibrium quantity of 3 million bushels of wheat per month are shown at point E, the intersection of the market demand curve for wheat (D) and the market supply curve of wheat (S) in Fig. 2-10.

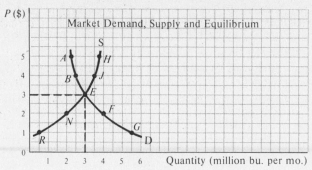

Fig. 2-10

2.8. With reference to Fig. 2-10, explain (*a*) why prices of $5 and $4 per bushel are not equilibrium prices and how the price is pushed down toward the equilibrium level in a free-enterprise system, (*b*) why prices of $1 and $2 per bushel are not equilibrium prices and how the price is pulled up toward equilibrium, and (*c*) why the equilibrium price of wheat is $3 per bushel and the equilibrium quantity is 3 million bushels of wheat per month.

(*a*)   Figure 2-10 shows that at the price of $5 per bushel, the quantity demanded of wheat falls short of the quantity of wheat supplied and leads to a surplus of 1.5 million bushels of wheat per month (*AH*).   This surplus of unsold wheat drives the price down.   As the price falls, the quantity demanded rises (a movement down the market demand curve) and the quantity supplied falls (a movement down the market supply curve).   At the price of $4 per bushel, there is still a surplus (even though the surplus has been reduced to 1 million bushels—*BJ* in Fig. 2-10) and so the pressure on price is still downward.   The price of wheat continues to fall until the wheat surplus is completely eliminated at the price of $3 per bushel (point *E*).

(*b*)   Starting at the opposite extreme, Fig. 2-10 shows that at the price of $1 per bushel, the quantity demanded of wheat exceeds the quantity of wheat supplied and leads to the very large shortage of −5.0 million bushels of wheat per month (*RG*).   Because of this unsatisfied demand, consumers bid wheat prices up.   As the price rises, the quantity demanded falls (a movement upward on the demand curve) and the quantity supplied rises (a movement upward on the supply curve). At the price of $2 per bushel, there is still a shortage (even though the shortage has been reduced to 2 million bushels—*NF* in Fig. 2-10) and so the pressure on price is still upward.   As the price of wheat continues to rise, the quantity demanded continues to fall and the quantity supplied continues to rise until the wheat shortage has been completely eliminated at the price of $3 per bushel (point *E*).

(*c*)   The equilibrium price of wheat is $3 per bushel because only at this price is the quantity of wheat that consumers are *willing* to purchase per month (3 million bushels—point *E* on D) exactly equal to the quantity that producers are *willing* to supply per month (3 million bushels—point *E* on S).   Note that at any other price, the *willingness* of consumers is not matched by the *willingness* of producers, even though the quantity bought equals the quantity sold.   For example, at the low price of $2 per bushel, producers will supply only 2 million bushels of wheat per month (point *N* in Fig. 2-10) and consumers cannot purchase more than the 2 million bushels produced.   As a result, the quantity bought of 2 million bushels of wheat equals the quantity sold of 2 million bushels of wheat at the price of $2 per bushel.   But this is not an equilibrium point because *consumers are willing to purchase more wheat at the low price of $2 per bushel.*

2.9. Why, in all these problems, do we talk about wheat?   Could we have talked about cars?

Wheat is used as the hypothetical commodity because there are many producers and consumers of wheat, each too small to affect its price.   In addition, wheat is a homogeneous product.   That is, the wheat of one producer is identical and indistinguishable from the wheat of others.   Similar products that we could have talked about are corn and potatoes.   We could also have referred to the identical shares of the stock of a particular corporation, because here too, there are numerous buyers and sellers at a particular point in time, each too small individually to affect its price.

On the other hand, it would not have served our purpose to talk about cars because there are only four car producers in the U.S. and each of them is large enough to determine and set the price of its cars.   Cars are also differentiated.   Chevrolets are not identical to Fords and Chevrolet Novas are different from Chevrolet Impalas.   Thus we could not talk of the demand for cars in general.

In talking about wheat, we have a homogeneous product whose price is determined exclusively by impersonal market forces.   In later chapters, we will see how the operation of the market mechanism is modified when such market imperfection as few sellers and differentiated products are introduced.   However, an understanding of how prices are determined in free-enterprise competitive markets is essential to understanding how they are determined in more realistic market situations.

SHIFTS IN DEMAND AND EQUILIBRIUM

2.10.   (a) What causes the market demand curve for a commodity to increase (i.e. to shift up)? (b) To decrease (i.e. to shift down)?   (c) Distinguish between an increase in the quantity demanded and an increase in demand.   (d) Distinguish between a decrease in the quantity demanded and a decrease in demand.

(a)   In defining the market demand curve for a commodity, it was implicitly assumed that the number of consumers in the market, their tastes, money incomes, and the prices of substitute and complementary commodities remained unchanged.   *Substitute commodities* are those which satisfy the same basic want, such as coffee and tea, wine and beer, etc.   *Complementary commodities* are those which are used together, such as coffee and sugar, cars and gasoline.   These are to be distinguished from independent or unrelated commodities such as sodas and cars, pencils and refrigerators.   The market demand curve for a commodity increases or shifts up if (1) the number of consumers of the commodity increases (as through population growth), (2) consumers' tastes for the commodity increase (as when concern over weight induces people to drink diet soda), (3) consumers' incomes rise (as the economy grows), (4) the price of a substitute commodity increases (e.g. we replace tea for coffee in consumption when the price of coffee rises), or (5) when the price of a complementary commodity falls (for example, consumers bought more compact cars when gasoline prices rose).   An increase in demand means, then, that at any given price, consumers demand more of the commodity per unit of time.

(b)   The market demand curve for a commodity decreases or shifts down if (1) the number of consumers buying the commodity falls, (2) consumers' tastes for the commodity decrease, (3) consumers' incomes fall, (4) the price of a substitute commodity falls, or (5) the price of a complementary commodity rises.   A decrease in demand means, then, that at any given price, consumers demand less of the commodity per unit of time.

(c)   An increase in the quantity demanded refers to a movement downward along a given demand curve as a result of a decrease in the commodity price, while holding constant everything else that affects demand.   An increase in demand refers to an upward and rightward shift in the entire demand curve and indicates that at any commodity price, consumers purchase more of the commodity per unit of time.

(d)   A decrease in quantity demanded refers to a movement upward along a given demand curve as a result of an increase in the commodity price, while holding constant everything else that affects demand.   A decrease in demand refers to a downward and leftward shift in the entire demand curve and indicates that at any price, consumers purchase less of the commodity per unit of time.

2.11.   In Table 11, QS is the market supply schedule of wheat given in Table 10, while QD' is a new market demand schedule for wheat.   Find the new equilibrium price and quantity of wheat (a) by preparing a table which shows the levels of surplus or shortage and pressure on price and (b) by drawing a graph which includes the original market demand curve (D) of Fig. 2-10.

(a)   In Table 12, we see that at a price of $5, there is a surplus and a downward pressure on price. At prices below $4, there are shortages and an upward pressure on price.   Only at the price of $4 is there neither a surplus nor a shortage.   Thus, the equilibrium price is now $4 per bushel and the new equilibrium quantity is 3.5 million bushels per month.

Table 11

Price ($ per bu.)	QD' (million bu. per mo.)	QS (million bu. per mo.)
5	3.00	3.75
4	3.50	3.50
3	4.50	3.00
2	6.00	2.00

Table 12

Price ($ per bu.)	QD' (million bu. per mo.)	QS (million bu. per mo.)	Surplus (+) or Deficit (−)	Pressure on Price
5	3.00	3.75	+0.75	downward
4	3.50	3.50	0.00	equilibrium
3	4.50	3.00	−1.50	upward
2	6.00	2.00	−4.00	upward

(b) In Fig. 2-11, the new equilibrium price of $4 and the new equilibrium quantity of 3.5 million bushels per month are given at point J where D' and S intersect. The effect of an increase in demand is shown clearly by the inclusion of the original demand curve from Fig. 2-10. As D shifted up to D', the equilibrium price rose by $1 and the equilibrium quantity by 0.5 million bushels per month (see the two arrows along the axes in Fig. 2-11).

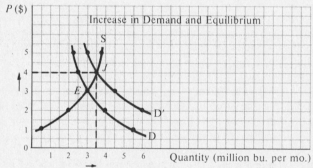

Fig. 2-11

2.12. Suppose that instead of increasing (as in Problem 2.11), the market demand curve for wheat had decreased to QD" in Table 13, while supply remained unchanged at QS. Derive the new equilibrium price and quantity of wheat (a) in tabular form and (b) graphically, including the original market demand curve of Fig. 2-10.

Table 13

Price ($ per bu.)	QD" (million bu. per mo.)	QS (million bu. per mo.)
5	1.10	3.75
4	1.25	3.50
3	1.50	3.00
2	2.00	2.00
1	3.00	0.50

(a) In Table 14, we see that at prices of $5, $4 and $3, there is a surplus and a downward pressure on price. At the price of $1, there is a shortage and an upward pressure on price. Only at the price of $2 is there neither a surplus nor a shortage. Thus, the equilibrium price is now $2 per bushel and the new equilibrium quantity is 2 million bushels per month.

Table 14

Price ($ per bu.)	QD″ (million bu. per mo.)	QS (million bu. per mo.)	Surplus (+) or Deficit (−)	Pressure on Price
5	1.10	3.75	+2.65	downward
4	1.25	3.50	+2.25	downward
3	1.50	3.00	+1.50	downward
2	2.00	2.00	0.00	equilibrium
1	3.00	0.50	−2.50	upward

(b) In Fig. 2-12, the new equilibrium price of $2 and the new equilibrium quantity of 2 million bushels per month is given at point N, where D″ and S intersect. The effect of the decrease in demand is shown clearly by a comparison of the two demand curves. As D shifted down to D″, the equilibrium price fell by $1 and the equilibrium quantity decreased by 1 million bushels per month (see the two arrows in Fig. 2-12).

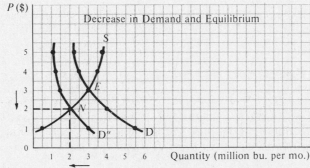

Fig. 2-12

SHIFTS IN SUPPLY AND DEMAND, AND EQUILIBRIUM

2.13. (a) What causes the entire market supply curve of a commodity to increase (i.e. shift down)? (b) To decrease (i.e. shift up)? (c) Distinguish between an increase in the quantity supplied and an increase in supply. (d) Distinguish between a decrease in the quantity supplied and a decrease in supply.

(a) In defining the market supply curve for a commodity, it was implicitly assumed that the number and size of producers of the commodity, technology, factor prices and the prices of other commodities related in production all remain unchanged. Commodities related in production are those which generally use the same factors of production, such as corn and wheat. The market supply curve for a commodity increases or shifts down if (1) the number and/or size of producers of the commodity increase, (2) technology in the production of the commodity improves, (3) the prices of factors used in the production of the commodity fall, and (4) the prices of commodities related in production fall. An improvement in technology or a reduction in factor prices reduces costs of production and leads to an increase in the supply of the commodity. A decrease in the price of corn leads to an increase in the supply of wheat because it becomes more rewarding for producers to shift resources from corn into wheat production. An increase in supply then means that at any given price, producers supply more of the commodity per unit of time.

(b) The market supply curve of a commodity decreases or shifts up if (1) the number and/or size of producers of the commodity decrease, (2) factor prices rise, or (3) the prices of other commodities related in production rise.   Technology is not included in the above list because once a particular technology is used in the production of a commodity, it is not generally unlearned so as to cause a worsening of technology (and a decrease in supply).   A decrease in supply means, then, that at any given commodity price, producers will supply less of it per unit of time.

(c) An increase in the quantity supplied of a commodity refers to a movement upward along a given supply curve as a result of an increase in the commodity price, while holding constant everything else that affects supply.   An increase in supply refers to a downward and rightward shift in the entire supply curve and indicates that at any commodity price, producers supply more of the commodity per unit of time.

(d) A decrease in quantity supplied refers to a movement downward along a given supply curve as a result of a decrease in commodity price, while holding constant everything else that affects supply.   A decrease in supply refers to an upward and leftward shift in the entire supply curve and indicates that at any commodity price, producers supply less of the commodity per unit of time.

2.14.   In Table 15, QD is the market demand schedule of wheat given in Table 10, while QS' is a new market supply schedule.   Derive the new equilibrium price and quantity of wheat (a) in tabular form, showing the levels of surplus and shortage and the pressure on price and (b) graphically, including the original market supply curve(s) of Fig. 2-10.

Table 15

Price ($ per bu.)	QD (million bu. per mo.)	QS' (million bu. per mo.)
4	2.50	4.75
3	3.00	4.50
2	4.00	4.00
1	5.50	3.00

(a) We can see from Table 16 that the new equilibrium price is $2 and the new equilibrium quantity is 4 million bushels per month.   At any other price, there is either a surplus or a shortage and a pressure on price to move toward its equilibrium level.

Table 16

Price ($ per bu.)	QD (million bu. per mo.)	QS' (million bu. per mo.)	Surplus(+) or Deficit(−)	Pressure on Price
4	2.50	4.75	+2.25	downward
3	3.00	4.50	+1.50	downward
2	4.00	4.00	0.00	equilibrium
1	5.50	3.00	−2.50	upward

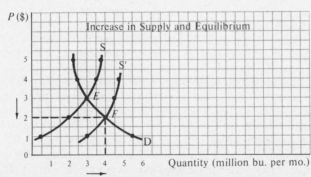

Fig. 2-13

(b)   In Fig. 2-13, the new equilibrium price of $2 and the new equilibrium quantity of 4 million bushels per month is given at point *F*, where D and S' intersect.   The effect of the increase in supply is shown clearly by comparing the two supply curves.   As S increased or shifted down to S', the equilibrium price fell by $1 and the equilibrium quantity increased by 1 million bushels per month (see the two arrows along the axes in Fig. 2-13).

2.15.   Suppose that instead of increasing, the market supply curve in Problem 2.14, had decreased as indicated by QS″ in Table 17, while the market demand remained unchanged at QD. Find the new equilibrium price and quantity of wheat (*a*) in tabular form and (*b*) graphically, including S and showing by arrows the changes in the equilibrium price and quantity.

Table 17

Price ($ per bu.)	QD (million bu. per mo.)	QS″ (million bu. per mo.)
5	2.25	3.00
4	2.50	2.50
3	3.00	1.50
2	4.00	0.25

(*a*)   Table 18 and Fig. 2-14 should by now be self-explanatory.

Table 18

Price ($ per bu.)	QD (million bu. per mo.)	QS″ (million bu. per mo.)	Surplus (+) or Deficit (−)	Pressure on Price
5	2.25	3.00	+0.75	downward
4	2.50	2.50	0.00	equilibrium
3	3.00	1.50	−1.50	upward
2	4.00	0.25	−3.75	upward

(*b*)   See Fig. 2-14.

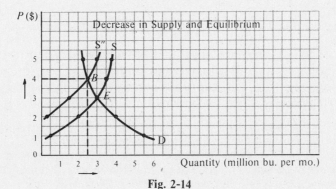

Fig. 2-14

2.16.   (*a*) On the same set of axes, draw D, D', D″ and S, S', S″ from the Problems 2.11–2.15. Indicate the equilibrium price and quantity when the relevant curves are (*b*) D and S, (*c*) D' and S (*d*) D″ and S, (*e*) D and S', (*f*) D and S″, (*g*) D' and S', (*h*) D″ and S', (*i*) D' and S″ (*j*) D″ and S″.   (*k*) What general conclusions can you reach with regard to the effect on the equilibrium price and quantity of an increase or decrease in demand and/or supply?

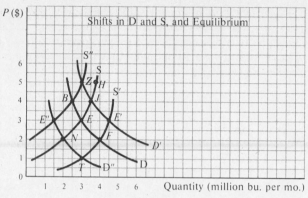

Fig. 2-15

(a) See Fig. 2-15.
(b) For D and S, the equilibrium price is $3 and the equilibrium quantity is 3 million bushels per month (point E in Figs. 2-15 and 2-10).
(c) For D' and S, the equilibrium price is $4 and the equilibrium quantity is 3.5 million bushels per month (point J in Figs. 2-15 and 2-11).
(d) For D" and S, the price is $2 and the quantity is 2 (point N in Figs. 2-15 and 2-12).
(e) For D and S', the price is $2 and the quantity is 4 (point F in Figs. 2-15 and 2-13).
(f) For D and S", the price is $4 and the quantity is 2.5 (point B in Figs. 2-15 and 2-14).
(g) For D' and S', the price is $3 and the quantity is 4.5 (point E' in Fig. 2-15).
(h) For D" and S', the price is $1 and the quantity is 3 (point T in Fig. 2-15).
(i) For D' and S", the price is $5 and the quantity is 3 (point Z in Fig. 2-15).
(j) For D" and S", the price is $3 and the quantity is 1.5 (point E" in Fig. 2-15).
(k) From Fig. 2-15 and the above results, the following general conclusions can be reached: (1) an increase in demand (D) by itself causes the equilibrium price (P) and quantity (Q) to increase; (2) an increase in S causes P to fall and Q to rise; a decrease in S has the opposite effect; (3) an increase in D and S will cause Q to rise for both reasons but P can rise, fall or remain unchanged depending on the relative increases in D and S; a decrease in D and S has the opposite effect; (4) an increase in D and a fall in S causes P to rise for both reasons, but Q can increase, decrease or remain unchanged depending on the relative change in D and S (the results are the opposite with the opposite shifts).

2.17. In recent years, (a) the price of gasoline has increased and the quantity purchased per year has also increased, indicating that the demand curve for gasoline is positively sloped, while (b) the price of pocket calculators has decreased and purchases have increased, indicating that the demand curve is negatively sloped.   Do you agree with these statements?   Explain.

(a) Through the years, as national income rose and the number of cars in operation and leisure time increased, our demand for gasoline increased (even though the proportion of compact cars increased).   Given the market supply of gasoline, this increase or upward shift in the market demand for gasoline, by itself, tended to increase both its price and quantity.   Through time, however, the supply of gasoline also increased (primarily as a result of larger imports).   By itself, the increase in the market supply of gasoline tended to reduce gasoline price and increase quantity.   Since demand increased much more than supply, both prices and quantities rose. Thus, it can be shown graphically that the rise in the quantity of gasoline purchased in the face of rising prices does not mean that the demand curve for gasoline is positively sloped but that it resulted from shifts in the demand for gasoline outstripping the increased gasoline supply. It is extremely important in the real world to isolate carefully the effect of shifts in demand from movements along the same demand curve and not jump to hasty conclusions that the law of demand has been refuted.

(b) The demand for pocket calculators increased but its supply increased much more from tremendous technological improvements that sharply cut production costs.   Thus, it can be shown graphically that the reduction in calculator prices and increased quantities purchased do not represent a movement downward along a given demand curve for calculators but, once again, represent the net result of shifts in both demand and supply over time.

THE PRICE-MECHANISM AND ITS FUNCTIONING

2.18. (a) How are the prices of factors of production determined in a free-enterprise economy? (b) How does the demand for factors of production arise?   Why is the demand for a factor negatively sloped?   (c) How does the supply of factors of production arise?   Why are factor supply curves positively sloped?

(a) In a free-enterprise economy, the prices of factors of production are determined by the market demand for and supply of these factors.   That is, the wage of each particular type of labor, the interest on each type of capital and the rent on each type of land is determined at the intersection of the market demand and supply for that particular factor.   Simultaneously, the equilibrium quantity of each factor is also determined.

(b) Business firms demand factors of production in order to produce the goods and services that society demands.   Thus, the demand for factors of production is a derived demand—derived from the demand for the commodity it is used to produce.   The demand for factors of production, as the demand for a final commodity, is negatively sloped because the quantity of the factor demanded by firms over a given time period is greater at lower factor prices.   This is the case because when the price of a factor of production falls, firms substitute this for other factors in production.   (This is the *substitution effect*.)   For a given level of expenditures, the firm can also buy more of the factor.   (This is called the *production effect* and is analogous to the income effect in demand theory).

(c) Individuals and households sell the use of the factors they own to businesses which demand them in order to produce the commodities that society wants to purchase.   They sell their labor time, lend their capital and rent the land they may own.   Of course, an individual who owns no capital or land receives an income based only on wages.   The supply curve for a factor of production is positively sloped because to induce owners of a factor to supply a greater quantity of factors, they must be paid a higher price per unit.   For example, overtime may be paid at the rate of one-and-a-quarter or one-and-a-half.

2.19. Discuss (a) the pros and (b) the cons of the price-mechanism in a free-enterprise economy.

(a) The basic arguments for the price system are that it (1) leads to an efficient allocation of resources and (2) permits and thrives on individual freedoms.   Literally millions of decisions are made every day through the operation of the price-mechanism in solving society's fundamental questions of what, how and for whom to produce.   It does this without any central authority coordinating these decisions and it does it impersonally and inconspicuously.   The individual is free to sell the use of the factors he or she owns to firms willing to pay the highest price and to use the income received to buy any commodity and in any quantity for which he or she can pay.   These efficiency considerations are so great that even such an otherwise centralized economy as the U.S.S.R. appears to be trying to leave some decision-making to the price system.

(b) Critics of the price system point out that (1) it leads to an unequal distribution of income (some live in luxury while others live in poverty); (2) it cannot ensure continued employment of labor and other resources; (3) firms grow large enough to restrict output and raise prices while unions distort wages and preclude the efficient allocation of resources; and (4) prices often reflect only private rather than social costs and benefits.   (For example, private production costs may not include the costs of pollution created and the private benefits of education, through higher incomes, do not include the social benefits of education.   In these cases, the price system cannot lead to the most efficient allocation of resources.   In addition, public services such as defense, roads, etc. cannot be provided by the individual.   It is to overcome these shortcomings that governments of western societies often seek to modify the operation of the market mechanism.)

2.20. How does the government in our mixed system try to overcome the criticisms levied against the price system in Problem 2.19(*b*)?   What is the justification for and the result of these actions?

Actions taken by the U.S. government to overcome criticisms of the price system include the following:

(1) In the name of fairness and equity, the government redistributes income from the rich to the poor in order to reduce the income inequality that results from the operation of the market mechanism. It does this through progressive taxation (i.e. the *rate* of taxation is greater on higher incomes than on lower incomes), inheritance taxes and welfare programs for the poor.   Income inequalities would certainly be much greater without government intervention.

(2) The government is also responsible for devising general policies to eliminate or reduce unemployment and/or inflation.   These policies will be explained in Chapters 6, 10 and 11, where it will also be shown that these policies are not always completely successful.

(3) The government seeks, through antitrust laws, to prevent firms from becoming so large that they can restrict quantities and raise prices.   It also occasionally seeks to break up those firms that already have such monopoly power.   The government also regulates those firms which for technological reasons need to be very large or to be the sole producer of a commodity or service. For example, to have many suppliers of electricity (or even more than one) in a city is so inefficient that the government allows only a single firm to operate but regulates its pricing and service policies to protect consumers.

(4) The government also tries to reduce the discrepancy between private costs and benefits on the one hand, and social costs and benefits on the other, through taxes and subsidies.   Thus, the government often taxes polluters and subsidizes education.   It also provides such public services as defense, roads, etc.

2.21. (*a*) Why do local governments often impose rent control laws?   What is their effect? (*b*) How does a price floor for agricultural commodities help farmers?   What problem does it create?

(*a*) Rent control laws place ceilings on rents paid for housing and prevent rents from rising to their equilibrium level.   These laws are directed at reducing housing costs for poor families.   However, as seen in Fig. 2-3, whenever the price of a commodity or service is set below its equilibrium level, a shortage results.   This is the basic reason for the housing shortage in New York City and in other parts of the nation where such rent control laws are in effect.

(*b*) A price floor for agricultural commodities is set above the equilibrium price by the government in order to raise farmers' incomes.   However, as seen in Fig. 2-3, this leads to a surplus of the commodity.   In the past, the Federal government has purchased the surplus of agricultural commodities arising from its price support programs.   This leads to higher prices for consumers, distortions in the economy and waste through spoilage of agricultural products.   In the case of both rent controls and price floors for agricultural commodities, the government *replaces* the operation of the market mechanism.   More often, the government prefers to work through the market mechanism by modifying its operation with taxes and subsidies.

Chapter 3

National Income Accounting

3.1 MEASURING NATIONAL OUTPUT

National output is the sum of goods and services produced in an economy. National income accounting provides aggregate measures of the market value of the final goods and services produced in the economy during a one-year period, with *gross national product* (GNP), *net national product* (NNP), and *national income* (NI) as different measures of this aggregate output. In a simplified model with no government and no investment (i.e. no saving), the market value of the final goods and services produced is equal to *both* the total expenditures for final goods and services and the sum of wages, interest, rent and profits received by economic resources for producing these final goods and services.

EXAMPLE 1. In a simple model with no government and no investment (saving), suppose that aggregate output consists of 100 items that have a market price of $2 per unit. The cost of producing this output consists of wages, $120; interest, $35; rent, $20; and profit, $25.

Earnings or income approach. The market value of national output equals $200 when the receipts of the factors of production are summed. (Wages $120 + interest $35 + rent $20 + profit $25 = $200.)

Expenditure or flow of product approach. Suppose households are the sole owners of the factors of production. Their income from production (wages, interest, rent and profit) equals $200. If households spend their entire income, expenditures and, therefore, the market value of national output, equals $200.

Figure 3-1 presents the simplified model of national output as a flow of expenditure and income. In this simplified model, the business sector is the sole producer of goods and services and hires the factors of production (capital, labor, natural resources, and entrepreneurial ability) owned by the household sector. Households in turn spend their entire incomes for consumption and receive goods and services produced by the business sector. The upper portion of the circular flow shows that national output is equal to the sum of household consumption expenditures for goods and services while the lower portion measures national output by summing the household sector's receipts of wages, rent, interest and profit. The inner portion of the circular flow traces the exchange of factor services for final output.

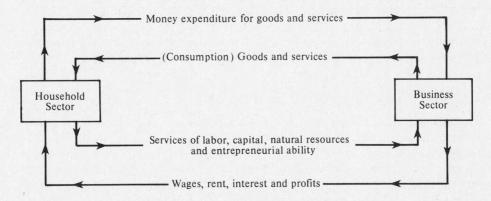

Fig. 3-1

Saving (not spending for consumption) permits investment in buildings, equipment and inventories.   If saving is added to the model in Fig. 3-1, investment spending becomes a second component of the flow of money expenditures for goods and services.   Investment in buildings, equipment and inventories (*gross investment*, I_g) is equal to capital additions (*net investment*, I_n) plus capital replacement (depreciation, D), or $I_g = I_n + D$.   Inclusion of capital replacement in reporting the value of national output necessitates differentiating *gross national product* (GNP) from *net national product* (NNP).   That is, GNP = NNP + D.   Both GNP and NNP measure the total market value of all final goods and services produced in an economy during a one-year period.   NNP is considered by many to be a more useful measure because it omits capital replacement and measures only the flow of output available for consumption and capital accumulation.

Addition of a government sector that imposes indirect taxes upon the production process requires that NNP be differentiated from *national income* (NI).   National income is the sum of wages, interest, rent and profits earned by the factors of production; NI equals NNP less indirect taxes. Thus, in a model with saving and a government sector, GNP approached from the expenditure side equals consumption plus gross investment plus government spending for goods and services plus net exports.   That is, GNP = $C + I_g + G + X_n$.   In the earnings or cost approach, GNP equals depreciation plus indirect taxes plus national income.

EXAMPLE 2.   In a model with saving and a government sector, assume that aggregate output consists of 1100 items that have an average price of $1 a unit.   Assume also the following annual data: replacement investment, $40; indirect taxes, $22; gross investment, $100; consumption, $850; government spending, $143; net exports, $7.   Factor costs are wages, $750; interest, $120; rent, $60; and profit, $108.

Calculation of NI, NNP and GNP is demonstrated, using the two approaches of Example 1.

Earnings or income approach	*Expenditure or flow of product approach*
NI = wages + rent + interest + profit	GNP = C $\quad + I_g \quad + G \quad + X_n$
= $750 + $60 + $120 + $108	= $850 + $100 + $143 + $7
= $1038	= $1100
NNP = NI + indirect taxes	NNP = GNP − D
= $1038 + $22	= $1100 − $40
= $1060	= $1060
GNP = NNP + D	NI = NNP − indirect taxes
= $1060 + $40	= $1060 − $22
= $1100	= $1038

Gross national product, net national product and national income are reported as annual flows; they exclude intermediate goods, transfers, and some goods that do not involve a market exchange.   Double counting (see Problem 3.7) is avoided by omitting intermediate goods (i.e. goods that are not ready for their final use).   Transfers, such as the transfer of financial securities and used goods, are excluded from GNP because they do not involve current output (see Problem 3.10).   However, omission of some goods that do not involve a market transaction, such as do-it-yourself home repairs, results in an understatement of GNP (see Problem 3.9).

3.2 PERSONAL INCOME AND DISPOSABLE INCOME

While individuals (households) are the owners of economic resources in a free-enterprise economic system, national income does not equal personal income (i.e. the amount of income received by households during a given year).   Adjustments must be made to national income to determine personal income because some individuals will receive transfer payments from corporations and/or the government although they have produced no good or service; other individuals receive less than their total earned income since they must make social security contributions to the government or the corporation will pay only a portion of corporate profits to its stockholders.   To obtain personal income, then, corporate profits and contributions to social security must be deducted from national

income while dividends, government and business transfers, and government and consumer installment interest payments are added.

EXAMPLE 3.   Given: national income, $560; corporate profits, $74; contributions to social security, $29;
government and business transfers, $40; government and consumer installment interest payments, $21; and dividends received by households, $19.   Personal income is computed as follows:

National income			$560
Less:	Corporate profits	$74	
	Social security contributions	29	(103)
Plus:	Government and business transfers	40	
	Government and consumer interest	21	
	Dividends	19	80
Personal income			$537

Disposable personal income is the amount of money households have available for spending.
It is found by deducting personal taxes from personal income.   *Personal taxes* consist of personal
income taxes, personal property taxes and inheritance taxes.   Households use disposable income
to consume, save and make interest payments on their debt obligations.

EXAMPLE 4.   Suppose that personal income equals $537, personal taxes total $66, while consumption equals
$432 and interest payments total $12. Personal saving is computed as follows:

Personal income		$537
Less: Personal taxes		66
Disposable personal income		471
Less: Consumption	$432	
Interest payments	12	(444)
Personal saving		$ 27

3.3   CHANGES IN GNP

In the expenditure approach to national output, GNP is the sum of price times the quantity of
final output (Σpq).   Changing values for GNP are the result of changes in price and/or quantity.
Since we are interested in knowing whether GNP changes are due to price or quantity, economists
have found it useful to report GNP in current and constant dollars.   GNP in current dollars is the
sum of current quantities multiplied by current prices.   Constant dollar GNP is the result of multiplying current quantities by prices for a selected year (see Problem 3.14).   Constant dollar GNP
measures the economy's real level of aggregate output (see Problem 3.15).

EXAMPLE 5.   Suppose that in Year 4, aggregate output consists of the five goods shown below with their
respective prices.   Current dollar GNP is the sum of the values found by multiplying Year 4 output by Year 4
prices.

Good	Year 4 Output	Year 4 Prices	Value
A	30	$2.00	$ 60.00
B	20	1.50	30.00
C	40	1.00	40.00
D	28	1.20	33.60
E	60	0.50	30.00
	Current dollar GNP		$193.60

For Year 4, constant dollar GNP is found by multiplying the current (Year 4) year's output by base-year prices. Assuming that Year 1 is the base year, constant dollar GNP during Year 4 is calculated as shown below.

Good	Year 4 Output	Year 1 Prices	Value
A	30	$1.50	$ 45.00
B	20	1.00	20.00
C	40	0.80	32.00
D	28	1.00	28.00
E	60	0.50	30.00
		Constant dollar GNP	$155.00

Data on the price and quantity of each final good are unavailable in the real world. Economists derive constant dollar GNP by dividing current dollar GNP by a price level index. The price level index (price deflator) used is a weighted one, and, therefore, is representative of the relative importance of numerous output components.

EXAMPLE 6. Constant dollar GNP is current dollar GNP divided by a price deflator and is computed as follows:

	Current Dollar GNP*	GNP Price Deflator	Constant (1972) Dollar GNP*
1965	$ 688	74.31	$ 926
1966	753	76.76	981
1967	796	79.00	1008
1968	868	82.56	1051
1969	936	86.70	1080
1970	982	91.39	1075
1971	1063	96.06	1107
1972	1171	100.00	1171
1973	1307	105.80	1235
1974	1413	116.02	1218
1975	1529	127.18	1202
1976	1706	133.88	1274

*in billions of dollars

Important Economic Terms

Constant dollar GNP. A measure of the total market value of all final goods and services produced in an economy during a year in the prices of a selected (base) year.

Current dollar GNP. A measure of the total market value of all final goods and services produced in an economy during a year in current year prices.

Depreciation. In national income accounting, the market value of capital used up in producing current output.

Disposable personal income. In the national income accounts, the sum of income households have to spend after payment of personal taxes.

Gross investment. The sum of *all* private sector spending on new buildings, machinery and additions to inventories during a year.

Gross national product. The total market value of all final goods and services produced in an economy during a year.

National income.   The sum of income of (or payments to) the factors of production.   It measures the cost to the economy of producing final output during a year.

Net national product.   The market value of all final goods and services produced in an economy during a year which are available for society's consumption or addition to its capital stock.   NNP equals GNP less depreciation.

Net investment.   The sum of *net* private sector spending on new buildings, machinery and additions to inventories during a year.   Net investment equals gross investment less depreciation.

Personal income.   In the national income accounts, the sum of income received by households during a year before the payment of personal taxes.

Real output.   In the national income accounts, aggregate production measured in constant dollars.

Review Questions

1. Gross national product is the market value of
   (a)   all transactions in an economy during a one-year period,
   (b)   all goods and services exchanged in an economy during a one-year period,
   (c)   all final goods and services exchanged in an economy during a one-year period,
   (d)   all final goods and services produced in an economy during a one-year period.

   Ans.   (d)

2. In a model in which there is no government, investment or capital replacement, the market value of final output is (a) the total money value of the flow of final production, (b) the sum of the receipts of the factors of production, (c) the sum of wages, rent, interest and profit, (d) none of the above, (e) all of the above.

   Ans.   (e)

3. In a model in which there is government, investment, and a foreign sector, GNP is the sum of
   (a)   consumption, gross investment, government spending for goods and services, and net exports,
   (b)   consumption, net investment, government spending for goods and services, and net exports,
   (c)   national income and indirect taxes,
   (d)   wages, rent, interest, profit, and depreciation.

   Ans.   (a)

4. Net investment is the
   (a)   gross sum of spending on buildings plus equipment less inventory changes,
   (b)   net sum of spending on buildings plus equipment less inventory changes,
   (c)   gross sum of spending on building plus equipment plus inventory changes,
   (d)   gross sum of spending on buildings plus equipment plus inventory changes less capital replacement.

   Ans.   (d)

5. Double accounting is avoided by (a) excluding financial transfers, (b) using the value added approach to GNP measurement, (c) excluding the market value of previously produced goods, (d) omitting goods that do not involve a market exchange.

   Ans.   (b)

6. Personal income
   (a)   is the amount of income received by the household sector during a given year,
   (b)   is the amount of income households have available for spending during a given year,
   (c)   equals national income less indirect taxes,
   (d)   is the sum of wages plus interest received by the household sector during a given year.

   Ans.   (a)

7. If personal income equals $550 while personal income taxes equal $70, consumption is $430, interest payments total $10 and personal saving is $40, disposable income equals (a) $500, (b) $480, (c) $470, (d) $440.

   Ans.   (b)

8. Constant dollar GNP is found (*a*) by multiplying current dollar GNP by a price deflator, (*b*) by dividing current dollar GNP by a price deflator, (*c*) by limiting the quantity of dollars available for purchasing the quantity of output, (*d*) only in those countries where there are price controls.

   Ans. (*b*)

9. Constant dollar and current dollar GNP have which of the following relationships with regard to the base year. (*a*) Constant dollar GNP exceeds current dollar GNP. (*b*) Constant dollar GNP equals current dollar GNP. (*c*) Constant dollar GNP is less than current dollar GNP. (*d*) Constant dollar GNP is unrelated to current dollar GNP.

   Ans. (*b*)

10. Suppose current dollar output is $500 in year 1, the base year. If the price deflator has doubled by year 8 while real output has increased 50%, current dollar output during year 8 equals (*a*) $2000, (*b*) $1500, (*c*) $1000, (*d*) $750.

    Ans. (*b*)

Solved Problems

MEASURING NATIONAL OUTPUT

3.1. (*a*) With reference to Table 1, assuming no depreciation and indirect business taxes, find the market value of final output if the incomes specified result from production and represent the only costs of producing final output.

Table 1

Good	Income				Final Goods	
	Wages	Interest	Rent	Profit	Annual Output	Market Price
A	$50.20	$3.10	$1.80	$4.90	30 units	$2.00
B	16.30	8.05	1.65	4.00	20 units	1.50
C	32.00	3.00	1.80	3.20	40 units	1.00
D	25.60	3.20	1.75	3.05	28 units	1.20
E	24.15	2.50	1.10	2.25	60 units	0.50

(*b*) Find the market value of final output if annual production consists of the final goods specified in Table 1.

(*c*) Why are the expenditure and income approaches alternate ways of measuring the market value of final output?

(*a*) In a no depreciation, no indirect business taxes model, the market value of final output from the income approach is the sum of the receipts of labor (wages), capital (interest), natural resources (rent), and entrepreneurs (the residual, profits). Wages received in producing goods A through E equals $148.25 ($50.20 + $16.30 + $32.00 + $25.60 + $24.15), interest is $19.85, rent is $8.10, and profits are $17.40. The summing of wages, rent, interest and profit gives a market value of final output of $193.60.

(*b*) The market value of *a* good is the price at which it is exchanged in the market place. The total market value of *a* good equals its market price times total output. Thus, the total market value of Good A is $60.00 (30 units × $2.00 per unit), while it is $30 for B, $40 for C, $33.60 for D and $30 for E. The total market value of Goods A through E is $193.60.

(*c*) Producing and selling outputs are alternate ways of viewing the economic process. From the production point of view: economic resources (labor, capital, natural resources and entrepreneurial ability) are paid to produce goods and services. From the sales point of view: goods and services are sold to final users. By including profit as a cost, costs of production will always equal the dollar value of sales. The income and expenditure approaches, thereby, become alternate ways of measuring national output since the income approach uses production costs (wages, rent, interest and profit) as its measure while the expenditure approach uses the dollar value of final sales (consumption, gross investment, government spending for goods and services, and net exports).

3.2.   (*a*) Explain the terms gross private domestic investment (GPDI) and net private domestic investment (NPDI).   (*b*) Distinguish Gross National Product from Net National Product.

   (*a*)   *Gross private domestic investment* is the sum of a given year's nongovernmental (private sector) spending on (1) new buildings (business and residential), (2) machinery, equipment and tools, and (3) the change in inventories.   *Net private domestic investment* equals GPDI less capital consumption allowances (depreciation, *D*) where *D* represents the sum of capital stock used up (consumed) in producing a given year's national output.   NPDI (or net investment) is the addition to an economy's stock of capital.   GPDI includes capital additions (net investment) and capital replacement (depreciation).

   (*b*)   GNP and NNP are gross and net measures respectively of the total market value of final goods and services produced in an economy during a one-year period.   GNP includes the market value of all final output while NNP excludes that production which represents capital replacement. Thus, NNP = GNP − D.

3.3.   (*a*) What are indirect business taxes?   (*b*) Why must indirect business taxes be added to national income to obtain NNP?

   (*a*)   Indirect business taxes are taxes levied on goods and services during output or at final sale and are thereby passed on to the final buyer through higher prices.   Examples of indirect business taxes include excise taxes, sales taxes, business property taxes, import duties and license fees.

   (*b*)   Since indirect business taxes are included in the price of final output, the factor cost of producing a final good (wages + interest + rent + profit) is less than the market value of the good by the amount of indirect business taxes collected by the government.   National income (the sum of factor payments: wages, interest, rent and profit) plus indirect business taxes equal NNP.

3.4.   From the flow of expenditure and income presented in Fig. 3-2, find national income, net national product and gross national product using (*a*) the flow-of-product approach and (*b*) the flow-of-income approach.

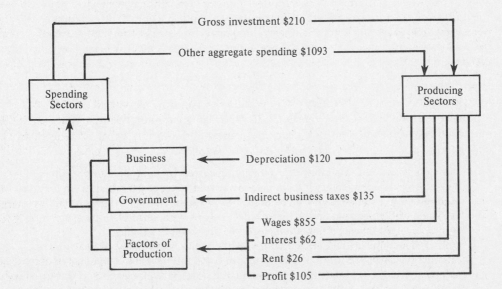

Fig. 3-2

(a) Flow of product:

$$GNP = \text{Gross investment} + \text{other aggregate spending}$$
$$= \$210 + \$1093$$
$$= \$1303$$
$$NNP = GNP - \text{depreciation}$$
$$= \$1303 - \$120$$
$$= \$1183$$
$$NI = NNP - \text{indirect business taxes}$$
$$= \$1183 - \$135$$
$$= \$1048$$

(b) Flow of income:

$$NI = \text{Returns to factors of production}$$
$$= \text{wages} + \text{interest} + \text{rent} + \text{profit}$$
$$= \$855 + \$62 + \$26 + \$105$$
$$= \$1048$$
$$NNP = NI + \text{indirect business taxes}$$
$$= \$1048 + \$135$$
$$= \$1183$$
$$GNP = NNP + D$$
$$= \$1183 + \$120$$
$$= \$1303$$

3.5.   What are the four components of aggregate spending?

The components of aggregate spending are (1) gross private domestic investment, (2) personal consumption expenditures, (3) government purchase of goods and services and (4) net exports.   *Gross private domestic investment* (I) is the sum of private sector spending for buildings, machinery and inventory (see Problem 3.2).   *Personal consumption expenditures* (C) includes household spending on durable consumer goods (automobiles), nondurable consumer goods (bread) and services (doctors).   *Government purchase of goods and services* (G) includes currently produced goods and services sold to the government sector.   Government transfers (welfare payments) are not included in this sum because the actual expenditure will take place in another sector.   *Net exports* (X_n) is the value of total exports (goods and services sent) less total imports (goods and services received).   A positive net export balance indicates that on balance a part of national output is being consumed outside the domestic economy.

3.6.   (a) Does GNP measure the flow of spending or the flow of output?   (b) Which of the following are included in this year's GNP: (1) a car manufactured this year, (2) a car manufactured last year and sold this year, (3) a used car sold this year, (4) a used car given a major tune-up at a service station this year.   Explain.

(a) During a given year, final output is either transferred by producers to consuming units or held by the producer in inventory.   During a given year some of the output from previous years and used goods are transferred via spending to consuming units.   Thus, spending involves the exchange of both current and earlier output.   However, since GNP measures only the flow of output for a given year, it is not a measure of the flow of spending.

(b) Only transactions (1) and (4) are components of this year's flow of final output.   Any good [transaction (1)] or service [transaction (4)] produced this year is a component of current aggregate output.   The car sold this year but manufactured last year [transaction (2)] was included in last year's GNP.   Transferring ownership of a used good [transaction (3)] does not involve current production and is not a component of current GNP.

3.7. (a) Distinguish between a final good and an intermediate good.   (b) Do (1) a loaf of bread and (2) a bag of flour represent final or intermediate goods?   Explain.   (c) Why would inclusion of final and intermediate goods in measuring GNP involve double counting?

   (a) A final good is one that does not require further processing and is purchased for final use (e.g. clothing by a consumer or a machine by a manufacturer).   An intermediate good is one that (1) requires further processing during the year before it is ready for final use, (2) is being purchased for modification before final use, or (3) will be resold during the year for a profit.

   (b) Bread and flour could be either final or intermediate goods, depending upon the purchaser's use of the good.   For example, the loaf of bread is a final good if purchased by a household for consumption; it is an intermediate good if purchased by a luncheonette which will resell the bread in sandwich form.   Similarly, a bag of flour is a final good when purchased by a household for family use but an intermediate good when purchased by a baker.

   (c) Intermediate goods are components of final goods.   If the value of both intermediate and final goods is included in the measurement of the value of final output, there would be a double counting of value and an overstatement of GNP.

3.8. Most output goes through several stages of production before reaching final form.   Suppose Good A goes through three stages.   In Stage 1, the raw material is produced; Stage 2 involves processing of the raw material; while Stage 3 involves its manufacture into final form. Related costs are given in Table 2.

Table 2

Stage	Cost per unit			
	Wage	Interest	Rent	Profit
1	$1.00	$0.08	$0.25	$0.18
2	0.25	0.20	0.03	0.04
3	0.75	0.35	0.06	0.09

For a single unit of Good A, find (a) the value at each stage of production, (b) the value added at each stage, and (c) the final value.   (d) What is the relationship between value added and the income approach to the measurement of GNP?

   (a) The value of a good at each stage of production is the sum of the *value added* (wage + interest + rent + profit cost) at the current stage plus the value of the good from the previous stage of production.   Thus, the value of one unit of Good A at Stage 1 is $1.51 ($1.00 + $0.08 + $0.25 + $0.18) while the value at Stage 2 is $2.03 ($1.51 from Stage 1 plus $0.25 + $0.20 + $0.03 + $0.04) and the value at Stage 3 is $3.28 ($2.03 from Stage 2 plus $0.75 + $0.35 + $0.06 + $0.09).

   (b) The value added at each stage is the sum of the wages, interest, rent, and profit cost during each stage.   Thus the value added is $1.51 at Stage 1, $0.52 at Stage 2 and $1.25 at Stage 3.

   (c) The value of a final good is the sum of the value added at each stage of production.   The value of each unit of final Good A is $3.28, the sum of the value added at Stage 1 of $1.51 plus that added at Stage 2, $0.52; plus that added at Stage 3, $1.25.

   (d) The value added to a product at each stage of production is the sum of factor costs (wages + rent + interest + profit).   The value added measure is in effect the income approach to measuring GNP.

3.9. Does GNP measure the output of all final goods and services?

   There are a number of productive activities that do not involve a market transaction (e.g. do-it-yourself home repairs, productive services of the housewife, etc.).   Since GNP includes only output that involves a market exchange, such productive activities are not included and their exclusion results in an understatement of the value of final output.

3.10. Why should nonproductive transfers be excluded from GNP?

Nonproductive transfers involve the transfer of funds from one party to another and include transactions such as public assistance (welfare payments), private transfers (a college scholarship), security trading (buying and selling of financial securities), and the exchange of used goods.   Since nonproductive transactions represent fund transfers that do not directly involve current output, they are not included in measures of current national output.

PERSONAL INCOME AND DISPOSABLE INCOME

3.11. Given the following data for 1974, find (a) national income, (b) NNP, (c) GNP, (d) personal income, (e) personal disposable income, and (f) personal saving.   Data are in billions of current dollars.

Capital consumption allowance	$119.5
Wages	855.7
Business interest payments	61.6
Indirect business taxes	135.0
Rental income	26.5
Corporate profits	105.4
Proprietors' income	93.0
Corporate dividends	32.7
Social insurance contributions	101.0
Personal taxes	170.7
Consumer interest payments	26.0
Interest paid by government and consumers	42.3
Government transfer payments	134.6
Business transfer payments	5.2
Personal consumption expenditures	877.0

(a) National income = Wages + business interest payments + rental income
$$+ \text{ corporate profits} + \text{proprietors' income}$$
$$= \$855.7 + \$61.6 + \$26.5 + \$105.4 + \$93.0$$
$$= \$1142.2$$

(b) NNP = National income + indirect business taxes
$$= \$1142.2 + \$135.0$$
$$= \$1277.2$$

(c) GNP = NNP + Capital consumption allowance
$$= \$1277.2 + \$119.5$$
$$= \$1396.7$$

(d) Personal income:

National income		$1142.2
Minus: Corporate profits	$105.4	
Social insurance contributions	101.0	(206.4)
Plus: Government transfer payments	$134.6	
Business transfer payments	5.2	
Interest paid by government and consumers	42.3	
Corporate dividends	32.7	214.8
Personal income		$1150.6

(e) Personal disposable income = Personal income − personal taxes
$$= \$1150.6 - \$170.7$$
$$= \$979.9$$

(f) Personal saving = Personal disposable income − (consumption expenditures + consumer
                            interest payments)
                     = $979.9 − ($877.0 + $26.0) = $979.9 − $903.0
                     = $76.9

3.12. In calculating personal income, why are corporate profits and contributions for social security deducted from national income?   Why are government and business transfers, dividends, and interest payments of government and consumers added to national income?

Personal income is the aggregate income received by households during a given year.   National income is the sum of payments made to the factors of production.   In a free-enterprise economy, economic resources are owned by households, but government and the corporate form of business organization intercept some of the national income flow as the government mandates that households make contributions for social insurance and the corporation elects to retain profits.   Some of the funds diverted to the government and corporation are returned, however, through transfer payments, interest and corporate dividends.   In deriving personal income, then, additions and subtractions must be made to the sum of national income since government and the corporation alter the disbursement of national income, i.e. the returns to the factors of production.

3.13. Why are consumer interest payments viewed as a use of disposable personal income along with consumption expenditures and saving?

Consumer interest payments represent funds transferred from one household to another as the result of one household borrowing savings from another.   For example, suppose Household A borrows $1000 from Household B and A agrees to pay interest of $80 per annum on the sum borrowed until the principal is repaid.   The $80 received by B is included as personal income. (Note that consumer interest was added to national income to calculate personal income in Problem 3.11.)   Household A, in making the $80 interest payment, is using disposable income to consume, save and make interest payments to B.   In an economy in which there is considerable consumer borrowing (as there is in the United States), consumer interest payments are a use of disposable personal income along with consumption and saving.   In the following chapters, however, it is assumed that households do not borrow from one another and that personal disposable income is either consumed or saved.

CHANGES IN GNP

3.14. Suppose that an economy's final output consists of the four goods presented in Table 3. (a) Find GNP in current dollars.   (b) Find GNP in constant dollars, using Year 3 as the base year.   (c) Which measure of GNP is more useful?

Table 3

Good	Year 1		Year 2		Year 3		Year 4		Year 5	
	p	q	p	q	p	q	p	q	p	q
A	$2.00	30	$2.00	30	$2.20	30	$2.25	40	$2.25	50
B	1.50	20	1.50	25	1.60	25	1.60	30	1.70	40
C	1.00	40	1.10	40	1.20	50	1.25	60	1.30	70
D	1.20	28	1.20	30	1.20	30	1.25	30	1.25	30

(a) GNP in current dollars is the sum of the current price times the current quantity of each good. During Year 1, current dollar GNP equals $163.60; this is the sum of $2.00 × 30 units + $1.50 × 20 units + $1.00 × 40 units + $1.20 × 28 units.   During Year 2, current dollar GNP is $177.50; during Year 3, $202.00; during Year 4, $250.50; and during Year 5, $309.00.

(b) Using Year 3 as the base year, constant dollar GNP is the sum of the annual quantity of each good times the Year 3 price of each good.   As calculated below, GNP in Year 3 dollars is $179.60 for Year 1.   Constant dollar GNP is $190.00 in Year 2, $202.00 in Year 3, $244.00 in Year 4, and $294.00 in Year 5.

Year 1 Output in Year 3 Prices

Good	Year 3 Price	Year 1 Quantity	Value in Year 3 Dollars
A	$2.20	30	$ 66.00
B	1.60	20	32.00
C	1.20	40	48.00
D	1.20	28	33.60
		Year 1 GNP in Year 3 dollars	$179.60

(c) Constant dollar GNP excludes the effect of price changes in summarizing the value of output; current dollar GNP includes it. Since the standard of living in an economy depends upon the output of goods and services (i.e. the quantity of real output) rather than their current monetary value, constant dollar GNP is a more meaningful aggregate measure of final output.

3.15. Table 4 presents the value of Good C in current dollars.

(a) Compute a price index for Good C using Year 3 as the base year.

(b) Compute the value of Good C in Year 3 dollars by (1) multiplying the quantities for Good C by Year 3 dollars and by (2) dividing the current dollar values by the price index found in part (a).

(c) Show that the methods used in part (b) are equivalent ways of computing a constant dollar value for Good C.

Table 4

Current Dollar Values for Good C			
Year	Price	Quantity	Current Dollar Value
1	$1.00	40	$ 40.00
2	1.10	40	44.00
3	1.20	50	60.00
4	1.25	60	75.00
5	1.30	70	91.00
6	1.35	70	94.50
7	1.40	80	112.00

(a) A *price index* measures the relationship between a given year's price and the price for a selected base year. It is found by dividing the current year's price by the base-year price and then multiplying by 100. For Good C, the price index is as follows:

Year			Price index
1	($1.00/$1.20)100	=	83.3
2	($1.10/$1.20)100	=	91.7
3	($1.20/$1.20)100	=	100.0
4	($1.25/$1.20)100	=	104.2
5	($1.30/$1.20)100	=	108.3
6	($1.35/$1.20)100	=	112.5
7	($1.40/$1.20)100	=	116.7

(b)

(1) Year	Quantity of C		Year 3 Price		Value in Year 3 Dollars
1	40	×	$1.20	=	$48
2	40	×	1.20	=	48
3	50	×	1.20	=	60
4	60	×	1.20	=	72
5	70	×	1.20	=	84
6	70	×	1.20	=	84
7	80	×	1.20	=	96

(2) Year	Current Value of C		Price Index		Value in Year 3 Dollars
1	$ 40.00	÷	83.3	=	$48
2	44.00	÷	91.7	=	48
3	60.00	÷	100.0	=	60
4	75.00	÷	104.2	=	72
5	91.00	÷	108.3	=	84
6	94.50	÷	112.5	=	84
7	112.00	÷	116.7	=	96

(c) Using Year 3 as the base year, constant dollar value for Good C (V_c) in Year 1 equals the quantity of C in Year 1 times the price in Year 3. That is, $V_c = Q_{yr\,1} \times P_{yr\,3}$.

Constant dollar value for Good C is also found by dividing the price index in Year 1 into the current value of Good C during Year 1.   That is,

$$V_c = \frac{V_{current}}{P_{index\ yr\ 1}}$$

Since

$$V_{current} = Q_{yr\,1} \times P_{yr\,1}$$

and

$$P_{index\ yr1} = \frac{P_{yr\,1}}{P_{yr\,3}}$$

then

$$V_c = \frac{Q_{yr1} \times P_{yr1}}{P_{yr\,1}/P_{yr\,3}} = Q_{yr\,1} \times P_{yr\,3}$$

Dividing a price index into current market value is equivalent to multiplying annual output by a base-year price.

3.16 Table 5 presents disposable personal income in current and constant dollars. (a) Find the implicit price deflator.   (b) Identify the base year.

Table 5

Disposable Personal Income (billion $)		
Year	Current Dollar	Constant Dollar
1965	$ 472	$612
1966	510	644
1967	544	670
1968	588	695
1969	630	712
1970	686	742
1971	743	769
1972	801	801
1973	902	855
1974	983	841
1975	1081	856
1976	1182	891

(a) The implicit price deflator is found by dividing current dollar income by constant dollar income. For the data in Table 5, the implicit price deflators are as given in Table 6 as follows:

Table 6

Year	1965	1966	1967	1968	1969	1970	1971	1972	1973	1974	1975	1976
Price Deflator	77.12	79.19	81.19	84.60	88.48	92.45	96.62	100.00	105.50	116.88	126.28	132.66

(b) Current dollar income is always equal to constant dollar income during the base year.   In Table 5, constant and current dollar disposable personal income are equal for 1972; therefore, the base year is 1972.

Chapter 4

Saving, Consumption and Investment

4.1 INTRODUCTION

This chapter begins an analysis of the determinants of output, employment, and income in an economy. It is assumed here and in Chapters 5 and 6 that the employment of labor is directly linked to output (i.e. the production of goods and services). Increases (decreases) in the level of output result in increases (decreases) in the employment of labor. We assume a closed economy (no foreign trade) and defer the analysis of the government sector to Chapter 6.

4.2 CIRCULAR FLOW IN A PRIVATE SECTOR MODEL

In the private sector (household and business) model presented in Fig. 4-1, production (output) requires that the business sector hire economic resources (labor, capital and land) from the household sector. The business sector's *ability to produce* depends upon the quantity of economic resources supplied by the household sector, i.e. $Y = f(N, K, R)$. This says that output Y is a function of (depends upon) the quantity of labor units employed N, the amount of capital available K, and natural resources R. Businesses' *willingness to produce* depends in turn upon their ability to sell output. The circular flow of Fig. 4-1 shows that the business sector must receive from the sale of goods and services it produces an amount equal to the economic resources used in the production of goods and services.

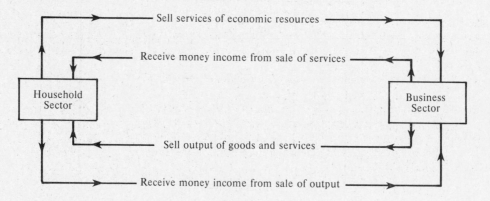

Fig. 4-1

EXAMPLE 1. Suppose households supply resource services that will produce 100 units of goods and services. Businesses will hire these resources only if they are able to sell the 100 units produced.

In the aggregate, household income is used to buy consumer goods or is saved. In Fig. 4-2(*a*), household saving is a leakage from the circular flow since the amount saved by households is not returned to the business sector. In Fig. 4-2(*b*), however, investment spending replaces the sum of the saving leakage.

EXAMPLE 2. Suppose businesses pay economic resources $300 to produce 200 units of goods and services. If households spend $250 of their income for consumption and save $50, investment spending must equal $50 for the business sector to receive a sum of money equal to that paid out for the services of economic resources.

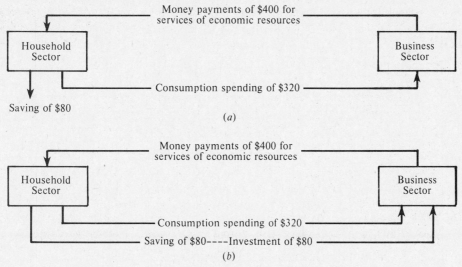

(a)

Fig. 4-2

4.3   SAVING AND INVESTMENT IN CLASSICAL ANALYSIS

Prior to the 1930s, a majority of economists believed that spending levels would be sufficient to bring about the full employment of labor.   This position was based upon *Say's Law,* which stated "supply creates its own demand."   This means that owners of economic resources supply their services because they wish to purchase output and will voluntarily reduce the supply of economic resources when fewer goods are demanded.

EXAMPLE 3.   Say's Law assumed that individuals work to buy goods and services.   Therefore, an increase in labor services that would produce an additional 75 units would automatically result in an increased demand for the additional output.   Changes in resource supply would always be associated with equal changes in the demand for output.

From Say's Law, it was assumed that in a money economy households would postpone consumption (save) only if paid an interest return and that the quantity of household saving was directly related to the interest paid on saving.   Businesses, it was believed, would invest larger sums the lower the rate of interest.   With saving positively related to the rate of interest and investment negatively related, the rate of interest was the mechanism for equating saving and investment.

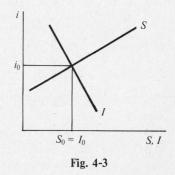

EXAMPLE 4.   Schedules for saving and investment are presented in Fig. 4-3.   Forces of supply and demand result in an interest rate i_0 at which the saving leakages are replaced by an equal amount of injected investment spending.   In the classical model, the rate of interest is the price mechanism for returning saving leakages to the circular flow.

Fig. 4-3

4.4   KEYNESIAN ANALYSIS OF CONSUMPTION AND SAVING

In 1936, J. M. Keynes, in *The General Theory of Employment Interest and Money,* questioned the classical assumption that households save for the same reasons that businesses invest.   There are many reasons why a household might not consume (see Problem 4.8).   Keynes saw disposable income as the principal determinant of consumption.   He called this relationship between consumption and disposable income *the propensity to consume* or *the consumption function* and the relationship between saving and disposable income *the propensity to save* or *the saving function*.

EXAMPLE 5. Suppose that Household A has the consumption and saving schedules given in Table 1.

Table 1

Disposable Income	Consumption	Saving
$ 8,000	$8,000	$ 0
8,500	8,300	200
9,000	8,600	400
9,500	8,900	600
10,000	9,200	800
10,500	9,500	1000
11,000	9,800	1200

Its consumption and saving functions would be expressed graphically as shown in Fig. 4-4.

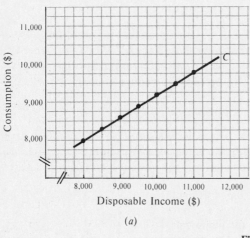
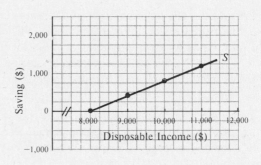

(a)   (b)

Fig. 4-4

When analyzing saving and consumption, it is useful to compute four propensities. The *average propensity to consume* (APC) is the ratio of consumption C to disposable income Y_d; the *average propensity to save* (APS) is the ratio of saving S to disposable income Y_d. *The marginal propensity to consume* (MPC) is the ratio of the change in consumption (ΔC) to the change in disposable income (ΔY_d); *the marginal propensity to save* (MPS) is the ratio of the change in saving (ΔS) to the change in disposable income (ΔY_d).

EXAMPLE 6. Using the consumption schedule in Table 1, we can compute Household A's average propensity to consume (C/Y_d) and marginal propensity to consume ($\Delta C/\Delta Y_d$), as shown in Table 2.

By aggregating household consumption and saving preferences, we can derive an aggregate consumption function in the same way that we derived a market demand schedule in Chapter 2. The aggregate consumption function then measures the planned consumption of households at different levels of disposable income.

Table 2

APC	Disposable Income	Consumption	MPC
$\dfrac{\$\ 8000}{\$\ 8000} = 1.0$	$\ 8,000	$8,000	$\dfrac{\$300}{\$500} = 0.60$
$\dfrac{\$\ 8300}{\$\ 8500} = 0.98$	8,500	8,300	$\dfrac{\$300}{\$500} = 0.60$
$\dfrac{\$\ 8600}{\$\ 9000} = 0.96$	9,000	8,600	$\dfrac{\$300}{\$500} = 0.60$
$\dfrac{\$\ 8900}{\$\ 9500} = 0.94$	9,500	8,900	$\dfrac{\$300}{\$500} = 0.60$
$\dfrac{\$\ 9200}{\$10,000} = 0.92$	10,000	9,200	$\dfrac{\$300}{\$500} = 0.60$
$\dfrac{\$\ 9500}{\$10,500} = 0.90$	10,500	9,500	$\dfrac{\$300}{\$500} = 0.60$
$\dfrac{\$\ 9800}{\$11,000} = 0.89$	11,000	9,800	$\dfrac{\$300}{\$500} = 0.60$

EXAMPLE 7. The aggregate consumption function C_1 presented in Fig. 4-5 indicates that households plan to consume $275 billion when disposable income is $300 billion and $350 billion when disposable income is $400 billion.

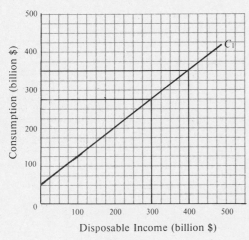

Fig. 4-5

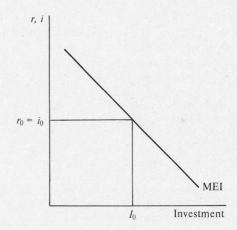

Fig. 4-6

4.5   INVESTMENT

Investment is largely dependent upon businesses' expectations of profit from adding to their capital stock and the interest cost of the funds invested.   Profit from capital additions (net investment) is generally measured as a rate of return r, called *the marginal efficiency of investment* (MEI). Aggregating each firm's MEI schedule, we have a downward-sloping aggregate MEI (investment demand) schedule.   Since the rate of interest i is the cost of using funds, investment will be at the level at which the marginal efficiency of investment equals the rate of interest, i.e. where $r = i$.

EXAMPLE 8.   Given the aggregate MEI schedule in Fig. 4-6, the quantity of investment is I_0 when the rate of interest is i_0 and equal to the MEI r_0 of the last unit of capital added.

Over time, investment may be volatile because of changing expectations (see Problem 4.16).   In Chapters 5 and 6, however, we assume that expectations and the rate of interest are constant and that there is a constant level of planned investment.

Important Economic Terms

Average propensity to consume.   The ratio of consumption to disposable income at a given level of income (i.e. APC $= C/Y_d$).

Consumption.   The amount households spend on newly produced goods and services.

Consumption function.   The relationship between the amount that households consume and different levels of disposable income.

Investment.   The addition to the economy's stock of capital.

Marginal efficiency of investment.   The expected rate of return from an addition to the stock of capital.

Marginal propensity to consume.   The ratio of a change in consumption to a change in disposable income (i.e. MPC $= \Delta C/\Delta Y_d$).

Marginal propensity to save.   The ratio of a change in saving to a change in disposable income (i.e. MPS $= \Delta S/\Delta Y_d$).

Saving.   The amount of current disposable income that is not consumed.

Saving function.   The relationship between the amount that households save and different levels of disposable income.

Say's Law.   Supply creates its own demand and there can be no oversupply of goods and services.

Review Questions

1. In a private-enterprise economy, businesses' willingness to produce depends upon
    (a)   government decisions on the optimum quantity of output,
    (b)   the quantity of economic resources supplied,
    (c)   their ability to sell output,
    (d)   the quantity of economic resources available for production and businesses' ability to sell output.
    Ans.   (d)

2. Businesses will continue producing at the current level of output if
    (a)   they receive a sum of money equal to that paid out for the services of economic resources,
    (b)   saving leakages are replaced by investment spending,
    (c)   they are able to sell what has been offered for sale,
    (d)   all of the above.
    (e)   none of the above.
    Ans.   (d)

3. According to Say's Law, (a) supply creates its own demand, (b) saving flows always equal investment flows, (c) spending is the principal factor determining output levels, (d) output is influenced by saving leakages.
    Ans.   (a)

4. Say's Law suggests that if people elect to postpone consumption, (a) they will not save, (b) they will not invest, (c) investment spending will always be sufficient to replace saving leakages, (d) investment spending will not be sufficient to replace saving leakages and unemployment will result.
    Ans. (c)

5. The consumption function specifies that consumption spending is
    (a)   negatively related to the level of disposable income,
    (b)   positively related to the level of disposable income,
    (c)   negatively related to the rate of interest,
    (d)   positively related to the rate of interest.
    Ans.   (b)

6. If a household consumes $10,000 when its level of disposable income is $11,000 and $10,500 when its level of disposable income is $12,000, its marginal propensity to consume is (*a*) 0.50, (*b*) 0.75, (*c*) 0.80, (*d*) 0.91.

Ans. (*a*)

7. A marginal propensity to consume of 0.80 indicates that
  (*a*) a household will consume 0.80 of any increase in its level of disposable income and 0.20 of any decrease in its level of disposable income,
  (*b*) a household will save a major portion of any change in its level of disposable income,
  (*c*) a household consumes 0.80 of its level of disposable income,
  (*d*) a household will consume 0.80 of any increase in its level of disposable income.

Ans. (*d*)

8. The average propensity to consume is the ratio of (*a*) a change in consumption to a change in disposable income, (*b*) a change in consumption to total disposable income, (*c*) total consumption to total disposable income, (*d*) total consumption to a change in disposable income.

Ans. (*c*)

9. The aggregate saving function is
  (*a*) the level of planned saving for every change in disposable income,
  (*b*) the level of planned saving at different levels of disposable income,
  (*c*) the ratio of total saving to total disposable income,
  (*d*) the ratio of a change in planned saving to a change in disposable income.

Ans. (*d*)

10. The level of investment spending depends upon (*a*) the marginal efficiency of investment, (*b*) the interest cost of funds, (*c*) the expected returns from additions to capital stock, (*d*) all of the above.

Ans. (*d*)

Solved Problems

CIRCULAR FLOW IN A PRIVATE SECTOR MODEL

4.1. Suppose that (1) households own all economic resources in the economy, (2) the price level is constant, and (3) the circular flow is given by Fig. 4-7.

Household Money Income   ≡   Value (Cost) of Output

```
┌─────────────┐                    ┌─────────────┐
│  Household  │                    │  Business   │
│   Sector    │                    │   Sector    │
└─────────────┘                    └─────────────┘
```

Aggregate Spending   ≡   Revenues of Firms

Fig. 4-7

  (*a*) Explain the identities: Household money income ≡ value of output and aggregate spending ≡ revenues of firms.

  (*b*) Why is it necessary for firms to receive revenues equal to their disbursement of funds?

  (*a*) The business sector pays households for supplying services to produce output. The value of output equals the sum of payments made to factors plus profits. In a model where households receive the payments to factors (wages, rent, interest and profits), the money income of households is equal to the costs and, therefore, the value of output.

  Aggregate spending is the sum spent by households for goods and services produced in the business sector. Since the business sector is the sole producer of goods and services, aggregate spending is equivalent to the revenues received by the business sector.

(*b*)   Given a constant price level, firms are unable to sell their entire output if their revenues are less than their costs of output.   During the next production period, the business sector will hire fewer economic resources and decrease production.   It is therefore necessary that the business sector receive revenues equal to their costs if they are to maintain current output levels.

4.2.   Suppose households own economic resources and the business sector produces 500 units priced at $1.50 per unit.
   (*a*)   What is the money value of output?
   (*b*)   What is the money income of the household sector?
   (*c*)   What is aggregate spending if households spend 90% of their income?
   (*d*)   What revenues are received by the business sector?
   (*e*)   Is there a saving leakage from the circular flow?
   (*f*)   What should happen to the level of output if firm's receipts are less than their costs of production?
   (*g*)   What volume of investment spending is necessary to stabilize output at 500 units?

   (*a*)   The money value of output equals the quantity of output times the unit price.   Thus, the value of output equals $500 \times \$1.50 = \$750$.
   (*b*)   Household money income equals the money value of output.   In this case, it is $750.
   (*c*)   Households are spending $675.00, 0.90 times the $750 money income.
   (*d*)   Business sector revenues equal the sum of aggregate spending.   Business sector revenues in this case equal $675.
   (*e*)   Households save what they do not consume.   Households' spending is $675 and saving is $75; the $75 in saving is a "leakage" from the circular flow.   The business sector is receiving $675 in revenues; this is less than their $750 payments.   Business firms are also holding output valued at $75.
   (*f*)   Output should fall because the business sector is unable to sell its current production of goods and services.
   (*g*)   Investment spending must total $75 in order to reinject the $75 saving leakage into the circular flow.

4.3.   (*a*)   What is a saving leakage?   (*b*)   Why must investment spending equal the saving leakage?

   (*a*)   A saving leakage is a sum received by households that is not returned (spent) to the business sector.   When households are the sole recipients of income, the saving leakage is the sum saved by the household sector.
   (*b*)   Investment spending returns saving to the circular flow.   It thus prevents output levels from dropping, since failure to purchase the business sector's output of goods and services leaves the business sector with unsold output; this will result in a reduction of output in the next time period.

4.4.   What determines the level of output (*a*) if the supply of economic resources is constant? (*b*) When there is an increase in the supply of economic resources?

   (*a*)   Potential supply is constant when there is no change in the supply of economic resources.   The utilization of this constant supply depends upon the business sector's ability to sell what has been produced.
   (*b*)   An increase in the supply of economic resources increases potential supply.   Utilization of increased productive capacity, however, requires that the business sector be able to sell what has been produced.

SAVING AND INVESTMENT IN CLASSICAL ANALYSIS

4.5.   (*a*)   Explain the economic motivation implied by Say's Law.
   (*b*)   What does Say's Law suggest about the employment of economic resources?
   (*c*)   Is there need for a full-employment policy in classical analysis?

(a) Say's Law holds that supply creates its own demand. The economic motivation suggested is that individuals supply resource services so that they may purchase goods and services.   Assuming that work is burdensome, resources are supplied to the extent individuals desire to purchase goods and services.   Thus, supply (supplying resources for production) creates its own demand (demand for the output of goods and services).

(b) If full employment means that those who are actively seeking work are employed, Say's Law suggests that full employment is the normal condition of a private enterprise economy.   Those who want to purchase goods and services are employed; those who do not seek material goods voluntarily withdraw their services from the market and are not viewed as unemployed.

(c) Since the normal condition is full employment, there is no need for an economic policy aimed at generating full employment.

4.6.   (a) What is the rationale for saving and investment in classical analysis?   (b) Why should saving leakages always equal investment spending in the classical model?

(a) According to classical analysis, the motivation for working is the desire to obtain goods and services, i.e. to consume.   Households will postpone consumption (i.e. save) because by lending they can obtain an interest return on the sum lent which allows them to purchase larger quantities of goods and services in the future. In the classical model, businesses borrow to purchase new capital (new machines, etc.) because they expect that the returns from the new capital will exceed the interest costs.

(b) Saving is positively related to the rate of interest and investment is negatively related to the rate of interest.   Since the interest rate is the only variable determining saving and investment, the quantity of saving is always equal to the quantity of investment at the full-employment level of income.

4.7.   In Fig. 4-8 the initial equilibrium rate of interest is i_0.   In terms of the graph, (a) what happens to the volume of saving and investment and the rate of interest if (1) there is an increase in investment, and (2) households are less willing to postpone consumption?   Treat each situation separately. (b) Does investment spending continue to equal saving leakages?

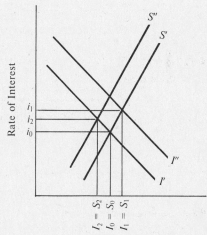

Fig. 4-8

(a) In (1), the investment schedule shifts to the right to, say, I''.   The rate of interest would increase to i_1 while the volume of saving and investment would increase to I_1 and S_1.

In (2), the saving schedule would shift leftward to S'' because of the decreased preference for saving. Given: investment schedule I', the rate of interest increases to i_2 and the volumes of saving and investment decrease to I_2 and S_2.

(b) Since saving and investment are determined by interest rate levels, the equality of the flow of saving and investment is assured by the rate of interest.

KEYNESIAN ANALYSIS OF CONSUMPTION AND SAVING

4.8.   (a) Might households save for reasons other than an interest return?   (b) Why is income the principal determinant of saving?   (c) What is the difference between saving and savings?

(a) People save to accumulate funds (1) to make future purchases, (2) to finance a child's education, (3) to retire, (4) to provide for possible sickness, etc.   In most instances, people's decisions to save are not influenced by interest rate levels.

(b) In Keynesian analysis, saving is viewed as a residual, i.e. an amount not consumed. Keynes suggested, and statistics have shown, that disposable income is the most important determinant of consumption.

(c) *Saving* is the amount saved between two periods of time while *savings* is the amount that has been saved at a given point in time. Thus, saving is a flow which measures the amount saved from a flow of income. Savings is a stock which measures the amounts that have been accumulated over time.

4.9. What is the implication of retaining the linkage of investment to the rate of interest and making saving a function of the level of income?

In advanced economies, savers and investors are, in most instances, distinct groups. Saving and investing decisions are thereby unrelated and the motivations of savers and investors are also different. As a result, there is no rate of interest which will assure that the volume of saving leakages at full employment equals those of investment injections. This raises the possibility that saving could equal investment at income levels other than those of full employment.

4.10. Suppose a household has the consumption function given in Fig. 4-9.
(a) Find consumption when disposable income is $12,000 and $14,000.
(b) What is consumption when disposable income is $10,000? How can a household consume more than its disposable income, i.e. dissave?
(c) What is true of every point on the 45° line?

(a) When disposable income is $12,000, consumption is $12,000. When disposable income is $14,000, consumption is $13,000.

(b) This household consumes $11,000 when its disposable income is $10,000. A household can dissave (consume more than its income) by drawing down accumulated savings from earlier periods or by borrowing.

(c) Any point on the 45° line is equidistant from the consumption and disposable income axes if the same scales of measurement are used on both axes. For example, at point A, $C = Y_d$.

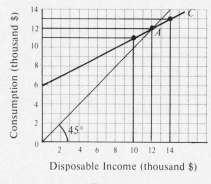

Fig. 4-9

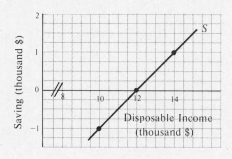

Fig. 4-10

4.11. (a) What is the relationship between consumption, saving and disposable income? Using Fig. 4-9, (b) find saving when disposable income is $10,000, $12,000 and $14,000, (c) identify the dissaving and saving areas; and (d) derive a saving function graphically.

(a) Disposable income is either consumed or saved. Thus, $Y_d = C + S$ or $S = Y_d - C$.

(b) Since $S = Y_d - C$, saving is −$1,000 when disposable income is $10,000, 0 when disposable income is $12,000, and $1000 when disposable income is $14,000. Saving is the vertical distance between the consumption function and the 45° line.

(c) The dissaving area is the vertical distance between the consumption line and the 45° line to the left of Y_d at which $C = Y_d$ (point A in Fig. 4-9).   The saving area is the vertical distance between the consumption line and the 45° line to the right of point A.

(d) The linear saving function is derived in Fig. 4-10 by plotting the saving levels found in part (b) and connecting the points.

4.12. Using the consumption function in Fig. 4-9, (a) find the APC and the APS when the levels of disposable income are $12,000 and $14,000, and (b) Calculate the MPC between these incomes.   (c) What does the marginal propensity to consume measure? (d) What is the relationship between the APC and the APS?

(a) The APC $\equiv C/Y_d$ and the APS $\equiv S/Y_d$.   When disposable income is $12,000 and $C = $12,000, the APC $= $12,000/$12,000 = 1$ and the APS $= 0/$12,000 = 0$.   When disposable income is $14,000, the APC $= $13,000/$14,000 = 0.93$ and the APS $= $1000/$14,000 = 0.07$.

(b) The MPC $= \Delta C/\Delta Y_d$.   Consumption increases $1000 when there is a $2000 increase in disposable income.   Thus, the MPC $= $1000/$2000 = 0.50$.

(c) The marginal propensity to consume measures the ratio of the change in consumption to the change in income, i.e. the fraction of each extra dollar of income that will be consumed.   The MPC is the slope of the consumption function.

(d) Since disposable income is either consumed or saved, the average propensity to consume plus the average propensity to save must equal one (i.e. APC + APS $= C/Y_d + S/Y_d = 1$).

4.13. Suppose a household consumes $9000 when the level of disposable income is $10,000.
(a) Find consumption when disposable income is $10,500, $11,000, $11,500 and $12,000 if the MPC is 0.60.
(b) What is the amount of saving at each level of disposable income?
(c) Find the APC and APS at each income level.
(d) What is the MPS?

(a) Since 0.60 of every change in income is consumed, for every $500 increase in disposable income, $300 is consumed.   Consumption is, therefore, $9300 when $Y_d = $10,500, $9600 when $Y_d = $11,000, $9900 when $Y_d = $11,500, and $10,200 when $Y_d = $12,000.

(b) Saving is $1200 when $Y_d = $10,500, $1400 when $Y_d = $11,000, $1600 when $Y_d = $11,500, and $1800 when $Y_d = $12,000.

(c) The APC and APS are as follows:

Y_d	APC	APS
$10,500	$ 9300/$10,500 = 0.89	$1200/$10,500 = 0.11
$11,000	$ 9600/$11,000 = 0.87	$1400/$11,000 = 0.13
$11,500	$ 9900/$11,500 = 0.86	$1600/$11,500 = 0.14
$12,000	$10,200/$12,000 = 0.85	$1800/$12,000 = 0.15

(d) If 0.60 of every increase in income is consumed, the MPS is 0.40 because the MPS plus the MPC must equal 1.

4.14. Explain the difference between autonomous consumption and induced consumption.

Autonomous consumption is that quantity of consumer spending that is unrelated to the level of disposable income.   Induced consumption is that quantity of consumption associated with disposable income.   In Fig. 4-11, autonomous consumption is OC when disposable income is 0.   At disposable income Y_1, induced consumption is AB and autonomous consumption remains OC.   Induced consumption at disposable income level Y_2 is DE.

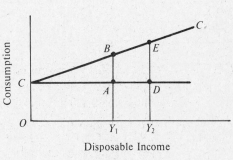

Fig. 4-11

INVESTMENT

4.15. (*a*) What is the marginal efficiency of investment?

(*b*) Why does the rate of interest determine the level of investment?

(*a*) The marginal efficiency of investment is the expected rate of return from an investment over the life of a project. For example, the expected rate of return on an investment proposal is 10% if a machine that costs $1000 has a one-year expected life and is expected to earn a $100 profit, i.e. $r = \$100/\$1000 = 0.10$ or 10%.

(*b*) Interest is the sum paid for the use of funds. Assuming that funds must be obtained to purchase new capital, firms employ funds to the amount at which the expected rate of return r from an investment proposal equals the cost i of funds, i.e. $r = i$. Given a marginal efficiency of investment schedule, the rate of interest determines the quantity of investment.

4.16. (*a*) Why might the volume of investment fluctuate over time? (*b*) Under what circumstances would investment be constant?

(*a*) There may be shifts in the aggregate marginal efficiency of investment schedule over time as a result of changes in expectations, technology, cost of new capital goods and corporate income tax rates. If businesses expect a weakening of consumption demand or an increase in production costs, the net profit of investment projects will decline and the aggregate marginal efficiency of investment schedule will shift to the left. Technological advances and the introduction of new products increase the number of potential investment projects and shift the marginal efficiency of investment schedule to the right. Actual or expected changes in the production costs of new machines affect the profitability of investment proposals. An increase in production costs lowers profitability and shifts the marginal efficiency of investment schedule leftward while decreases in the cost of producing new capital shift the marginal efficiency of investment schedule to the right. The level of corporate income taxes is a factor in determining the net profitability of investment proposals. If corporate income taxes are expected to increase, net profitability of investment proposals falls and the marginal efficiency of investment schedule shifts to the left.

(*b*) Given the stable marginal efficiency of investment schedule I_1 and a constant rate of interest i_0 in Fig. 4-12, the amount of investment equals I_0. The amount of investment is a constant if there is no change in the rate of interest and in the factors affecting the aggregate marginal efficiency of investment schedule.

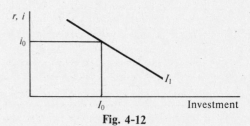

Fig. 4-12

Chapter 5

The Determination of National Income

5.1 AGGREGATE SUPPLY, AGGREGATE DEMAND AND EQUILIBRIUM

Aggregate supply is the quantity of goods and services producers make available for sale and is equal to the money income received by the owners of the factors of production. Aggregate demand is the sum buyers plan to spend on output. The equilibrium level of income (output) is the income (output) level at which aggregate supply equals aggregate demand. That is, where the total output of goods and services (the flow of money income) equals the total quantity of goods and services demanded (the return flow of spending).

EXAMPLE 1. The equilibrium level of income is $520 in the schedules of aggregate supply and aggregate demand presented in Table 1 and graphed in Fig. 5-1. At aggregate supply levels below $520, spending demands are not met because the amount demanded exceeds the amount supplied. At income levels above $520, firms are unable to sell the entire output available for sale.

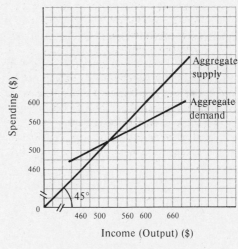

Table 1

Aggregate Supply Schedule	
Output (Income)	Aggregate Supply
$480	$480
500	500
520	520
540	540
560	560
Aggregate Demand Schedule	
Output (Income)	Aggregate Demand
$480	$500
500	510
520	520
540	530
560	540

Fig. 5-1

Aggregate demand consists of consumption and investment spending in a model of the economy in which all income from production is paid to the household sector. We shall assume that (1) there is a constant level of planned investment spending, and that (2) household aggregate consumption is positively related to the receipt of money income. As shown in Example 2, there is only one level of income where aggregate supply Y equals aggregate demand $C+I$.

EXAMPLE 2. The aggregate demand data of Example 1 are presented in Table 2 and Fig. 5-2. The equilibrium level of income remains at $520. At supply levels below $520, consumption plus investment spending exceeds what is being offered for sale. At supply levels above $520, consumption plus investment spending is less than output. For example, when businesses produce $540, firms are forced to hold as inventory the $10 of output they were unable to sell.

Table 2

Aggregate Supply (Output/Income)	Consumption	Investment	Aggregate Demand ($C + I$)
$480	$450	$50	$500
500	460	50	510
520	470	50	520
540	480	50	530
560	490	50	540

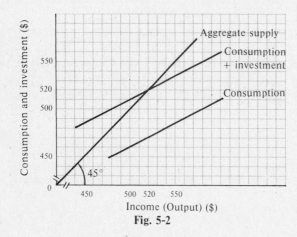

Fig. 5-2

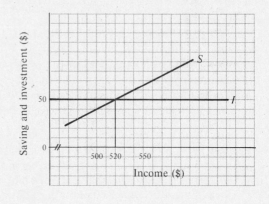

Fig. 5-3

5.2   SAVING, INVESTMENT AND EQUILIBRIUM

The equilibrium level of income can be found by a saving/investment (leakages/injection) approach as well as by equating aggregate supply and aggregate demand.   Saving is a leakage from the circular flow.   Investment spending is an injection into the circular flow that offsets a saving leakage.   The equilibrium level of income occurs where planned saving (total leakages) equals planned investment (total injections).

EXAMPLE 3.   In Table 3, *planned saving*, the difference between consumption and the income obtained from production, is added to the data of Example 2.   Planned saving equals planned investment at the $520 equilibrium level of income.   At income levels below $520, planned saving is less than planned investment, i.e. investment injections exceed saving leakages.   At income levels above $520, planned saving exceeds planned investment and saving leakages are greater than investment injections. See also Fig. 5-3.

Table 3

Aggregate Supply (Income/Output)	Consumption	Saving	Investment
$480	$450	$30	$50
500	460	40	50
520	470	50	50
540	480	60	50
560	490	70	50

5.3   THE MULTIPLIER EFFECT

Changes in investment demand or consumption demand change the equilibrium level of income.   Although either the consumption (or saving) function or investment schedule can shift, we shall assume that the autonomous change in aggregate demand orginates with investment.

EXAMPLE 4. Given the saving function and investment spending in Example 3, a $10 increase in investment shifts the investment schedule I' upward to I'' (see Fig. 5-4), resulting in a higher equilibrium level of income.

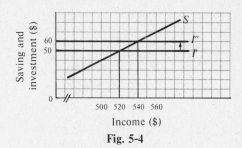

Fig. 5-4

Changes in investment demand, such as that assumed in Example 4, result in a change in the equilibrium level of income that is several times larger than the change in investment.   In Example 4, the $10 increase in investment spending raises the equilibrium level of income $20.   The multiplied effect of a change in autonomous spending occurs because consumption is dependent upon the level of income.   The multiplier measures the rate of change in income resulting from a change in autonomous spending.   In the model analyzed above, the multiplier equals 1/MPS or 1/(1-MPC).

EXAMPLE 5. Suppose investment increases $10 and the MPC is 0.50.   Households, in receiving additional income from the increase in investment, consume 0.50 of the change in income, which leads to further increases in production (income).

    Round 1: Increased investment causes an increase in the level of output (income).
    Round 2: Increased income from Round 1 induces consumption spending which in turn raises output (income).
    Round 3: Increased income from Round 2 induces consumption, further adding to the level of output (income).

In terms of a $10 increase in investment spending,

    Round 1: A $10 increase in investment causes a $10 increase in income.
    Round 2: The increased $10 income from Round 1 induces an additional $5 of consumption (MPC×$\Delta Y$ = 0.50×$10) which in turn raises the income level $5.
    Round 3: The increased $5 income from Round 2 induces an additional $2.50 of consumption (0.50×$5), which in turn raises the income level $2.50.

Summarizing,

	ΔI	ΔC	ΔY
Round 1	$10.00		$10.00
Round 2		$5.00	5.00
Round 3		2.50	2.50
Successive rounds		2.50	2.50
Sums	$10.00	$10.00	$20.00

A $10 increase in investment spending, given an MPC = 0.50, induces an additional $10 of consumption spending and results in a $20 increase in the equilibrium level of income.

5.4 EQUILIBRIUM INCOME AND FULL EMPLOYMENT

Since saving and investment are not related to a common variable, it is highly unlikely that equilibrium will occur at a full-employment level of income.   A *recessionary gap* exists if the full-employment level of income is above the equilibrium level of income.   An *inflationary gap* exists when full-employment income is less than the equilibrium income level.

EXAMPLE 6. In Fig. 5-5(a), the equilibrium level of income is below the $500 full-employment level of income.   There is a $25 recessionary gap because a $25 increase in autonomous aggregate demand is needed to bring the economy to full employment.
    In Fig. 5-5(b), aggregate demand exceeds the economy's capacity to produce.   There is a $15 inflationary gap because a $15 decrease in autonomous aggregate demand is needed to bring the economy to the $500 full-employment level of income.

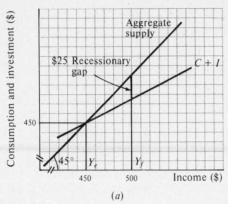
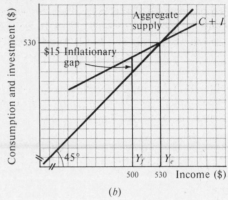

Fig. 5-5

Important Economic Terms

Aggregate demand.   In a private sector model, the dollar value of planned consumption by households and planned investment by businesses (i.e. aggregate demand equals $C + I$).

Aggregate supply.   The dollar value of output offered for sale by the business sector.

Autonomous spending.   Spending that is unrelated to the level of income.

Equilibrium income.   The income level that will be sustained because aggregate supply equals planned aggregate demand or alternatively, because planned saving equals planned investment.

Inflationary gap.   The decrease in autonomous spending needed to bring the economy to a noninflationary, full-employment level of income.   It is the vertical distance between the $C + I$ line and the 45° aggregate supply line at the full-employment level of income.

Multiplier.   The ratio of the change in income to the change in autonomous spending.   In the private sector model, the multiplier equals 1/MPS or 1/(1-MPC).

Recessionary gap.   The increase in autonomous spending needed to bring the economy to the full-employment level of income.   It is the vertical distance between the $C + I$ line and the 45° aggregate supply line at the full-employment level of income.

Unplanned inventory investment.   The balancing item that brings about the equality of actual and planned saving to actual investment.

Review Questions

1. In a private sector ($C + I$) model, the equilibrium level of income occurs where (a) planned consumption equals planned investment, (b) aggregate supply equals planned investment, (c) aggregate supply equals aggregate demand, (d) saving equals investment.

    Ans.   (c)

2. Suppose aggregate supply is $540, consumption is $460 and planned investment is $70. In this economy, ($a$) planned saving equals planned investment, (b) there is unplanned investment in inventories, (c) there is unplanned saving, (d) unplanned saving equals planned investment and unplanned investment.

    Ans.   (b)

3. If actual output is to the right of the intersection of aggregate supply and the $C + I$ (aggregate demand) line, (*a*) there is excess output, (*b*) there is unplanned investment in inventories, (*c*) planned saving exceeds planned investment, (*d*) all of the above, (*e*) none of the above.

    Ans. (*d*)

4. If actual output is to the left of the intersection of the saving function and the investment line, (*a*) there is excess output, (*b*) there is unplanned investment in inventories, (*c*) planned saving exceeds planned investment, (*d*) all of the above.

    Ans. (*b*)

5. If the marginal propensity to consume is 0.80, the multiplier equals (*a*) 2, (*b*) 3, (*c*) 4, (*d*) 5.

    Ans. (*d*)

6. There is a multiplier effect from changes in autonomous investment because (*a*) aggregate supply is dependent upon the level of income, (*b*) autonomous consumption is dependent upon the level of income, (*c*) consumption is dependent upon the level of income, (*d*) unplanned investment in inventories is dependent upon the level of income.

    Ans. (*c*)

7. The multiplier measures the (*a*) rate of change in income resulting from a change in autonomous spending, (*b*) rate of change in consumption resulting from a change in income, (*c*) rate of change in income resulting from a change in induced consumption, (*d*) rate of change in autonomous investment resulting from a change in income.

    Ans. (*a*)

8. If the MPC is 0.50, a $10 increase in autonomous investment will result in a (*a*) $10 increase in the equilibrium level of income, (*b*) $20 increase in the equilibrium level of income, (*c*) $10 increase in the level of autonomous consumption, (*d*) $20 increase in the level of induced consumption.

    Ans. (*b*)

9. A recessionary gap exists when (*a*) aggregate supply exceeds autonomous demand, (*b*) the $C + I$ line intersects aggregate supply at an income level to the right of the full-employment level of income, (*c*) the $C + I$ line intersects aggregate supply at an income level to the left of the full-employment level of income, (*d*) the $C + I$ line intersects aggregate supply at the full-employment level of income.

    Ans. (*c*)

10. If there is a $20 inflationary gap and the MPC is 0.50, (*a*) there is a $20 excess of aggregate demand, (*b*) there is a $20 deficiency in aggregate demand, (*c*) there is a $40 excess of aggregate demand, (*d*) there is a $40 deficiency in aggregate demand.

    Ans. (*d*)

Solved Problems

AGGREGATE SUPPLY, AGGREGATE DEMAND AND EQUILIBRIUM

5.1. (*a*) Find the equilibrium level of production if the data in Table 4 represents the business sector's willingness to sell different levels of output.

Table 4

Total production (units)	350	360	370	380	390
Demand (units)	360	365	370	375	380

(b) Assuming a price level of $2, convert Table 4 into a schedule of aggregate supply and aggregate demand.

(c) Interpret the relationship between aggregate supply and aggregate demand if the business sector produces above a $740 level of income.

(a) Equilibrium output occurs at 370 units, when the business sector is able to sell its total production.

(b) Aggregate supply is the output offered for sale while aggregate demand is the quantity demanded at different levels of income. See Table 5.

Table 5

Aggregate Supply (Output/Income)	Aggregate Demand
$700	$720
720	730
740	740
760	750
780	760

(c) Beyond a $740 level of income (output), aggregate supply exceeds aggregate demand. When aggregate supply is $760, $10 (5 units) of output is not sold; $20 remains when $780 is supplied. Beyond a $740 level of income (output), firms are unable to sell their entire output and must hold the excess as inventory. During future production periods, output levels will be lowered in order to reduce these forced inventory accumulations (i.e. unplanned investment in inventories).

5.2. Refer to the data in Table 6. (a) Find the equilibrium level of income. (b) What gives rise to unplanned investment in inventories? (c) What is the level of unplanned investment in inventories when the income level is $450, $500 and $550? (d) What is the meaning of an equilibrium level of income?

Table 6

Aggregate Supply (Output/Income)	Consumption	Investment	Aggregate Demand (C + I)
$400.00	$350.00	$75.00	$425.00
450.00	387.50	75.00	462.50
500.00	425.00	75.00	500.00
550.00	462.50	75.00	537.50
600.00	500.00	75.00	575.00
650.00	537.50	75.00	612.50

(a) The equilibrium level of income is $500, at which aggregate supply equals aggregate demand.

(b) Unplanned investment in inventories is the difference between aggregate supply and aggregate demand. When aggregate demand exceeds aggregate supply, businesses are *forced to draw down* desired inventory levels to meet demand. When aggregate supply exceeds aggregate demand, businesses are *forced to add* to planned inventory holdings because they have been unable to sell the entire ouput. Unplanned investment in inventories is zero when aggregate supply equals aggregate demand (i.e. when there is an equilibrium level of income).

(c) Unplanned investment in inventories is −$12.50 when aggregate supply is $450, 0 when it is $500 and +$12.50 when it is $550. Thus, planned inventory is drawn down $12.50 when the production level is $450 while businesses are forced to add $12.50 to their desired inventory holdings when production is $550.

(d) A equilibrium level of income is the level of output where the quantities of goods and services offered for sale (aggregate supply) are equal to consumption and investment expenditures (aggregate demand). An equilibrium level of income will be sustained as long as there is no change in aggregate supply or aggregate demand.

5.3.   Graph the data from Problem 5.2, and indicate the equilibrium levels of income, consumption and investment.

  In Fig. 5-6, the aggregate supply schedule is the 45° line through the origin.   The equilibrium level of income is $500 and is determined by the intersection of the aggregate supply and aggregate demand $(C+I)$ lines.   Consumption spending at the equilibrium level of income is $425, and is found by reading across the consumption function from the $500 income level.   Investment is $75, the difference between the consumption function C and the $C+I$ line.

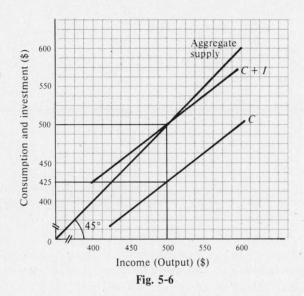

Fig. 5-6

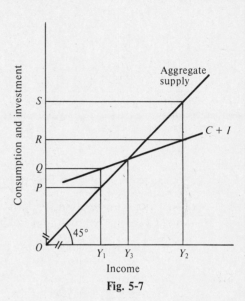

Fig. 5-7

5.4.   (a) From Fig. 5-7, find the levels of aggregate demand and unplanned inventory investment when production is Y_1 and Y_2.   (b) Do either of these income levels represent an equilibrium position?

  (a)   At income level Y_1, aggregate demand is OQ while aggregate supply is OP; unplanned inventory investment is PQ.
        At income level Y_2, aggregate demand is OR and aggregate supply is OS; unplanned inventory investment is RS.

  (b)   Neither Y_1 nor Y_2 is an equilibrum level of output. Y_3 is the equilibrium level of income because aggregate supply equals aggregate demand at Y_3.

5.5.   Suppose that consumption spending is given by the equation $C = \$100 + 0.50Y$ and I is $75.   (a) Plot $C+I$ on a graph and find the equilibrium level of income.   (b) Find the equilibrium level of income by solving the equilibrium equation: aggregate supply $Y =$ aggregate demand $C+I$.

  (a)   In Fig. 5-8, consumption is $100 when $Y = 0$ and $150 when $Y = 100$.   Connecting these points, we obtain the linear consumption function C_1.   Adding $75 of investment to the consumption function gives the aggregate spending line $C+I$.   Aggregate supply equals aggregate demand at the $350 income level.

  (b)   Aggregate supply = aggregate demand.

$$
\begin{aligned}
Y &= C + I \\
  &= \$100 + 0.50\,Y + \$75 \\
Y - 0.50\,Y &= \$100 + \$75 \\
0.50\,Y &= \$175 \\
Y &= \$175/0.50 = \$350
\end{aligned}
$$

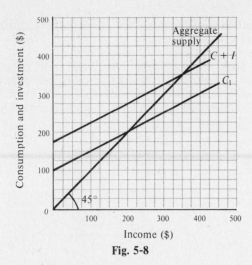

Fig. 5-8

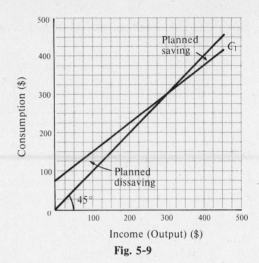

Fig. 5-9

SAVING, INVESTMENT AND EQUILIBRIUM

5.6. From the consumption function in Fig. 5-9, (a) derive a saving function and (b) find the level of saving when output is $200, $300 and $400.

(a) From the consumption function we see that consumption is $300 when income is $300 and is $375 when income is $400. Since saving equals income minus consumption, saving is 0 when income is $300 and is $25 when income is $400. Connecting these points with a straight line, we have the linear saving function S_1 in Fig. 5-10.

(b) Saving is the distance between the consumption line and the 45° aggregate supply line. In Fig. 5-9, when aggregate supply (income) is $200, consumption is $225 and saving is −$25. When income is $300, consumption is $300 and saving is 0. When income is $400, consumption is $375 and saving is $25.

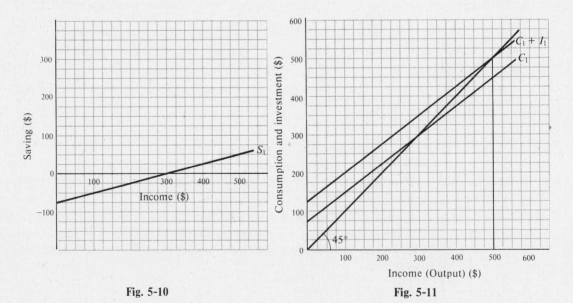

Fig. 5-10

Fig. 5-11

5.7. From Fig. 5-11, (a) find the level of planned saving and planned investment when the income level is $400, $500 and $550, and (b) Identify the equilibrium level of income. (c) Why does planned saving equal planned investment at equilibrium?

(a) Planned investment is the difference between consumption function C_1 and aggregate demand line $C_1 + I_1$. Planned investment is a constant $50. Planned saving is the distance between the consumption function line C_1 and the 45° aggregate supply line. Planned saving is $25 when income is $400, $50 when income is $500 and $67.50 when income is $550.

(b) Equilibrium occurs at an income level of $500, at which aggregate supply equals aggregate demand. At the equilibrium level of income, planned saving equals planned investment.

(c) An income level is sustained (there is equilibrium) when aggregate supply equals aggregate demand. When planned saving (saving leakages) is less than planned investment, firms reduce planned inventory holdings to meet demand (i.e. investment plans are frustrated). When planned saving exceeds planned investment, saving leakages exceed investment injections and firms are forced to hold an inventory larger than planned. Equilibrium occurs where planned saving leakages are matched by planned investment injections.

5.8. (a) From Fig. 5-12, find *planned* saving and *planned* investment as well as *actual* saving and *actual* investment at a $350, $400 and $450 income level. (b) Why does actual saving always equal actual investment? (c) What is the equilibrium level of income?

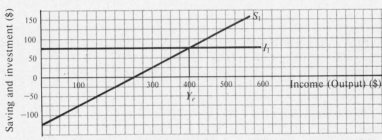

Fig. 5-12

(a) Planned investment is $75 regardless of the level of income. From saving function S_1, planned saving is $50 when income is $350, $75 when income is $400 and $100 when income is $450.

Actual saving and actual investment are the amounts realized. We shall assume that planned saving is always realized, i.e. actual saving equals planned saving. Actual investment, however, has planned and unplanned components; the unplanned component depends upon spending levels. For example, if businesses' planned investment is $75 but inventory must be drawn down $10 to meet demand, actual investment is $65 and is equal to the sum of planned ($75) and unplanned (−$10) investment. Actual and planned saving and investment for the income levels specified are given in Table 7.

Table 7

Income	Planned Saving	Actual Saving	Planned Investment	Unplanned Investment	Actual Investment
$350	$ 50	$ 50	$75	−$25	$ 50
400	75	75	75	0	75
450	100	100	75	25	100

(b) Unplanned inventory investment is the balancing item that equates actual saving and investment. If households do not consume and save instead, businesses must voluntarily or involuntarily invest in current output. Thus, actual saving must always equal actual investment. It is only when business investment is at desired levels that this equality results in an equilibrium level of income.

(c) The equilibrium level of income is $400 because planned saving equals planned investment at the $400 income level.

THE MULTIPLIER EFFECT

5.9.   Suppose there is a $25 increase in investment and the investment schedule in Fig. 5-13 shifts up from I_1 to I_2.   (a) Find the equilibrium level of income before and after the change in investment.   (b) Relate the change in income to the change in investment ($\Delta Y/\Delta I$) to find the multiplier effect of the autonomous change in investment.

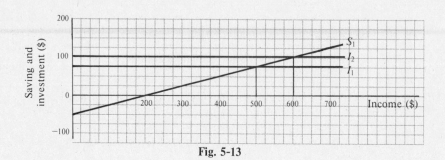

Fig. 5-13

(a)   Given investment schedule I_1, equilibrium income equals $500 and increases to $600 when a $25 increase in investment shifts the investment schedule to I_2.

(b) $\Delta Y = \$100$ and $\Delta I = \$25$.   The $25 autonomous increase in investment has a multiplier effect of 4 because $\Delta Y/\Delta I = \$100/\$25 = 4$.   That is, every $1 increase in investment raises the income level $4.

5.10.   Why does an autonomous change in investment have a multiple effect upon the equilibrium level of income?

An autonomous change in investment (the shift of the investment schedule in Fig. 5-13) has a multiple effect upon equilibrium income because consumption is dependent on the receipt of income.   Using the situation in Problem 5.9, the $25 increase in investment necessitates increased output.   Output is increased by hiring additional economic resources which are supplied by the household sector.   The $25 paid households for the production of an additional $25 of investment goods is partially consumed (MPC $\times \Delta Y$) and partially saved (MPS $\times \Delta Y$).   The increased consumption results in additional output and, therefore, in increased income for the household sector. This additional income in turn induces additional consumption spending.   Thus, the initial increase in investment induces enough consumption spending to bring about a multiple increase in the level of income.

The multiplier effect of the $25 increase in investment in Problem 5.9 is traced below.   Note that the change in planned investment equals the change in planned saving.

Round	ΔI	ΔY	ΔC		ΔS
1	$25.00 ⟶	$25.00 ⟶	$18.75	and	$6.25
2		18.75 ⟶	14.06	and	4.69
3		14.06 ⟶	10.55	and	3.51
4		10.55 ⟶	7.91	and	2.64
Successive Rounds		31.64 ⟶	23.73	and	7.91
Sum	$25.00	$100.00	$75.00		$25.00

5.11.   The multiplier effect of autonomous changes in spending (e.g. $\Delta Y/\Delta I$) equals 1/MPS or $1/(1-\text{MPC})$. (Recall that MPC + MPS = 1.) (a) Find the value of the multiplier when the MPC = 0.50, 0.75 and 0.80.   (b) What change in the equilibrium level of income results from a $10 increase in investment when the MPC = 0.50, 0.75 and 0.80?   (c) What is the relationship between the size of the multiplier and the MPC?   (d) What is the multiplier effect when the MPC = 0?

(a) When the marginal propensity to consume is 0.50, the value of the multiplier equals $1/(1-0.50)$ = 2. When the MPC = 0.75, the multiplier is $1/(1-0.75) = 4$; it is $1/(1-0.80) = 5$ when the MPC = 0.80.

(b) The change in the equilibrium level of income ΔY equals the change in investment ΔI times the multiplier.   Thus,

$$\text{when the MPC} = 0.50,\ \Delta Y = \Delta I[1/(1-\text{MPC})]\ = \$10\,[1/(1-0.50)] = \$20$$
$$\text{when the MPC} = 0.75,\ \Delta Y = \Delta I[1/(1-\text{MPC})]\ = \$10\,[1/(1-0.75)] = \$40$$
$$\text{when the MPC} = 0.80,\ \Delta Y = \Delta I[1/(1-\text{MPC})]\ = \$10\,[1/(1-0.80)] = \$50$$

(c) Part (a) shows a direct relationship between the size of the MPC and the multiplier, i.e. the larger the MPC, the greater the multiplier.

(d) There is a multiplier effect of 1 when the MPC = 0, $[k_e = 1/(1-\text{MPC}) = 1/(1-0) = 1]$. Thus, $\Delta Y = \Delta I \times 1 = \Delta I$.

5.12.   Suppose households elect to save more and shift the saving function in Fig. 5-14 from S_1 to S_2.

(a) What is planned saving for saving functions S_1 and S_2 at a $600 income level?

(b) What happens to the equilibrium level of income as a result of the shift in the saving function?

(c) Compare the levels of planned saving at equilibrium income before and after the shift of the saving function.

(d) Can a society increase saving by becoming more thrifty?

(e) Why is there a "paradox of thrift"?

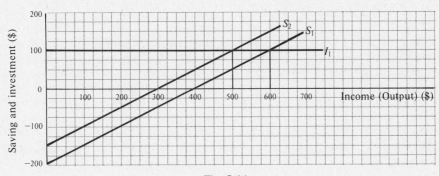

Fig. 5-14

(a) At a $600 income level, saving is $100 for saving function S_1 and $150 for S_2.   Households in effect have decided to increase the amount saved at each income level.

(b) The equilibrium level of income falls from $600 to $500.

(c) Planned saving is $100 at both equilibrium levels of income.   Since planned investment remains at $100, the income level must generate $100 in planned saving at the equilibrium level of income.   After the shift of the saving function, the $100 in planned saving occurs at a lower level of income.

(d) If there is no change in planned investment, a society cannot increase saving by decreasing consumption.   By decreasing consumption, the economy simply moves to a lower level of income.

(e) Thrift (saving) is necessary for investment (additions to the economy's stock of capital).   Therefore, saving is a necessary condition for capital expansion.   An increase in saving, however, with no change in planned investment is not beneficial to society since it will result in a decrease in income and employment.   Similarly, while saving is beneficial for each member of a society, in the aggregate, saving is detrimental to general welfare because it increases unemployment.

EQUILIBRIUM INCOME AND FULL EMPLOYMENT

5.13. (*a*) What is a recessionary gap?   Given the aggregate supply and aggregate demand schedules in Fig. 5-15, find (*b*) the economy's equilibrium level of income, (*c*) the magnitude of the recessionary gap if a $500 income level represents full employment, and (*d*) the change in autonomous spending needed to bring the economy to full employment, if the marginal propensity to consume is 0.50.

   (*a*)   There is a *recessionary gap* when aggregate supply is above the aggregate demand line at full employment.   A *recessionary gap* exists when the equilibrium level of income is below the full-employment income level and indicates that economic resources are not at full employment.

   (*b*)   The equilibrium level of income is $450.

   (*c*)   A recessionary gap is the distance between the aggregate supply and aggregate demand lines at full employment.   In Fig. 5-15, the recessionary gap is $25.

   (*d*)   The needed change in autonomous spending is the $25 recessionary gap identified in part (*c*).   The multiplier is 2 when the MPC = 0.50.   Thus, the $25 increase in autonomous spending times a multiplier of 2 produces a $50 change in the equilibrium level of income.   The $25 change in autonomous spending moves the economy from the current $450 equilibrium position to the $500 full-employment level of income.

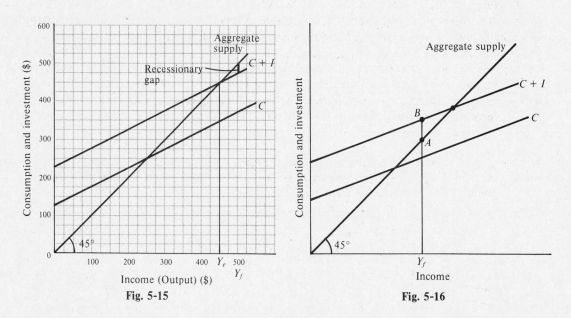

Fig. 5-15   Fig. 5-16

5.14. Suppose that in Fig. 5-16, Y_f is the full-employment level of income.   (*a*) Why is the distance *AB* between aggregate supply and aggregate demand at full employment an inflationary gap?   (*b*) What tends to happen to prices when there is an inflationary gap?

   (*a*)   An inflationary gap exists when the aggregate demand schedule is above aggregate supply at the full-employment level of income.   The distance *AB* in Fig. 5-16 measures the reduction in autonomous demand needed to bring the economy to an equilibrium level at which there is full employment and no inflationary pressures due to excessive demand.

   (*b*)   When there is an inflationary gap, aggregate demand exceeds aggregate supply at full employment.   Because the economy cannot expand output and there is unsatisfied demand, prices will tend to rise.

Chapter 6

Fiscal Policy and National Income

6.1 INTRODUCTION

Through the Employment Act of 1946, the United States government assumed responsibility for promoting "maximum employment, production and purchasing power." This chapter analyzes the fiscal measures the Federal government can take to promote economic stability.

6.2 GOVERNMENT SPENDING, TAXES AND THE LEVEL OF INCOME

In adding a public sector to the economic model in Chapter 4, government spending and taxes become two additional variables affecting the level of income and employment. Increased government spending shifts the aggregate demand schedule upward by the same amount as an equal increase in net investment (see Example 1). Decreased taxes cause upward shifts in aggregate demand because personal income taxes affect households' disposable income (see Problem 6.1), which in turn alters the levels of saving and consumption (see Example 2). In the leakages-injection approach to income determination, increased government spending, an injection, shifts the investment plus government spending schedule upward while decreased taxes, a leakage, shifts the saving plus taxes schedule to the right (see Problem 6.3).

EXAMPLE 1. Government spending G, like consumption C and net investment I, is a component of aggregate demand. Increases in government spending, such as ΔG in Fig. 6-1, shift the aggregate demand schedule upward from $C + I + G$ to $C + I + G + \Delta G$.

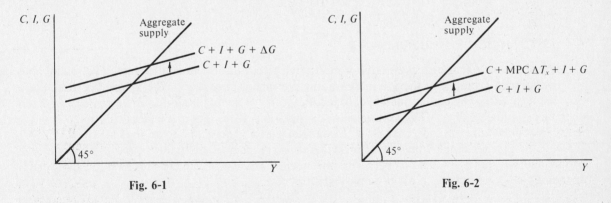

| Fig. 6-1 | Fig. 6-2 |

EXAMPLE 2. Taxes affect household disposable income and therefore the level of consumption and saving. The vertical shift in aggregate demand from a change in taxes equals $-\text{MPC}\Delta T_x$. In Fig. 6-2, the decrease in taxes ΔT_x causes an upward shift of aggregate demand from $C + I + G$ to $C + \text{MPC}\Delta T_x + I + G$.

6.3 DISCRETIONARY FISCAL POLICY

Discretionary fiscal policy involves deliberate changes in the level of government spending and/ or government's net tax revenues in order to reach a desired level of income. Government's net tax revenues equal gross tax receipts less transfers; net tax revenues fall when gross tax receipts decrease and/or government transfer payments increase. If a recessionary gap exists, the government can increase aggregate demand to the full-employment level of income by increasing government spending or decreasing net tax revenues (see Example 3).

EXAMPLE 3.   Suppose that D_1 in Fig. 6-3 is the current level of aggregate demand and the $750 income level represents full employment.   There is a $10 recessionary gap at the $700 equilibrium level of income.
    Discretionary Policy A: *Increased Government Spending*.   A $10 increase in government spending would shift the aggregate demand schedule from D_1 and D_2 and bring the economy to the $750 full-employment level of income.
    Discretionary Policy B: *Decrease in Gross Tax Receipts*.   If the marginal propensity to consume is 0.80, a $12.50 decrease in gross tax receipts (a tax cut) will reduce net tax revenues $12.50, cause a $10 increase in the consumption schedule (0.80 × $12.50) and shift the aggregate demand schedule from D_1 to D_2.
    Discretionary Policy C: *Increase in Government Transfer Payments*.   If the marginal propensity to consume is 0.80, a $12.50 increase in government transfer payments (e.g. an increase in welfare payments) will reduce net tax revenues $12.50, cause a $10 increase in the consumption schedule (0.80 × $12.50) and shift the aggregate demand schedule from D_1 to D_2.

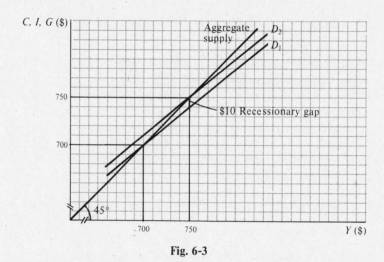

Fig. 6-3

6.4   FISCAL POLICY MULTIPLIERS

    Discretionary fiscal measures have a multiplier effect upon the equilibrium level of income. For instance, in Example 3, the $10 increase in government spending or the $12.50 decrease in net tax revenues raised the equilibrium level of income $50.   The multiplier for changes in government spending k_e equals $1/(1 - \text{MPC})$ as it does for changes in private sector spending (ΔI or ΔC).   The multiplier for net tax revenue changes k_{tx} is smaller and negative and equal to $-\text{MPC}/(1 - \text{MPC})$. If we know the full-employment level of income, the respective multipliers, and the current level of income, we should be able to prescribe the needed change in net tax revenues or government spending that would produce a full-employment level of income.

EXAMPLE 4.   Suppose the equilibrium level of income is $700, the MPC is 0.75, and the full-employment level of income is $760.   An additional $60 in income will bring the economy to full employment.   With the expenditure multiplier equal to 4 and the tax multiplier equal to -3, this is achieved by a $15 increase in government spending or a $20 decrease in net taxes (a $20 decrease in gross tax receipts or a $20 increase in government transfers).
    Since $\Delta Y = k_e \Delta G$, the required increase in government spending to achieve the full-employment level of income is

$$\Delta G = \Delta Y / k_e$$

where $\Delta Y = \$60$ (the required increase in income) and $k_e = 1/(1 - \text{MPC}) = 1/(1 - 0.75) = 4$.   Thus, $\Delta G = \$60/4 = \$15$.

Since $\Delta Y = k_{tx}\Delta T_x$, the required decrease in net tax revenues to achieve the full-employment level of income is

$$\Delta T_x = \Delta Y / k_{tx}$$

where ΔY equals \$60 (the required increase in income) and k_{tx} equals -3 [since $k_{tx} = -\text{MPC}/(1 - \text{MPC}) = -0.75/(1 - 0.75) = -3$], so that $\Delta T_x = \$60/-3 = -\$20$.

The fiscal measures prescribed in Example 4 may result in budget deficits (see Problem 6.7) which are unacceptable to individuals who believe that government expenditures should be totally financed by taxes.   Equal changes in government spending G and net taxes T_x, however, are not neutral in their effect upon the level of income (see Example 5) because the balanced budget multiplier is 1 (see Problem 6.8).   It follows, therefore, that the absolute increase in government spending and taxes is minimized by instituting fiscal measures that result in budget deficits rather than by fiscal measures that generate a balanced budget (see Problem 6.9).

EXAMPLE 5. Suppose that the current level of income is \$700 and that net taxes and government spending both equal \$60.   If the MPC is 0.80, the expenditure multiplier $[k_e = 1/(1 - \text{MPC})]$ equals 5 while the tax multiplier $[k_{tx} = -\text{MPC}/(1 - \text{MPC})]$ equals -4.   A \$10 increase in government spending *and* net taxes maintains a balanced budget and raises the level of income \$10.

The effect of a \$10 increase in government spending is

$$\Delta Y = k_e \Delta G = 5 \times \$10 = \$50$$

The effect of a \$10 increase in taxes is

$$\Delta Y = k_{tx}\Delta T_x = -4 \times \$10 = -\$40$$

The net effect of a \$10 increase in government spending and taxes is

$$\Delta Y = k_e \Delta G + k_{tx}\Delta T_x = 5 \times \$10 + (-4) \times \$10 = \$50 - \$40 = \$10$$

6.5 BUILT-IN STABILIZERS

An income tax and such social programs as unemployment compensation, welfare payments, and subsidies to families generate automatic changes in tax revenues as the economy moves away from (or toward) the full-employment level of income (see Problem 6.12).   These automatic changes in net tax revenues moderate fluctuations in households' disposable income and aggregate consumption and curb the severity of economic fluctuations (see Example 6).   While beneficial in the short run, built-in stabilizers may be a "fiscal drag" in the long run because they may prevent aggregate demand from growing at the same rate as aggregate supply (see Problem 6.13).   As a result of the potential long-run effects of built-in stabilizers, economists have found it useful to analyze the need for discretionary economic policy in terms of a full-employment budget rather than the actual budget (see Problem 6.14).

EXAMPLE 6. Suppose the government guarantees that it will pay labor force participants who become unemployed one-third of their weekly employed income up to a maximum of \$150 for a period not to exceed six months.   Given such a guarantee, the government automatically pays unemployment benefits to those who lose jobs as economic activity declines.   It therefore follows that government's net tax revenues fall during an economic contraction because the government returns a portion of its gross receipts to the unemployed. Households' aggregate income also falls, but by less than if transfer payments were not paid to the unemployed.   Thus, unemployment insurance moderates changes in households' aggregate disposable income, reduces declines in aggregate consumption, and thereby reduces economic instability.

6.6 THE PUBLIC DEBT

The government sector finances its expenditures by taxing, borrowing or printing money.   Views on borrowing as an alternative to taxing are analyzed in this section; money creation is treated in Chapter 9.

Historically, it was believed that the government sector should balance its budget annually, i.e. tax revenues should equal government spending in each fiscal year.   Since the 1930s, however, there has been greater acceptance of the philosophy of cyclically balanced budgets; functional finance later became acceptable as the economics of fiscal policy was better understood (see Problem 6.15).   Functional finance discredits the importance of the public debt and focuses instead upon the use of fiscal measures to achieve full employment.   The lack of concern about the public debt by proponents of functional finance, however, increases the likelihood of unsupervised growth of government expenditures and net tax revenues.

Important Economic Terms

Balanced-budget multiplier. The principle that equal changes in government spending and taxes alter the equilibrium level of income by the amount of the balanced change in the budget.

Built-in stabilizers.   The automatic changes in net tax revenues that result from changes in the level of income which moderate fluctuations in aggregate demand and stabilize economic activity.

Discretionary fiscal policy.   A deliberate change in the level of government spending and/or taxes by Congress to reach a desired level of income.

Employment Act of 1946.   Legislation which committed the United States government to promoting maximum employment, productivity and purchasing power.

Fiscal drag.   An economic condition which occurs when aggregate demand fails to grow at a rate equal to that of aggregate supply because the rising receipts from a progressive income tax exceed the growth of government spending.

Fiscal policy. The use of changes in government spending and taxes to achieve the economic goals of the Employment Act of 1946.

Full-employment budget.   An estimate of what the goverment's net tax receipts and expenditures would be if the economy were at full employment.

Functional finance.   A fiscal philosophy reflecting the belief that a balanced Federal budget is of secondary importance to the goal of a noninflationary, full-employment economy.

Public debt.   The amount owed by the government to lenders as a result of past budget deficits.

Tax multiplier.   The multiple effect upon income of discretionary changes in taxes. The tax multiplier equals $-\text{MPC}/(1-\text{MPC})$.

Review Questions

1. An increase in government spending shifts the aggregate demand schedule (a) upward by the increase in government spending, (b) downward by the increase in government spending, (c) upward by the increase in government spending times the expenditure multiplier, (d) downward by the increase in government spending times the expenditure multiplier.

    Ans.   (a)

2. In the leakages-injection approach to income determination, an increase in taxes shifts (a) the investment plus government spending schedule upward, (b) the investment plus government spending schedule downward, (c) the saving plus taxes schedule to the right, (d) the saving plus taxes schedule to the left.

    Ans.   (d)

3. An inflationary gap can be eliminated by (a) equal increases in net tax revenues and government spending, (b) an increase in government spending and a decrease in net tax revenues, (c) equal decreases in net tax revenues and government spending, (d) a decrease in net tax revenues.

    Ans. (c)

4. Discretionary fiscal policy includes (a) automatic changes in gross tax receipts that result from the income tax structure, (b) payment of unemployment insurance, (c) deliberate changes in the level of government spending and net tax receipts, (d) making welfare payments, (e) none of the above.

    Ans. (c)

5. Suppose the equilibrium level of income is $600, the MPC is 0.80, and the full-employment level of income is $680.   Full employment can be achieved by a $16 increase in government spending or which of the following changes in net tax revenues? (a) $20 decrease, (b) $20 increase, (c) $16 increase, (d) $16 decrease.

    Ans. (a)

6. Which of the following situations will result in a $50 increase in the equilibrium level of income when the MPC equals 0.80?
    (a) $10 increases in net tax revenues and government spending.
    (b) $12.50 increases in net tax revenues and government spending.
    (c) $12.50 increase in net tax revenues and $10 increase in government spending.
    (d) $12.50 increase in net tax revenues and $20 increase in government spending.

    Ans. (d)

7. If the MPC is 0.70, the balanced-budget multiplier is (a) 1, (b) 1.5, (c) 2, (d) 2.5.

    Ans. (a)

8. Built-in stabilizers are
    (a) discretionary fiscal actions available to the President,
    (b) automatic increases in government spending on public works projects,
    (c) discretionary changes in taxes,
    (d) automatic changes in tax revenues that occur when the economy moves away from full employment.

    Ans. (d)

9. According to the proponents of functional finance,
    (a) the public debt is secondary to the goal of full employment,
    (b) the public budget should be balanced annually,
    (c) the public budget should be balanced cyclically,
    (d) the government should neutralize the effect of the public debt on the private sector.

    Ans. (a)

10. The public debt imposes a burden on future generations if
    (a) the government balances the budget over the business cycle,
    (b) it is completely owed to citizens of the issuing country,
    (c) it is largely owed to foreigners,
    (d) taxes do not have to be increased in the future to cover higher interest payments on the debt.

    Ans. (c)

Solved Problems

DISCRETIONARY FISCAL POLICY

6.1. Suppose that a household with a marginal propensity to consume of 0.80 consumes its entire disposable income at a disposable income level of $10,000.

    (a) Calculate the levels of disposable income Y_d, consumption C, and saving S when the household's earned income is $11,000, $12,000, $13,000, $14,000 and $15,000 and it pays no taxes.

    (b) Redo part (a), assuming that the household pays $1000 in taxes to the government at each level of earned income.

    (c) What effect does a $1000 tax at the $11,000 level of earned income have upon the levels of consumption and saving?

    (d) Graph the data derived in parts (a) and (b) so that disposable income is measured on the x axis.

    (e) Redo part (d) so that earned income is measured on the x axis.

    (f) Compare the data in parts (d) and (e).

    (a) See Table 1. When there are no taxes, earned income equals disposable income. With an MPC of 0.80, $800 of each additional $1000 is consumed and $200 is saved. Since $C = Y_d$ when $Y_d = \$10,000$, C is $10,800 when $Y_d = \$11,000$.

Table 1

Earned Income	Y_d	C	S
$11,000	$11,000	$10,800	$ 200
$12,000	$12,000	$11,600	$ 400
$13,000	$13,000	$12,400	$ 600
$14,000	$14,000	$13,200	$ 800
$15,000	$15,000	$14,000	$1,000

    (b) See Table 2. Disposable income equals earned income less taxes ($Y_d = Y - T_x$). If taxes equal $1000, $C = Y_d$ when earned income is $11,000.

Table 2

Earned Income	T_x	Y_d	C	S
$11,000	$1,000	$10,000	$10,000	$ 0
12,000	1,000	11,000	10,800	200
13,000	1,000	12,000	11,600	400
14,000	1,000	13,000	12,400	600
15,000	1,000	14,000	13,200	800

    (c) The change in consumption equals the change in taxes multiplied by a negative MPC; the change in saving equals the change in taxes multiplied by a negative MPS. Thus, a $1000 increase in taxes decreases consumption $800 ($-0.80 \times \$1000 = -\$800$) and saving $200. At the $11,000 level of earned income, the imposition of $1000 in taxes reduces consumption from $10,800 to $10,000 and saving from $200 to $0.

    (d) In Fig. 6-4, the data on C and Y_d from Tables 1 and 2 produce one straight-line consumption function. This is expected since the MPC [MPC $= \Delta C / \Delta Y_d$] is 0.80 for all levels of diposable income.

    (e) In Fig. 6-5, there is an $800 downward shift in the consumption line from C_1 (when there are no taxes) to C_2 (when taxes of $1000 are imposed).

(*f*) When disposable income is measured along the *x* axis, there is no shift of the consumption function when there is a tax change. When earned income is measured along the *x* axis, however, the consumpton function shifts downward by −MPC times any increase in taxes. [Note that there is no shift of the consumption function in Fig. 6-4 when taxes increase $1000, but in Fig. 6-5 at the $11,000 level of earned income, consumption falls from $10,800 to $10,000 (−MPC ΔT_x) as a result of the $1000 tax.] In graphing aggregate consumption with aggregate income, then, the aggregate consumption function will shift downward by −MPC ΔT_x when taxes increase and upward by −MPC ΔT_x when taxes decrease.

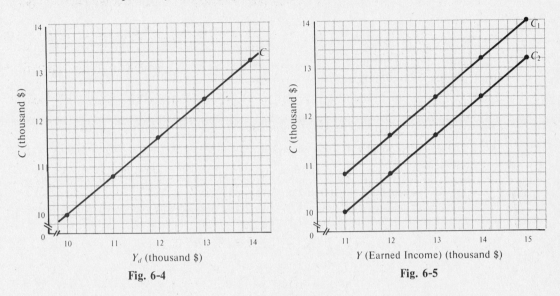

Fig. 6-4   Fig. 6-5

6.2 What effect do the following have upon the aggregate demand schedule? Treat each event separately. (*a*) a $15 increase in government spending. (*b*) a $10 increase in investment. (*c*) a $15 decrease in net taxes when the marginal propensity to consume is 0.80.

(*a*) The aggregate demand schedule shifts by the amount of the change in government spending. In this case, there is a $15 upward shift of the aggregate demand schedule.

(*b*) Changes in investment cause shifts in the aggregate demand schedule equal to the change in investment. Here, there is a $10 upward shift of the aggregate demand schedule.

(*c*) Tax changes cause the aggregate demand schedule to shift by −MPC ΔT_x. Since net taxes decrease $15, there is a $12 [$12 = −0.80 (−$15)] upward shift of the aggregate demand schedule.

6.3. In the expanded model with a public sector, the leakage-injection approach to income determination requires that leakages (household saving S_H + taxes T_X) equal injections (net investment I + government spending G).

(*a*) Why are taxes viewed as a leakage while government spending is considered an injection?

(*b*) Starting from an initial position where $G = 0$ and $T_x = 0$, show the effect of G and T_x increases on leakage-injection schedules by discussing the effect of (1) a $10 increase in government spending in Fig. 6-6 and (2) a $20 increase in taxes when the MPC is 0.50 in Fig. 6-7.

(*a*) When the government taxes and does not spend the tax receipts, payments resulting from production are not being returned through spending. That is, there is a leakage from the circular flow just as there is when households save some of their disposable income. The spending of tax receipts, i.e. government spending, returns payments to the circular flow. Government expenditures, like investment, then, are an injection of spending.

(*b*) In (1), a $10 increase in government spending from 0 to $10 shifts spending schedule I upward by $10 in Fig. 6-6 to $I + G$. In (2), a $20 increase in taxes from 0 to $20, when the MPS is 0.50, shifts the saving schedule upward from S_H in Fig. 6-7 to $S_H + T_x$ (the vertical shift equals −MPSΔT_x).

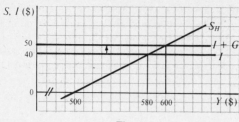

Fig. 6-6   Fig. 6-7

6.4. Suppose that D_1 in Fig. 6-8 is a schedule of aggregate demand and there is full employment at a $600 level of income.
  (a)   Is there an inflationary or recessionary gap?
  (b)   What discretionary fiscal measure can be used to eliminate the gap? Assume the MPC is 0.80.
  (c)   If investment spending should fall by $10, what discretionary policy action is needed?

  (a)   There is a $12 inflationary gap since aggregate demand exceeds aggregate supply at the $600 full-employment level of income.
  (b)   A $15 increase in net taxes ($-\text{MPC}\Delta T_x$) or a $12 decrease in government spending are alternate means of eliminating the inflationary gap.
  (c)   If investment spending should fall by $10, the inflationary gap is reduced to $2.   Net taxes would now have to increase by only $2.50 or government spending would need to decrease by only $2.00.

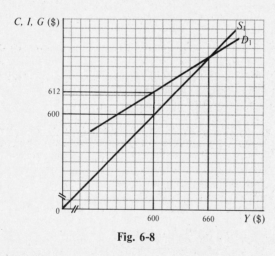

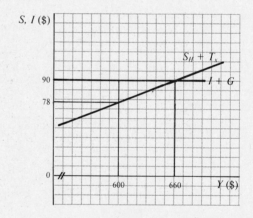

Fig. 6-8   Fig. 6-9

6.5. Given: the leakage injections schedules in Fig. 6-9 with full employment achieved at the $600 level of income.
  (a)   Is there an inflationary or recessionary gap?
  (b)   What change in government spending or taxes is needed to bring the economy to the $600 level of full employment?   Assume that the MPC = 0.80.

  (a.) There is an inflationary gap since injections ($I + G$) exceed leakages ($S_H + T_x$) at the full-employment level of income.   The inflationary gap equals $12.
  (b)   The situation in Fig. 6-9 is a leakage-injection presentation of the situation in Problem 6.4.   Thus, a $15 increase in net taxes or a $12 decrease in government spending is needed to eliminate the inflationary gap.

6.6. In Fig. 6-10, suppose that government spending and taxes equal zero and there is a $20 recessionary gap.   If government increases its spending $20 to eliminate this gap, where does it obtain the funds to meet these expenditures?

By increasing spending, government increases the level of income, which in turn increases the quantity of household saving. At the new $600 full-employment and equilibrium level of income, saving has increased from $80 to $100. Thus, if government spends and does not tax to close a recessionary gap, it may borrow the additional saving generated by its stimulative economic policy. That is, borrowing rather than taxation may be the source of financing an expansion in government spending.

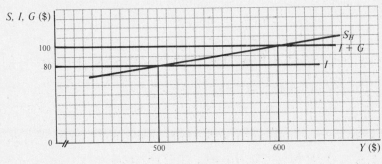

Fig. 6-10

FISCAL POLICY MULTIPLIERS

6.7.   Suppose the current level of income equals $700, aggregate consumption is $570, investment equals $70, government spending is $60, and taxes equal $60.

(a) Find the tax and expenditure multipliers if the MPC is 0.80.

(b) What effect will a $10 increase in government spending have upon the equilibrium level of income?

(c) What changes are there in aggregate consumption and saving as a result of the increase in government spending?

(d) How is the $10 increase in government spending financed?

(e) To avoid a deficit, suppose a $10 increase in taxes accompanies the $10 increase in government spending. What effect will these fiscal measures have upon the equilibrium level of income?

(a)   When the MPC is 0.80, the tax multiplier is -4 and the expenditure multiplier is 5.

$$k_{tx} = -\text{MPC}/(1 - \text{MPC}) = -0.80/(1 - 0.80) = -4$$

$$k_e = 1/(1 - \text{MPC}) = 1/(1 - 0.80) = 5$$

(b)   The change in income resulting from a change in government spending is found by solving $\Delta Y = k_e \Delta G$ for ΔY, as follows:

$$\Delta Y = k_e \Delta G = 5 \times \$10 = \$50$$

(c)   Assuming no change in investment and taxes, changes in income are due to changes in government spending and to induced consumption (see Problem 5.10), i.e. $\Delta Y = \Delta G + \Delta C$. Since ΔG equals $10, ΔC must equal $40. Given an MPC of 0.80, $40 of induced consumption requires $10 in additional saving. The $10 increase in government spending induces a $40 increase in aggregate consumption and a $10 increase in aggregate saving.

(d)   Since there is no change in taxes, additional government expenditures must be financed by borrowing. The $10 increment in household saving may be borrowed to finance the $10 increase in government spending.

(e)   A tax increase has a negative influence upon aggregate spending while an increase in government spending has a positive influence. Thus, we have the net change in income equal to

$$\Delta Y = k_e \Delta G + k_{tx} \Delta T_x$$

Substituting, $\Delta Y = (5 \times \$10) + (-4 \times \$10) = \$10$

Since the value of the expenditure multiplier exceeds the value of the tax multiplier by one, equal $10 increases in government spending and taxes have a positive $10 effect upon the level of income.

6.8. (a) Find the expenditure and tax multiplier when the MPC equals (1) 0.50, (2) 0.75, (3) 0.60.
(b) Find the balanced budget multiplier for each of the situations in part (a).
(c) Why does the balanced budget multiplier always equal 1?

(a)

$$(1) \; k_e = 1/(1 - 0.50) = 2; \quad k_{tx} = -0.50/(1 - 0.50) = -1$$
$$(2) \; k_e = 1/(1 - 0.75) = 4; \quad k_{tx} = -0.75/(1 - 0.75) = -3$$
$$(3) \; k_e = 1/(1 - 0.60) = 2\tfrac{1}{2}; \quad k_{tx} = -0.60/(1 - 0.60) = -1\tfrac{1}{2}$$

(b) When there are equal changes in taxes and government spending, the net change in income is given by

$$\Delta Y = k_e \Delta G + k_{tx} \, \Delta T_x$$

Since $\Delta G = \Delta T_x$, we can substitute so that

$$\Delta Y = k_e \Delta G + k_{tx} \Delta G$$

Dividing both sides of the equation by ΔG, we obtain the multiplier effect of equal changes in G and T_x, i.e. the balanced budget multiplier:

$$\Delta Y/\Delta G = k_e + k_{tx}$$

Substituting the values for k_e and k_{tx} into the balanced budget multiplier, we obtain the following values for the situations in part (a):

$$\Delta Y/\Delta G = k_e + k_{tx}$$
$$(1) \; 1 = 2 - 1 \qquad (2) \; 1 = 4 - 3 \qquad (3) \; 1 = 2\tfrac{1}{2} - 1\tfrac{1}{2}$$

(c) Using the expression derived in part (b) for the balanced budget multiplier, $\Delta Y/\Delta G = k_e + k_{tx}$, and substituting the formulas for k_e and k_{tx},

$$\Delta Y/\Delta G = 1/(1 - \text{MPC}) + [-\text{MPC}/(1 - \text{MPC})]$$

Simplifying, $$\Delta Y/\Delta G = (1 - \text{MPC})/(1 - \text{MPC}) = 1$$

6.9. Suppose that the MPC is 0.80 and a $50 recessionary gap exists between the current and full-employment levels of income.
(a) Find the magnitude of the fiscal measure needed to bring the economy to full employment if the policy to be used is (1) increased government spending, (2) a decrease in taxes, (3) a balanced budget.
(b) Why are fiscal measures (1) and (2) preferable to measure (3)?
(c) Is fiscal measure (1) preferable to measure (2)?

(a) The income level must be increased $50 ($\Delta Y = \$50$) to achieve the full-employment level of income.
(1) Government spending must be increased $10.

$$k_e \Delta G = \Delta Y$$
$$5 \Delta G = \$50$$
$$\Delta G = \$50/5 = \$10$$

(2) Taxes must be cut $12.50.

$$k_{tx} \Delta T_x = \Delta Y$$
$$-4 \, \Delta T_x = \$50$$
$$\Delta T_x = \$50/-4 = -\$12.50$$

(3) The balanced budget multiplier equals 1. To achieve a $50 increase in income, $\Delta G = \Delta T_x = \$50$.

(b)   Measure (3) requires a larger expansion of government expenditures and taxes than either (1) or (2).   Securing economic stability through (3) results in the diminished importance of the private sector.   Assuming that we wish to achieve full employment with minimum expansion of the government sector, (1) and (2) are preferable to (3).

(c)   Tax cuts return funds to the private sector and allow an expansion in household spending.   If expansion of the private sector is advocated, tax cuts are to be preferred to an increase in government spending.   Policy (1) should be supported only if there is a recognized need for an increase in public sector goods.

6.10.   Predict the effect of each of the following events:

(a) In an inflationary economy, there are equal increases in government spending and taxes.

(b) In an inflationary economy, there is an increase in taxes.

(c) In a recessionary economy, there are equal decreases in government spending and taxes.

(a)   An inflationary economy is characterized by excess aggregate demand.   Equal increases in government spending and taxes will further stimulate demand through the balanced budget multiplier and add to inflationary pressures.

(b)   An increase in taxes reduces household saving and consumption.   In an inflationary situation, tax increases would decrease aggregate consumption and alleviate inflationary pressures.

(c)   In a recession, there is inadequate aggregate demand.   Equal decreases in government spending and taxes would further reduce demand through the balanced budget multiplier and increase the size of the recessionary gap.

BUILT-IN STABILIZERS

6.11.   What is the difference between a lump-sum tax and an income tax?

A *lump-sum tax* is a constant tax (e.g. a property tax) which is not related to income.   An *income tax*, which may be progressive, proportional or regressive, is related directly to earned income.   Income taxes are progressive if taxes increase at a faster rate than income does.

Lump-sum, proportional and progressive income taxes are illustrated in Fig. 6-11.   Note that lump-sum taxes stay at $1000 as income increases from $10,000 to $11,000.   If there is a 10% proportional tax on income, taxes increase from $1000 to $1100 as income increases from $10,000 to $11,000.   The assumed progressive income tax increases from $1000 to $1200 (by 20%) when income increases from $10,000 to $11,000 (by 10%).

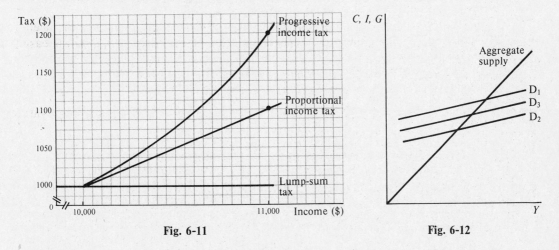

Fig. 6-11   Fig. 6-12

6.12.   Suppose that the level of government spending is fixed and there is a decline in the level of net investment.

(a) What should happen to the level of income and the employment of labor?

(b) What should happen to government's net tax receipts if the government sector provides unemployment compensation?

(*c*) What should happen to the government's net tax receipts if its gross tax receipts come from a progressive income-tax structure?

(*d*) Why are unemployment compensation and income taxes classified built-in stabilizers?

(*a*) A decrease in net investment shifts the aggregate demand schedule downward and reduces the equilibrium level of income. Since employment is tied directly to the level of income, there is also a decrease in the level of employment.

(*b*) Unemployment compensation is paid to workers who become unemployed and are unable to obtain other jobs. Net tax receipts equal gross tax receipts minus such government transfers as unemployment compensation. A fall in net investment that causes a decline in aggregate income and employment results in an automatic decrease in the government's net tax receipts when there is an unemployment compensation program.

(*c*) A progressive income tax structure exists when tax changes are more than proportional to changes in the level of income. Associated with a fall in aggregate income, then, is a more than proportional decrease in the government's gross tax receipts.

(*d*) Holding other variables constant, a decline in net investment shifts aggregate demand downward from D_1 to D_2 in Fig. 6-12. A fall in income, however, is associated with automatic decreases in government's net tax revenues because unemployment compensation payments increase and income tax receipts decline and, thereby, moderate the shift in the aggregate demand schedule to D_3. Thus, unemployment insurance and income taxes are built-in stabilizers since they moderate the effects of autonomous changes upon the equilibrium level of income.

6.13. (*a*) If there is a progressive income tax structure, what will happen to the government's gross tax receipts as the income level expands?

(*b*) Suppose that government spending does not increase at the same rate as receipts from a progressive income tax structure. What will happen to the growth of aggregate demand over time?

(*c*) What causes "fiscal drag"?

(*a*) Government's gross tax receipts will increase at a rate greater than the rate of increase in the level of income.

(*b*) The balanced budget multiplier shows that equal increases in government spending and taxes result in an increase in income equal to the balanced change in G and T_x. If taxes increase at a more rapid rate than government spending, aggregate demand will grow more slowly and may even decrease if the growth in tax revenue is excessive.

(*c*) The ability of an economy to produce goods and services increases over time. Aggregate demand must, therefore, grow at the same rate as supply if the economy is to remain at full employment. "Fiscal drag" exists when the public sector's spending and revenue structure is such that growth in aggregate demand is constrained by rising tax receipts and the rising equilibrium level of income is below the economy's expanding capacity to produce.

6.14. Explain the concept and use of the full-employment budget.

The full-employment budget estimates what the levels of government spending and taxes would be if the economy were at full employment. It is used to analyze the government budget to determine whether tax receipts are excessive and act as a deterrent to achieving the full-employment level of income. For example, the current budget may show a deficit; at full employment, however, the budget may show a surplus and it is this surplus which prevents the economy from achieving the full-employment level of income.

THE PUBLIC DEBT

6.15. (*a*) What argument can be made against an annually balanced budget for the Federal government?

(*b*) What are the advantages and disadvantges of a cyclically balanced budget?

(a) An annually balanced budget may prove to be contrary to the aims of the Employment Act of 1946.   The built-in stabilizers and a budget always in balance may aggravate inflationary and recessionary tendencies.   For example, tax revenues automatically fall with aggregate income. If government spending were cut along with the decrease in tax revenue, the equal decreases in taxes and government spending through the balanced budget multiplier would have a negative effect upon an already contracting economy.   Similarly, rising tax revenues during an economic expansion would necessitate increased government spending to keep the budget in balance and would further stimulate aggregate demand.   Given the built-in stabilizers, then, an annually balanced budget would be procyclical, and create greater fluctuations in the level of economic activity.

(b) A cyclically balanced budget overcomes the procyclical disadvantages of an annually balanced budget by incurring deficits during contractions, surpluses during expansions and a balanced budget over the cycle.   Budget deficits during periods of rising unemployment are countercyclical because the falling aggregate demand is offset by falling tax revenues, and surpluses during expansions prevent excessive increases in aggregate demand which would be inflationary.   While theoretically appealing, a cyclically balanced budget may be impractical in the real world.   Recessionary and inflationary gaps are not necessarily of the same magnitude and duration to assure a balanced budget over time.   If the Employment Act of 1946 is adhered to, balancing of government receipts and expenditures over time should become secondary to the achievement of a noninflationary, full-employment economy.

6.16.   (a) Explain functional finance.   (b) What is the relationship of functional finance to the Employment Act of 1946?

(a) The functional finance approach to the public debt holds that financing of government spending is secondary to the fiscal actions needed to achieve a noninflationary, full-employment economy.   Government spending and tax levels are to be determined by the strength of aggregate demand in the private sector.   A resulting surplus or deficit in the public budget is simply the result of fiscal actions taken to achieve full employment.

(b) Functional finance is an outgrowth of the 1946 Employment Act, which committed the government to promoting maximum employment, production and purchasing power.   That is, the government is to take whatever policy actions are needed to achieve these stated goals, and budget surpluses and deficits are secondary to this central concern.

6.17.   (a) Might disregard of the magnitude of the public debt eventually lead to default and Federal bankruptcy?   (b) Does a large public debt place a burden on future generations?

(a) Default occurs when a borrower fails to meet its financial commitments.   Bankruptcy exists when a borrower's debts far exceed its ability to meet these obligations.   The Federal government will neither default nor face bankruptcy since it has the power to tax and print money.   Suppose the Federal government has no tax revenue to meet interest payments on its debt.   It can secure whatever funds it needs by raising taxes.   Alternatively, since it is the sole issuer of paper currency, it can print additional paper currency and use it to meet its interest payments.   Thus, with virtually unlimited sources of funds, the Federal government is not prone to default or bankruptcy.

(b) Public debt comes into existence when the Federal government spends more than its tax revenues and borrows savings from the private sector.   The immediate burden is upon individuals who elect to save and not consume.   If the debt is never retired and is owed to citizens of the issuing country, then the only burden imposed by debt creation is upon those who elected to save when the debt was issued.

A burden is shifted to future generations, however, if the borrowed funds come from savers who do not reside in the borrowing country and future taxes must be increased to meet the interest payments on the debt.   When funds are borrowed externally (from foreigners), future generations will have to save to repay these loans.   Similarly, higher taxes on future generations to meet interest payments reduce the disposable incomes of a large proportion of the labor force.

Chapter 7

The Business Cycle

7.1 FULL EMPLOYMENT

The ultimate employment goal of the Employment Act of 1946 is generally viewed as a commitment to full employment.   Unemployed workers may be classified as frictionally, cyclically or structurally unemployed (see Problem 7.1).   Labor is *frictionally unemployed* when it is temporarily out of work, between jobs, or in the process of changing jobs.   Workers who have lost jobs due to changes in the demand for particular products or to technological advance are classified as *structurally unemployed;* unemployment caused by insufficient aggregate demand is called *cyclical unemployment*.   Since frictional and structural unemployment are integral to a changing and free society, full employment generally occurs at a rate of unemployment greater than zero (see Problem 7.2).

Prior to the 1970s, a 4% rate of unemployment was generally accepted as the benchmark for full employment in the United States; recent experience suggests that this benchmark rate should be higher (see Problem 7.3).   Potential GNP and the GNP gap are calculated using a 4% rate of unemployment as the measure of full employment (see Example 1).   *Potential GNP* is a measure of output at full employment; the *GNP gap* is a measure of the dollar value of lost output when the unemployment rate is greater than 4%.

EXAMPLE 1.   Potential GNP is found by multiplying 96% of the civilian labor force times the total number of manhours worked annually times the average productivity of labor.   Thus, if the civilian labor force is 95,000 workers, 1870 total manhours are worked annually by each worker, and the average productivity of labor is $9.921, potential GNP equals

$$0.96(95,000) \times 1870 \times \$9.921 = \$1,691,967,000$$

If actual GNP is $1650 million dollars, the GNP gap equals $41,967,000.

7.2 INFLATION

Inflation occurs when there is an increase in the general price level (i.e. when the cost of a given quantity [basket] of goods and services increases).   Inflation is also defined as a reduction in the purchasing power of a unit of money, which means that a given quantity of money purchases a smaller basket of goods and services (see Example 2).

EXAMPLE 2.   Suppose the typical household uses $1250 to purchase one housing unit for $350, 75 food units for $400 and 50 units of miscellaneous goods and services for $500.   If the price of the housing unit increases to $375, the cost of 75 food units increases to $420, and there is no change in the cost of 50 miscellaneous units, the typical household is no longer able to purchase the same quantity of goods and services with $1250.   That is, the purchasing power of $1250 has fallen.   Inflation occurs, then, when a given quantity of money will purchase a smaller quantity of goods and services; it results when the price of one or more of a given set of goods and services increases and the price increases are not offset by decreases in the prices of other items in the given set.

An increase in the general price level may be classified as demand-pull inflation or cost-push inflation.   *Demand-pull inflation* occurs when aggregate demand exceeds the economy's ability to produce and causes the price level to increase.   *Cost-push inflation* originates on the supply side of the market and occurs when one or more groups of resource owners use their market power to receive a higher return for their factor (see Problem 7.6).   Regardless of the cause of inflation, a rising price level generally harms creditors and recipients of a fixed money income (see Problem 7.9).

EXAMPLE 3.   Suppose in Fig. 7-1, D_1 represents the aggregate demand for goods and services, S_1 represents aggregate supply, and p_1 is the initial general price level.

Demand-pull inflation.   In Fig. 7-1(a), a rightward shift of aggregate demand from D_1 to D_2 with no change in aggregate supply causes the price level to increase from p_1 to p_2.   The rightward shift of aggregate demand causes excess demand equal to $y_1 y_2$ at price level p_1.   The increase in the price level to p_2 eliminates the excessive demand and brings about the equality of the quantities demanded and supplied.

Cost-push inflation.   In Fig. 7-1(b), suppliers require a price of p_3 to continue supplying a y_1 level of output.   That is, there is an upward shift of aggregate supply from S_1 to S_2.   There is insufficient aggregate demand for output y_1 at price level p_3, and the price level increases to p_2 to bring about an equality of the quantity demanded and supplied.

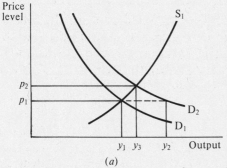

Fig. 7-1

7.3   BUSINESS CYCLES

Throughout its history, the American economy has experienced periods of price inflation and deflation and periods of high and low employment.   These recurrent but nonperiodic ups (expansions) and downs (contractions) of economic activity have been called business cycles. There are four phases of a business cycle: trough, expansion, peak and contraction.   See Fig. 7-2.

While the business cycle is a very complex phenomenon, changes in investment are generally recognized as a major cause of fluctuations.   Other contributors to the recurrence of the cycle include innovations, changes in expectations, the money supply and government spending (see

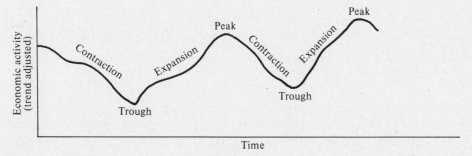

Fig. 7-2

Problem 7.13).   While these factors may initiate a new cyclical phase, it is the interrelatedness of producing units that diffuses the effects and makes a movement self-reinforcing (see Problem 7.12).

7.4   THE ACCELERATION PRINCIPLE

The acceleration principle is the most prominent theory used to explain the periodicity of changes in investment over the business cycle.   In *the accelerator theory,* the stock of capital a society desires to have is directly related to the level of output.   A firm's decision to add to its stock of capital (i.e. net investment) depends upon its sale of output.

EXAMPLE 4.   Suppose the XYZ Corporation keeps its stock of capital equipment at a level equal to twice its volume of sales.   If XYZ begins operations at the start of Year 1 and its sales grow by $5000 a year from Year 1 through Year 12, XYZ would invest $10,000 a year, and its stock of capital equipment would increase from $10,000 at the end of Year 1 to $120,000 at the end of Year 12.   If each machine lasts ten years, XYZ, beginning in Year 11, would have replacement investment (depreciation investment) as well as net investment.   See Table 1.

Table 1

XYZ Corporation					
Year	Sales	Stock of Capital (end of year)	Net Investment	Replacement Investment	Gross Investment
1	$ 5,000	$ 10,000	$10,000	$ 0	$10,000
2	10,000	20,000	10,000	0	10,000
3	15,000	30,000	10,000	0	10,000
4	20,000	40,000	10,000	0	10,000
5	25,000	50,000	10,000	0	10,000
6	30,000	60,000	10,000	0	10,000
7	35,000	70,000	10,000	0	10,000
8	40,000	80,000	10,000	0	10,000
9	45,000	90,000	10,000	0	10,000
10	50,000	100,000	10,000	0	10,000
11	55,000	110,000	10,000	10,000	20,000
12	60,000	120,000	10,000	10,000	20,000

Given the fixed capital to sales ratio, sales must grow by a constant amount for net investment to remain at a given level.   (Note in Example 4 that net investment is $10,000 a year when sales increase $5,000 a year.)   If sales grow less rapidly, net investment falls.   When sales fall below previous peak levels, firms may omit replacement of worn-out equipment.   Thus, any slowing of sales growth causes declines in net investment and aggregate demand.   The accelerator theory, therefore, demonstrates that prosperity is destined to end whenever there is a slowdown in the growth of sales.

EXAMPLE 5.   Suppose the sales of XYZ Corporation increase $5000 in Year 13, $4000 in Year 14, $3000 in Year 15, $2000 in Year 16, $1000 in Year 17 and do not increase at all in Year 18.   If sales during Year 12 are $60,000, the stock of capital is $120,000 and the capital/sales ratio is 2, net investment will fall from $10,000 during Year 13 to 0 in Year 18.   See Table 2.

The accelerator theory is used to explain fluctuations in inventories over the business cycle (see Problem 7.16).   The accelerator has also been combined with the multiplier to explain why an upward or downward movement in economic activity is self-reinforcing (see Problem 7.17).

Table 2

		XYZ Corporation			
Year	Sales	Stock of Capital (end of year)	Net Investment	Replacement Investment	Gross Investment
13	$65,000	$130,000	$10,000	$10,000	$20,000
14	69,000	138,000	8,000	10,000	18,000
15	72,000	144,000	6,000	10,000	16,000
16	74,000	148,000	4,000	10,000	14,000
17	75,000	150,000	2,000	10,000	12,000
18	75,000	150,000	0	10,000	10,000

Important Economic Terms

Acceleration principle.   A slowing down in the absolute increase in sales (or consumption) produces a decline in net investment.

Business cycles.   Recurrent but nonperiodic fluctuations in economic activity that occur over a number of years.

Cost-push inflation.   Inflation that occurs when price increases are caused by increased payments to economic factors or the government, which originates with labor, businesses or material suppliers who possess monopolistic market power or the government through taxes or regulation.

Cyclical unemployment.   Unemployment that arises when there is insufficient aggregate demand.

Demand-pull inflation.   Inflation that arises when aggregate demand exceeds the economy's capacity to produce.

Depression.   A condition in which the economy has high rates of unemployment and output levels which are substantially below its capacity to produce.

Frictional unemployment.   The temporary unemployment of workers that results from seasonal factors, job switching or new individuals in the labor force.

GNP gap.   A measure of the dollar value of lost output when the unemployment rate exceeds 4%.   The GNP gap equals potential GNP less actual GNP.

Potential GNP.   A measure of the output that could be produced at full employment when a 4% rate of unemployment is assumed to be full employment.

Prosperity.   A condition in which the economy is operating at or near full employment and producing at or near its maximum level of output.

Structural unemployment.   The unemployment caused by changing patterns of demand and/or technological advance.

Review Questions

1. Frictional unemployment occurs when (*a*) there is a fall in aggregate demand, (*b*) workers are seasonally unemployed, (*c*) workers lack required skills, (*d*) aggregate demand exceeds aggregate supply.
   Ans. (*b*)

2. In a changing, free society, an economic policy aimed at maximum employment strives to
   (*a*) achieve a zero rate of unemployment,
   (*b*) eliminate frictional unemployment but recognizes that some cyclical and structural unemployment will exist,
   (*c*) eliminate cyclical unemployment but recognizes that some frictional and structural unemployment will exist,
   (*d*) eliminate structural unemployment but recognizes that some frictional and cyclical unemployment will exist.

   Ans. (*c*)

3. Potential GNP is that quantity of goods and services that the economy could produce if the economy had an unemployment rate of (*a*) 4%, (*b*) 3%, (*c*) 2%, (*d*) 1%.
   Ans. (*a*)

4. Inflation is a situation in which
   (*a*) there is a decrease in the purchasing power of the monetary unit,
   (*b*) there is a decrease in the general price level,
   (*c*) a given quantity of money purchases a larger quantity of goods and services,
   (*d*) increases in the general price level exceed increases in the rate of economic growth.
   Ans. (*a*)

5. Cost-push inflation occurs when
   (*a*) consumers use their market power to push up prices,
   (*b*) resource owners use their market power to push up prices,
   (*c*) aggregate supply increases at a faster rate than aggregate demand,
   (*d*) aggregate demand increases at a faster rate than aggregate supply.
   Ans. (*b*)

6. A business cycle is
   (*a*) an annual fluctuation in economic activity,
   (*b*) a recurrent, nonperiodic fluctuation in economic activity during a period of less than one year,
   (*c*) a recurrent, nonperiodic fluctuation in economic activity during a period exceeding one year,
   (*d*) a secular deviation from a long-term trend.
   Ans. (*c*)

7. During the contraction phase of the business cycle,
   (*a*) unemployment, interest rates and the price level are rising,
   (*b*) economic activity, interest rates and the level of employment are rising,
   (*c*) economic activity, interest rates and the level of employment are falling,
   (*d*) the price level, interest rates and the level of employment are falling.
   Ans. (*c*)

8. In the acceleration principle, there is a fixed relationship between (*a*) capital stock and the level of sales, (*b*) capital stock and the level of inventory investment, (*c*) capital stock and the level of profits, (*d*) capital stock and technological change.
   Ans. (*a*)

9. If there is a fixed relationship of 3 between capital stock and sales,
   (*a*) $1000 in sales will necessitate a $3000 level of net investment,
   (*b*) $1000 in sales will necessitate a $3000 level of gross investment,
   (*c*) $1000 increase in sales will necessitate a $3000 level of net investment,
   (*d*) $1000 increase in sales will necessitate a $3000 level of gross investment.
   Ans. (*c*)

10. In the accelerator theory,
    (a) a slowing down of the increase in sales causes a decline in net investment,
    (b) a slowing down of the rate of increase in sales causes a decline in net investment,
    (c) a decline in net investment causes a decline in sales,
    (d) the change in net investment is proportionate to the change in sales.
    Ans. (a)

Solved Problems

FULL EMPLOYMENT

7.1. Explain frictional, cyclical and structural unemployment.

Frictional unemployment occurs in a free society when at any time some workers are temporarily laid off or are between jobs and expect to find employment soon. For example, automobile workers are seasonally unemployed during model changeover periods; so are some construction workers during periods of bad weather. New entrants into the labor force are counted as unemployed while they look for their first jobs. Some workers dissatisfied with their current jobs quit prior to finding new ones and are counted as unemployed. It is estimated that at any time frictional unemployment in the United States is about 3% of the civilian labor force.

Cyclical unemployment is caused by insufficient aggregate demand. Fiscal policy, discussed in Chapter 6, is aimed at eliminating cyclical unemployment, which is considered to be the major cause of unemployment in the United States.

Labor is classified as structurally unemployed when it lacks the skills needed to qualify for available job openings. Changing demand and technology are the principal causes of structural unemployment. A major reduction in the demand for a product will reduce the demand for labor within an industry. The introduction of new technology makes some labor skills obsolete. If workers displaced by structural changes lack the skills required for other jobs, they become structurally unemployed; such workers must be retrained to be reemployed.

7.2. Should the government introduce policies to eliminate frictional and structural as well as cyclical unemployment?

The objective of fiscal policy is to stabilize aggregate demand and thereby eliminate cyclical unemployment. Frictional and structural unemployment, however, are essential to a changing, free society. If workers are to be free to change jobs or reject their initial job offerings, some workers must be frictionally unemployed at any point in time. Likewise, businesses should not retain employees during slack demand periods if they are to strive for productive efficiency. Structural unemployment is necessary in an economy experiencing technological advance and a growth in output. While some frictional and structural unemployment must exist at any point in time, government should institute programs to minimize the number so unemployed. For example, it should facilitate the dissemination of information on job availability to reemploy more rapidly the labor that is frictionally unemployed. Similarly, it should provide job retraining programs to reemploy the structurally unemployed. The government should not use fiscal policy to minimize frictional and structural unemployment since insufficient aggregate demand is not the cause of these workers being unemployed.

7.3. Does a 4% rate of unemployment always represent full employment?

In the United States prior to the 1970s, the usual rate of unemployment at the peak of the business cycle averaged 4%. This led economists to use the 4% rate of unemployment as a benchmark for full employment.   In the 1970s, however, changes in the composition of the labor force and technology suggested that full employment was occurring at a higher rate of unemployment.   For example, the rising minimum wage eliminated a large number of jobs for the unskilled during a period in which the proportion of teenagers in the United States population was increasing.   Rapid technological advances since the 1960s have caused larger proportions of unskilled workers to remain unemployed.   It is argued that full employment may well exist at a 5% or even 6% rate of unemployment.

7.4.   Suppose that potential output equals $750 and actual output is $720.   If you know that the tax multiplier is -3, would you support a $10 decrease in taxes to close the $30 GNP gap?

Potential output is calculated using a 4% rate of unemployment as the full-employment level of income.   Before advocating a $10 tax cut, it is necessary to examine why the unemployment rate exceeds 4%.   If the higher unemployment rate is identified as cyclical unemployment, the $10 tax cut is justified.   If analysis suggests that frictional and structural unemployment are abnormally high and causing the gap, a tax cut is not advised.   Economic policy should strive instead to retrain the structurally unemployed, disseminate information on available job opportunities for those frictionally unemployed and take whatever other measures are needed to reduce the abnormally high rates of frictional and structural unemployment.

7.5.   Why is cyclical unemployment considered undesirable?

Unemployment has economic and social costs.   The economic costs are losses to society in general and to individual members in particular.   For instance, unemployment results in lost output which cannot be recovered in future time periods.   It also means lost increases in productive capacity that result from lower levels of net investment and thereby a reduced rate of economic growth. Productive capacity is also lost because labor skills deteriorate when they are unemployed.   The unemployed suffer individual losses through a reduction in their standard of living.   During a period of rising unemployment, these individual losses are not shared equally by all economic groups; greater economic burdens fall upon minorities, women and teenagers.   The unequal effect of unemployment is the major argument against allowing greater than normal rates of unemployment.

Larger-scale unemployment may also involve social and political unrest.   A prolonged period of unemployment could result in radical changes in the form of government.   It also undermines the social fabric of society and destroys motivation and self-worth.   This damage may not be overcome when jobs become available.

INFLATION

7.6.   Explain the basic causes of demand-pull and cost-push inflation.

Demand-pull inflation develops when economic resources are fully employed and there is (1) an increase in aggregate demand, (2) aggregate demand grows at a faster rate than aggregate supply, or (3) bottlenecks (see Chapter 12) develop prior to full employment.   Demand-pull inflation, then, occurs when price increases are needed to ration goods and services since the desire to purchase exceeds the ability to supply.

Cost-push inflation comes from the supply side and may be due to the market power of labor unions, business firms or suppliers of raw materials, or to government regulation or taxation of business.   If firms with sufficient market control find profit levels low, they may be able to increase profits by raising the prices of the goods and services they produce.   A similar effect occurs if government raises business taxes or if labor or suppliers of material inputs increase their prices and these higher prices result in higher costs which are passed on to the consumer.   Cost-push inflation arises when monopolistic power permits supply prices to be influenced by the actions of firms, labor unions, raw material suppliers or government.

7.7.   Describe the effect of each of the following on the price level, assuming an initial position of full employment and using Fig. 7-3 as your point of reference.   Treat each situation separately.   (*a*) There are increases in the quantities of economic resources.   (*b*) An increase in aggregate demand exceeds an increase in aggregate supply.   (c) Suppliers of raw materials use their market power to increase substantially the price of material inputs.   (d) Labor unions gain large wage increases by collective bargaining.

(a)   An increase in economic resources raises potential supply.   The rightward shift of aggregate supply S_1 in Fig. 7-3, with no change in aggregate demand, results in a decrease in the general price level.   That is, there is deflation.

(b)   The rightward shift of aggregate demand is greater than the rightward shift of aggregate supply.   There is an increase in the general price level.

(c)   Higher raw material prices raise production costs and thereby decrease aggregate supply.   There is an increase in the general price level.

(d)   Higher wages for labor diminish aggregate supply and increase the general price level.

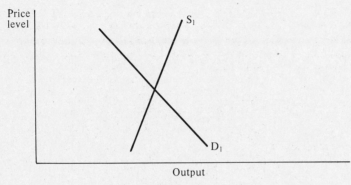

Fig. 7-3

7.8.   Explain (a) consumer price index, (b) wholesale price index, (c) creeping inflation, (d) hyperinflation.

(a)   The consumer price index is a weighted average of prices for items consumed by a typical urban family.   The consumer price index, used to indicate the "cost of living," is used by labor in wage negotiations.

(b)   The wholesale price index is a weighted average of prices in wholesale markets.   The index is based upon the prices of over 2200 commodities and includes the prices of raw materials, semi-finished products and finished goods.

(c)   Creeping inflation exists when there are annual increases of 2% to 4% in the general price level.   Based upon the assumption that production-cost increases lag price increases, some economists advocate creeping inflation because it raises profit levels which in turn stimulate investment.   There is decreasing support for this position among economists who note that creeping inflation can lead to higher rates of inflation when continuous price increases are anticipated and their effects are incorporated into wage demands.

(d)   Hyperinflation or galloping inflation exists when the rate of price increase is high or prices are increasing at increasing rates through time.   Money prices eventually become a poor measure of value.   With no dependable monetary system available to facilitate exchange, the economy plunges into a severe depression.

7.9.   (a) What effect does inflation have upon the following: (1) fixed income groups, (2) debtors, (3) creditors?   (b) How can one be protected from the redistribution effect of inflation?

(a)   Inflation can affect real income and wealth.   Real income is the amount of goods and services that can be purchased with a given money income.   If the price level doubles and there is a constant level of money income, real income is halved because only one-half of the quantity of goods and services can be purchased.   Similarly, wealth kept in such money-denominated claims as bonds is inversely related to the price level.   That is, as the price level increases, the purchasing power of money-denominated assets decreases.

(1) Inflation lowers the real incomes of individuals on fixed money incomes. That is, fixed income groups are able to purchase fewer goods and services as the price level increases.

(2) Debtors are individuals who owe fixed sums of money to other parties. Debtors benefit from inflation since their real indebtedness decreases as the price level increases. Prolonged inflation, then, results in partial cancellation of real debt. For example, the United States government greatly benefited from the inflation of the 1970s because its real indebtedness to the private sector fell as prices rose.

(3) Creditors are lenders. Lenders lose during inflation because they will be repaid a fixed sum of dollars which will have a lower purchasing power.

(b) Protection from the redistribution effect of inflation can be obtained by an indexation of money obligations. Indexation ties money obligations to a price level so that the sum of a money obligation increases proportionally with the price level. For example, a $10,000 salary would increase to $11,000 if the money wage was indexed and there was a 10% increase in the price level.

BUSINESS CYCLES

7.10. Explain the terms (a) seasonal fluctuation, (b) secular trend and (c) business cycle.

(a) A seasonal fluctuation is a variation in business or economic activity which takes place within a one-year period. Seasonal fluctuations are usually recurrent and are the result of weather (when there are harvest or production seasons) or custom (when buying is bunched into such holiday periods as Christmas or Easter).

(b) A secular trend is the growth or decline of an economic series over a period of years. In the United States, there has been an upward secular trend for GNP during the twentieth century.

(c) Business cycles are fluctuations of economic activity that occur over a period of several years. These recurrent but nonperiodic oscillations occur around the secular trend of GNP.

7.11. (a) Explain the terms depression and prosperity. (b) Describe the four phases of the business cycle.

(a) Depressions are periods of high unemployment in which economic output is substantially below the full-employment level and the economy's capacity to produce. The United States last experienced a depression during the 1930s when the unemployment rate reached almost 25% in 1933. Prosperity generally refers to periods when economic output is at or close to the full-employment level. The United States economy experienced prosperity during a majority of the post-World War II years.

(b) The four phases of the business cycle are expansion, peak, contraction (recession) and trough. The *expansion period* is characterized by increases in employment, production, prices, the money supply, interest rates and profits. The *peak period* occurs at that point where production and employment reach their highest levels relative to the levels in preceding and succeeding months. The *contraction (recession) phase* is characterized by falling employment, output, interest rates and profits. The *trough* occurs where actual output and employment are at their lowest level relative to the levels in preceding and succeeding months.

7.12. (a) Why are the effects of the business cycle diffused throughout the economy? (b) Why are capital goods and durable goods industries hit harder by a recession than industries that produce nondurable goods and services?

(a) Production in a decentralized economy occurs in stages in which individual producing units usually produce a small component of the final good. There are, therefore, intricate links in the production process. Since complex interrelatedness between businesses exists, the actions of one producing unit affect the economic activity of others. It follows that a decrease in the demand for a final good affects a large number of suppliers of the intermediate goods needed for final output. If there is an overall decline in aggregate demand, the effects of this decline are diffused through a complex host of supporting suppliers and the decline in economc activity is felt throughout the economy.

(b) Capital goods (machines, tools, etc.) and durable goods (cars, TV's, etc.) are purchases that can be postponed. (It is especially easy to postpone replacement purchases of capital and durable goods.) Nondurable consumer goods and services (food, shelter, etc.) are generally not postponable since they tend to be essential to one's everyday life. Thus, when the economy contracts and individuals lose their jobs, nonessential purchases are cut first.   This creates a larger contraction in durable goods and capital goods industries than in firms producing nondurable goods and services.

7.13.   Why are innovations and changes in government spending and the money supply considered potential causes of business cycles?

An innovation is the introduction of a new product or a new way of producing, marketing or financing an old product.   Innovations and changes in government spending and the money supply are viewed as possible causes of business fluctuations because a change in any one can alter aggregate demand and the equilibrium level of income.   For example, a wave of innovation creates large increases in aggregate demand as do large increases in government spending and the money supply. Since major innovations tend to be bunched together, investment levels tend to be abnormally high and low through time.   When innovation slows, investment demand can be expected to fall and cause lower levels of economic activity and employment.   Similarly, government spending may experience substantial increases and decreases through time.   A war effort, for example, necessitates large increases in government spending which abate at the end of the war.   Chapter 8 demonstrates how large increases or decreases in the money supply are responsible for alterations in aggregate demand.   Innovations and changes in government spending and the money supply, then, are nonperiodic factors that can cause the economy to move into an expansionary or contractionary phase of the business cycle.

THE ACCELERATION PRINCIPLE

7.14.   (*a*) Suppose $200,000 of capital stock has been accumulated uniformly over ten years and each unit in this stock has a useful life of ten years.   If the firm's capital/sales ratio is 2, find the firm's level of net and gross investment for 1975 through 1980 if sales are as follows: 1974, $100,000; 1975, $100,000; 1976, $110,000; 1977, $130,000; 1978, $140,000; 1979, $140,000; and 1980, $130,000.

   (*b*) Would the changes in investment be larger or smaller if the firm's capital/sales ratio equaled 3?

   (*a*)   Refer to Table 3.   There are no additions to the firm's capital stock during 1975, 1979 and 1980 since sales level off during these years.   Replacement investment is $20,000 a year since $20,000 in capital was acquired uniformly during the previous ten years.   Capital replacement falls to 0 during 1980 as a result of the decline in sales volume.

Table 3

Year	Sales	Change in Sales	Required Stock of Capital	Net Investment	Replacement Investment	Gross Investment
1975	$100,000	$ 0	$200,000	$ 0	$20,000	$20,000
1976	110,000	10,000	220,000	20,000	20,000	40,000
1977	130,000	20,000	260,000	40,000	20,000	60,000
1978	140,000	10,000	280,000	20,000	20,000	40,000
1979	140,000	0	280,000	0	20,000	20,000
1980	130,000	−10,000	260,000	0	0	0

   (*b*)   If the firm's capital/sales ratio were 3, there would be even larger changes in the firm's net investment.   For example, the firm's increase in sales in 1976, 1977 and 1978 would require respective net investment of $30,000, $60,000 and $30,000 rather than the $20,000, $40,000 and $20,000 required when the capital/sales ratio was equal to 2.

7.15.   Explain what will happen to the level of net investment if (*a*) sales volume remains constant, (*b*) sales increase by a decreasing sum each year, (*c*) sales increase by a constant sum each year, (*d*) sales increase at a constant rate each year.

   (*a*)   Net investment equals 0.   With no increases in sales there is no reason to add to the firm's capacity to produce.

(b) The need for additional capacity is growing but by a decreasing sum each year.   Net investment is falling.

(c) There is a need for a constant sum of additional productive capacity each year.   Net investment is a constant sum each year.

(d) There are increasing needs for productive capacity.   Net investment is increasing each year.

7.16. (a) Suppose a firm wishes to have $2 in inventory for every $10 in sales.   What is the firm's desired inventory when sales equal $20,000?

(b) Find the level and the change in desired inventory if a firm's sales are as given in Table 4.

Table 4

Year	Quarter I	Quarter II	Quarter III	Quarter IV
1977	$20,000	$21,000	$23,000	$26,000
1978	28,000	30,000	30,000	30,000
1979	28,000	27,000	28,000	30,000

(c) Changes in sales volume obviously affect the firm's level of employment.   When would the employment level drop for the firm?   When would it decrease for the firm's suppliers of material inputs?

(a) Since the firm's desired ratio of inventory to sales is 0.20, the firm would wish to hold a $4000 inventory when sales equal $20,000.

(b) See Table 5.

Table 5

Period	Sales	Desired Inventory	Desired Change in Inventory
1977 Q I	$20,000	$4,000	—
Q II	21,000	4,200	$200
Q III	23,000	4,600	400
Q IV	26,000	5,200	600
1978 Q I	$28,000	$5,600	$400
Q II	30,000	6,000	400
Q III	30,000	6,000	0
Q IV	30,000	6,000	0
1979 Q I	$28,000	$5,600	−$400
Q II	27,000	5,400	− 200
Q III	28,000	5,600	200
Q IV	30,000	6,000	400

(c) We shall assume that the firm's employment of labor is directly related to its level of output. This firm reaches peak sales during the second quarter of 1978.   Material suppliers to this firm reach their peak level of employment during the fourth quarter of 1977 when the increase in inventory is largest.

7.17. Suppose the aggregate capital to sales ratio is 2 and sales growth results in the net investment levels presented in Table 6.   What effect will the changes in net investment have upon the equilibrium level of income if the expenditure multiplier is 2?

There is no change in the equilibrium level of income if net investment and other aggregate demand variables are constant.   An expansion of net investment changes the level of income by the expenditure multiplier k_c times the change in net investment ΔI.   The effect of the changes in net investment in Table 6 upon aggregate income are presented in Table 7.

Table 6

Period	Aggregate Sales	Required Stock of Capital	Net Investment
Year 1 Q I	$ 750	$1500	—
Q II	760	1520	$20
Q III	770	1540	20
Q IV	790	1580	40
Year 2 Q I	$ 810	$1620	$40
Q II	840	1680	60
Q III	870	1740	60
Q IV	910	1820	80
Year 3 Q I	$ 940	$1880	$60
Q II	970	1940	60
Q III	990	1980	40
Q IV	1000	2000	20

Table 7

Period	Net Investment	ΔI	$k_e \Delta I = \Delta Y$
Year 1 Q I	—	—	
Q II	$20	—	
Q III	20	0	0
Q IV	40	$20	$40
Year 2 Q I	$40	0	0
Q II	60	$20	$40
Q III	60	0	0
Q IV	80	20	$40
Year 3 Q I	$60	−$20	−$40
Q II	60	0	0
Q III	40	− 20	− 40
Q IV	20	− 20	− 40

Thus, if the equilibrium level of income was initially $750, the equilibrium level of income over the three years would appear as shown in Fig. 7-4.

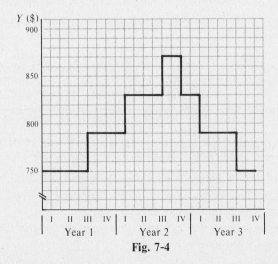

Fig. 7-4

Midterm Examination— Macroeconomics

1. (*a*) What are the basic economic questions that each society must answer?   (*b*) Why are they a problem in every society, regardless of its form of organization?   (*c*) How are these questions answered in a free-enterprise economy?   (*d*) In a mixed-enterprise system? In a centralized economy?

2. Given the market demand and supply schedules for corn in Table 1, (*a*) indicate whether at each price there is a surplus(+) or shortage(−) and the pressure on price toward its equilibrium level.   (*b*) Show the equilibrium price and quantity of corn graphically; how is this equilibrium reached?   (*c*) What does the negative slope of the market demand for corn indicate?   Why?   What happens to the equilibrium price and quantity of corn if its market demand increases?   What can cause this increase?   (*d*) What does the positive slope of the supply curve for corn indicate?   What is the reason for this upward slope? What happens to the equilibrium price and quantity of corn if its market supply increases? What can cause this increase?

Table 1

Price ($ per bu.)	Quantity Demanded of Corn in the Market (million bu. per mo.)	Quantity Supplied of Corn to the Market (million bu. per mo.)
4	1	5
3	2	4
2	3	3
1	4	2

3. (*a*) What is national income accounting?   (*b*) What are the two alternative ways of measuring GNP?   (*c*) What is the difference between national income and personal income? (*d*) Explain the difference between current dollar GNP and constant dollar GNP.

4. (*a*) Explain the determinants of saving and investment in the classical model.   (*b*) What is the role of the rate of interest in the classical model?   (*c*) Explain Keynes' theory of consumption and saving.

5. (*a*) Given the following schedule of aggregate consumption and a $120 level of investment, explain why at a $600 level of output some output will be unsold.

Income	$480	$520	$560	$600	$640	$680
Aggregate consumption	380	410	440	470	500	530

   (*b*) Graph the data in part (*a*) as an aggregate demand schedule.   Show aggregate supply as a 45° line through the origin.   What is the equilibrium level of income?
   (*c*) What is an equilibrium level of income?
   (*d*) Why does an autonomous change in investment cause a multiplied change in the equilibrium level of income?

94

6.   (*a*)   What are discretionary fiscal measures and what effect do they have upon the level of income?

         (*b*)   Assume that the marginal propensity to consume is 0.75.   What effect will the following events have upon the level of income: (1) a $20 increase in taxes, (2) a $15 increase in government spending, (3) a $20 increase in government spending and taxes?

         (*c*)   Why do equal changes in G and T_x alter the level of income?

         (*d*)   What are built-in stabilizers?

7.   (*a*) What is the difference between frictional, structural and cyclical unemployment?

         (*b*) What is a business cycle?   (*c*) Explain the accelerator theory of investment.

Answers

1.   (*a*)   The basic economic questions that must be answered by every society are what to produce, how to produce and for whom to produce.   What to produce refers to which goods and services and how much of each to produce.   How to produce refers to what combination of various resources and techniques to use in production.   For whom to produce refers to how much of the wants of each consumer are to be satisfied.   Society must also provide for the maintenance and growth of the system.

         (*b*)   The what, how and for whom to produce are problems because every society has only limited resources.   As a result, it cannot produce all the goods and services and as much of each commodity that society wants.   Society must also produce goods and services as efficiently as possible to economize on scarce resources.   Since resources, and therefore commodities, are scarce, not all the wants of all individuals can be satisfied.   Finally, the more future growth society wants, the more it must sacrifice present consumption to improve technology and skills and increase its stock of capital equipment.

         (*c*)   In a free-enterprise economy (i.e. one in which the government does not directly control economic activity), the questions of what, how and for whom to produce and how to maintain and provide for the growth of the system are solved by the price-mechanism.   Only those commodities for which consumers are willing to pay a price per unit sufficient to cover the cost of producing them are normally produced or supplied.   Since the price of resources normally reflects their relative scarcity, goods and services should be produced with the technique and resource combination which minimizes costs of production and thus economizes on scarce resources.   The for whom to produce is solved by the economy producing those goods and services that satisfy the wants of those people who have the money to pay for them.   The system is maintained by the fact that commodity prices usually include the cost of replacing capital equipment depreciated or used up in the course of producing current production.   Finally, prospects of higher wages and profits induce people to acquire new skills, accumulate capital and develop and introduce better technology—which are required for growth.

         (*d*)   In a mixed-enterprise system such as our own, the government (through taxes, subsidies, etc.) modifies and in some instances (through direct controls) replaces the operation of the price-mechanism in solving the questions of what, how and for whom to produce and how to maintain the system and provide for its growth.   In a completely centralized economy, a planning committee makes these decisions.   We in the West believe that this is inefficient.   Our feeling seems to be confirmed by the fact that the Soviet Union (never a completely centralized economy) has been moving recently toward even more decentralized control of its economy and toward greater reliance on the price-mechanism to answer society's basic questions.

2.   (*a*)   See Table 2.

         (*b*)   The equilibrium price of corn is $2 and the equilibrium quantity is 3 million bushels per month and is given at the intersection of D and S in Fig. M-1.   At $P > \$2$, there is a corn surplus which drives P down.   As P falls, QD increases, QS decreases and the surplus diminishes until it is completely eliminated at $P=\$2$.   At $P < \$2$, there is a corn shortage which drives P upward.   As P rises, QD falls, QS increases until the shortage is eliminated at $P=\$2$.   Thus, $P=\$2$ is the only price at which the quantity consumers are willing and able to buy equals the quantity suppliers are willing to sell.

Table 2

Price ($ per bu.)	QD (million bu. per mo.)	QS (million bu. per mo.)	Surplus (+) or Shortage (−)	Pressure on Price
4	1	5	4	downward
3	2	4	2	downward
2	3	3	0	equilibrium
1	4	2	−2	upward

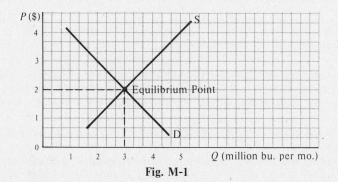

Fig. M-1

(c) The negative slope of D indicates that price and quantity are inversely related; that is, when the price of corn falls, the quantity demanded increases.   This results because when the price of corn falls, we consume more corn as a substitute for wheat.   Also, when the price of corn falls, consumers buy more corn with a given money income.   If D shifts up, both P and Q rise. D shifts up if the number of consumers buying corn rises, if their tastes for corn increase, if consumers' money income rises, if the prices of wheat and other corn substitutes rise, or if the prices of other commodities consumed together with corn (i.e. complementary commodities) rise.

(d) The positive slope of the S curve indicates that in order to induce producers to supply more corn, they must be paid higher corn prices.   This results because of rising production costs.   An increase in supply refers to a downward and rightward shift in S.   This causes P to fall and Q to rise.   The market supply of corn increases when the number and/or size of corn producers increases, if the technology of corn production improves, if the prices of factors used to produce corn fall, or if there is a fall in the prices of wheat and other commodities requiring generally the same factors of production as corn.

3.   (a) National income accounting is a system of accounts used to measure various aspects of aggregate economic activity.   The principal summary national income accounts are *Gross National Product* (GNP), *Net National Product* (NNP), *National Income* (NI) and *Personal Income* (PI).   GNP is a measure of the total market value of all final goods and services produced in an economy during a year.   The difference between GNP and NNP is depreciation—a sum that represents the amount of capital replacement included in current output.   National income is the amount paid to economic resources during the current year and thereby measures the factor cost of producing final output.   Personal income is the gross income (income prior to payment of personal taxes) received by households from final output.

(b) The market value of final output is measured by a total flow of income and a total flow of expenditures.   The total flow of income approach measures the income received by economic resources in producing final output; it is the sum of wages, rent, interest and profit.   The flow of expenditure approach measures the amount of final output received by households, businesses, government and foreigners as the sum of consumption investment, government and net export spending, i.e. $C+I+G+X_n$.

(c) National income is the sum of wages, rent, interest and profit paid to economic resources in producing final output.   Personal income is that part of national income received by households.   Thus, national income minus the net receipts of the government and the business sector equals the personal income of households.

(*d*) National income accounting uses the market prices of goods and services as the unit for measuring the value of final output. Current dollar GNP uses current year prices in measuring the value of final output; constant dollar GNP is measured in terms of the prices of a selected (base) year.

4. (*a*) In the classical model, saving is directly related to the level of the rate of interest; investment is inversely related. The economic behavior determining these relationships is as follows: It was believed that households worked primarily to earn a money income which would be used to purchase goods and services. Households could be induced to postpone consumption (save) by the payment of interest which would permit a higher level of future consumption. It was believed that households were more willing to postpone consumption the higher the rate of interest, i.e. saving was positively related to the rate of interest. As profit maximizers, businesses would borrow and therefore add to their capital stock as long as the expected return from net investment exceeded the cost of borrowing (the rate of interest). Since a larger number of investment projects are profitable when borrowing costs are lower, net investment was viewed as being inversely related to the rate of interest.

(*b*) The rate of interest was the price-mechanism that replaced saving leakages from the circular flow with an equal amount of investment injections. Households saved (postponed consumption) only when induced to do so with interest payments. Businesses borrowed and thereby invested as long as expected returns from capital additions exceeded the cost of borrowing. Since the interest rate was the only variable determining saving and investment, the quantity of saving was always equal to the quantity of investment at the full-employment level of income.

(*c*) Disagreeing with classical analysis, Keynes held that income was a more important determinant of consumption and saving than the rate of interest. He postulated that consumption and saving were positively related to the level of income; he further theorized that consumption changed by a smaller absolute amount than income. This relationship of ΔC to ΔY ($\Delta C/\Delta Y$) was called the marginal propensity to consume and had a value less than one. The relationship between consumption and income was called the consumption function; the relationship between saving and income was named the saving function.

5. (*a*) At a $600 level of output (income), aggregate supply exceeds aggregate demand, and firms are unable to sell the entire output available for sale. When firms' production totals $600, households' income equals $600. According to the aggregate consumption function, households plan to consume $470 when income equals $600. At the $600 level of output, aggregate demand (consumption $470 plus investment $120) totals $590; aggregate supply is $600, and firms have unsold output of $10.

(*b*) See Fig. M-2. An equilibrium level of output exists when aggregate supply equals aggregate demand. When production equals $560, households' income equals $560 and aggregate consumption is $440. At the $560 level of output, aggregate demand is $560 (consumption $440 plus investment $120) which is equal to aggregate supply.

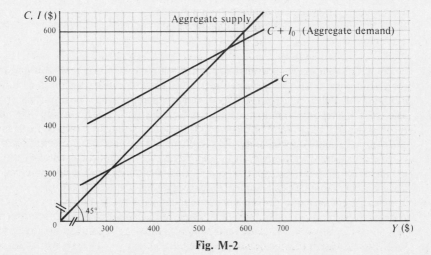

Fig. M-2

(c) An equilibrium level of income occurs when aggregate supply equals aggregate demand; it is the level of output where the quantities of goods and services offered for sale are equal to planned spending on consumption and investment.   An equilibrium level of income is sustained as long as there is a balance of aggregate supply and aggregate demand.

(d) An autonomous change in investment has a multiplied effect upon the level of income because consumption is dependent upon the level of income.   An increase in investment, for example, raises aggregate demand, the level of output, and therefore the income of households.   Since household consumption is directly related to income received, aggregate consumption also rises, further increasing the level of production.   Additional increases in income and consumption occur but they are of decreasing magnitude.   Thus, the initial increase in investment causes successive rounds of induced consumption spending which results in a multiple increase in the level of income.

6.   (a) Discretionary fiscal measures involve deliberate changes in the level of government spending and/ or government's net tax revenues to either increase or decrease the level of aggregate demand. Increased government spending raises the level of aggregate demand while increases in net tax revenues decrease household disposable income and thereby reduce the level of aggregate demand.   Since discretionary changes in government spending and taxes represent autonomous changes in aggregate demand, these changes will have a multiplied effect upon the level of income.

(b) When the MPC is 0.75, the expenditure k_e and tax k_{tx} multipliers are as follows.

$$k_e = 1/(1-\text{MPC}) = 1/(1-0.75) = 4 \qquad k_{tx} = -\text{MPC}/(1-\text{MPC}) = -0.75/(1-0.75) = -3$$

(1) A $20 increase in taxes lowers the level of income $60.

$$\Delta Y = k_{tx}\Delta T_x = -3(+\$20) = -\$60$$

(2) A $15 increase in government spending raises the level of income $60.

$$\Delta Y = k_e\Delta G = 4(\$15) = \$60$$

(3) A $20 increase in government spending and taxes raises the level of income $20.

$$\Delta Y = k_e\Delta G + k_{tx}\Delta T_x = 4(\$20) + (-3)(\$20) = \$80 - \$60 = \$20$$

(c) Equal changes in government spending and taxes alter the level of income by the change in government spending and taxes.   This balanced budget effect is due to the fact that the expenditure multiplier exceeds the tax multiplier by one, i.e. $k_e + k_{tx} = 1$.   Proof: $k_e + k_{tx} = [1/(1-\text{MPC})] + [-\text{MPC}/(1-\text{MPC})] = (1-\text{MPC})/(1-\text{MPC}) = 1$.

(d) Built-in stabilizers are the changes in government's net tax revenues that occur automatically when there are autonomous changes in aggregate demand.   Unemployment compensation is an example of a built-in stabilizer since this government transfer increases when aggregate demand falls and unemployment rises and decreases when aggregate demand rises and unemployment falls.   Unemployment insurance and other built-in stabilizers moderate the effect that autonomous changes in aggregate demand have upon the level of income; they reduce the contractionary effect of a decrease in aggregate demand and dampen the expansionary effect of an increase in aggregate demand.

7.   (a) Frictionally unemployed workers are those who are between jobs and can expect to find employment soon; such workers may be out of work due to seasonal demand for the good they produce, may have quit a previous job and are seeking a new position, or may be new entrants into the labor force who have not secured their first job.   Structurally unemployed workers are those displaced by structural changes in the economy and lack the required skills for other jobs; such workers may be replaced by a technologically more efficient machine or may have lost their job due to a permanent reduction in the demand for the good they helped produce.   Cyclically unemployed workers are those who have lost their jobs as a result of a decrease in aggregate demand; economic policy is aimed at increasing aggregate demand to reemploy workers whose unemployment is due to insufficient aggregate spending.

(b) A business cycle is an economic fluctuation in aggregate economic activity that occurs over a period of several years.   These recurrent but nonperiodic oscillations are generally divided into four phases: expansion, peak, contraction and trough.   The expansion phase is characterized by rising aggregate demand and employment while the contraction phase is characterized by falling aggregate demand and employment.

(c) The accelerator theory of investment links the level of net investment to changes in the level of consumption spending (or sales), i.e. $I = f(\Delta C)$. If consumption fails to increase by a constant amount or a constant rate over time, the level of investment spending will fluctuate, causing fluctuations in the level of economic activity. For example, suppose $2 in capital is required to produce $1 of a consumption good. If the change in consumption over six periods is $10, $20, $30, $20, $10 and $5, net investment is $20, $40, $60, $40, $20 and $10, respectively. Although consumption is increasing over the six periods, investment spending rises from $20 to $60 and then falls to $10. The acceleration principle is the most prominent theory used to explain the periodicity of changes in net investment over the business cycle.

Chapter 8

The Role and Importance of Money

8.1 MONEY

Money serves three distinct functions: medium of exchange, standard of value and store of value. As a *medium of exchange*, the monetary unit is used to pay economic resources for services rendered and thus becomes the mechanism for distributing the final output of goods and services. As a *standard of value*, the monetary unit is the common denominator used to measure prices, costs, revenues and incomes. As a *store of value*, the monetary unit can be stored for possible future use.

Laws and customs establish what is actually used as money. It is possible, however, to differentiate between two distinct monetary standards: a commodity standard and an inconvertible paper standard (see Problem 8.3). Since the 1930s, the United States has been on an inconvertible paper standard; the major components of the money supply have consisted of debts of the Federal government or privately owned commercial banks (see Problem 8.4). Defined as currency plus demand deposits adjusted, the M_1 definition of money includes coins and paper currency issued by the government and commercial banks' demand (i.e. checking) deposits (see Problem 8.7). Since savings and time deposits at commercial banks and thrift institutions are very close substitutes for demand deposits (i.e. near monies), broader definitions of the money supply also exist. The M_2 definition adds time and savings deposits (excluding large negotiable CDs) at commercial banks to M_1; the M_3 definition adds deposits of nonbank thrift institutions (mutual savings banks, savings and loan shares and credit union shares) to M_2.

EXAMPLE 1. The M_1, M_2 and M_3 stocks of money in the United States for April, 1978 were as follows (data are in billions of dollars):

$$M_1 = \text{currency} + \text{demand deposits adjusted}$$
$$= \$91.0 + \$256.8 = \$347.8$$
$$M_2 = M_1 + \text{time and savings deposits at commercial banks}$$
$$\text{(excluding negotiable certificates of deposit)}$$
$$= \$347.8 + \$486.3 = \$834.1$$
$$M_3 = M_2 + \text{deposits at nonbank thrift institutions}$$
$$= \$834.1 + \$584.6 = \$1418.7$$

8.2 THE EQUATION OF EXCHANGE

The central importance of money as a medium of exchange is formalized in the equation of exchange, $M \cdot V = \text{GNP}$, in which M is the stock of money, V is the velocity of money (the average number of times a unit of money is used during the year to purchase final goods and services), and GNP is the nominal value of the final output of goods and services in a given year (see Example 2). The nominal value of GNP can also be expressed as $P \cdot Q$, in which P is a weighted average of the prices of final output and Q is the quantity of final output (see Problem 8.9). Whether it is presented as $M \cdot V = \text{GNP}$ or $M \cdot V = P \cdot Q$, the equation of exchange is an identity and should be written $M \cdot V \equiv P \cdot Q$. (The three bars indicate that the equation is a tautology; see Problem 8.10.)

EXAMPLE 2. Suppose the stock of money is $312 and final output consists of the following components: consumption, $1080; investment, $240; government spending, $366, and net exports, $7.

Nominal GNP would equal $1693, as follows:

$$GNP \equiv C + I + G + X_n$$
$$\equiv \$1080 + \$240 + \$366 + \$7 \equiv \$1693$$

The velocity of money would be 5.426 since

$$V \equiv GNP/M$$
$$\equiv \$1693/\$312 \equiv 5.426$$

and the equation of exchange would appear as

$$M \cdot V \equiv GNP$$
$$\$312(5.426) \equiv \$1693$$

Thus, a $312 money supply circulated on the average 5.426 times in the distribution of a $1693 output of final goods and services.

8.3   THE QUANTITY THEORY OF MONEY

Quantity theorists use the equation of exchange to explain price movements over time.   In the rigid presentation of the quantity theory, V and Q are assumed constant; money supply increases, therefore, bring about proportional increases in the price level (see Example 3).

EXAMPLE 3.   Suppose the money supply is $400 and output consists of 800 units at an average price of $1.50 a unit. $P \cdot Q$ would equal $1200 [$1.50 × 800]; V would be 3 [$V = P \cdot Q/M = \$1200/\$400$].   The equation of exchange would appear as

$$M \cdot V = P \cdot Q$$
$$\$400 \times 3 = \$1.50 \times 800$$
$$\$1200 = \$1200$$

If V is constant, the economy is at full employment and Q does not change, a doubling of the money supply from $400 to $800 would double average prices from $1.50 to $3.   The rigid version of the quantity theory assumes that V and Q are constant and thereby concludes that money supply changes result in proportional changes in the price level.

The flexible version of the quantity theory recognizes the possibility of changes in V and Q over time.   In a growing economy, Q increases over time.   Velocity, dependent upon alterations in payment patterns, is also likely to change over the long run.   Holding that velocity changes are predictable, quantity theorists maintain that growth in nominal GNP is closely associated with increases in the stock of money (see Example 4).   Since nominal GNP equals $P \cdot Q$, quantity theorists suggest that a relatively stable price level can be achieved if money supply increases are closely tied to growth of the economy's capacity to expand output.   Thus, the flexible version of the quantity theory suggests that money is an important determinant of spending and price level changes over time.

EXAMPLE 4.   Suppose that the current money supply is $400, V is 4 and nominal GNP equals $1600.   A quantity theorist would predict that nominal GNP would increase to $2016 five years from now if the money supply grew 20% over the period and V was expected to increase to 4.2 by the end of the period.

$$GNP = (M + \Delta M) \cdot V$$
$$= (\$400 + \$80) \, 4.2$$
$$= \$2016$$

8.4   THE FINANCIAL SYSTEM

A well-developed financial system is necessary for a market economy to be efficient.   Such a system facilitates the transfer of funds from savers to investors and reduces the likelihood of extreme variability in the use of the money supply.   Since a large volume of saving is done by those who do not have ready access to investment opportunities, financial instruments provide a means of channeling saving to productive investment outlets (see Example 5).   Financial markets facilitate the issuance of new financial instruments as well as the exchange of existing ones.   Financial intermediaries are institutions that issue a safe and liquid claim which is a close substitute for money. In doing so, they help minimize the likelihood that savers will hold money as a store of value (hoard it) and not channel their savings to those who wish to invest (see Problem 8.17).

EXAMPLE 5.   In the two-sector circular flow depicted in Fig. 8-1, households earn $750, of which they consume $670 and save $80.   The $80 saving reenters the circular flow through $80 in real investment.   Assuming that savers are not the same individuals who invest, financial instruments are needed to transfer funds from savers to investors. Such money transfers are accomplished through various debt (bonds, promissory notes) and equity (stock) instruments.

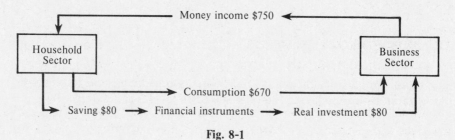

Fig. 8-1

Important Economic Terms

Commodity standard.   A monetary standard by which money is defined in terms of a specific commodity, such as gold.

Demand deposit.   A commercial bank liability which is payable to the owner upon demand or is transferred to another party by the writing of a check.

Equation of exchange.   A tautology specifying that the amount of money spent on goods and services is equal to the market value of goods and services sold, i.e. $M \cdot V \equiv P \cdot Q$.

Financial instrument.   A document issued by one who secures funds from another party who has saved.

Financial intermediary.   A financial institution that issues a financial claim upon itself upon the receipt of funds.   Its economic function is to accumulate savings to lend to those who wish to borrow.

Financial market.   A market in which newly issued financial instruments transfer current saving to those who wish to borrow or in which previously issued financial instruments are exchanged.

Inconvertible paper standard.   A monetary standard by which money consists of debt of the government or commercial banks and is not convertible into a specific commodity.

Near money.   A financial asset that cannot be used as a medium of exchange but is a close substitute for money because it is easily changed into money with little to no loss of original nominal value.

Quantity theory of money.   Its rigid presentation states that there is a proportional relationship between the stock of money and the price level.   The flexible version of the quantity theory states that nominal GNP bears a close relationship to the quantity of money, and that strict control of the money supply is needed to control the price level.

Review Questions

1. As a standard of value, money provides (*a*) its holder with perfect liquidity, (*b*) a common denominator for measuring value, (*c*) a mechanism for allocating resources and distributing output, (*d*) a medium for exchanging final output.

    Ans.   (*b*)

2. What is used as money is determined by (*a*) laws and customs, (*b*) government's acceptance of a commodity standard, (*c*) government's acceptance of an inconvertible paper standard, (*d*) its use as a store of value.

    Ans.   (*a*)

3. An inconvertible paper standard consists of a money supply that (*a*) is backed by gold, (*b*) is backed by gold but is not convertible into gold, (*c*) includes the debts of the government and/or commercial banks, (*d*) includes only the debts of commercial banks which have gold backing.

    Ans.   (*c*)

4. In the United States, the M_1 definition of money is (*a*) paper currency, (*b*) paper currency and demand deposits, (*c*) paper currency, demand deposits and deposits at nonbank thrift institutions, (*d*) paper currency, demand deposits, deposits at nonbank thrift institutions and time and savings deposits at commercial banks.

    Ans.   (*b*)

5. The velocity of money measures (*a*) the use of each unit of money in purchasing final output, (*b*) the average use of money in purchasing final output, (*c*) the average use of money by consumers in purchasing consumer goods, (*d*) the average use of money by the business sector.

    Ans.   (*b*)

6. In the equation of exchange, GNP equals (*a*) $4000 if M is $100 and the average use of money is 4, (*b*) $1000 if M is $100 and the average use of money is 5, (*c*) $500 if M is $100 and the average use of money is 5, (*d*) $400 if M is $100 and the average use of money is 2.

    Ans.   (*c*)

7. In the rigid version of the quantity theory of money, (*a*) changes in nominal GNP are proportional to changes in the money supply, (*b*) changes in nominal GNP are proportional to changes in velocity, (*c*) changes in V are proportional to changes in the money supply, (*d*) changes in the price level are proportional to changes in the money supply.

    Ans.   (*d*)

8. In the flexible version of the quantity theory of money, (*a*) changes in nominal GNP are closely associated with changes in the money supply, (*b*) changes in V are closely associated with changes in the money supply, (*c*) changes in the price level are closely associated with changes in the money supply, (*d*) changes in nominal GNP are proportional to changes in velocity.

    Ans.   (*a*)

9. If the current money supply is $400, velocity is 4 and there is a 10% growth in the money supply and a 25% increase in velocity, nominal GNP should increase from (*a*) $1200 to $1600, (*b*) $1600 to $1760, (*c*) $1600 to $2200, (*d*) $1760 to $2200.

    Ans.   (*c*)

10. Which of the following statements is *incorrect*?
    (*a*) A financial system helps facilitate the transfer of funds from savers to investors.
    (*b*) Financial intermediaries issue financial claims which help reduce the likelihood that savers will hold money as a store of value.
    (*c*) Financial markets allow the exchange of previously issued financial instruments.
    (*d*) None of the above.

    Ans.   (*d*)

Solved Problems

MONEY

8.1. (*a*) How does money assist in efficiently allocating resources and goods?   (*b*) Why is the standard-of-value function central to the efficient performance of a decentralized economy?

    (*a*) Producers use money rather than goods to pay owners of economic resources for their services.   Owners of economic resources are therefore able to seek the employment that maximizes their money incomes rather than the one that provides them with payments in a specific good. The use of money not only fosters the efficient allocation of economic resources, but also avoids the complexities and inefficiencies of barter in the distribution of final output.   In addition, the recipients of a money income have the freedom to control their timing of purchases as well as the combinations of goods purchased.

    (*b*) The physical sciences require units of measurement to relate and understand physical phenomenon, e.g. the speed of sound and light, the weight and size of objects, the calories found in foods. Money is a convenient means of measuring the worth of economic goods and services.   In hiring resources and exchanging goods and services, money serves as a measure of their values and thereby facilitates economic decision-making.

8.2. (*a*)   Explain the store-of-value function of money.
      (*b*)   Can other financial assets serve as a store of value?
      (*c*)   What is the difference between money and other financial assets as stores of value?

    (*a*) Money is generalized purchasing power that is acceptable at any time for the purchase of goods and services.   Thus, money, as a store of value, permits consuming units to postpone spending and allows them to keep savings in a form in which there is no loss of nominal value.

    (*b*) Other financial assets, such as time and savings deposits at commercial banks or thrift institutions, have a fixed nominal value and thereby represent generalized purchasing power.   These financial assets also serve as a store of value since they are readily converted into money with no loss of nominal value.

    (*c*) Unlike money, other financial assets are not accepted as a medium of exchange; they are a safe store of nominal value but must be converted into money to be used in exchange during some future period.

8.3. What is (*a*) a monetary standard?   (*b*) A commodity standard?   (*c*) An inconvertible paper standard?

    (*a*) A monetary standard is the accepted laws, practices and customs that define money in an economy.   That is, a monetary standard is what a country decides to use as money.   It could be paper currency, gold, bricks or anything else accepted as the medium of exchange.

    (*b*) With a commodity standard, the monetary unit is defined in terms of a specific commodity.   In most commodity standards, paper currency circulates as money but can be converted into a specific commodity.   For example, if the United States adopted a gold standard and defined the dollar as 24 grains of gold, holders of dollars could convert each dollar into 24 grains of gold. When a country adopts a commodity standard, the money supply depends upon the defined commodity content of the paper currency, the available quantity of that commodity and the commercial use of the commodity.

    (*c*) With an inconvertible paper standard, there is no government commitment to convert the monetary unit into a specified commodity at a fixed price.   An inconvertible paper standard is usually composed of promissory notes issued by the government and/or commercial banks.   Discretionary management of the money supply is possible with an inconvertible paper standard since there is no physical (commodity) limit to the creation of money.

8.4. (*a*)   Suppose 1 ounce of gold is equal to $20 in a country on a gold standard.   Using "T" accounts, show how the discovery of 100 ounces of gold by households can increase paper currency $2000.   Assume that households deal directly with the government in exchanging gold for dollars.

(b) Suppose a country is on an inconvertible paper standard.   Show via "T" accounts how the government can increase the money supply by exchanging $2000 in paper currency for $2000 of previously issued interest-bearing government debt owned by the household sector.   Assume that the government sector deals directly with the household sector in the exchange of promissory notes.

(c) Referring to parts (a) and (b), explain the difference in money creation between a commodity standard and an inconvertible paper standard.

(a) The household sector gives up ownership of 100 ounces of gold valued at $2000 *in exchange for* $2000 in paper currency issued by the government sector.   The government sector in receiving the gold has a $2000 increase in assets and a $2000 increase in liabilities as a result of issuing paper currency.   Evidenced by its issuance of paper currency, government has become a depository for gold.

HOUSEHOLD SECTOR			GOVERNMENT SECTOR		
Assets		Liabilities	Assets		Liabilities
Gold	−$2000		Gold	+$2000	Paper currency +$2000
Paper currency	+$2000				

(b) The household sector exchanges government securities valued at $2000 *in exchange for* $2000 in paper currency issued by the government sector.   In exchanging previously issued government securities for paper currency, the government sector retires previously issued debt and issues paper currency.

HOUSEHOLD SECTOR			GOVERNMENT SECTOR		
Assets		Liabilities	Assets		Liabilities
Government securities	−$2000				Government securities −$2000
Paper currency	+$2000				Paper currency +$2000

(c) In part (a), the government owns gold equal in value to the paper currency it issued.   In part (b), there is no asset with a value equal to the $2000 in paper currency issued by the government.   With an inconvertible paper standard, paper currency is a liability of the government; there is no specific asset "backing" the money supply.   With a commodity standard, the government holds a specific asset (in this case gold) as "backing" for the paper currency that has been issued.

8.5.   (a) Why are demand deposits included in the M_1 definition of money?   (b) What "backing" is there for coins, paper currency and demand deposits?   (c) How can money have value without commodity "backing"?

(a) Demand deposits are check-writing accounts at commercial banks.   In most cases checks are as acceptable as paper currency in purchasing goods and services.   Since demand deposits are accepted as a medium of exchange, they are included along with coins and paper currency in the M_1 definition of money.

(b) In the United States, coins, paper currency and demand deposits have no specific commodity backing.   While coins have a metallic content, the market value of the coined metal is considerably less than the face (monetary) value of the coin.   Paper currency is a liability (debt) of Federal Reserve Banks while in the United States demand deposits are liabilities (debts) of privately owned commercial banks.

(c) Anything has value if there is a limited supply and an unlimited demand for it.   The basis of value for an inconvertible paper standard is that government is willing to limit its supply, owners of economic resources are willing to receive it in payment for services and spending units are willing to use it to obtain goods and services.

8.6.   (a) What are near monies?   (b) Why are some near monies included in the broader M_2 definition of the money supply?

(a)   Near monies are financial assets that cannot be used as a medium of exchange but are close substitutes for money because they are easily transferred into money with little or no loss of original nominal value.   Time and savings deposits in commercial banks are close substitutes for demand deposits in the same bank.   Other close substitutes include deposits at thrift institutions, credit union shares and United States savings bonds.

(b)   Economists have recognized that the volume of savings and time deposits at commercial banks may be an important factor affecting aggregate demand.   Since the money supply is controlled because of the effect of its size upon aggregate demand and economic activity, economists have considered it prudent to expand the traditional M_1 definition of money to include these near monies. M_2 is an expansion of M_1 that includes time and savings deposits at commercial banks.   Since it is not clear which near monies should be included, the expansion of the definition of money becomes arbitrary.   Recognizing this, the Federal Reserve publishes a monthly series on five expanded definitions of the money supply.

8.7.   The Federal Reserve defines M_1 and M_2 as follows:

M_1 equals the sum of demand deposits in the commercial banking system *plus* currency outstanding *plus* foreign deposits at Federal Reserve Banks *less* Treasury, Federal government and interbank demand deposits in the banking system and currency held by the Federal government and the commercial banking system.

M_2 equals M_1 plus savings and time deposits (except negotiable certificates of deposit in denominations of $100,000 or more) in the commercial banking system.

From the data in Table 1, find (a) M_1 and (b) M_2.

Table 1

(1)	Total currency in circulation	$ 60.0
(2)	Currency held by the government sector	4.0
(3)	Currency held by the commercial banking system	3.0
(4)	Total demand deposits in the commercial banking system	210.0
(5)	Treasury demand deposits at the commercial banking system	8.0
(6)	Interbank demand deposits	15.0
(7)	Foreign deposit balances at Federal Reserve Banks	1.0
(8)	Savings and time deposits at the commercial banking system	360.0
(9)	Negotiable certificates of deposit in denominations of $100,000 or more	62.0

(a)

$$M_1 = (1) + (4) + (7) - [(2) + (3) + (5) + (6)]$$
$$= \$60 + \$210 + \$1 - [\$4 + \$3 + \$8 + \$15] = \$241$$

(b)

$$M_2 = M_1 + (8) - (9)$$
$$= \$241 + \$360 - \$62 = \$539$$

THE EQUATION OF EXCHANGE

8.8. Find the velocity of money when (*a*) the stock of money is $200 and nominal GNP equals $800, (*b*) the stock of money is $225 and nominal GNP equals $1000, and (*c*) the stock of money is $250 and nominal GNP equals $1500.

Velocity equals nominal GNP divided by the money supply. Therefore, (*a*) $V = GNP/M = \$800/\$200 = 4.0$, (*b*) $V = GNP/M = \$1000/\$225 = 4.44$, (*c*) $V = GNP/M = \$1500/\$250 = 6.0$.

8.9. Suppose an economy's output consists of the following goods, which were sold at the prices stated in Table 2.

Table 2

Good	A	B	C	D	E
Price ($)	1.00	0.75	5.00	2.25	1.50
Quantity	50	50	50	50	50

(*a*) Find the average price *P* and total units of output *Q* for this economy. (*b*) Find GNP by summing the price times output for each good. (*c*) Find GNP by multiplying the average price *P* times the total units of output *Q*.

(*a*) The average price for final output is

$$P = \frac{p_A + p_B + p_C + p_D + p_E}{5}$$

$$= \frac{\$1.00 + \$0.75 + \$5.00 + \$2.25 + \$1.50}{5}$$

$$= \$10.50/5 = \$2.10$$

Total output $Q = 250$ units, the sum of the individual quantities produced.

(*b*) The nominal value of final output for Goods A through E is presented in Table 3.

Table 3

Good	Price (*p*)	Quantity (*q*)	Nominal Value (*p* × *q*)
A	$1.00	50	$ 50.00
B	0.75	50	37.50
C	5.00	50	250.00
D	2.25	50	112.50
E	1.50	50	75.00
			Σpq = GNP = $525.00

(*c*) GNP equals the average price *P* times the total units of output *Q*. $GNP = P \cdot Q = \$2.10(250) = \$525.00$.

8.10. Why is the equation of exchange a tautology?

The left side of the equation of exchange ($M \cdot V$) is composed of the economy's stock of money times its average use in purchasing the final output. Thus, $M \cdot V$ represents the amount *spent* on final goods and services. The right side of the equation of exchange (GNP) represents the nominal value of the final output of goods and services, i.e. the nominal amount *received* from the sale of final output. Since, *ex post*, the amount spent must equal the amount received, $M \cdot V$ must always equal GNP. Thus, the equation of exchange is a tautology because the equation is true as a result of the way the terms are defined.

THE QUANTITY THEORY OF MONEY

8.11. (*a*) Why does the rigid version of the quantity theory of money conclude that there is a proportional relationship between the money supply and the price level? (*b*) Would one expect price level changes to be proportional to increases in the money supply in the long run?

(*a*) The rigid version of the quantity theory of money suggests that the average use *V* of the money stock and full-employment output are constant. Given no change in *V* or *Q*, the average price of output *P* must be proportional to changes in the money supply.

(*b*) Full-employment output *Q* increases through time and *V* could increase or decrease. It is unlikely, therefore, that *M* and *P* will have a proportional relationship in the long run.

8.12. With reference to the rigid version of the quantity theory of money, what should happen to the average price of output if the money supply is currently $100 and there is an increase of (*a*) $50, (*b*) $100, or (*c*) $200?

(*a*) There is a 50% increase in the money supply ($\Delta M/M = \$50/\$100 = 0.50 = 50\%$). The average price of output should increase 50%.

(*b*) There is a 100% increase in the money supply; the average price should double.

(*c*) There is a 200% increase in the money supply; the average price should triple.

8.13. Suppose in a full-employment economy, government expenditures increase substantially and the government elects to finance these expenditures by increasing the money supply from $200 to $400. (*a*) What should happen to the average price of output? (*b*) What is the cause(s) of increases in the price level in an economy which is at or near full employment?

(*a*) Assuming no change in *V*, the average price of output should double because the economy is at full employment. Average prices, however, may more than double if *V* increases. *V*, the average turnover of the money stock, is likely to increase in the short run if prices are already rising or are expected to rise. In such a situation, people spend money income upon receipt since they will lose purchasing power if money is held for any length of time.

(*b*) If *Q* is constant, *V* and *M* are the only causes of rising prices. Historically, *V* has not had wide fluctuations in the short run. Substantial increases in the money supply are the only cause of rapidly rising prices in the short run.

8.14. Suppose the money supply is initially $250, the average price of output is $4.25 and *Q* equals 400.

(*a*) Find *V* and the nominal value of GNP.

(*b*) Find GNP, *P* and *Q* if *V* is constant and there is a 15% growth in output and a 20% increase in the money supply.

(*c*) Find GNP, *P* and *Q* if *V* increases to 7 and there is a 15% growth in output and a 20% increase in the money supply.

(*d*) Could stable prices (average price of $4.25) be achieved in situations (*b*) and (*c*)?

(*a*) The nominal value of GNP equals $P \cdot Q$. Given $P = \$4.25$ and $Q = 400$, nominal GNP equals $1700. *V* equals GNP/$M = \$1700/\$250 = 6.8$.

(*b*) A 15% growth in output and a 20% increase in the money stock increase *Q* from 400 to 460 and *M* from $250 to $300. With *V* remaining constant at 6.8, we have

$$P \cdot Q = M \cdot V$$
$$P(460) = \$300(6.8)$$
$$460P = \$2040$$
$$P = \$4.435$$

The average price of output increases from $4.25 to $4.435.

(*c*) With *Q* increasing to 460, *M* to $300 and *V* to 7, we have

$$P \cdot Q = M \cdot V$$
$$P(460) = \$300(7)$$
$$460P = \$2100$$
$$P = \$4.565$$

The average price of output increases from \$4.25 to \$4.565.

(d) According to the flexible version of the quantity theory, a stable price level is achieved by tying growth of the money stock to projections of V and Q. In situation (b), V is expected to remain constant. P would also remain constant if money growth matches expected growth in Q. Thus, prices would remain at \$4.25 if M increased by 15%.

In situation (c), V is projected to increase to 7. Solving for M, we find that the money supply should have increased from \$250 to \$279.29 to keep average prices at \$4.25, as follows:

$$M \cdot V = P \cdot Q$$
$$M(7) = \$4.25(460)$$
$$7M = \$1955$$
$$M = \$279.29$$

THE FINANCIAL SYSTEM

8.15. (a) What is a financial instrument? (b) What are debt and equity financial intruments?

(a) A financial instrument is a document issued by a household, business or government in exchange for funds (money saving) from savers.

(b) A debt financial instrument is a contract between the borrower and lender which specifies the amount that the borrower must repay, the interest to be paid on the sum borrowed and the maturity of the obligation. While also involving the transfer of funds, an equity financial instrument does not contractually require repayment of the amount borrowed nor require a specific interest payment. Rather, the saver receives a financial instrument that specifies partial ownership and control of the firm and a promise of sharing in the firm's profits.

8.16. Using "T" accounts, show the following transactions: (a) Household B borrows \$100 from Household A, issues a promissory note, and agrees to repay the \$100 plus \$6 in interest in 6 months. (b) Six months later, Household B repays A the principal plus interest.

(a) Household A exchanges the asset money for B's promissory note. Household B's assets and liabilities increase \$100: its money assets have increased upon receipt of the loan; its liabilities are larger because it gave the promissory note to Household A.

(b) Six months later, Household A exchanges B's promissory note for the \$100 lent plus \$6 in interest. Household B's liabilities and assets decrease \$106 in repaying the loan.

HOUSEHOLD A

	Assets		Liabilities
(a)	Money	−\$100	
	Promissory note of Household B	+\$100	
(b)	Promissory note of B plus interest due	−\$106	
	Money	+\$106	

HOUSEHOLD B

	Assets		Liabilities	
(a)	Money	+\$100	Promissory note	+\$100
(b)	Money	−\$106	Promissory note plus interest owed	−\$106

8.17.   (*a*) What are financial intermediaries?   (*b*) Show through "T" accounts how a savings bank acts as a financial intermediary by accepting deposits and making loans.   (*c*) What is the importance of financial intermediaries to the economic process?

(*a*)   Financial intermediaries are financial institutions that issue a financial claim against themselves upon the receipt of funds; they reinvest these deposited funds in financial instruments.   There is a wide array of financial intermediaries: commercial banks, mutual savings banks, savings and loan associations, life insurance companies and investment companies, to name a few.

(*b*)   (1) We shall assume that Household A deposits $10,000 in a savings bank.   Household A gives up the asset money in exchange for a deposit in the savings bank.   The savings bank accepts the $10,000 money deposit and credits $10,000 to the deposit account of Household A.

(2) We shall further assume that the savings bank makes a $10,000 loan to Household B.   Household B receives money and signs a $10,000 promissory note (an IOU).   The savings bank exchanges the asset money for the promissory note of Household B.

Transactions (1) and (2) demonstrate how financial intermediaries bring together those who save and those who wish to borrow funds.   As an intermediary, they reduce the likelihood that savers will fail to make funds available for investment.

HOUSEHOLD A

	Assets		Liabilities
(1) {	Money	−$10,000	
	Deposit in savings bank	+$10,000	

SAVINGS BANK

	Assets		Liabilities	
(1)	Money	+$10,000	Deposit of Household A	+$10,000
(2) {	Money	−$10,000		
	Promissory note of Household B	+$10,000		

HOUSEHOLD B

	Assets		Liabilities	
(2)	Money	+$10,000	Promissory note	+$10,000

(*c*)   Financial intermediaries supply a financial claim that is relatively safe (there is little probability of loss of principal) and highly liquid (a financial claim that is quickly converted into money without loss of nominal value).   In doing so, they minimize the likelihood that savers will hold money (hoard) and thereby divert funds from the circular flow.

8.18.   How does the financial system help an economy operate efficiently?

An economic system is judged efficient when it achieves maximum use of economic resources and maximum satisfaction of consumer wants.   Financial instruments and institutions generate efficiency by (1) increasing consumer satisfaction from earned income, (2) increasing the stability of economic activity, (3) facilitating capital formation, and (4) achieving the best allocation of money savings. Elaborating:

(1) The financial system increases consumer satisfaction by facilitating the allocation of spending over time.   It allows some units to spend more than their current incomes (dissave) and allows other spending units to increase their levels of spending by earning interest on money savings.

(2) The creation of safe and liquid financial claims by financial intermediaries reduces the likelihood that some savers will hold idle money balances.   By rechanneling savings into the circular flow, spending flows are stabilized.   This in turn stabilizes employment and economic activity.

(3) Financial instruments encourage the lending of money savings to units that spend in excess of their incomes.   A large proportion of the funds so borrowed are used by business firms to add to the economy's stock of capital.   This increases productive capacity.

(4) Since the profit motive guides the operation of financial institutions, money savings are distributed to those capital uses that have the greatest productivity.

8.19.   (*a*) What is a financial market?   (*b*) Distinguish between a money market and a capital market.

(*a*) A financial market is a place where financial instruments are exchanged.   In *primary* financial markets newly issued financial instruments are exchanged for money and current saving is transferred to those who wish to borrow.   There are also *secondary* financial markets in which previously issued debt and equity financial instruments are exchanged (traded) for money (i.e. in which the current owner of a debt or equity instrument is able to sell a financial claim to another individual).

(*b*) The money market is a financial market that consists of financial instruments that mature in one year or less.   In the capital market, the maturity of financial instruments issued or traded exceeds one year.

Chapter 9

Commercial Banks and
the Money Supply

9.1 INTRODUCTION

Like other financial institutions, commercial banks accept deposits and make loans.   Commercial banks, however, are unique because their loans increase demand deposits and the money supply.   This chapter focuses upon commercial banks and their involvement in money creation.

9.2 REGULATION OF DEMAND DEPOSIT VOLUME

Paper currency is a bearer instrument but demand-deposit money can be transferred to another party only by the written request of the current owner to the commercial bank (see Problem 9.3). Since demand deposits are a safer way of holding money, they are the most frequently used form of money; demand deposits account for over 90% of all money transactions in the United States.

Commercial banks, unless regulated, are in a position to create demand deposits (money) at their discretion (see Problem 9.5).   In the United States, commercial bank deposit expansion is state or Federally regulated by the imposition of a reserve requirement.   The *reserve requirement* is a rule that requires a commercial bank to limit its demand deposits to a fixed multiple of one of its liquid assets (see Example 1).   Given its desire for income and profits and its understanding that demand deposits are the preferred form of money, a commercial bank will tend to expand its loans and demand deposits by an amount equal to its holding of excess reserves (see Example 2).

EXAMPLE 1. Suppose the government specifies that a commercial bank's demand deposit volume cannot exceed 20% of its holding of currency, i.e. there is a 0.20 reserve requirement and currency is designated the reserve asset.   If the First National Commercial Bank has the assets and liabilities shown below and the reserve requirement is 0.20, actual reserves (i.e. currency) equal $1,000 while required reserves are $800 (0.20 × $4000 demand deposits).

First National Commercial Bank

Assets		Liabilities	
Currency	$1000	Demand deposits	$4000
Loans	2000		
Investment	1000		

EXAMPLE 2. A commercial bank that holds reserves greater than required (excess reserves equal actual reserves less required reserves) is in a position to expand loans up to the amount of its excess reserves.   Thus, in Example 1, the First National Commercial Bank, holding $200 of excess reserves, could increase loans by $200 to $2200 and expand demand deposits by $200 to $4200.   A commercial bank will not expand demand deposits by more than its excess reserves because it is unsure whether expenditures by the borrower of the newly created demand deposit will result in a reserve loss to another commercial bank.   See Section 9.3.

The Federal Reserve System, composed of twelve district Reserve Banks, implements monetary policy and thereby is the central bank for the United States.   While not all commercial banks are members of the Federal Reserve System, those that are usually keep a majority of their reserve assets on deposit at a district reserve bank (see Example 3).   This institutional arrangement does not alter commercial bank behavior in lending excess reserves; it does, however, facilitate the transfer of funds from one commercial bank to another (see Problem 9.8).

EXAMPLE 3. Suppose Commercial Bank A has $2000 in currency, $4000 in loans and investments, a $6000 demand-deposit liability, and the reserve requirement on demand deposits is 0.20.

COMMERCIAL BANK A

Assets		Liabilities	
Actual reserves:		Demand deposits	$6000
Currency	$2000		
Loans & investments	4000		

If Commercial Bank A joins the Federal Reserve System, it may elect to deposit any part of its currency in the district reserve bank.   Suppose it deposits $1600 of its currency at the reserve bank.   In doing so, the form of reserves has changed but the total has stayed constant at $2000.   Since Commercial Bank A's actual reserves are $2000 and required reserves equal $1200 ($0.20 \times \$6000$ demand deposits), it is in a position to expand loans and deposits up to $800, the amount of its excess reserves.

COMMERCIAL BANK A

Assets		Liabilities	
Actual reserves:		Demand deposits	$6000
Currency	$ 400		
Deposit at the Federal Reserve	1600		
Loans & investments	4000		

9.3   DEMAND DEPOSIT CREATION BY THE COMMERCIAL BANKING SYSTEM

Commercial banks in the United States are privately owned.   Seeking profits for stockholders, they tend to expand loans and create deposits whenever excess reserves are held because loans produce the interest income which is the source of bank earnings (see Problem 9.9).   Since there are over 14,000 commercial banks, demand-deposit expansion by one bank usually results in a reserve loss to another commercial bank.   With each commercial bank making loans equal in amount to its excess reserves, demand-deposit expansion becomes a multiple of the increase in the reserves held by the commercial banking system (see Problem 9.10).   Viewed in the aggregate, the potential increase in demand deposits for the commercial banking system is specified as $\Delta D = d\Delta R$ where ΔD is the potential change in demand-deposit volume, d is the reciprocal of the reserve requirement (i.e. $d = 1/r$) and ΔR is the change in reserves for the commercial banking system.

EXAMPLE 4. Suppose the reserve requirement is 0.10 and there is a $250 increase in actual reserves.   The commercial banking system could experience a $2500 increase in demand deposits, as shown below.

$$\Delta D = d\Delta R$$

Since $\Delta R = \$250$ and $d = 1/r = 1/0.10 = 10$,

$$\Delta D = 10(\$250) = \$2500$$

9.4   MONEY CREATION

Given an M_1 definition of money, a change in the money supply consists of a change in demand deposits plus currency, i.e. $\Delta M = \Delta D + \Delta C$. As explained in Section 9.3, an increase in commercial bank reserves may cause a multiple increase in demand deposits.   Since currency holdings are generally positively related to the volume of demand deposits, some of the additional reserves created by the Federal Reserve will be held as currency (see Example 5).   Given the possibility that commercial banks may also hold excess reserves, the change in the money supply is given as

$$\Delta M = \Delta B \left[\frac{1 + c}{r + c + e} \right]$$

where r is the reserve requirement on demand deposits, c is the ratio of currency to demand deposits and e is the ratio of excess reserves to demand deposits. ΔB consists of reserves held by the commercial banking system plus currency in circulation.   See Problem 9.16.

EXAMPLE 5.   Suppose (1) the Federal Reserve increases the commercial banking system's currency reserves $1000, and (2) the demand for currency increases $200 when demand deposits increase.   With a net increase of $800 in reserves, (3) the commercial banking system expands demand deposits by $4000.   *Note* that the potential increase in demand deposits would be $5000 if there was no currency outflow associated with the expansion of demand deposits.

THE COMMERCIAL BANKING SYSTEM

	Assets			Liabilities
(1)	Currency reserves	+$1000	Demand deposits	+$1000
(2)	Currency reserves	−$ 200	Demand deposits	−$ 200
(3)	Loans	+$3200	Demand deposits	+$3200

9.5   MANAGING A COMMERCIAL BANK'S ASSETS

While profits are a commercial bank's principal objective, survival requires that each bank remain solvent and hold adequate liquidity for those instances when depositors wish to convert deposits into currency.   Solvency is achieved by lending to borrowers whose probability of default is minimal, i.e. by holding noncash debt assets that have a high likelihood of repayment.   Liquidity is secured by holding some marketable securities that can be converted into cash quickly without loss of nominal value.   Thus, the bank's asset portfolio (composition of assets) depends upon the investment opportunities open to it and the need for safety and liquidity in the bank's day-to-day operation.

Important Economic Terms

Demand-deposit multiplier.   The multiple effect that a change in the commercial banking system's reserves has upon demand-deposit volume, i.e. $\Delta D/\Delta R = d$.   The value of the demand-deposit multiplier is $1/r$.

Excess reserves.   The quantity of reserves held by a commercial bank in excess of its required reserves. Excess reserves equal actual reserves held by a commercial bank less required reserves.

Fractional-reserve banking.   A condition where a commercial bank's required reserves are less than its demand deposit volume, which thereby permits the commercial banking system to expand demand deposits by a multiple of the additional reserves it may receive.

Money multiplier.   The multiple effect that a change in reserves has upon the money supply, i.e. $\Delta M/\Delta R = m$.   Given an M_1 definition of money, the money multiplier equals $(1+c)/(r+c+e)$.

Reserve requirement.   The rule established by the banking authority whereby a commercial bank must maintain a minimum relationship between reserves and demand deposits.   This specified relationship between reserves and demand deposits is called the *reserve ratio*.

Reserves.   Those assets that a commercial bank may hold to satisfy a reserve requirement.   In the United States, reserves equal currency (paper money and coins) plus commercial bank deposits at Federal Reserve Banks.

Review Questions

1. Reserve requirements are imposed on commercial banks to (a) control demand-deposit expansion, (b) regulate commercial banks' profits, (c) encourage the use of demand deposits as a medium of exchange, (d) discourage the use of demand deposits as a medium of exchange.
   Ans. (a)

2. If the reserve requirement for demand deposits is 0.15, commercial banks'
   (a) total assets must equal at least 15% of their demand deposit liabilities,
   (b) demand deposit liabilities must equal at least 15% of their asset holdings,
   (c) demand deposits must equal at least 15% of a designated reserve asset,
   (d) designated reserve assets must equal at least 15% of demand deposits.
   Ans. (d)

3. Which of the following statements is *correct*?
   (a) A commercial bank holds excess reserves if its required reserves exceed actual reserves.
   (b) A commercial bank holds excess reserves if its actual reserves exceed required reserves.
   (c) A commercial bank will expand loans and deposits if required reserves exceed actual reserves.
   (d) A commercial bank will expand loans by the amount of the inflow of actual reserves.
   Ans. (b)

4. If the reserves of a commercial bank total $250, demand deposits equal $2000, and the reserve requirement is 0.10, excess reserves equal (a) $250, (b) $200, (c) $50, (d) 0.
   Ans. (c)

5. If a commercial bank's actual reserves equal $400, demand deposits equal $3500, and r is 0.10, the commercial bank is in a position to expand its loans by (a) $4000, (b) $500, (c) $250, (d) $50.
   Ans. (d)

6. If the commercial banking system receives $400 in additional reserves and the reserve requirement is 0.20, maximum deposit expansion for the commercial banking system is (a) $2000, (b) $1200, (c) $320, (d) $80.
   Ans. (a)

7. If $c = 0.05$, $e = 0$, $r = 0.20$ and commercial banks receive an additional $100 in actual reserves, the commercial banking system will expand demand deposits by (a) $100, (b) $400, (c) $420, (d) $500.
   Ans. (d)

8. If $c = 0.05$, $e = 0$, $r = 0.20$, a $100 increase in ΔB will result in an increase in the money supply of (a) $100, (b) $400, (c) $420, (d) $500.
   Ans. (c)

9. If $c = 0.05$, $e = 0$, $r = 0.20$, a $100 increase in ΔB will result in a
   (a) $5 increase in nonbank holdings of currency and a $95 increase in demand deposits,
   (b) $20 increase in nonbank holdings of currency and a $380 increase in demand deposits,
   (c) $20 increase in nonbank holdings of currency and a $400 increase in demand deposits,
   (d) $25 increase in nonbank holdings of currency and a $475 increase in demand deposits.
   Ans. (c)

10. Which of the following statements is *incorrect?*
    (a) A commercial bank may hold excess reserves as a source of liquidity.
    (b) A commercial bank must remain solvent to be profitable in the long run.
    (c) A commercial bank must hold liquid assets to meet unexpected deposit outflows.
    (d) A commercial bank's secondary reserves consist of its excess reserves and marketable money-market securities.
    Ans. (d)

Solved Problems

REGULATION OF COMMERCIAL BANK DEPOSITS

9.1. Explain the meaning of "T" accounts (1) and (2) below.

(1) NATIONAL COMMERCIAL BANK

Assets		Liabilities	
Currency	$10,000	Demand deposits	$87,000
Loans	60,000	Net worth	5,000
Investments	20,000		
Other assets	2,000		
	$92,000		$92,000

(2) NATIONAL COMMERCIAL BANK

Assets		Liabilities	
Currency	+ $100	Demand deposits	+ $100

"T" account (1) presents the values of the bank's *stock* of assets, liabilities and net worth. It is, in effect, the bank's balance sheet. The "T" account in (2) shows the *flow* (net change) in asset and liability accounts. A flow "T" account specifies what is happening to a specific asset or liability account, i.e. whether it is increasing (+) or decreasing (−). In monetary analysis, "T" accounts are generally used to present the net change (flow) in specific accounts that results from a given transaction.

9.2. Suppose Commercial Bank A has the following balance sheet:

COMMERCIAL BANK A

Assets		Liabilities	
Currency	$12,000	Demand deposits	$74,000
Loans	50,000	Net worth	5,000
Investments	15,000		
Other assets	2,000		
	$79,000		$79,000

(*a*) Using a flow "T" account, show the effect of the following situation: Depositors in Commercial Bank A convert $500 in demand deposits into currency.   (*b*) Present Commercial Bank A's balance sheet after the deposit outflow assumed in part (*a*).

(*a*) Currency has decreased $500 as have demand deposits.

COMMERCIAL BANK A

Assets		Liabilities	
Currency	− $500	Demand deposits	− $500

(*b*) The currency account is lowered from $12,000 to $11,500 and demand deposits decrease from $74,000 to $73,500.

COMMERCIAL BANK A

Assets		Liabilities	
Currency	$11,500	Demand deposits	$73,500
Loans	50,000	Net worth	5,000
Investments	15,000		
Other assets	2,000		
	$78,500		$78,500

9.3. Why is a demand deposit a safer form of money than currency?

Currency is a bearer instrument (there is no specification of ownership on the instrument) with ownership transferred from one party to another without endorsement.   Checking deposit money is a liability of a commercial bank; ownership of the deposit is transferred from one party to another by an order from the original owner and endorsement by the recipient of the check.   It therefore follows that demand deposit money is a safer medium of exchange since a check specifies who is to receive a specified sum.   Suppose, for example, that an envelope containing a $500 check and $500 in currency is lost.   The finder of the envelope can claim ownership of the currency since there is no way of determining the ownership of these funds.   But the $500 check must be endorsed by the finder in order to acquire the specified sum; this is impossible if the finder is not the person named on the face of the check.

9.4. (a) How does one transfer ownership of a demand deposit by writing a check?
    (b) Use "T" accounts to illustrate the following transactions:

    (1) Individual A discharges a $100 debt to B by issuing a check payable to B.
    (2) Individual B takes A's check to a commercial bank, endorses it and receives $100 in paper currency.
    (3) The commercial bank deducts $100 from A's account and returns the cancelled check to A.

(a) In issuing a check, the owner of a demand deposit orders the commercial bank to transfer a specified sum to the party named on the face of the check.   The recipient of the check presents this order to the commercial bank (with the bank requiring proper identification) and receives either paper currency or a credit to its deposit at that bank.

(b)

INDIVIDUAL A

	Assets		Liabilities	
(1)	Check payable to B	−$100	Amount owed to B	−$100
(3)	Demand deposit of A	−$100		
	Check issued to B	+$100		

INDIVIDUAL B

	Assets		Liabilities
(1)	Check of A	+$100	
	IOU of A	−$100	
(2)	Check of A	−$100	
	Paper currency	+$100	

COMMERCIAL BANK

	Assets		Liabilities		
(2)	Paper currency	−$100	Demand Deposit of A	−$100	(3)
	Check of A	+$100			
(3)	Check of A	−$100			

Note that A's demand deposit is not reduced $100 until the commercial bank has followed the order written on the face of the check (i.e. until the commercial bank has "cashed" the check).

9.5. (a) Why might loan expansion by a commercial bank result in an increase in the money supply? (b) Suppose the XYZ Corporation asks the First National Commercial Bank for a $1000 loan. Show through "T" accounts how deposit expansion takes place if First National Commercial Bank credits XYZ's demand deposit account in making the loan. (c) Why does the Federal government impose a reserve requirement on commercial banks?

(a) In taking out a loan, the borrower acquires a sum of funds to be used to purchase goods, services, etc. With the exception of commercial banks, all lenders must part with money (currency or a demand deposit) in making a loan. Since commercial banks accept demand deposits, they can also make a loan by increasing their demand deposit liability. Thus, commercial banks are in the unique position of creating money when they make loans.

(b)

FIRST NATIONAL COMMERCIAL BANK

Assets		Liabilities	
Loan to XYZ Corporation	+$1000	Demand deposit of XYZ Corporation	+$1000

XYZ CORPORATION

Assets		Liabilities	
Demand deposit in First National Commercial Bank	+$1000	Loan payable to First National Commercial Bank	+$1000

(c) The government imposes a reserve requirement on commercial banks to regulate demand deposit volume. As we saw in Chapter 8, excessive increases in the money supply are inflationary.

9.6. (a) Suppose the First National Bank's assets and liabilities are as follows:

FIRST NATIONAL BANK

Assets		Liabilities	
Currency	$ 3,000	Demand deposits	$25,000
Other assets	24,000	Other liabilities and net worth	2,000
	$27,000		$27,000

If currency is designated as reserves and the reserve requirement is 0.10, find First National Bank's (1) actual reserves, (2) required reserves and (3) excess reserves.
(b) Explain fractional-reserve banking.
(c) Why will a commercial bank's loan expansion not exceed its excess reserves?

(a) The First National Bank's (1) actual reserves are $3000, (2) required reserves equal $2500 (0.10 × $25,000), and (3) excess reserves are $500 ($3000 actual reserves less $2500 required reserves).

(b) In fractional-reserve banking, the reserves which banks are required to hold need be only a fraction (less than one) of their demand-deposit liabilities. Thus, there is the potential for a multiple change of demand deposit/loan volume whenever there is a change in a commercial bank's holding of reserves. By way of contrast, 100%-reserve banking stipulates that commercial banks have reserves equal to 100% of their demand-deposit liabilities. In 100%-reserve banking, commercial banks are only depositories for currency and therefore are unable to engage in lending.

(c) Since there are many different commercial banks accepting demand deposits, it is highly probable that the demand deposit created by loan expansion will be transferred to a party with a checking account in another commercial bank. Thus, deposit expansion will not exceed excess reserve holdings because the commercial bank is expecting the newly created demand deposit to result in a reserve loss equal to the sum lent.

9.7.   Describe the structure of the Federal Reserve System.

The Federal Reserve System consists of a Board of Governors, a Federal Open Market Committee, 12 district Federal Reserve Banks with 24 branches through the United States and over 5,500 member commercial banks.   The seven-member Board of Governors, appointed by the President of the United States (with the consent of Congress), oversees the various central bank supervisory functions.   The twelve-member Federal Open Market Committee, which includes the Board of Governors, is responsible for directing the system's open-market operations which are the basis for United States monetary policy (see Chapter 10).   District Federal Reserve banks are depositories for member banks, make loans to member banks during periods of adverse reserve flows and issue almost all of the paper currency used in the United States.

9.8.   Fund transfers from one commercial bank to another are usually made through reserve deposits at the Federal Reserve.   Use "T" accounts to show the following transactions: (1) Commercial Bank A makes an $800 loan to XYZ Corporation, (2) XYZ purchases supplies valued at $800 from ABC and makes payment with a check drawn upon Commercial Bank A, (3) ABC deposits the check in its account at Commercial Bank B, (4) Commercial Bank B receives $800 from Commercial Bank A through a reserve transfer at the district Federal Reserve Bank.

COMMERCIAL BANK A

	Assets		Liabilities	
(1)	Loan to XYZ Corporation	+$800	Demand deposit of XYZ Corporation	+$800
(4)	Deposit reserves at Federal Reserve	−$800	Demand deposit of XYZ Corporation	−$800

XYZ CORPORATION

	Assets		Liabilities	
(1)	Demand deposit at Commercial Bank A	+$800	Loan from Commercial Bank A	+$800
(2)	Demand deposit at Commercial Bank A	−$800		
	Supplies	+$800		

ABC CORPORATION

	Assets		Liabilities
(2)	Supplies	−$800	
	Check drawn on Commercial Bank A	+$800	
(3)	Check drawn on Commercial Bank A	−$800	
	Demand deposit at Commercial Bank B	+$800	

COMMERCIAL BANK B

	Assets		Liabilities	
(3)	Check drawn on Commercial Bank A	+$800	Demand deposit of ABC Corporation	+$800
(4)	Check drawn on Commercial Bank A	−$800		
	Deposit reserves at Federal Reserve Bank	+$800		

DISTRICT FEDERAL RESERVE BANK

Assets		Liabilities
	Deposit reserves of Commercial Bank A	$-\$800$ ⎫
	Deposit reserves of Commercial Bank B	$+\$800$ ⎭ (4)

DEMAND DEPOSIT CREATION BY THE COMMERCIAL BANKING SYSTEM

9.9. Why is it generally assumed that a commercial bank will lose reserves equal in amount to its expansion of loans and deposits?

With nearly 15,000 commercial banks in the United States, it is highly probable that the borrower will issue a check to someone whose account is not at the originating commercial bank. Since sums are transferred from one commercial bank to another by transferring funds in reserve accounts, the deposit-creating commercial bank can expect to lose reserves through loan/deposit expansion.

9.10. Suppose the reserve requirement is 0.20 and commercial banks charge an annual 8% rate of interest on loans.
(a) What is a commercial bank's interest return on a one-year loan of (1) $1000, (2) $1500 and (3) $2000?
(b) Assume that a commercial bank's reserves and demand deposits increase $2500. Find the *net change* in the bank's assets and liabilities if, as a result of the reserve gain, it makes loans of (1) $1000, (2) $1500 or (3) $2000. Assume a reserve loss equal to the sum loaned. Treat each situation separately.
(c) Why will a commercial bank lend by expanding deposits even though it expects to lose reserves in doing so?
(d) Might a commercial bank expand loans by less than its holding of excess reserves?

(a) The annual interest return on a loan equals the nominal value of the one-year loan multiplied by the annual rate of interest. (1) The interest return on the $1000 loan is $80 ($1000 × 0.08 = $80). The interest return on (2), the $1500 loan, is $120 and (3) $160 on the $2000 loan.

(b) (1) The *net change* in the commercial bank's assets and liabilities is Reserves, +$1500; Loans, +$1000; and Demand deposits, +$2500.

COMMERCIAL BANK A

Assets		Liabilities	
Reserves	+$2500	Demand deposits	+$2500
Loans	+$1500	Demand deposits	+$1500
Reserves	-$1500	Demand deposits	-$1500

(2) The *net change* in the commercial bank's assets and liabilities is Reserves, +$1000; Loans, +$1500; and Demand deposits, +$2500.

COMMERCIAL BANK A

Assets		Liabilities	
Reserves	+$2500	Demand deposits	+$2500
Loans	+$1000	Demand deposits	+$1000
Reserves	-$1000	Demand deposits	-$1000

(3) *The net change* in the commercial bank's assets and liabilities is Reserves, +$500; Loans, +$2000; and Demand deposits, +$2500.

COMMERCIAL BANK A

Assets		Liabilities	
Reserves	+$2500	Demand deposits	+$2500
Loans	+$2000	Demand deposits	+$2000
Reserves	−$2000	Demand deposits	−$2000

(c) A commercial bank's asset/liability position is the same whether it holds excess reserves or lends with reserve losses equal to loan expansion. [Compare the commercial bank's net change in assets/liabilities in situations (1), (2) and (3) in part (b) of this problem.] A commercial bank has the choice of holding assets with or without an interest return (there is no interest return on reserves). As calculated in part (a), the alternative returns are 0 if there is no loan expansion, $80 if loan expansion is $1000, $120 if loans increase $1500, and $160 if loans increase $2000, the sum of excess reserves. A commercial bank intent on maximizing the interest return on assets will elect to expand loans by the sum of its excess reserves.

(d) It is possible that a commercial bank may elect to hold excess reserves if it expects reserve/ deposit outflows to exceed those due to loan/deposit expansion. For example, the $2500 reserve/ deposit gain in part (b) may be only temporary. Thus, while we shall assume that a commercial bank's loan/deposit expansion equals the sum of excess reserves held, this may not occur if the commercial bank anticipates a need for liquidity, i.e. additional reserve/deposit losses.

9.11. Suppose that (i) the reserve requirement on demand deposits is 0.20; (ii) currency plus deposits at the district Federal Reserve Bank is the designated reserve asset; (iii) commercial banks expand loans and demand deposits by the amount of their excess reserves upon the receipt of additional reserves; and (iv) deposit expansion by a commercial bank results in a reserve loss equal to the increase in demand deposits since, by assumption, the eventual owner of the newly created demand deposit has an account with another commercial bank.

(a) Present the following flows in "T" accounts.

(1) Commercial Bank A receives a $1000 deposit of currency which it deposits with a district Federal Reserve Bank; the net effect is Deposits at the Federal Reserve, + $1000; Demand deposits, + $1000.

(2) Commercial Bank A, with $800 in excess reserves, expands loans and demand deposits, $800.

(3) Commercial Bank A loses reserves totalling $800 to Commercial Bank B since the final owner of the $800 demand deposit has a checking account with Commercial Bank B.

(4) Commercial Bank B, with $640 in excess reserves, expands loans and demand deposits, $640.

(5) Commercial Bank B loses reserves totalling $640 to Commercial Bank C since the final owner of the $640 demand deposit has a checking account with Commercial Bank C.

(6) Commercial Bank C, with $512 in excess reserves, expands loans and demand deposits, $512.

(7) Commercial Bank C loses reserves totalling $512 to Commercial Bank D since the final owner of the $512 demand deposit has a checking account with Commercial Bank D.

(8) Commercial Bank D, with $409.60 in excess reserves, expands loans and demand deposits, $409.60.

(9) Commercial Bank D loses reserves totalling $409.60 to Commercial Bank E since the final owner of the $409.60 demand deposit has a checking account with Commercial Bank E.

(10) Commercial Bank E, with $327.68 in excess reserves, expands loans and demand deposits, $327.68.

(b) Construct a table showing the net change in demand deposits and reserves for Commercial Banks A through E as a result of the flows in part (a).

(a)   COMMERCIAL BANK A

	Assets		Liabilities	
(1)	Reserves	+$1000	Demand deposits	+$1000
(2)	Loans	+$ 800	Demand deposits	+$ 800
(3)	Reserves	−$ 800	Demand deposits	−$ 800

COMMERCIAL BANK B

	Assets		Liabilities	
(3)	Reserves	+$800	Demand deposits	+$800
(4)	Loans	+$640	Demand deposits	+$640
(5)	Reserves	−$640	Demand deposits	−$640

COMMERCIAL BANK C

	Assets		Liabilities	
(5)	Reserves	+$640	Demand deposits	+$640
(6)	Loans	+$512	Demand deposits	+$512
(7)	Reserves	−$512	Demand deposits	−$512

COMMERCIAL BANK D

	Assets		Liabilities	
(7)	Reserves	+$512.00	Demand deposits	+$512.00
(8)	Loans	+$409.60	Demand deposits	+$409.60
(9)	Reserves	−$409.60	Demand deposits	−$409.60

COMMERCIAL BANK E

	Assets		Liabilities	
(9)	Reserves	+$409.60	Demand deposits	+$409.60
(10)	Loans	+$327.68	Demand deposits	+$327.68

(b) Table 1 presents the net change in demand deposits and reserves for Commercial Banks A through E. While total reserves increase $1000, the net increase in demand deposits is $3689.34. If reserve transfers are continued beyond Commercial Bank E, the final outcome would be a $5000 increase in demand deposits from a $1,000 increase in reserves.

Table 1

Commercial Bank	Net Change in Reserves Held	Net Change in Demand Deposits
A	$ 200.00	$1000.00
B	160.00	800.00
C	128.00	640.00
D	102.40	512.00
E	409.60	737.28
	$1000.00	$3689.28

9.12. Suppose all the commercial banks in the United States are merged into one monopoly bank. Would the effect of a $1000 increase in reserves/deposits differ from that found in Problem 9.11 if the monopoly bank repeatedly expands loans/deposits by the sum of its excess reserves?

We shall assume, as in Problem 9.11, that the Monopoly Commercial Bank initially receives an additional $1000 in reserves and deposits.

Round 1: Having $800 excess reserves, the monopoly commercial bank expands loans and demand deposits $800.

Round 2: With no loss of reserves from the $800 loan expansion since it is the only commercial bank, the monopoly commercial bank has excess reserves of $640.   The monopoly commercial bank expands loans and demand deposits $640.

Round 3: There is no loss of reserves from the $640 loan expansion.   Excess reserves equal $512 and loans increase $512.

Round 4: No loss of reserves from the $512 loan expansion.   Loans are increased $409.60, the amount of excess reserves.

Round 5: No reserve loss from the $409.60 loan expansion; loans are increased $327.68, the sum of the excess reserves.

The $1000 reserve/deposit inflow and the resulting deposit creation in Rounds 1 through 5 are presented in the following "T" account.   The expansion by a monopoly commercial bank is the same as the expansion by a series of nonmonopoly banks in Problem 9.11.   Whether there is 1 or 15,000 commercial banks serving a country, an inflow of reserves will result in a multiple increase in demand deposits.

MONOPOLY COMMERCIAL BANK

Assets		Liabilities	
Reserves	+$1000.00	Demand deposits	+$1000.00
Loans	+$ 800.00	Demand deposits	+$ 800.00
Loans	+$ 640.00	Demand deposits	+$ 640.00
Loans	+$ 512.00	Demand deposits	+$ 512.00
Loans	+$ 409.60	Demand deposits	+$ 409.60
Loans	+$ 327.68	Demand deposits	+$ 327.68

9.13.   (*a*) Find the value of the demand-deposit multiplier *d* when the reserve requirement is (1) 0.05, (2) 0.10, (3) 0.20, and (4) 0.25.   (*b*) Find the potential change in the volume of demand deposits when reserves increase $100 and the reserve requirement is (1) 0.05, (2) 0.10, (3) 0.20, and (4) 0.25.   (*c*) Reserves are often called "high-powered" money.   How high powered are changes in reserves?

(*a*) $d = 1/r$.   (1) When $r = 0.05$, $d = 1/0.05 = 20$.   (2) $d = 10$ when $r = 0.10$, (3) $d = 5$ when $r = 0.20$.   (4) $d = 4$ when $r = 0.25$.

(*b*)   The potential change in demand deposits $\Delta D = d \Delta R$, where d is the deposit multiplier and ΔR is the change in reserves.   (1) When $r = 0.05$ and $\Delta R = \$100$, $\Delta D = 20(\$100) = \$2000$.   (2) $\Delta D = \$1000$ when $r = 0.10$ and $\Delta R = \$100$.   (3) $\Delta D = \$500$ when $r = 0.20$ and $\Delta R = \$100$.   (4) $\Delta D = \$400$ when $r = 0.25$ and $\Delta R = \$100$.

(*c*)   As demonstrated in part (*b*), a change in reserves is "high powered" because it results in a multiple change in potential demand-deposit volume.   These reserves are more "high powered," the lower the reserve requirement.

MONEY CREATION

9.14.   Why might a commercial bank hold excess reserves?

Currency reserves are ultimate liquidity for a commercial bank.   A commercial bank may elect to hold excess reserves to meet unexpected currency demands (demand deposits unexpectedly converted into currency) or to satisfy possible reserve losses that would result from the transfer of deposits to competing commercial banks.   Commercial banks may also hold excess reserves to meet the future loan demand of borrowers.   While excess reserves provide no interest return, they contribute to the long-run continuance and profitability of a commercial bank.

9.15. Suppose aggregate currency holdings equal $20,000, $25,000, and $30,000 when demand-deposit volume is $80,000, $100,000 and $120,000 respectively.   (*a*) If this behavior continues, what amount of currency should be held when the demand deposit volume is $160,000?   (*b*) What is the currency ratio?

    (*a*) $1 in currency is held for every $4 in demand deposits.   Thus, currency holdings should equal $40,000 when the demand deposit volume is $160,000.

    (*b*) The currency ratio c equals C/D.   Substituting for the values given, $c = 0.25$.

9.16. (*a*) Find an equation for the change in demand deposits if there is a constant reserve requirement for demand deposits, a constant relationship c of currency to demand deposits and a constant relationship e between excess reserves and demand deposits.   (*b*) Given the behavior in part (*a*), find an equation for an M_1 definition of the money supply.

    (*a*) Total reserves R are held by commercial banks to support demand deposits rD and as excess reserves eD; they also circulate as currency cD.   Thus, a change in reserves is held as required reserves, excess reserves and currency.   Thus,

$$\Delta R = r\,\Delta D + e\,\Delta D + c\,\Delta D$$

Simplifying $$\Delta R = \Delta D\,(r + e + c)$$

so that $$\Delta D = \Delta R/(r + e + c)$$

    (*b*) With an M_1 definition of money, $M = C + D$.

$$\Delta M = \Delta C + \Delta D$$

By definition, $$\Delta C = c\,\Delta D$$

and $$\Delta D = \Delta R/(r + e + c)$$

Substituting,

$$\Delta M = c\,\Delta D + \Delta R/(r + e + c)$$
$$= c[\Delta R/(r + e + c)] + \Delta R/(r + e + c)$$

so that $$\Delta M = \Delta R\,[(1 + c)/(r + e + c)]$$

9.17. The money multiplier m equals $(1 + c)/(c + r + e)$.

    (*a*) Find the money multiplier when (1) $r = 0.10$, $c = 0.05$ and $e = 0.05$; (2) $r = 0.10$, $c = 0.05$ and $e = 0$; and (3) $r = 0.10$, $c = 0$ and $e = 0$.

    (*b*) What effect does the size of the currency and excess-reserve ratio have upon the magnitude of the money multiplier?

    (*c*) Using the money multipliers calculated in part (*a*), find the change in the money supply from a $100 increase in currency reserves.

    (*a*) (1) $m = (1 + c)/(c + r + e)$.   When $r = 0.10$, $c = 0.05$, and $e = 0.05$,
$$m = 1.05/(0.05 + 0.10 + 0.05) = 5.25$$

        (2) $m = 1.05/(0.05 + 0.10 + 0) = 7.0$.

        (3) $m = 1/(0 + 0.10 + 0) = 10$.

    (*b*) As shown in the calculations in part (*a*), the magnitude of the money multiplier m is inversely related to the values of c and e, i.e. the larger c and e, the smaller the value of m.   Such a relationship exists since c and e represent alternate uses of reserves (as currency holdings or excess reserves) which reduce the quantity of reserves available for commercial bank deposit expansion.

    (*c*) $\Delta M = m\,\Delta R$ is the formula used for finding changes in the money supply where $m = (1 + c)/(c + r + e)$.   Using the situations in part (*a*), money supply changes are (1) $\Delta M = m\,\Delta R = 5.25(\$100) = \$525$, (2) $\Delta M = m\,\Delta R = 7(\$100) = \$700$, and (3) $\Delta M = m\,\Delta R = 10(\$100) = \$1000$.

MANAGING A COMMERCIAL BANK'S ASSETS

9.18. (a) What role does solvency play in the financial management of a commercial bank? (b) What differentiates a solvent from an insolvent commercial bank?

(a) Funds are deposited with a commercial bank on the supposition that they will be safe (the bank will remain solvent) and liquid (deposit liabilities can be converted into cash upon request). Solvency and liquidity must be central to the management of a commercial bank's assets for it to remain trustworthy and thereby retain deposited funds.

(b) A commercial bank is solvent as long as the market or realizable value of its assets exceeds outstanding liabilities.   A commercial bank becomes insolvent when its assets are inadequate to meet all outstanding liabilities.

9.19. (a) Why must a commercial bank be concerned about liquidity?   (b) Which assets are the commercial bank's principal sources of liquidity?   (c) Is there a conflict between the profit and liquidity motives?

(a) A commercial bank must not only remain solvent but be able to pay out cash to those who wish to withdraw deposits and to satisfy borrowers' loan demands.   Liquidity requires that a commercial bank hold assets that are the equivalent of and /or can be converted into currency with little to no loss of nominal value.

(b) A commercial bank's asset portfolio consists of noninterest-bearing reserves (currency plus deposits at the Federal Reserve), marketable short-term securities (money-market instruments), short- and long-term loans to customers and miscellaneous fixed income obligations.   Noninterest-bearing reserves are immediately available to permit deposit withdrawals or satisfy loan demands if the amount held exceeds reserve requirements.   Generally, a money-market instrument (marketable short-term securities) is convertible into a reserve asset at or close to its nominal value.   Noninterest-bearing reserves and marketable short-term securities, categorized as the bank's primary and secondary reserves, are the commercial bank's principal sources of liquidity.

(c) Generally, a profit-seeking commercial bank will minimize its holdings of excess reserves and rely upon secondary reserves for liquidity.   Short-term securities, however, usually offer a lower return than loans on longer-term securities and the commercial bank's goal of profit maximization is thus constrained by its need to maintain adequate liquidity.

9.20. Show how a commercial bank can use its secondary reserves to meet (a) a $200 cash withdrawal and (b) a request for a $100 loan.   Assume that the commercial bank acquires additional reserves by selling short-term securities to others.

(a) Suppose Individual A converts a $200 demand deposit into currency.   Commercial Bank Z is deficient $160 in required reserves.   (Note that required reserves decrease $40 when there is a $200 decline in demand deposits and the reserve ratio is 0.20.)   Commercial Bank Z can meet this reserve deficiency by selling $160 of short-term securities to others for $160 in currency.

COMMERCIAL BANK Z

Assets		Liabilities	
Reserves	−$200	Individual A's demand deposit	−$200
Currency (reserves)	+$160		
Short-term securities	−$160		

INDIVIDUAL A

Assets		Liabilities
Demand deposit	−$200	
Currency	+$200	

OTHERS

Assets		Liabilities
Short-term securities	+$160	
Currency	−$160	

(b) The $100 loan request is satisfied by selling $100 of short-term securities to others for currency. The $100 addition to primary reserves is sufficient to meet the $100 expansion in loans and demand deposits.

COMMERCIAL BANK Z

Assets			Liabilities	
Short-term securities	−$100		Demand deposits	+$100
Currency	+$100			
Loans	+$100			

Chapter 10

The Federal Reserve and Monetary Policy

10.1 INTRODUCTION

In the United States, the Federal Reserve Banks are responsible for instituting monetary policies designed to promote full employment and price stability. This chapter focuses upon the techniques that the Federal Reserve employs to implement monetary policy. The discussion of how monetary policy affects economic activity is introduced in Chapter 11.

10.2 CONTROLLING DEMAND-DEPOSIT VOLUME

The money supply model $\Delta M = \Delta R \left[(1 + c)/(r + c + e)\right]$ developed in Section 9.4 shows that money supply changes depend upon the changes in reserves ΔR, the currency ratio c, the reserve requirement r and the excess reserve ratio e. Since R and r are directly controlled by the Federal Reserve, demand-deposit and, therefore, money-supply changes are implemented by altering commercial bank reserves or the reserve requirement on demand deposits. Tools available for instituting changes in demand deposits include reserve-requirement variation, open-market operations, and discount-rate policy.

Reserve-Requirement Variation. Increases in the reserve requirement on demand deposits reduce the multiplier effect of a given level of reserves while decreases expand the multiplier effect. Although reserve requirement variation is a powerful tool for instituting changes in demand deposits, it is infrequently used. Reserve requirement changes affect *all* commercial banks, and it is therefore viewed as too blunt a means of instituting changes in the money supply.

EXAMPLE 1. Suppose the reserve requirement on demand deposits is 0.20 and the commercial banking system's balance sheet is as follows:

COMMERCIAL BANKING SYSTEM

Assets		Liabilities and Net Worth	
Reserves	$10,000	Demand deposits	$45,000
Short-term securities	7,000	Net worth	5,000
Loans	25,000		$50,000
Other assets	8,000		
	$50,000		

If the Federal Reserve increases the reserve requirement to 0.25, the commercial banking system is deficient in its reserve holdings. Assuming that commercial banks are unable to obtain additional reserves, demand-deposit volume must be reduced to $40,000 to meet the new reserve requirement. This $5000 decrease in commercial bank assets and demand deposits can be achieved by liquidating short-term securities and/or by not renewing loans that have become due (see Problem 10.3). Thus, by increasing the reserve requirement on demand deposits, the Federal Reserve can reduce demand deposits and contract the money supply.

Open-Market Operations. Open-market operations are the Federal Reserve's principal means of effecting changes in demand deposits. Following the directives of the Federal Open-Market Committee, the Federal Reserve Bank of New York purchases or sells government securities. Purchases increase commercial bank reserves; sales decrease them. If commercial banks hold no excess reserves, these reserve changes result in a multiple change in demand deposits.

EXAMPLE 2. Suppose the Federal Reserve Bank of New York purchases government securities valued at $100 from the commercial banking system.   The related transactions are as follows: (1) The commercial banking system's asset, government securities, decreases by $100 and the Federal Reserve's asset, government securities, increases by $100.   (2) The Federal Reserve pays for these government securities by crediting the commercial banks' deposit accounts at the Fed by $100 and the commercial banks' asset, Deposit at the Federal Reserve, increases by $100.   (3) Given a 0.20 reserve requirement and no excess reserves in the commercial banking system, commercial bank loans and demand deposits increase $500.

COMMERCIAL BANKING SYSTEM

	Assets		Liabilities		
(1)	Government securities	−$100			
(2)	Deposit at the Federal Reserve	+$100			
(3)	Loans	+$500	Demand Deposits	+$500	(3)

FEDERAL RESERVE SYSTEM

	Assets		Liabilities		
(1)	Government securities	+$100	Commercial bank deposit	+$100	(2)

Discount-Rate Policy.   When short of reserves, commercial banks may borrow (discount) from the Federal Reserve.   The rate of interest charged on such loans is called the discount rate, and generally follows other market rates of interest.   Changes in the discount rate are newsworthy and are generally interpreted as indicating the direction which the Federal Reserve believes interest rates will take (see Problem 10.7).

EXAMPLE 3. Suppose Commercial Bank A is deficient $1000 in reserves.   Rather than contract demand deposits by selling short-term securities, Commercial Bank A obtains $1000 in additional reserves by discounting (borrowing) at the Federal Reserve.   In doing so, Commercial Bank A's reserve assets and its liability to the Federal Reserve both increase by $1000.   The Federal Reserve's liability, Deposit of Commercial Bank A, increases $1000, as does its asset Discounts.

COMMERCIAL BANK A

Assets		Liabilities	
Deposit at the Federal Reserve	+$1000	Discount (loan from Federal Reserve)	+$1000

FEDERAL RESERVE

Assets		Liabilities	
Discounts (Loans to member banks)	+$1000	Deposit of Commercial Bank A	+$1000

10.3   DYNAMIC AND DEFENSIVE OPEN-MARKET OPERATIONS

Commercial bank reserves are affected by factors other than Federal Reserve purchases and sales of government securities.   The Federal Reserve's principal asset and liability accounts that affect the size of member bank reserves are found in Table 1.   Member bank reserves increase whenever there is an increase in a Federal Reserve asset account or a decrease in a liability account; reserves decrease when a Federal Reserve asset account decreases or a liability account increases (see Problem 10.10).   Since accounts such as Discounts, Federal Reserve notes, and U.S. Treasury Deposits are not directly controlled by the Federal Reserve, changes in these accounts can cause undesired movements in member bank reserves, necessitating *defensive* open-market operations to offset the change in commercial bank reserves (see Example 4).   *Dynamic* open-market operations occur when the Federal Reserve initiates changes in the level of member bank reserves (see Problem 10.11).

Table 1: Combined Balance Sheet of Twelve Federal Reserve Banks
May 31, 1978
(billion $)

Assets		Liabilities and Net Worth	
Gold certificates and other cash	$ 13.3	Federal Reserve notes	$ 94.6
U.S. Government securities	110.7	Deposits:	
Discounts, loans and acceptances	1.4	Member bank reserves	
Miscellaneous other assets	14.4	(Commercial bank deposits)	30.1
Total	$139.8	U.S. Treasury	2.4
		Foreign and other	1.1
		Miscellaneous liabilities	8.9
		Capital accounts	2.7
		Total	$139.8

Source: *Federal Reserve Bulletin;* June, 1978.

EXAMPLE 4. Suppose the U.S. Treasury transfers $100 from its demand-deposit account in the commercial banking system to the Federal Reserve.   (1) The transfer of funds from the commercial bank to the Federal Reserve reduces the commercial banks' demand-deposit and reserve accounts while on the Federal Reserve balance sheet member bank reserves decrease by $100 and Treasury deposits increase by $100.   The effect of the relocation of the Treasury deposit from commercial banks to the Federal Reserve is a $100 decrease in commercial bank reserves.   (2) If the Federal Reserve does not want member bank reserves to decrease, it can institute a defensive open-market operation by purchasing from households government securities valued at $100 to restore commercial bank reserves to their previous level.

COMMERCIAL BANKING SYSTEM

	Assets		Liabilities		
(1)	Demand deposits at Federal Reserve	−$100	Demand deposits of Treasury	−$100	(1)
(2)	Demand deposits at Federal Reserve	+$100	Demand deposits of Households	+$100	(2)

FEDERAL RESERVE

	Assets		Liabilities		
			Member-bank reserves	−$100	(1)
			Treasury deposit	+$100	(1)
(2)	Government securities	+$100	Member-bank reserves	+$100	(2)

10.4 SELECTIVE CREDIT CONTROLS

Qualitative controls selectively allocate credit and are of minor importance in contrast to the policy tools discussed in Section 10.2.   Moral suasion and margin requirements are the selective controls still at the Federal Reserve's disposal.   *Moral suasion* is used periodically to encourage commercial banks to conform more closely to a stated monetary policy.   *Margin requirements* seek to regulate the flow of commercial bank credit to the stock market by setting the maximum percentage of a security purchase that can be financed through a loan.

Important Economic Terms

Defensive open-market operations.   Federal Reserve purchases or sales of government securities to prevent undesired changes in the level of commercial bank reserves.

Discount rate.   The rate of interest charged by the Federal Reserve on loans to commercial banks that are members of the Federal Reserve System.

Dynamic open-market operations.   Federal Reserve purchases or sales of government securities to bring about changes in the level of commercial bank reserves.

Member bank reserves.   The deposits of member commercial banks with the Federal Reserve plus the cash these banks have in their vaults.

Open-market operations.   The purchase or sale of government securities by the Federal Reserve to increase or decrease member-bank reserves.

Reserve-requirement variation.   A technique available for changing the volume of demand deposits.   An increase in the reserve requirement decreases the demand-deposit multiplier and reduces the volume of demand deposits; a decrease in the reserve-requirement increases the demand-deposit multiplier and expands demand deposits.

Selective credit controls.   Specific measures aimed at influencing the flow of funds into selected credit sectors.

Review Questions

1. If the volume of commercial bank reserves is held constant,
    (a) an increase in the reserve requirement reduces the demand-deposit multiplier and decreases excess reserves,
    (b) a decrease in the reserve requirement reduces the demand-deposit multiplier and decreases excess reserves,
    (c) an increase in the reserve requirement increases the demand-deposit multiplier and decreases excess reserves,
    (d) an increase in the reserve requirement increases the demand-deposit multiplier and decreases excess reserves.

    Ans.   (*a*)

2. Suppose commercial banks hold no excess reserves and reserves total $1000.   If the reserve requirement is decreased from 0.25 to 0.20, demand deposits (*a*) increase from $1000 to $1250, (*b*) decrease from $1000 to $750, (*c*) increase from $4000 to $5000, (*d*) decrease from $5000 to $4000.
    Ans.   (*c*)

3. Which of the following measures will *not* help a commercial bank to overcome a deficit reserve position? (*a*) Borrowing from the Federal Reserve, (*b*) selling holdings of short-term securities, (*c*) an increase in the reserve requirement on demand deposits, (*d*) failing to renew maturing business loans.
    Ans.   (*c*)

4. Holding other things constant, a Federal Reserve purchase of government securities will increase
    (a)   the Federal Reserve's liabilities, member bank reserves and government securities.
    (b)   the Federal Reserve's assets, member bank reserves and government securities.
    (c)   the commercial bank's liability, member bank reserves.
    (d)   the commercial bank's asset, member bank reserves.
    Ans.   (*d*)

5. If the reserve requirement is 0.20 and the Federal Reserve purchases government securities valued at $100 from a commercial bank, the commercial bank would (*a*) hold $80 in excess reserves, (*b*) hold $100 in excess reserves, (*c*) expand demand deposits $80, (*d*) expand demand deposits $400.
    Ans.   (*b*)

6. A decrease in the discount rate reduces the cost of (a) commercial bank borrowing from the Federal Reserve, (b) household borrowing from the Federal Reserve, (c) household borrowing from commercial banks, (d) Treasury borrowing from commercial banks.

    Ans. (a)

7. An increase in the discount rate generally indicates that (a) the Federal Reserve is no longer making loans to commercial banks, (b) the market rate of interest is due to fall, (c) the Federal Reserve is following a tight-money policy, (d) the Federal Reserve is following an easy-money policy.

    Ans. (c)

8. An increase in which of the following accounts at the Federal Reserve results in an *increase* in member bank reserves? (a) Treasury deposits, (b) Federal Reserve notes, (c) foreign deposits, (d) the Federal Reserve gold certificate account.

    Ans. (d)

9. What effect will a $50 increase in discounts (loans to member banks) and a $75 decrease in Federal Reserve notes have on member-bank reserves? (a) $125 increase, ($b$) $125 decrease, ($c$) $25 decrease,   ($d$) $25 increase.

    Ans. (c)

10. Selective credit controls (a) regulate the quantity of credit created by commercial banks. (b) regulate the quantity of demand deposits created by commercial banks, (c) selectively allocate credit to commercial banks, (d) selectively allocate credit among borrowers.

    Ans. (d)

Solved Problems

CONTROLLING DEMAND-DEPOSIT VOLUME

10.1. Suppose the commercial banking system holds no excess reserves.
   (a) What is demand-deposit volume when reserves total $1000 and the reserve requirement is (1) 0.20, (2) 0.16 and (3) 0.10?
   (b) Find deposit volume when the reserve requirement is 0.20 and reserves total (1) $1000, (2) $1250 and (3) $2000.
   (c) Compare the calculations of parts (a) and (b).

   (a) In a simplified model of demand-deposit volume, $D = R/r$.   Thus, in (1) demand deposits total $5000 ($D = R/r = \$1000/0.20 = \$5000$) while they total $6250 for (2) and $10,000 for (3).
   (b) When there is a constant 0.20 reserve requirement and commercial bank reserves increase from $1000 to $1250 to $2000, demand-deposit volume increases from (1) $5000 to (2) $6250 ($D = R/r = \$1250/0.20 = \$6250$) to (3) $10,000.
   (c) The situations in parts (a) and (b) show that there are two alternate ways of increasing demand-deposit volume: by lowering the reserve requirement or by increasing the volume of reserves held by the commercial banking system.   By lowering the reserve requirement in part (a) from 0.20 to 0.16 to 0.10 with commercial bank reserves held at $1000, demand-deposit volume increased from $5000 to $6250 to $10,000.   The same increase in demand-deposit volume is achieved in part (b) by increasing the commercial banking system's reserves and holding the reserve requirement at 0.20.

10.2. (a) Assume that commercial banks hold no excess reserves.   Find the demand deposit multiplier when the reserve requirement is (1) 0.20, (2) 0.19 (3) 0.18 (4) 0.17, (5) 0.16, and (6) 0.15.
   (b) Using the demand-deposit multipliers calculated in part (a), find demand deposits when the commercial banking system's reserves total $10,000.

(c) If the commercial banking system's reserves total $10,000 and the reserve requirement is 0.20, what is the needed change in the reserve requirement to increase demand-deposit volume from $50,000 to $51,280?

(a) If the commercial banking system holds no excess reserves, the demand-deposit multiplier d equals $1/r$. d is (1) 5 when r equals 0.20, (2) 5.263 when r equals 0.19, (3) 5.556 when r equals 0.18, (4) 5.882 when r equals 0.17, (5) 6.250 when r equals 0.16, and (6) 6.667 when r is 0.15.

(b) $D = R/r$. When reserve assets total $10,000, demand-deposit volume is (1) $50,000 if $r = 0.20$, (2) $52,632 if $r = 0.19$, (3) $55,556 if $r = 0.16$, (4) $58,824 if $r = 0.17$, (5) $62,500 if $r = 0.16$, and (6) $66,667 if $r = 0.15$.

(c) Given $D = R/r$, the needed reserve requirement for a specific level of R is found by solving $r = R/D$.   Since R is $10,000 and the desired level of D is $51,280, the reserve requirement must be decreased from 0.20 to about 0.195.

10.3. (a) Use "T" accounts to show how the following events reduce a commercial bank's demand deposits.   Treat each situation separately.
(1) A commercial bank short of reserves sells short-term securities valued at $500 to households.   Households pay for these securities by drawing down their demand-deposit balance at the commercial bank.
(2) The 90-day, $600 loan to the XYZ Corporation becomes due.   XYZ repays the loan to the commercial bank by writing a check against its demand-deposit balance.

(b) When the Federal Reserve changes the reserve requirement and there is no change in commercial bank reserves, how does a commercial bank bring about a change in demand-deposit liabilities?

(a)

(1) COMMERCIAL BANK

Assets		Liabilities	
Short-term securities	−$500	Demand deposits of Households	−$500

HOUSEHOLDS

Assets		Liabilities
Short-term securities	+$500	
Demand deposit at Commercial Bank	−$500	

(2) COMMERCIAL BANK

Assets		Liabilities	
Loan to XYZ	−$600	Demand deposit of XYZ	−$600

XYZ CORPORATION

Assets		Liabilities	
Demand deposit at Commercial Bank	−$600	90-day Commercial Bank Loan	−$600

(b) When reserve-requirement variation is used to change demand deposits, the commercial banking system brings about changes by expanding or contracting its assets (loans or short-term securities) and demand-deposit accounts.   For example, an increase in the reserve requirement may make commercial banks short of reserves.   This reserve deficiency is remedied either by not renewing loans or by selling short-term securities in the open market.   Decreases in the reserve requirement create excess reserves; commercial banks react by expanding loans and demand deposits.

10.4. (*a*) Show the following transactions in "T" accounts.

   (1) The Federal Reserve purchases government securities valued at $250 from the household sector and pays for these securities with a check drawn upon itself.

   (2) Households deposit the Federal Reserve check in a demand-deposit account at a commercial bank.

   (3) The commercial bank presents the Federal Reserve check for payment.   The Federal Reserve makes payment by increasing the commercial bank's deposit account at the Fed.

(*b*) If commercial banks hold no excess reserves and the reserve requirement is 0.20, what is the eventual effect of the $250 purchase of government securities upon the volume of demand deposits?

(*c*) Why are open-market operations considered superior to reserve-requirement variations as a means of changing demand-deposit volume?

(*a*)

HOUSEHOLDS

	Assets		Liabilities
(1)	Government securities	−$250	
(1)	Check payable at Federal Reserve	+$250	
(2)	Check payable at Federal Reserve	−$250	
(2)	Demand deposit	+$250	

COMMERCIAL BANK

	Assets		Liabilities		
(2)	Check payable at Federal Reserve	+$250	Demand deposit of Households	+$250	(2)
(3)	Check payable at Federal Reserve	−$250			
(3)	Deposit at Federal Reserve	+$250			

FEDERAL RESERVE

	Assets		Liabilities		
(1)	Government securities	+$250	Check issued to Households	+$250	(1)
			Check issued to Households	−$250	(3)
			Deposit of Commercial Bank	+$250	(3)

(*b*) Demand deposits increase $1250. $\Delta D = \Delta R/r = \$250/0.20 = \$1250$.

(*c*) Reserve-requirement variation affects *all* commercial banks whereas open-market operations immediately affect *only* those commercial banks that are directly involved in the purchase or sale of government securities.   Thus, the effects of open-market operations filter through the commercial banking system and are more easily reversed when the Federal Reserve decides to change the direction of monetary policy.

10.5. (*a*) Use "T" accounts to show the net effect of the following open-market operations.

   (1) The Federal Reserve purchases government securities valued at $100 from the commercial banking system.

   (2) The Federal Reserve purchases government securities valued at $100 from households.

(*b*) What is the commercial bank's excess reserves in each situation in part (*a*) if the reserve requirement is 0.20?

(*c*) What is the commercial banking system's loan expansion in part (*a*) if the reserve requirement is 0.20 and commercial banks hold no excess reserves?

(*d*) Find the eventual change in demand deposits in the two situations in part (*a*).

(*e*) Does the purchase of government securities from commercial banks *or* households result in the larger expansion of commercial bank loans?

(*a*)

FEDERAL RESERVE

Assets		Liabilities		
(1)	Government securities	+$100	Deposit of Commercial Banks +$100	(1)
(2)	Government securities	+$100	Deposit of Commercial Banks +$100	(2)

COMMERCIAL BANKS

Assets		Liabilities		
(1)	Government securities	−$100		
(1)	Deposit at Federal Reserve	+$100		
(2)	Deposit at Federal Reserve	+$100	Deposit of Households +$100	(2)

HOUSEHOLDS

Assets		Liabilities
(2)	Government securities	−$100	
(2)	Demand deposit at Commercial Banks	+$100	

(*b*) In situation (1), commercial banks hold $100 in excess reserves since an additional $100 in reserves has been received and there is no change in demand deposits.   In situation (2), commercial banks have $80 in excess reserves since $20 of the $100 increase in reserves is required for the $100 increase in the demand deposits of households.

(*c*) In situation (1), the commercial banking system is able to expand loans and deposits $500; loans and deposits increase $400 in situation (2).   Recall that loan/deposit expansion is determined by commercial bank holding of excess reserves.

(*d*) In both situations (1) and (2), the eventual expansion of demand deposits is $500.   In situation (1), the $100 in excess reserves results in a $500 increase in loans and demand deposits.   Situation (2) results in a $500 increase in demand deposits through the initial $100 deposit of households plus the $400 loan/demand deposit expansion due to the initial $80 in excess reserves.

(*e*) As shown in part (*c*), purchase of government securities from commercial banks results in the larger expansion of commercial bank loans.

10.6.   (*a*)   Explain the relationship between the discount rate and market rates of interest.   (*b*) Is discounting controlled by the Federal Reserve or does it occur at the discretion of commercial banks?   (*c*) Do commercial banks have alternatives to discounting at the Federal Reserve?

(*a*)   The Federal Reserve generally keeps the discount rate below market rates of interest in order to encourage commercial banks to borrow when they are "short" of reserves.   While market rates of interest may change from day to day and reflect movements in the supply and demand for funds, the discount rate is set by the Federal Reserve and is changed periodically to conform to market rates.

(b) The volume of discounting is largely determined by commercial banks' need to borrow reserves.   Thus, while the Federal Reserve can make the discount rate more or less attractive to commercial banks, each commercial bank must apply for a loan.   The Federal Reserve does exercise a degree of control over the volume of discounting, however, by its insistence that discounting is "a privilege and not a right."   Thus, during periods of monetary restraint, the Federal Reserve is in a position to limit the extent to which commercial banks obtain discounts.

(c) If a commercial bank is short of reserves, it can liquidate assets (e.g. sell short-term securities or fail to renew expiring loans) rather than discount at the Federal Reserve.

10.7.   What can one infer from changes in the discount rate?

Given that the discount rate is generally below market rates of interest and the availability of discounting is a privilege and not a right, commercial banks should borrow only when they fail to meet their reserve requirement.   Therefore, changes in the discount rate should not affect a commercial bank's willingness to borrow from the Federal Reserve.   Changes in the discount rate, however, may encourage commercial banks to increase their rate of borrowing if the differential between what they can earn on loans and the rate at which they can discount widens.   Thus, the Federal Reserve can institute a tight-money policy but moderate the tightness by not raising the discount rate as market rates of interest rise.   When the Federal Reserve, then, raises the discount rate to conform to rising market rates of interest, opinion is reinforced that interest rates will remain high or go higher and that the Federal Reserve is pursuing a more stringent monetary policy.   Thus, while the discount rate is not a central tool of monetary policy, it can be used to reinforce or moderate the monetary policy set by open-market operations.

DYNAMIC AND DEFENSIVE OPEN-MARKET OPERATIONS

10.8.   Explain the following asset and liability accounts which are found in Table 1's combined balance sheet of the twelve Federal Reserve Banks: (a) Gold certificates and other cash; (b) Discounts, loans and acceptances; (c) Federal Reserve notes; (d) Member bank reserves; (e) U.S. Treasury deposits; (f) Foreign and other deposits; (g) Capital accounts.

(a) Gold certificates are paper currency issued by the Treasury when it received gold.   In 1933, gold certificates were recalled from the public and are held today only by the Federal Reserve as receipts from the United States Treasury for the U.S.'s monetized gold stock.   Other items in this account include SDR's issued by the International Monetary Fund and miscellaneous currency.

(b) Discounts and loans represent the sum of lending to member commercial banks and others. Bankers' acceptances are short-term obligations in which a commercial bank substitutes its credit rating for that of a firm so that the borrowing firm may secure a short-term loan from another business.

(c) Federal Reserve notes are the main paper currency component of the United States' money supply.   They represent nothing more than claims against the Federal Reserve Banks.

(d) Member bank reserves are the deposit balances of commercial banks that are members of the Federal Reserve System.   Member bank reserves plus currency held by the commercial banking system equal the total reserves of the banking system.

(e) U.S. Treasury deposits are demand deposits of the United States government.   All Treasury checks are written against deposits with the Federal Reserve.

(f) Foreign and other deposits are demand deposits of foreign central banks, the International Monetary Fund, and commercial banks that are not members of the Federal Reserve System.

(g) Capital accounts equal the funds contributed by commercial banks upon joining the Federal Reserve System plus the retained earnings of the Federal Reserve Banks.   The capital account shows little growth over time since the Federal Reserve contributes all its excess profits to the Treasury.

10.9.   Suppose commercial banks keep all their reserves on deposit with the Federal Reserve. Show the effect of a $200 currency withdrawal upon a member commercial bank's reserve account with the Federal Reserve.

(1) A household's conversion of a $200 demand deposit to currency necessitates that the commercial bank obtain Federal Reserve notes.   Thus, the commercial bank's member bank reserve account at the Federal Reserve must decrease $200 and the Federal Reserve's Federal Reserve note account must increase $200 upon remittance of currency to the commercial bank.

(2) There is a decrease in the commercial bank's reserves as Federal Reserve notes are withdrawn by households.

FEDERAL RESERVE

Assets		Liabilities		
		Federal Reserve notes	+$200	(1)
		Member bank reserves	−$200	(1)

COMMERCIAL BANK

	Assets		Liabilities		
(1)	Member bank reserves	−$200			
(1)	Federal Reserve notes	+$200			
(2)	Federal Reserve notes	−$200	Demand deposit of households	−$200	(2)

10.10. What effect will the following events have upon member bank reserves?   Treat each situation separately and assume no changes in other Federal Reserve accounts.
(1) There is an increase in the Gold certificate and other cash account.
(2) There is a decrease in Discounts, loans and acceptances.
(3) There is a seasonal decrease in Federal Reserve notes outstanding.
(4) U.S. Treasury deposits at the Federal Reserve increase.

Holding other Federal Reserve accounts constant, an increase in an asset account or a decrease in a liability account increases member bank reserves whereas a decrease in an asset account or an increase in a liability account decreases member bank reserves.   Thus, (1) the increase in the asset account, Gold certificates and other cash, increases member bank reserves.   (2) The decrease in the asset account, Discounts, loans and acceptances, decreases member bank reserves.   (3) The decrease in the Federal Reserve liability account, Federal Reserve notes, increases member bank reserves. (4) The increase in the liability acount, U.S. Treasury deposits, decreases member bank reserves.

10.11. (*a*) Suppose member bank reserves are $28.2 billion at the end of April.   Find member bank reserves at the end of May if Federal Reserve asset and liability accounts are as shown below (all items are in billions of dollars).

Federal Reserve Assets

	April	May
Gold certificates and other cash	$ 13.3	$ 13.3
U.S. Government securities	110.7	110.7
Discounts, loans and acceptances	2.0	1.4
Miscellaneous other assets	11.4	11.4
	$137.4	$136.8

Federal Reserve Liabilities and Capital Accounts		
Federal Reserve notes	$ 92.3	$ 94.6
Deposits:		
Member Bank Reserves	28.2	?
U.S. Treasury	4.2	2.4
Foreign and other	1.1	1.1
Miscellaneous liabilities	8.9	8.9
Capital accounts	2.7	2.7
	$137.4	

(b) What open-market operation should the Federal Reserve institute to bring member bank reserves back to their April level?

(c) What open-market operation should the Federal Reserve follow to increase member bank reserves to $30.1 billion?

(d) Distinguish between defensive and dynamic open-market operations.

(a) Three Federal Reserve balance sheet accounts changed during the month: Discounts decreased $0.6 billion (a negative factor for MBRs); Federal Reserve notes increased $2.3 billion (a negative factor for MBRs); and U.S. Treasury deposits decreased $1.8 billion (a positive factor for MBRs).   Given −$0.6, −$2.3 and +$1.8, member bank reserves must have fallen $1.1 billion to $27.1 billion.

(b) The Federal Reserve should purchase government securities valued at $1.1 billion to offset the negative factors that decreased member bank reserves $1.1 billion.

(c) In addition to the defensive open-market purchases in part (b), the Federal Reserve should purchase an additional $1.9 billion of government securities to bring member bank reserves to the $30.1 billion level.

(d) Defensive open-market operations are purchases or sales of government securities that prevent factors such as Federal Reserve notes, Treasury deposits, etc. from bringing about undesired changes in the level of commercial bank reserves.   Dynamic open-market operations are Federal Reserve purchases and sales of government securities to change the level of commercial bank reserves.

SELECTIVE CREDIT CONTROLS

10.12. What is the objective of selective credit controls?

Supporters of selective credit controls believe that control of the money supply and bank credit is not adequate for achieving economic stability.   According to selective credit control proponents, individual spending areas are subject to periods of excessive or deficient demand relative to aggregate demand and cause greater economic instability than need be the case.   For example, a depressed housing market would be aided by a redirection of funds, such as the changing of real estate credit terms.   Excessive speculation in the stock market could be avoided by increasing margin requirements and thereby decreasing the flow of credit into the stock market.   The objective of selective credit controls is the same as that of quantitative controls: full employment and price stability.   Advocates of selective credit controls believe that selective intervention with the allocation of credit is a necessary adjunct to the control of the quantity of money and credit.

10.13. How has the Federal Reserve used moral suasion in the implementation of monetary policy?

Over the years the Federal Reserve has used moral suasion to discourage the use of credit in the stock markets, to limit the quantity of nonproductive loans, to discourage commercial bank loans to foreigners, etc.   All such uses supplemented general monetary control and were aimed at what the Federal Reserve viewed as a special problem.   For example, the Federal Reserve initiated a ''voluntary credit-restraint program'' during the Korean war which urged commercial banks to expand essential loans and limit nonessential loans to assist in the war effort.   In 1973, the Federal Reserve sent commercial banks a letter suggesting that they take greater care in extending lines of credit, and thereby slow down the expansion of commercial loans.   While it is difficult to evaluate the effectiveness of these selective communications, moral suasion has probably been a useful supplement to overall control of the money supply.

10.14. Explain how changes in margin requirements influence the flow of credit to the security markets.

During the 1930s, the Federal Reserve was authorized to place a margin requirement on loans where the principal purpose of the loan was the purchase of a security.   The specified margin represents the minimum percentage down payment that the purchaser of the security must supply.   Thus, if an individual wanted to purchase New York Stock Exchange shares valued at $3000, he could borrow no more than $2400 to purchase the stock if the margin requirement was 20%.   By varying the margin requirement, the Federal Reserve is able to influence the flow of speculative funds into the security markets; it can increase such flows when the margin requirement is lowered and decrease them when the margin requirement is raised.

10.15. How do consumer and real estate credit controls affect credit flows and durable goods/ housing demand?

For a number of years between 1941 and 1952, the Federal Reserve was authorized to set (1) minimum down payments and (2) maximum repayment periods on consumer installment and real estate loans.   Regulation of these terms allowed the Federal Reserve to control the level of credit demanded by installment and housing purchasers and influence spending on durable goods and housing.   By increasing the minimum down payment from 10% to 20% on an automobile, for example, the Federal Reserve could decrease the demand for automobiles since a portion of the households buying auto- mobiles would be unable to provide the higher down payment.   Similarly, by shortening the repayment period from 36 to 24 months, some households would be unable to purchase a car because they would be unable to make the higher monthly payments.   Thus, by controlling consumer installment and real estate credit terms, the Federal Reserve had a powerful tool for selectively influencing the level of spending on durable goods and housing.   These controls are no longer used as a result of the difficulty in administering and enforcing credit terms and of the criticism of proponents of a free market system.

Chapter 11

Synthesis of Monetary and Income Analysis

11.1 INTRODUCTION

This chapter presents the Keynesian and monetarist views of how money supply changes are translated into changes in the money level of GNP. Although Keynesian analysis suggests that fiscal policy is more effective than monetary policy, monetary policy is viewed as a way of altering the rate of interest and thereby changing the level of investment spending. Monetarists, on the other hand, argue that money is central to the operation of a market economy and see money supply changes as having a direct effect upon spending in the private sector.

11.2 THE EFFECT OF MONEY SUPPLY CHANGES: A KEYNESIAN VIEW

In a Keynesian model, the demand for money (see Problem 11.1) and investment demand (see Section 4.4) are inversely related to the rate of interest. By increasing the money supply, the Federal Reserve is able to lower the rate of interest; this increases the volume of investment spending, which induces additional consumption spending and raises the level of GNP. The focal point of monetary policy becomes the rate of interest that will bring forth the desired level of investment spending. As viewed by a Keynesian, the Federal Reserve influences the money level of income through the process shown in Fig. 11-1.

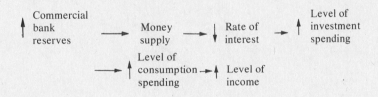

Fig. 11-1

EXAMPLE 1. Suppose that the rate of interest is initially 7% [Fig. 11-2(a)], investment spending totals $80 [Fig. 11-2(b)], and that the equilibrium level of income is $660[Fig. 11-2(c)], which is below the full-employment level. Suppose also that the Federal Reserve adopts an expansionary (easy) monetary policy in an effort to increase the level of income. By open-market operations, commercial bank reserves increase and the money supply increases from $200 to $225. Given the demand for money in Fig. 11-2(a), the rate of interest falls to 6%, and investment spending rises [see Fig. 11-2 (b)] to $90. The higher level of investment spending shifts the $C + I + G$ schedule in Fig. 11-2(c) to $C + I + G + \Delta I$, and raises the equilibrium level of income to $710. The additional aggregate spending is composed of a $10 increase in the level of investment spending and a $40 increase in the level of consumption spending.

While recognizing the possible usefulness of monetary policy, Keynesians advocate the use of fiscal policy for economic stabilization. Monetary policy is viewed as potentially weaker and/or less predictable in its effect upon the level of income. Monetary policy is a potentially weaker economic measure when the demand for money becomes highly sensitive to the rate of interest (see Problem 11.4) or when the investment demand schedule is insensitive to the rate of interest (see Problem 11.5). The effectiveness of monetary policy is also considered unpredictable because of the possibility of shifts in the demand for money or the investment demand schedule (see Problem 11.6).

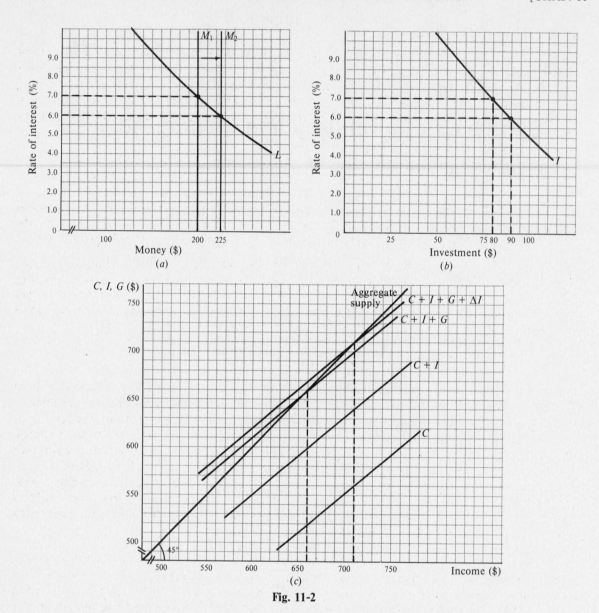

Fig. 11-2

11.3   THE EFFECT OF MONEY SUPPLY CHANGES: A MONETARIST VIEW

The monetarists consider money unique and hold that its demand is stable and insensitive to the rate of interest (see Problem 11.7).   Household and business sector spending, on the other hand, are considered highly responsive to monetary policy with money supply changes having a substantial and predictable effect upon the level of private $(C + I)$ spending (see Problem 11.9).   Figure 11-3 presents the monetarists' view of the transmission process.

Fig. 11-3

11.4 THE VELOCITY OF MONEY

Given divergent views on the demand for money, it follows that there should be disagreement about the velocity of money (see Problems 11.11 and 11.12).   In the Keynesian model, velocity is believed to be variable, whereas it is assumed to be predictable in the monetarist model.   Money supply changes, therefore, have either a predictable (monetarist) or a highly variable (Keynesian) effect upon the level of income.   Obviously an empirical question, a look at the velocity of money in the United States over the 1960–1977 period shows that the year-to-year change in velocity is somewhat variable (see Problem 11.14).

EXAMPLE 2.   Suppose the money level of income is $600 and the money supply equals $150.   Since $V = Y/M$, velocity is 4.

A monetarist would hold that a $10 increase in the money supply would result in a $40 increase in spending and a $640 level of income $[(M + \Delta M)V = Y = (\$150 + \$10)4 = \$640]$. (*Note:* In this example we assume that V is constant; monetarists recognize that V may change but contend that the change in V is relatively small and predictable.)

By comparison, a Keynesian would contend that a $10 increase in the money supply would have a smaller, less predictable effect upon income.   They would argue that a money supply increase that lowers the rate of interest would cause velocity to fall as well.   If we assume that V declines to 3.9, the result is that the $10 increase in the money supply raises the level of income to $624 rather than $640.   The actual fall in V determines the extent to which the expansive monetary policy results in a change in the level of income.

11.5 MONETARY VS. FISCAL POLICY

Monetarists and Keynesians also disagree about the strength of fiscal policy, the use of fiscal measures to stabilize a market economy, and the impact of discretionary monetary management. Monetarists contend that fiscal measures are weak and argue that an expansive fiscal policy forces interest rates up, "crowds out" private investment, and thereby results in only a small net change in the level of income (see Example 3).   According to Keynesians, an expansive fiscal policy not only stimulates the economy but can be used to achieve a better distribution of income and a better balance between public and private goods.   Monetarists, on the other hand, see government and, therefore, fiscal measures as inefficient, arbitrary allocators of economic resources (see Problem 11.16).   Although they advocate the exclusive use of monetary policy, monetarists view discretionary monetary management as a destabilizing factor (see Problem 11.17).

EXAMPLE 3.   Suppose the rate of interest is 8%, investment spending is $70, consumption is $540, government spending is $60, the equilibrium level of income is $670, and the expenditure multiplier is 4.   If full employment is defined as a $750 level of income and government spending is the selected fiscal policy, government spending must be increased $20 to close the $20 deflationary gap.   The expansive fiscal policy and resulting government deficit cause interest rates to rise to 9% and investment spending to decline to $55.   Thus, $15 in investment spending is "crowded out" by higher interest rates and income expands $20 rather than $80.   [*Note:* $\Delta Y = k_e \Delta G + k_e \Delta I$.   Since $\Delta G = +\$20$ and $\Delta I = -\$15$, the change in income equals $4(+\$20) + 4(-\$15) = +\$20$.]

Important Economic Terms

Crowding out.   The process by which increases in the public sector's deficit, due to a tax cut or an increase in government spending, raise interest rates and in turn reduce (crowd out) investment spending.

Keynesian theory.   An economic school of thought which advocates the use of fiscal policy rather than changes in the money supply to stabilize what is considered an inherently unstable market economy.

Monetarist theory.   The economic school of thought that views monetary policy as a more effective, predictable stabilization measure than fiscal policy, and advocates that the money supply increase at a rate consistent with increases in the economy's capacity to produce.

Transmission process. The manner in which stabilization measures are channeled through spending sectors to effect changes in an economy's level of income.

Review Questions

1. In the Keynesian model, the demand for money
   (a) is directly related to the rate of interest while investment demand is inversely related to the rate of interest,
   (b) and investment are directly related to the rate of interest,
   (c) and investment are inversely related to the rate of interest,
   (d) is inversely related to the rate of interest while investment demand is directly related to the rate of interest.

   Ans. (c)

2. How does monetary policy affect economic activity in the Keynesian model?
   (a) An expansion of the money supply raises the rate of interest, increases investment spending, and brings about a multiple increase in the level of income.
   (b) An expansion of the money supply lowers the rate of interest, increases investment spending, and brings about a multiple increase in the level of income.
   (c) An expansion of the money supply lowers the rate of interest, decreases investment spending, and brings about a multiple decrease in the level of income.
   (d) An expansion of the money supply lowers the rate of interest, increases investment and consumption spending, and brings about a multiple increase in the level of income.

   Ans. (b)

3. Keynesians view monetary policy as less effective than fiscal policy when the demand for money (a) and investment demand are interest inelastic, (b) and investment demand are interest elastic, (c) is interest elastic and investment demand is interest inelastic, (d) is interest inelastic and investment demand is interest elastic.

   Ans. (c)

4. Keynesian monetary policy is (a) essentially an interest rate and credit availability policy, (b) aimed at stabilizing the demand for money, (c) aimed at stabilizing the investment demand schedule, (d) directed toward controlling the level of consumption spending.

   Ans. (a)

5. Monetarists contend that money supply changes (a) have no effect upon the quantity of money demanded, (b) have an effect only upon household spending, (c) have an effect upon consumption and investment spending, (d) shift the demand for money schedule.

   Ans. (c)

6. In the monetarist model, the demand for money, (a) and private sector spending are interest inelastic, (b) and private sector spending are interest elastic, (c) is interest elastic and private sector spending is unresponsive to interest rate changes, (d) is interest inelastic and private sector spending is responsive to interest rate changes.

   Ans. (d)

7. Which of the following statements is *true*?
   (a) The demand for money is unrelated to the velocity of money.
   (b) The demand for money and velocity are directly related to the rate of interest.
   (c) The demand for money and velocity are indirectly related to the rate of interest.
   (d) The interest elasticity of the demand for money determines the extent to which interest rate changes affect the velocity of money.

   Ans. (d)

8. Which of the following statements is *true*?
   (*a*) In the Keynesian model, monetary policy is unpredictable due to variability in velocity.
   (*b*) In the Keynesian model, monetary policy is unpredictable due to the interest inelasticity of the demand for money.
   (*c*) In the monetarist model, monetary policy is predictable due to the sensitivity of velocity to the rate of interest.
   (*d*) In the monetarist model, money supply changes are partly dissipated by changes in the velocity of money.

   Ans. (*a*)

9. Which of the following statements is *not* true?
   (*a*) Monetarists favor stable monetary growth rather than discretionary monetary management.
   (*b*) Monetarists view monetary policy as a means of achieving a more efficient allocation of resources.
   (*c*) Monetarists contend that monetary policy crowds out private investment.
   (*d*) Monetarists contend that velocity is predictable.

   Ans. (*c*)

10. Crowding out occurs when
    (*a*) interest rate changes alter the quantity of money demanded.
    (*b*) fiscal measures alter investment spending through changes in the rate of interest.
    (*c*) fiscal measures change the velocity of money.
    (*d*) fiscal policy becomes inoperative due to an interest elastic demand for money.

    Ans. (*b*)

Solved Problems

THE EFFECT OF MONEY SUPPLY CHANGES: A KEYNESIAN VIEW

11.1. Why is there a demand for money?

Money is used for the exchange of goods and services in advanced economies. Households generally hold some idle money balances in order to budget the spending of money income over a pay period. For example, if a household receives $140 weekly and spends this income evenly over a seven-day period, a $70 average money balance is held over the pay period. In addition to this transaction motive, economists have also recognized that money is held for precautionary purposes as protection against such future events as illness or loss of job or to take advantage of unexpected opportunities. Economists have suggested that these transaction and precautionary needs are relatively immutable, are tied to the level of income, and are somewhat influenced by the rate of interest.

In the *General Theory of Employment, Interest and Money*, Keynes introduced the theory of a speculative demand for money by recognizing money as a possible alternative way to hold financial wealth. Whether a household holds money or financial securities depends upon its expectation about the future rate of interest and thereby the expected return to be received from money or financial securities as alternative stores of value. For example, if the future rate of interest is expected to rise substantially so that capital losses from holding financial securities exceed their interest return, investors are assured a better return by holding money. Thus, the lower the current rate of interest relative to the future rate, the greater the preference for money over financial securities. This suggests that the speculative demand for money is inversely related to the rate of interest.

11.2. (*a*) Suppose the demand for money is L_1 in Fig. 11-4(*a*). Find the rate of interest when the money supply is $150, $160 and $170.
   (*b*) Find the volume of investment from Fig. 11-4(*b*) when the rate of interest is 8%, 7% and 6%.
   (*c*) Suppose the Federal Reserve, through an easy money policy, lowers the rate of interest from 8% to 7%. Find the change in the equilibrium level of income if the expenditure multiplier is 5.

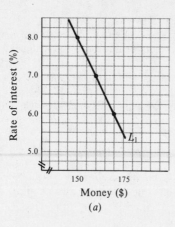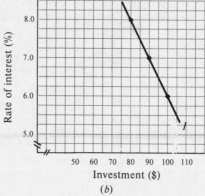

Fig. 11-4

(a) From Fig. 11-4(a), we see that increasing the money supply from \$150 to \$160 to \$170 lowers the rate of interest from 8% to 7% to 6%.

(b) Investment spending is \$80 when the rate of interest is 8%, \$90 when it is 7% and \$100 when i equals 6%.

(c) Chapter 5 demonstrated that $\Delta Y = k_e \Delta I$, i.e. that the change in income equals the expenditure multiplier times the change in investment spending. Since $k_e = 5$ and $\Delta I = \$10$, the change in the equilibrium level of income is \$50.

11.3. Given: the demand for money, investment demand and aggregate spending schedules in Fig. 11-5.

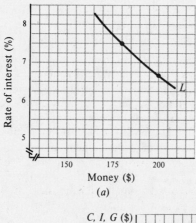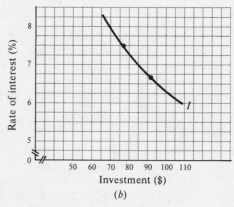

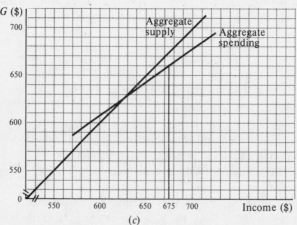

Fig. 11-5

(a) Suppose full employment occurs at the $675 level of income. If the current rate of interest is 7.5%, what rate of interest is needed to achieve full employment?

(b) In a Keynesian model, is monetary policy focused upon changing the rate of interest or the quantity of money?

(a) The deflationary gap is $15. By increasing investment spending $15, the deflationary gap is closed and full employment is reached. Figure 11-5(b) shows that investment is increased from $77 to $92 by lowering the rate of interest from 7.5% to 6.7%; this is accomplished by a $20 increase in the money supply.

(b) The primary concern of monetary policy in the Keynesian model is with changes in the cost and availability of credit rather than with changes in the stock of money. An elastic and/or unstable demand for money schedule in the Keynesian model may require large changes in the quantity of money to bring the rate of interest to a level that will generate full employment.

11.4. Given: demand for money schedules L' and L'', money supply M_o and equilibrium rate of interest i_o in Fig. 11-6. (a) Find the rate of interest when the money supply increases to M_1. (b) In a Keynesian model, why is the slope of the demand for money schedule important in an evaluation of the effectiveness of monetary policy?

(a) The rate of interest falls from i_0 to i_1 along demand for money schedule L' and from i_0 to i_2 along L''. The rate of interest has the greater decrease along the steeper demand for money schedule.

(b) The slope of the demand for money schedule determines the extent to which money supply changes bring about changes in the rate of interest. Monetary policy becomes a weak stabilization measure the flatter the demand for money schedule since large increases in the stock of money may be necessary to achieve the desired higher level of income. For example, if L' is the relevant demand for money schedule and i_2 is the policy objective, the money supply must be increased to M_2 to achieve the desired level of income.

11.5. Given: investment demand schedules I' and I'' and the rate of interest i_0 in Fig. 11-7. (a) Find the level of investment spending when the rate of interest is lowered to i_1. (b) What is the importance of the interest elasticity of investment demand to the effectiveness of monetary policy? (c) What can one infer about the effectiveness of monetary policy if the demand for money is interest elastic (relatively horizontal) and investment demand is interest inelastic?

(a) A decrease in the rate of interest to i_1 increases investment demand to I_1 if the investment demand schedule is I' and to I_2 if the investment demand schedule is I''.

(b) Figure 11-7 shows that investment is more responsive to interest rate changes when the schedule of investment spending is less steeply sloped (more interest elastic). Monetary policy is, therefore, more effective when investment demand is interest elastic.

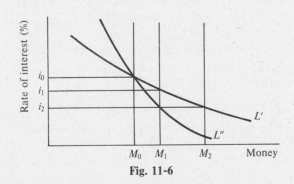

Fig. 11-6

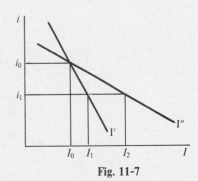

Fig. 11-7

(c) When the demand for money is interest elastic, money supply changes have only small effects upon the rate of interest.   When the investment schedule is interest inelastic, interest rate changes have small effects upon investment spending.   Thus, if the demand for money is interest elastic and investment demand is interest inelastic, one can predict that money supply changes will have little effect upon the level of income.

11.6. Given: investment demand schedule I' and rate of interest i_0 in Fig. 11-8.

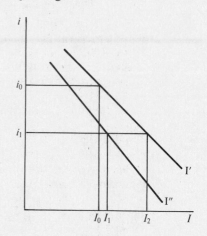

Fig. 11-8

(a) Suppose that the investment demand schedule shifts to I" at the same time that the Federal Reserve initiates an easy monetary policy which lowers the rate of interest to i_1.   Find the new level of investment spending.

(b) If the investment demand schedule is subject to shifts downward during periods of pessimism and upward during periods of optimism, how predictable are the effects of monetary policy?

(a) Investment spending will increase from I_0 to I_1 as the rate of interest falls to i_1.   Investment spending would have increased to I_2 if the investment demand schedule had been stable and not shifted downward.

(b) Monetary policy is highly unpredictable if the investment demand schedule is unstable.   To know the effect of a money supply change upon the level of income, one would have to know the direction and magnitude of the shift in the investment demand schedule.

THE EFFECT OF MONEY SUPPLY CHANGES: A MONETARIST VIEW

11.7. What does the monetarist view—that the demand for money is interest inelastic—suggest about the availability of money substitutes?

Section 8.1 listed the principal functions of money as a medium of exchange and store of value. Demand deposits and currency are the only financial assets that serve as mediums of exchange.   Money and such highly liquid financial assets as savings accounts, savings and loan shares, and short-term securities, serve as a store of value.   In taking the position that money is unique, monetarists are suggesting that money's principal function is that of a medium of exchange and that money is only marginally important as a store of value because there is a large array of interest-bearing financial assets that are substitutes for money.   In denying the importance of money's store of value function (which Keynesians emphasize) and focusing upon its transaction use for which there are no substitutes, monetarists take the position that the demand for money is interest inelastic.

11.8. (a) Column 1 of Table 1 presents the market values of financial assets in an economy in which the rate of interest is 7%.   What is the aggregate market value of the economy's financial assets?

(b) What effect should changes in the rate of interest have upon the market value of marketable, interest-bearing financial assets?

(c) Column 2 of the table presents the market values of financial assets in the economy after an expansive monetary policy has lowered the rate of interest to 6%.   What is the aggregate market value of the economy's financial assets?

(d) How does an increase in the money supply affect the aggregate market value of financial assets?

(e) How might changes in the aggregate market value of financial assets affect the private sector's ability to spend?

Table 1

Asset	Column 1	Column 2
Money	$ 100	$ 110
Savings obligations of financial intermediaries	1000	1000
Market value of public sector debt	400	435
Market value of private sector debt	1111	1212
Market value of equity securities	2000	2300
	$4611	$5057

(a) The aggregate market value of an economy's financial assets (i.e. financial wealth) is the sum of all interest and noninterest-bearing, marketable and nonmarketable financial assets.   Given the values in Table 1, the aggregate market value of financial assets is $4611.

(b) The market value of marketable, interest-bearing financial assets is the present value of future returns from these assets, i.e. $V = R_1/(1+r) + R_2/(1+r)^2 + \ldots + R_n/(1+r)^n$ where V is the market value of the financial asset, R_1, R_2 are the annual returns and r is the appropriate rate of discount applied to these future flows.   Holding other things constant, an increase in the rate of interest, and therefore the rate of discount r, lowers V.   Thus, the market value of marketable, interest-bearing financial assets is inversely related to the rate of interest.   Reductions in the rate of interest increase the market value of marketable financial assets and increases in the rate of interest lower them.

(c) The aggregate market value of the economy's financial assets increases from $4611 to $5057.

(d) An increase in the money supply affects the aggregate market value of financial assets in two ways: (1) directly, by the increase in the money supply (the money supply increases from $100 in Column 1 to $110 in Column 2); and (2) indirectly, by the decrease in the rate of interest (the reduction in the rate of interest increases the market value of marketable securities by $436).

(e) Changes in the aggregate market value of financial assets affect the private sector's wealth and therefore its ability to spend.   Thus, increases in the aggregate value of financial assets increase this ability, while decreases in the aggregate market value of financial assets reduce this ability to spend.

11.9. (a) Why does an easy monetary policy influence spending for things other than capital goods?   (b) Should monetary policy be a weak or powerful means of stabilizing economic activity?

(a) A reduction in the rate of interest stimulates investment spending by reducing the cost of funds.   Other spending is influenced by an expanded ability to buy.   (Remember that demand for a good is dependent upon one's *willingness* and *ability* to purchase the good.)   Since an easy monetary policy increases the aggregate market value of financial assets, an expansion of the money supply also increases spending for durable consumer goods, residential housing, etc., because of the household sector's increased ability to purchase output.

(b) Monetary policy should be an extremely effective tool of policy since it affects the private sector's ability to buy aggregate output as well as investment spending.

11.10. Given the effects of money supply changes developed in Problems 11.8 and 11.9, what should happen to the $C + I + G$ schedule in Fig. 11-9 as a result of an increase in the money supply?

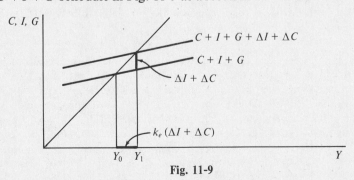

Fig. 11-9

An expansion of the money supply shifts the aggregate spending schedule upward. The shift equals $\Delta I + \Delta C$, the sum of increased spending on investment and consumption. The increase in the equilibrium level of income will be $k_e (\Delta I + \Delta C)$.

THE VELOCITY OF MONEY

11.11. Suppose that on the average households and others hold money balances equal to one-half their annual expenditure for final goods and services. (*a*) What is the average money balance held if the aggregate level of income is $500? (*b*) What is the money supply? (*c*) What is the velocity of money? (*d*) What is the relationship of velocity to the demand for money?

  (*a*) Since the average money balance held is $0.5Y$ (one-half the expenditure on GNP), households and others hold an average money balance of $250.

  (*b*) Since the money created by the central bank must be held by households and others (the supply of money must equal the demand for money), the money supply must equal $250.

  (*c*) Given the equation of exchange $M \times V = Y$, V equals 2 since M equals $250 and Y is $500.

  (*d*) V equals one divided by the proportion of income households and others hold as a money balance. Thus, V is 2 when $0.5Y$ is the average money balance held. V, therefore, is inversely related to the demand for money. It increases when there is a fall in the demand for money and decreases when larger money balances are demanded. For example, a decrease in the desire to hold money balances from $0.5Y$ to $0.4Y$ raises velocity from 2 to 2.5.

11.12. (*a*) Find V in the following situations:
  (1) The money balance held is $0.20Y$ when the rate of interest is 4%, $0.204Y$ when the rate of interest is 6% and $0.207Y$ when the rate of interest is 8%.
  (2) The money balance held is $0.20Y$ when the rate of interest is 4%, $0.23Y$ when the rate of interest is 6% and $0.26Y$ when the rate of interest is 8%.
  (*b*) Which of the situations in part (*a*) best represents the monetarists' position?

  (*a*) (1) Velocity is 5 when the rate of interest is 4%, 4.90 when it is 6% and 4.83 when it is 8%.
    (2) Velocity is 5 when the rate of interest is 4%, 4.35 when it is 6%, and 3.85 when it is 8%.

  (*b*) Monetarists contend that the demand for money, and therefore velocity, is little affected by interest rates whereas Keynesians argue that velocity is considerably influenced by them. Thus, a monetarist is closely identified with situation (1) in part (*a*) while a Keynesian is best associated with situation (2).

11.13. Suppose the money supply is currently $120, V is 5, and the aggregate level of income is $600.
  (*a*) Find the aggregate level of income if the money supply is increased $10 and V remains at 5.
  (*b*) Find the aggregate level of income if the money supply is increased $10 but V falls to 4.8 as the expansionary monetary policy lowers the rate of interest from 8% to 7%.
  (*c*) Why is the demand for money and therefore velocity crucial to an evaluation of the effect of changes in the money supply?

  (*a*) If V remains constant, the $10 increase in the money supply raises the aggregate level of income from $600 to $650 [$(M + \Delta M)V = Y = (\$120 + \$10)5 = \$650$].

  (*b*) If V falls to 4.8 as the money supply increases $10, the aggregate level of income increases from $600 to $624 [$(M + \Delta M)V = Y = (\$120 + \$10)4.8 = \$624$].

  (*c*) If the demand for money is influenced by interest rates, V is variable and the effect of money supply changes upon the aggregate level of income is less predictable. For example, the 8.5% growth in aggregate income in part (*a*) is reduced to a 4% rate of growth in part (*b*) as a result of the fall in velocity. Velocity is central to the formulation of a monetary policy when a specific growth in aggregate income is needed to achieve full employment.

11.14. GNP, the money supply (M_1) and velocity for 1960-1977 are presented in Table 2.   (a) Plot V and M_1.   (b) Interpret the resulting figure.

Table 2

Year	GNP*	M_1*	V
1960	$ 503.7	$144.2	3.49
1961	520.1	148.7	3.50
1962	560.3	150.9	3.71
1963	590.5	156.5	3.77
1964	632.4	163.7	3.86
1965	684.9	171.3	4.00
1966	749.9	175.4	4.28
1967	793.9	186.9	4.25
1968	864.2	201.7	4.28
1969	930.3	208.7	4.46
1970	977.1	221.4	4.41
1971	1054.9	235.4	4.48
1972	1158.0	255.8	4.53
1973	1294.9	271.5	4.77
1974	1277.9	284.4	4.91
1975	1513.5	295.0	5.13
1976	1706.5	312.6	5.46
1977	1889.6	336.7	5.61

*billions of dollars

(a)   See Fig. 11-10.

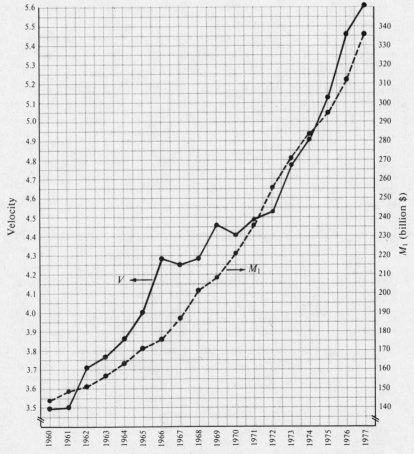

Fig. 11-10

(b) Both velocity and M_1 have increased over the 1960-1977 period. M_1 shows a more constant increase than velocity.   While velocity increases have been variable, the variation has not been as substantial as Keynesian analysis would suggest.   However, the existence of some variation indicates that a strict interpretation of the monetarists' position is not supported either.   The predictability of the effect of money supply changes upon the level of income appears to be somewhat between the positions suggested by monetarist and Keynesian analysis and is to date unresolved.

MONETARY VS. FISCAL POLICY

11.15. Suppose that an economy is below the full-employment level of income and the behavior of investment and velocity is as presented in Fig. 11-11.

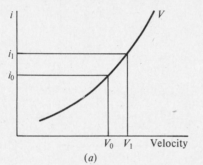 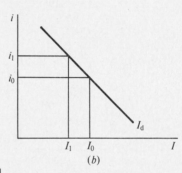

Fig. 11-11

(a) Referring to Fig. 11-11(a), determine what happens to the quantity of money demanded as the rate of interest increases from i_0 to i_1.

(b) Suppose that there is an increase in government spending which raises the rate of interest from i_0 to i_1. Using the equation of exchange as your point of reference, establish that the level of income is increasing.

(c) Using the investment behavior specified in Fig. 11-11(b), establish that the increase in the level of income is less than $k_e \Delta G$.

(d) Could the Federal Reserve have offset the crowding-out effect of increased government spending?

(a) In Fig. 11-11(a), velocity increases from V_0 to V_1 as the rate of interest rises from i_0 to i_1.   For velocity to increase, the quantity of money demanded (average money balance held) must be falling.   See Section 11.4.

(b) Given no change in the money supply, an increase in velocity must raise the level of income, e.g. $\bar{M} \cdot V\uparrow = Y\uparrow$.

(c) Investment spending falls from I_0 to I_1 as the rate of interest increases from i_0 to i_1.   The stimulative effect of increased government spending is partially offset by decreased investment.   Thus, $\Delta Y = k_e \Delta G - k_e \Delta I$.

(d) The Federal Reserve could offset the crowding-out effect of fiscal policy by increasing the money supply in order to keep the rate of interest at the i_0 level.

11.16. Are there philosophical differences between Keynesians and monetarists?

Keynesians are politically "liberal" and see the need for government interference to overcome the problems of social imbalance and the unequal distribution of disposable income.   Fiscal policy, therefore, permits policy makers to seek microeconomic policy objectives while stabilizing economic activity.   Monetarists are "conservative" and view the market, and not man, as the best allocator of resources and output.   Monetary management is the best means of achieving economic stabilization in a market system.   Philosophically, then, Keynesians advocate a mixed economy and monetarists prefer an economic system that most closely approximates a market economy.

11.17. What are the monetarists' objections to discretionary monetary management?

Economists agree that the effect of money supply changes on income are not instantaneous and that changes in income lag changes in the money supply.   Monetarists contend that discretionary increases in the money supply are destabilizing and cite studies on the lagged effect of money supply changes.   For example, Milton Friedman's pathbreaking study on the lagged effect of monetary policy indicates that the level of income lags changes in the money supply by 6 to 22 months.   One of the conclusions from this study is that discretionary monetary management is probably destabilizing since the Federal Reserve does not know when today's monetary policy will affect economic activity. Monetarists, such as Milton Friedman, therefore advocate stable monetary growth and would have the money supply grow at a fixed rate to eliminate potential destabilizing effects.

Chapter 12

Full Employment and Price Stability

12.1 SIMPLE DEMAND-PULL AND COST-PUSH MODELS OF INFLATION

Demand-pull inflation (defined in Chapter 7) is a process in which prices rise due to the inability of supply to expand to meet an increasing demand.   In a simple demand-pull inflation model, we assume that upward shifts of the aggregate spending ($C + I + G$) schedule raise the level of real income and employment and do not change prices as long as the economy is below full employment.   Once the full-employment level of output is reached, further increases in aggregate spending raise prices.

EXAMPLE 1. The economy's nominal level of income equals the average price of output times the real level of output, i.e. $Y = p \cdot y$.   Suppose full employment is defined as the y_f level of real output.   As aggregate spending in Fig. 12-1(a) increases from H_1 to H_2 to H_3, the nominal level of income increases from Y_1 to Y_2 to Y_3, and real output rises from y_1 to y_2 to y_3.   The average price of output remains at p_0.   The upward shifts of aggregate spending appear in Fig. 12-1(b) as rightward shifts of the aggregate demand schedule from D_1 to D_2 to D_3 along a horizontal aggregate supply schedule.   Increased aggregate spending to H_4 raises the nominal level of income to Y_4 [Fig. 12-1(a)] with the increase representing a rise in the average price of output from p_0 to p_1 [Fig. 12-1(b)] since real output cannot expand beyond y_f.

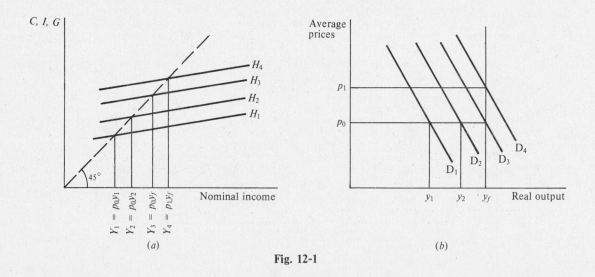

Fig. 12-1

As explained in Section 7.2, cost-push inflation develops when labor, business or material suppliers exert pressure upon the supply price of goods and services.   Given a constant level of aggregate spending (aggregate demand), upward pressure on the supply price of goods increases the average price of output and decreases the level of output.

EXAMPLE 2. Suppose an economy's aggregate demand and aggregate supply schedules are given as D' and S' in Fig. 12-2.   If raw material producers raise the supply price of basic goods, the aggregate supply schedule will shift upward to S''.   The new equilibrium will occur at the lower real income level y_1 and at a higher average price of p_1.

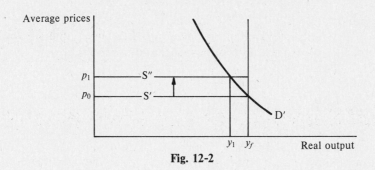

Fig. 12-2

12.2 BOTTLENECK INFLATION

The model in Section 12.1 assumes that spending increases have no effect upon the price level until the economy reaches the full-employment level of output.   This assumption is unrealistic for a large and complex economy like the United States'.   Bottlenecks (shortages of specific labor skills or supplies) are likely to develop as an economy nears full employment; this causes the prices of some goods and services to rise and therefore increases the price level before the full-employment level of output is reached (see Problem 12.6).   An economy continually in the vicinity of full employment strengthens the likelihood that cost-push inflation will develop (see Problem 12.10).

EXAMPLE 3.   Suppose an economy's aggregate supply schedule is S_1 in Fig. 12-3 and that its rising slope from y_2 to y_f reflects developing labor and material shortages.   An increase in aggregate demand from D_1 to D_2 raises the level of real output from y_1 to y_2 and has no effect upon the price level.   The increase in aggregate demand from D_2 to D_3 raises both the level of real output and prices because specific labor and/or material shortages develop as the economy moves toward y_f.

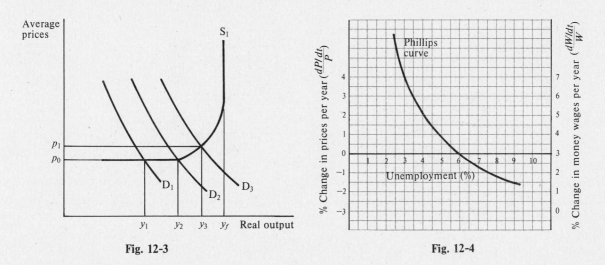

Fig. 12-3   **Fig. 12-4**

12.3 THE PHILLIPS CURVE

The analysis in Section 12.2 indicates that increases in aggregate spending when the economy is not at full employment raise prices as well as the level of real output.   A.W. Phillips, investigating unemployment and price/wage rate increases over time, found that low rates of unemployment in Great Britain were associated with high rates of price/wage rate increase while higher levels of unemployment were associated with lower rates of price/wage rate increase.   The Phillips curve, plotted in Fig. 12-4, indicates a short-run dilemma for policy makers: should economic policy strive for the lowest level of unemployment *or* stable prices?   (Note that in Fig. 12-4 the annual rate of price increase is read on the left-hand vertical axis while the annual rate of money wage increase is read on the right-hand vertical axis.)   The unemployment/inflation trade-off appears to exist only in the short run, though, because a continuous policy directed at low unemployment rates is likely to shift the Phillips curve upward and to result in stagflation (see Problem 12.13).

12.4 THE NATURAL RATE OF UNEMPLOYMENT

Some economists contend that the Phillips curve trade-off is an illusion; they suggest that the long-run Phillips curve is a vertical line at the natural rate of unemployment and that attempts in the 1970s to push the unemployment rate below the natural rate resulted in accelerating rates of inflation (see Example 4).   Keynesians have disagreed and contend that the inflation of the 1970s is best explained by the changing composition of the labor force and a lagged and/or imperfect cost-of-living feedback effect upon the price level (see Problem 12.15).   Both sides agree, however, that the long-run relationship between prices and unemployment rates is different than it is in the short run when economic policy is directed toward minimizing the level of unemployment.

EXAMPLE 4.   Suppose the economy in Fig. 12-5(a) is at the y_0 level of real output.   Government introduces a stimulative economic policy to shift aggregate demand from D_1 to D_2 which increases real output to y_1; in Fig. 12-5(b) it lowers the unemployment rate from 6% to 4% and raises the rate of price increase from 0% to 2%. Since aggregate supply S_1 was derived with the expectation of stable prices, a continuous 2% rate of price increase shifts aggregate supply to S_2 and returns real output and unemployment to their initial y_0 and 6% levels.   The expectation of a 2% rate of price increase has shifted the Phillips curve upward to P_2 on which a 2% rate of price increase is now consistent with a 6% level of unemployment.   Continuous attempts to lower the unemployment rate to 4% will result in continuous increases in the price level.   Expectations of such price increases shift the Phillips curve to P_3, P_4, etc.   The 6% natural rate of unemployment persists and there is no possibility of achieving a permanently lower level of unemployment.

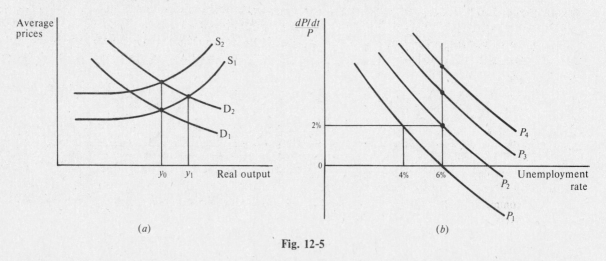

Fig. 12-5

EXAMPLE 5.   Suppose an economy currently has a 6% rate of unemployment and stable prices.   Government introduces a stimulative economic policy which lowers the unemployment rate to 4% and results in a 2% rate of inflation.   Labor is unable to secure a 2% increase in its money wage rate to recover lost purchasing power; the short-run Phillips curve P_1 in Fig. 12-6 shifts rightward to P_2 rather than P_a.   (Note: A shift to P_a would occur if labor received a 2% increase in its money wage rate.)   The rightward shift of the short-run Phillips curve from P_1 to P_2 raises the unemployment rate to 5% from the previous 4% rate that developed from government's expansionary economic policy. Successive increases in aggregate spending and the price level are also imperfectly translated into money wage rate increases and the short-run Phillips curve shifts to P_3 and P_4.   A long-run relationship P_L between the rate of inflation and the rate of unemployment evolves; this is the result of labor's failure to secure money wage rate increases equal to the rate of inflation.

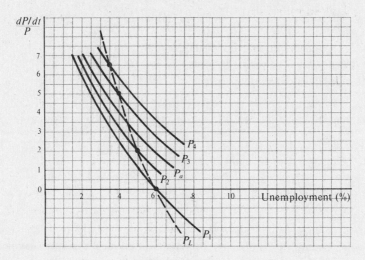

Fig. 12-6

Important Economic Terms

Bottleneck inflation.   The increase in the general price level caused by rising prices for goods and services produced by economic resources which become fully employed before the designated full-employment level of income is achieved.

Bottlenecks.   Specific labor market or material shortages that develop in an economy with unemployed resources.

Incomes policy.   A Federal government policy of wage-price guideposts or controls aimed at limiting price increases in an economy that is operating below full employment.

Natural rate of unemployment.   The rate of unemployment at which a vertical Phillips curve is found, indicating that inflation cannot be used to lower the level of unemployment in the long run.

Phillips curve.   An empirical relationship between the rate of change in wage rates and prices and the rate of unemployment, which shows an inverse relationship between the rate of unemployment and that of inflation.

Stagflation.   A situation in which high rates of unemployment and inflation occur simultaneously.

Review Questions

1. In a simple demand-pull model of inflation, an increase in aggregate spending at the full-employment level of output will
    (a)   have no effect upon prices and the real level of output,
    (b)   have no effect upon prices but increase the real level of output,
    (c)   have no effect upon the real level of output but increase prices,
    (d)   increase prices and the real level of output.

    Ans.   (*c*)

2. In a simple cost-push model of inflation, an increase in the supply price of output will
   (*a*) increase prices and the real level of output,
   (*b*) increase prices and decrease the real level of output,
   (*c*) increase prices and have no effect upon the real level of output,
   (*d*) have no effect upon prices and the real level of output.

   Ans. (*b*)

3. In a simple demand-pull model of inflation, an increase in aggregate spending results in proportional increases in
   (*a*) real output as long as the economy has not reached full employment,
   (*b*) the price level as long as the economy has not reached full employment,
   (*c*) the cost of real output as long as the economy has not reached full employment,
   (*d*) real output once the economy has reached full employment.

   Ans. (*a*)

4. Bottlenecks refer to (*a*) inadequate spending in a sector of the economy, (*b*) a shortage of materials in a full-employment economy, (*c*) an inadequate supply of labor in a full-employment economy, (*d*) an inadequate supply of specific resources in an economy below full employment.

   Ans. (*d*)

5. Bottlenecks (*a*) cause the cost of specific resources to increase, (*b*) cause the cost of specific resources to decrease, (*c*) cause aggregate spending to decrease, (*d*) prevent the economy from reaching full employment.

   Ans. (*a*)

6. As a result of bottlenecks, one would expect
   (*a*) prices to remain constant until full employment is reached,
   (*b*) prices to rise before the economy reaches full employment,
   (*c*) increased spending to have no effect upon the price level until all resources are employed,
   (*d*) increased spending to cause proportional increases in the price level although the economy is below full employment.

   Ans. (*b*)

7. The Phillips curve shows that
   (*a*) high unemployment rates are associated with low rates of inflation,
   (*b*) high unemployment rates are associated with high rates of inflation,
   (*c*) high unemployment rates are associated with large increases in money wage rates,
   (*d*) high inflation rates are associated with small increases in money wage rates.

   Ans. (*a*)

8. An increase in the cost of living (*a*) has no effect upon the Phillips curve in the long run, (*b*) shifts the Phillips curve upward in the long run, (*c*) shifts the Phillips curve downward in the long run, (*d*) increases the likelihood of bottleneck inflation.

   Ans. (*b*)

9. The natural rate of unemployment hypothesis suggests that
   (*a*) there is no inflation/unemployment trade-off in the long run,
   (*b*) money wage rate increases lag price increases in the long run,
   (*c*) money wage rate increases lead price increases in the long run,
   (*d*) the short-run Phillips curve is steeper than the long-run Phillips curve.

   Ans. (*a*)

10. Keynesians suggest that the high rates of unemployment and inflation in the 1970s were partially explained by
   (*a*) manpower projects that shifted the Phillips curve upward,
   (*b*) manpower projects that shifted the Phillips curve downward,
   (*c*) changes in the composition of the labor force that shifted the Phillips curve upward,
   (*d*) changes in the composition of the labor force that shifted the Phillips curve downward.

   Ans. (*c*)

Solved Problems

12.1. Suppose full employment occurs when the aggregate quantity of labor demanded equals the aggregate quantity of labor supplied. (a) Given the aggregate demand for labor N_d, the aggregate supply of labor N_s and aggregate production function $y(N)$ in Fig. 12-7, find the employment of labor when real output is y_1, y_2 and y_3. (b) What is the full-employment level of output?

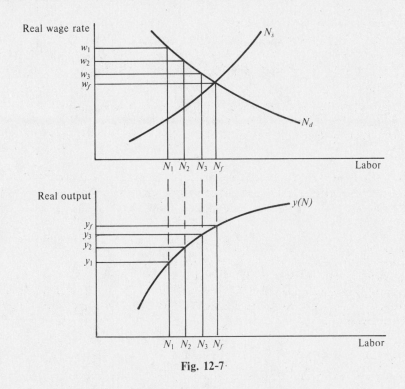

Fig. 12-7

(a) N_1 is the quantity of labor required to produce a y_1 level of real output; N_2 and N_3 are needed to produce y_2 and y_3, respectively.

(b) By definition, full employment exists at N_f, where the labor markets are in equilibrium. y_f is the level of real output consistent with the employment of N_f labor units.

12.2. Suppose the money supply is $200, velocity is 5, the average price of output is $2, and real output is $500. ($M \cdot V = p \cdot y = \$200 \times 5 = \$2 \times 500 = \$1000$.) If the full-employment level of real output is $550, what effect will an increase in the money supply to $210 and then to $220 have upon the price level and real output? Assume that velocity is constant and prices are stable until real income reaches full employment.

When velocity remains at 5 and the money supply increases from $200 to $210 and then to $220, nominal income increases from $1000 to $1050 and then to $1100. The initial $10 increase in the money supply raises nominal income $50 and is composed of a $50 increase in real output and no change in prices. (Real output increases from $500 to the full-employment $550 level of output since it is assumed that prices remain constant as long as there are unemployed resources.) The second $10 increase in the money supply raises nominal income another $50; this increase is composed of only an increase in the average price of output because the economy had reached the $550 full-employment level of real output.

12.3. (a) Suppose the money supply is $200, velocity is 5, the average price of output is $2 and real output is $500. Letting the $550 level of real output represent full employment, what effect will an increase in the average price of output to $2.10 have if there is no change in velocity or the money supply?

(b) Why do increases in the supply price of output cause real output to fall in the absence of an increase in the level of aggregate spending?

(c) Could real output have been sustained at the $500 level of real output by employing economic policy?

(a) Given the identity $M \cdot V = p \cdot y$, an increase in p with no change in M or V must reduce y. Since $M \cdot V = \$200 \times 5$ remains at $1000, the increase in p from $2 to $2.10 forces y to fall from $500 to $476.19.

(b) If nominal aggregate spending is constant (if there is no change in aggregate demand), spenders are less able to purchase output when there is an increase in the average price of output (an upward shift of aggregate supply).   This reduced ability to spend results in a decrease in the actual amount of goods and services purchased.

(c) Real output would stay at $500 if the money supply were increased $10 as cost pressures raise the average price of output from $2.00 to $2.10; or if V were increased (by using fiscal policy) to 5.25.

12.4. What effect will the following events have upon the average price of aggregate output? Assume the economy is initially at full employment.   Treat each situation separately.

(a) There is a 5% increase in the money supply and no change in the economy's ability to produce.

(b) There is a 5% increase in the money supply and a 10% increase in the economy's productive capacity.

(c) There is an increase in the supply price of output.

(d) There is an increase in the money supply and an increase in the supply price of output.

(a) This increase in the money supply stimulates aggregate spending and results in an increase in the price level.

(b) Since the increase in the economy's productive capacity exceeds the increase in aggregate spending, there is no reason for the price level to increase.   If prices are inflexible downward, prices will remain constant and unemployment will develop.

(c) Cost-push forces raise the price level.

(d) Demand-pull and cost-push forces raise the average price of aggregate output.

12.5. Given: the aggregate demand D_1 and aggregate supply S_1 schedules in Fig. 12-8 in which full employment exists at the y_f level of aggregate output.

(a) How can price increases caused by (1) a shift of aggregate demand from D_1 to D_2 or (2) a shift of aggregate supply from S_1 to S_2 be prevented?

(b) Suppose the cause of inflation is incorrectly diagnosed and policies designed to overcome demand-pull inflation are used when price increases are caused by cost-push factors. What will happen to prices and to the level of aggregate output?

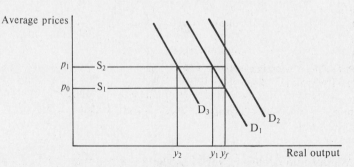

Fig. 12-8

(a) (1) To stop demand-pull inflation, the Federal government must prevent aggregate demand from increasing to D_2 and keep spending levels at D_1. The stimulative pressures shifting aggregate demand to D_2 must be offset by such restrictive economic policies as a decrease in the money supply and/or a decrease in government spending or increased taxes. (2) Monetary and fiscal policy are ineffective in combating cost-push inflation. Here the government must institute either a voluntary or mandatory incomes policy by which wage and price increases are restricted by the government and the upward shift of the aggregate supply schedule is minimized.

(b) Restricting aggregate spending to combat cost-push inflation does not stop prices from increasing but does worsen the decline in aggregate output. In Fig. 12-8, for example, suppose cost-push pressures are expressed by the upward shift of aggregate supply from S_1 to S_2. If a restrictive economic policy shifting aggregate demand to D_3 is used to combat the inflation, prices would still increase from p_0 to p_1 but real output would fall from y_f to y_2 rather than from y_f to y_1 (if no policy action was taken).

BOTTLENECK INFLATION

12.6. (a) What are bottlenecks and why do they develop as an economy approaches full employment? (b) What is bottleneck inflation?

(a) In a developed economy, labor, natural and capital resources are not homogeneous but highly specialized. In a country the size of the United States, some economic resources are geographically immobile. Thus, there is not one market for such an economic resource as labor but a large number of separate and distinct markets. In a market economy, the structure of demand is not constant and during an economic expansion spending is unlikely to increase uniformly for each item of output. Therefore, given the separate and distinct resource markets and changeable structure of demand, it follows that some economic resources are fully employed before the economy reaches the full-employment level of income. Bottlenecks, then, represent an inadequate supply of specific resources and/or goods in a market economy that is approaching the full-employment level of income.

(b) Bottleneck inflation is the overall increase in the general price level caused by the rising prices for goods and services produced by economic resources which become employed before the designated full-employment level of income is reached.

12.7. (a) Does an increase in the money wage rate always result in a proportional increase in the supply of output? (b) What relationship would you expect to find between productivity and money wage rates in a labor market approaching full employment?

(a) The influence of money wage rates upon the supply price of output depends upon whether money wage rate changes alter the labor cost per unit of output. If money wage rate increases cause the labor cost per unit of output to rise, the supply price of output must also increase. However, money wage rate increases have no effect upon the supply price of output as long as the labor cost per unit of output remains constant. For example, suppose labor is paid $6.00 per hour and produces 2 units of output per hour. The labor cost per unit of output is $3.00 ($6.00 money wage rate divided by the output of 2 units). If labor receives a 10% increase in its money wage rate for being 10% more productive, the labor cost per unit of output remains at $3.00 and there is no change in the supply price of output. (The $6.00 initial wage + $0.60 wage increase divided by 2 units + 0.2 unit increase in output = $6.60/2.2 units = $3.00.) Wage rate increases have no effect upon the supply price of output as long as the increase in productivity is equal to or greater than the increase in the money wage rate.

(b) A profit-maximizing firm would be expected to hire the most productive resources first and the least productive ones last. Money wage rates should increase as specialized labor resources become fully employed. As a specific labor market becomes fully employed, the firm's labor cost per unit of output should increase and necessitate an increase in the supply price of the firm's output.

12.8. (a) Suppose an economy's final output consists of the five goods listed in Table 1. Find the average price and nominal value of the final output.

(b) Since the economy is below the full-employment level of output, the Federal government stimulates aggregate spending. The new output levels are presented in Table 2. Find the average price and the nominal value of final output.

(c) Comparing Tables 1 and 2, what might one infer about the availability of unemployed resources to meet an increase in aggregate spending?

Table 1

Good	Unit price	Units of Output	Value of Output
A	$1.00	75	$ 75.00
B	2.50	50	125.00
C	1.25	60	75.00
D	3.00	40	120.00
E	2.00	125	250.00
		350	$645.00

Table 2

Good	Unit Price	Units of Output	Value of Output
A	$1.00	85	$ 85.00
B	2.50	60	150.00
C	1.50	62	93.00
D	3.00	50	150.00
E	2.25	128	288.00
		385	$766.00

(a) The nominal value of final output is the sum of the dollar output for the five goods produced. The nominal value of final output is initially $645. The average price of output is a weighted sum of the price of each good and can be found by dividing the nominal value of final output by the total units of output *or* by weighting each unit price by the ratio of each good's output to that of total output. The average price of output is $1.84.

(b) The nominal value of final output increases to $766 with the average price of output increasing to $1.99.

(c) Increased spending affects the demand for each good. This increases the outputs of goods A, B, and D without affecting their prices; it increases the prices and outputs for goods C and E. If economic resources were abundant, output should be able to increase without a rise in the supply price of output. It would appear that economic resources were less available to produce more of goods C and E, and their prices increased as a result.

12.9. Suppose an economy's full-employment level of output is $575, the money supply is currently at $250, velocity is 4, the average price of output is $2, and the real level of output is $500. What effect will a 10% increase in the money supply have on the economy's level of real output?

Assuming no change in velocity, the nominal value of final output must increase from $1000 to $1100. $[(M + \Delta M) \cdot V = Y = (\$250 + \$25) \times 4 = \$1100.]$ Without knowledge of the allocation of the increased spending and the ability of producers to meet the increased demand, there is no way of predicting whether the increase in nominal income reflects a rise in prices and /or an increase in real output. Policy makers, therefore, are unable to determine the effect of a stimulative policy upon real output when the economy is near full employment and the policy increases spending in the market.

12.10. Why is cost-push inflation likely to be associated with bottleneck inflation?

As an economy moves toward full employment, some economic resources become fully employed before others, and some producing sectors reach their productive capacity before the full-employment level of output.   Labor unions in these fully employed markets are in a position to use their market power to extract larger wage rate increases than market conditions would dictate.   Firms, enjoying a strong demand for output, are more willing to meet labor demands.   In the absence of excessive demand, unions are able to use their market power to improve wage positions when the economy is still below the full-employment level of income if their specific supply market is at or near full employment.

THE PHILLIPS CURVE

12.11.   (*a*) What does the Phillips curve show?   (*b*) What economic rationale can be advanced to explain the Phillips curve?

    (*a*)   The Phillips curve is derived from observation of wage rate price increases and unemployment rates over time.   Fitted to actual data, the curve shows that low unemployment rates are associated with high inflation rates and high unemployment rates with low inflation rates.   Thus, the goals of maximum employment and price stability appear to be mutually exclusive and necessitate establishment of priorities between the two policy objectives.

    (*b*)   Bottleneck and cost-push inflation are the rationale for a trade-off between full employment and price stability.   Bottlenecks appear before the full-employment level of output and create cost pressures upon the supply price of specific goods and services.   Union power capitalizes upon these developing shortages to push the supply price of specific goods beyond that dictated by market conditions.

12.12.   (*a*) What productivity increases are indicated by the Phillips curve presented in Fig. 12-9?

    (*b*) What would happen to the Phillips curve if the productivity of labor increases from 3% to 4%?

    (*c*) What other factors might cause a shift of the Phillips curve?

    (*d*) What policies might the Federal government adopt to minimize the trade-off between full employment and price stability?

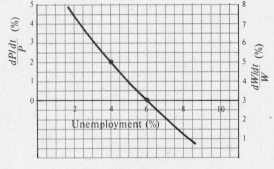

Fig. 12-9

    (*a*)   At the 6% level of unemployment, money wage rates are increasing at a 3% rate and prices are stable; at the 4% level of unemployment, money wage and price increases are 5% and 2% respectively.   The 3% difference between money wage and price increases measures the rate of increase in the average productivity of labor and indicates that businesses are able to absorb a 3% increase in money wages because labor productivity is also increasing 3%.

    (*b*)   If productivity increases to 4%, businesses are able to absorb a 4% increase in money wages with no change in prices.   The Phillips curve shifts downward with a 4% level of unemployment now consistent with a 1% rate of inflation.

    (*c*)   Since the unemployment/inflation rate trade-off is primarily due to bottlenecks and market power, changes in the importance of these factors will result in shifts of the Phillips curve.   For example, if factor markets become technically more specialized, bottlenecks are likely to develop earlier, have a larger effect upon the supply price of output, and bring about a rightward shift of the Phillips curve.   Similarly, the growth in market power of unions and/or businesses increases the likelihood of cost-push inflation and shifts the Phillips curve rightward.   Expectations of increased rates of inflation will also shift the Phillips curve rightward.

    (*d*)   Leftward shifts of the Phillips curve are achieved by the following policies: (1) Reduction in bottlenecks through manpower training programs, improved geographic mobility of factors and elimination of barriers to entry into specific labor markets; (2) reduction in the monopoly power of unions and businesses by more vigorously applying existing antitrust laws; and (3) adoption of an incomes policy in which wage rate and price increases are monitored by the Federal government.

12.13. (*a*) Why might continued inflation shift the Phillips curve upward?   (*b*) What is stagflation?

(*a*)   If individuals believe that high inflation rates are permanent, these inflation rates will be incorporated into the money wage demands of workers in an effort to secure a given real wage. Inflationary expectations shift the Phillips curve upward; the magnitude of the shift is dictated by the expected rate of inflation.

(*b*)   Stagflation consists of simultaneous rising unemployment and high rates of inflation, and is contrary to the apparent trade-off indicated by the Phillips curve.

THE NATURAL RATE OF UNEMPLOYMENT

12.14. (*a*) Why do those who believe in a natural rate of unemployment contend that the Phillips curve is vertical in the long run?   (*b*) Why will attempts to bring the unemployment rate below the natural rate result in accelerating rates of inflation?

(*a*)   The short-run Phillips curve suggests that a movement up the curve will lower unemployment and raise the rate of inflation.   This is true as long as labor fails to secure money wage rate increases to adjust for decreases in the real wage rate brought about by inflation.   Over time, one would expect sustained inflation to be recognized and incorporated into labor's money wage demands.   It is possible that money wage increases might lag inflation or coincide with the rate of inflation.   Those who believe that there is a natural rate of unemployment contend that money wage increases will be tied to inflationary expectations so that there is a high probability that the price expectations of labor and business will coincide.   If their contention is correct, inflation should have no effect upon the real wage and, therefore, not increase the quantity of labor employed.   Thus, in the long run, the Phillips curve is vertical since inflation has no influence upon the employment of labor.

(*b*)   Given the assumption that money wages and price increases coincide in the long run, there is only one equilibrium rate of employment (the natural rate of unemployment) at which the quantity of labor demanded equals the quantity of labor supplied.   Attempts by government to increase employment beyond the equilibrium rate (push unemployment below the natural rate) by increasing aggregate spending will only result in increases in the price level.

12.15.   What explanation do Keynesians offer for the high rates of unemployment and inflation in the United States during the 1970s?

Keynesians have attributed the high rate of inflation and unemployment in the 1970s to an upward shift of the Phillips curve which resulted from a change in the composition of the labor force and inflationary expectations.   Since the 1960s there has been a substantial change in the composition of the United States labor force.   Teenagers and women, who historically have had higher unemployment rates than men and older labor force participants, now represent a much larger proportion of the labor force.   Keynesians have suggested that this structural change has increased the likelihood of bottlenecks, and a given level of unemployment is now associated with a higher rate of inflation than before the change in the composition of the labor force.   Inflationary expectations are also a recognized force that causes an upward shift of the Phillips curve.   Unlike natural rate of unemployment advocates, though, Keynesians suggest that money wage increases lag and/or are below the inflation rate and contend that an unemployment/inflation trade-off still exists.   Keynesians have somewhat moderated their advocacy of very low rates of unemployment because of the harmful effects of the high rates of inflation experienced during the 1970s.

Chapter 13

Economic Growth

13.1 THE DETERMINANTS OF ECONOMIC GROWTH

The employment theory of Chapters 4 through 12 dealt with the utilization of the existing productive capacity of the economy.   Economic growth focuses upon the expansion of productive capacity over time.   An expansion of productive capacity Y_p requires an increase in natural resources R, human resources N, capital K, and/or technological advance T, i.e. $Y_p = f(R, N, K, T)$ (see Problem 13.2).   Economic growth is measured absolutely and relatively by the increase in the economy's real GNP and the increase in its real per capita output (see Problem 13.3).   Graphically, economic growth is shown as an outward shift of the economy's production possibility curve; it is assumed that the increased capacity is matched by a proportional rise in aggregate spending.

EXAMPLE 1. Suppose an economy's production possibility curve is PP' in Fig. 13-1; aggregate spending is composed of OA_0 units of private goods and OB_0 units of public goods.   Assume that a 10% increase in economic resources shifts the production possibility curve to TT' and raises capacity 10%.   If aggregate spending increases 10%, the output of private and public goods would rise to OA_1 and OB_1.

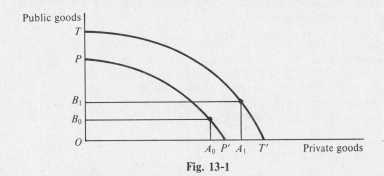

Fig. 13-1

13.2 POPULATION AND ECONOMIC GROWTH

While an economy's absolute productive capacity is directly related to its population size, the law of diminishing returns states that real per capita output will eventually fall if population increases and the quantity of other economic resources remains constant (see Problem 13.5).   Based upon the expectation of rapid population increase, early 19th-century economists predicted that population growth would result in economic stagnation and decline in the long run.   For example, the Malthusian theory of population was that population would increase at a rate faster than an economy's ability to grow food and that real income would fall to the subsistence level (see Problem 13.6).   While the gloomy projections of early 19th-century economists have been avoided by such highly industrialized countries as the United States, rapid population growth is a problem for many underdeveloped areas of the world (see Problem 13.9).

EXAMPLE 2. Suppose that technology and all economic resources but labor are constant over time.   Furthermore, assume that labor increases by 10% in each time period and output grows by 5%, 4% and 3% in successive time periods.   Starting in period t with an initial labor supply of 200 units and $1,000,000 in real output, labor and real output increase to 266 units and $1,124,760, respectively, by period $t + 3$.   As shown in Table 1, labor's more rapid growth causes a decline in output per labor input (output/labor) over the three time periods.   Whenever one economic resource is variable and technology and other economic resources are constant, output *eventually* grows at a rate slower than the rate at which the input of the variable economic resource grows; and per capita output falls.

Table 1

Time Period	Labor (in man-years)	Output (in constant $'s)	Output per Labor Input
t	200	$1,000,000	$5,000.00
$t + 1$	220	1,050,000	4,772.73
$t + 2$	242	1,092,000	4,512.40
$t + 3$	266	1,124,760	4,228.42

13.3   FULL-EMPLOYMENT GROWTH

In the Keynesian model of aggregate spending in Chapter 5, net investment was viewed as a source of demand for a fixed level of potential output.   In Section 13.1, net investment was seen as a source of increased productive capacity since net investment represents an addition to the economy's stock of capital.   In its capacity-creating effect, net investment is continuously raising the level of output and income associated with full employment (see Problem 13.10).   Net investment in its demand-creating role must therefore continuously increase if full-employment growth is to be achieved (see Example 3).   Equilibrium growth is achieved in a private sector ($C + I$) model of the economy by having net investment increase at a rate equal to the marginal propensity to save α times the marginal productivity of capital σ (see Problem 13.12).   Changes in either the marginal propensity to save or the marginal productivity of capital alter the economy's long-run rate of economic growth (see Problem 13.13).

EXAMPLE 3.   Suppose that (1) all economic resources increase proportionally, (2) technology is constant, and (3) aggregate spending consists only of consumption and investment.

In the initial time period t in Fig. 13-2(a), the stock of capital K_0 makes it possible for the economy to produce a Y_0 level of output.   The aggregate spending schedule in Fig. 13-2(b) during period t is initially $C + I_0$ and Y_0 is the equilibrium level of income.   During time period t, the economy's productive capacity Y_0 is fully utilized, i.e. there is full employment.

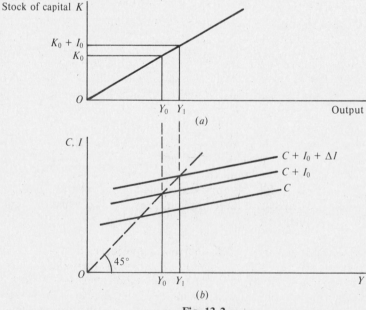

Fig. 13-2

In moving to the next time period $t + 1$, the capital stock increases to $K_0 + I_0$ as a result of net investment I_0 during period t. Potential output in time period $t + 1$ becomes Y_1. If the aggregate spending schedule does not shift upward during period $t + 1$, the equilibrium income will remain at Y_0 and there will be unused productive capacity of $OY_1 - OY_0$. An increase in investment spending of ΔI during period $t + 1$, however, will eliminate the recessionary gap and the economy will remain at full employment.

Net investment must increase at a rate equal to $\alpha\sigma$ in each successive period if the economy is to be continuously at full employment.

13.4 THE DESIRABILITY OF ECONOMIC GROWTH

The analysis of population in Section 13.2 suggests that economic growth is essential. There is, however, a growing debate among scientists and social scientists about the desirability and feasibility of sustained growth. Proponents of growth contend that growth is the best means of raising living standards and reducing poverty. Opponents argue that the costs of growth, such as pollution and a reduction in the quality of life, far outweigh the benefits (see Problem 13.14). Some scientists even see limits to the growth process and predict that per capita output will peak early in the 21st century (see Problem 13.15).

Important Economic Terms

Average productivity of capital.   Total output divided by the stock of capital.

Capital-output ratio.   The ratio of the economy's stock of capital to total output, e.g. a capital-output ratio of 4 indicates that 4 units of capital are used to produce 1 unit of output.

Economic growth.   The increase in an economy's level of output over time, which is generally measured by the absolute or relative increase in GNP or in real per capita output over time.

Full-employment growth.   A situation in which aggregate spending grows at the same rate as potential output and there is full utilization (full employment) of the economy's productive capacity over time.

Law of diminishing returns.   The tendency for incremental output to fall as additional inputs of a variable factor are used with a fixed quantity of other economic resources.

Malthusian theory of population.   The economy's ability to grow food increases at a slower rate than the increase in population size and results in an eventual decrease in the economy's standard of living.

Real per capita output.   Total output (GNP) divided by the total population.

Review Questions

1. There is an increase in the economy's productive capacity if there is (a) an increase in government spending, (b) a decrease in government spending, (c) an increase in the economy's capital stock, (d) an increase in the economy's rate of capital replacement.

    Ans.   (c)

2. There will be an increase in real per capita output if a 10% increase in the labor force is associated with a (a) 10% increase in output, (b) 10% increase in population and a 20% increase in output, (c) 20% increase in population and a 10% increase in output, (d) 10% increase in population and a 10% increase in output.

    Ans.   (b)

3. According to the law of diminishing returns, continuous increases in population size with no change in other resources or technology (a) eventually results in an increase in real per capita output, (b) eventually results in a decrease in real per capita output, (c) will have no effect upon an economy's ability to produce food, (d) eventually reduces an economy's ability to produce food.

    Ans. (b)

4. The Malthusian theory of population predicts that growth in food production will (a) keep up with population growth as a result of technological advance, (b) expand more rapidly than population growth if advanced technology is introduced in developing countries, (c) be at a faster rate than population growth, (d) be at a slower rate than population growth.

    Ans. (d)

5. According to the Malthusian theory of population, in the long run, real per capita income would (a) tend toward the subsistence level, (b) increase at an increasing rate, (c) increase at a decreasing rate, (d) not increase.

    Ans. (a)

6. A constant level of net investment
    (a) expands aggregate spending and aggregate productive capacity,
    (b) expands aggregate spending but has no effect upon aggregate productive capacity,
    (c) expands aggregate productive capacity but has no effect upon aggregate spending,
    (d) has no effect upon aggregate spending and aggregate productive capacity.

    Ans. (c)

7. Net investment must expand continuously in each time period because
    (a) aggregate spending must increase in an expanding economy,
    (b) capital formation is required in an expanding economy,
    (c) worn-out capital must be replaced in an expanding economy,
    (d) it is necessary if technological advance is to be realized.

    Ans. (a)

8. If the stock of capital is $400 and the full-employment level of income is $100, the average productivity of capital is (a) 4, (b) 5, (c) 0.25, (d) 0.20.

    Ans. (c)

9. If the marginal propensity to save is 0.20 and its capital output ratio is 2.0, to maintain full employment, investment must increase at a rate of (a) 4%, (b) 5%, (c) 10%, (d) 20%.

    Ans. (c)

10. Proponents of economic growth contend that growth is the best way (a) to overcome poverty and economic pollution, (b) to improve the quality of life, (c) to create jobs for those who are technologically unemployed, (d) to reduce poverty and raise per capita output.

    Ans. (d)

Solved Problems

THE DETERMINANTS OF ECONOMIC GROWTH

13.1. Compare the focus of national income theory and the theory of economic growth.

National income theory is concerned with short-run aggregate demand; economic growth focuses upon the expansion of aggregate supply over time. National income theory analyzes the determinants and adequacy of aggregate spending and takes as fixed the economy's production capacity. The objective of national income theory is the design of economic policies that will move the economy onto the production possibility curve. Economic growth takes a longer view of the economic process and evaluates the effect of resource growth upon productive capacity, the increase in individuals' standards of living, and the rate at which aggregate demand must increase to achieve maximum growth.   Economic growth analyzes outward shifts of the production possibility curve over time.

13.2.   (*a*) What factors determine an economy's ability to increase its productive capacity?
(*b*) What is the importance of economic growth?

(*a*) An economy's potential output Y_p depends upon the quantity and quality of natural R and human N resources, the stock of capital K, and technology T.   An economy's quantity and quality of natural resources are relatively fixed and are not a major source of increased productive capacity.   However, since some of these resources, such as petroleum deposits, may be undiscovered, natural resources are a source of economic growth when they are discovered.   An increase in an economy's population, in the population's participation in the labor force, and in the number of hours worked and an improvement in its quality expand an economy's productive capacity.   An improved quality of labor, the result of health care, education and training, fosters economic growth because it expands labor's productivity.   Capital formation, the accumulation of factories, machines, etc., is a key element in the growth process.   Through the accumulation of capital, an economy is able to use capital (e.g. a machine) to manufacture goods that labor would be less efficient in producing by itself.   By substituting capital for labor, productive capacity is enhanced since labor resources become available for the output of other goods.   It follows that the larger the accumulation of capital relative to labor (capital-deepening), the more rapid the rate of increase in productive capacity.   Technology is the development and application of new knowledge to enhance the productive process.   It may involve investment in new and more efficient machinery or more efficient ways of combining existing resources.

(*b*) Economic growth is a means of raising society's standard of living (more output per person) and meeting changes in society's demand for goods and services.   Unless productive capacity is expanded (the production possibility curve is shifted outward), the increased output of a good necessitates the decreased output of other goods in a full-employment economy.   Economic growth eliminates the need for the substitution of one good for another and raises society's standard of living.

13.3.   Suppose Country A and Country B experience the growth in real output presented in Table 2. Find each country's
(*a*) relative growth in output between 1955 and 1980,
(*b*) output per capita for 1955 and 1980, and
(*c*) relative growth in output per capita between 1955 and 1980.
(*d*)   Which measure of economic growth is more useful?

Table 2

	1955	1980
Country A Real GNP Population	$650,000,000 166,000	$1,300,000,000 224,000
Country B Real GNP Population	$528,614,000 135,000	$1,295,100,000 270,000

(*a*)   The relative increase in output is found by dividing 1980 output by that for 1955.   The relative increase in Country A's real GNP is 2.0 ($1,300,000,000/$650,000,000).   The relative increase in Country B's real GNP is 2.45 during the same period ($1,295,100,000/$528,614,000).

(*b*)   An economy's real output per capita is found by dividing real GNP by total population.   In Country A, per capita output is $3915.66 ($650,000,000/166,000) in 1955 and $5803.57 in 1980. In Country B, per capita output increased from $3915.66 in 1955 to $4796.67 in 1980.

(c) The relative increase in per capita GNP between 1955 and 1980 is found by dividing per capita output in 1980 by that in 1955. In Country A, the relative increase in per capita GNP is 1.48 while it is 1.22 in Country B.

(d) Economic growth is often measured in terms of the expansion of productive capacity of the economy. While useful, increases in real GNP do not measure the relative change in individual economic well-being, which is best measured by real per capita GNP. Parts (a) through (c) show how these measures of economic growth might differ between two countries. Country A's relative increase in real GNP was slower than B's but on a per capita basis A's relative growth exceeded that of B's. Which measure is more useful depends upon one's objective in measuring growth. If one's point of reference is growth in productive capacity, real (potential) GNP is the better measure. However, if the focus is upon standard of living, real per capita GNP is the better indicator of economic growth.

13.4. Suppose an economy is faced with the production possibility curve PP' in Fig. 13-3. (a) What implication does the selection of point B rather than point A have for the economy's rate of economic growth? (b) Should point B always be preferred to point A?

(a) Net investment is the addition to an economy's capital stock. Point B is the position for a more rapid expansion of capital stock and, therefore, a position for a more rapid rate of economic growth.

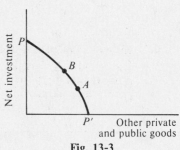

Fig. 13-3

(b) If a society must decide between points B and A, it is being asked to decide whether it wishes to forego present consumption for a more rapid rate of growth *or* have a relatively larger basket of present goods with a slower rate of growth. Individuals are being asked to compare the benefits of higher levels of output in the future with the benefits of a larger basket of goods for current use. The question is not easily resolved. It necessitates a ranking of economic priorities and it is possible that a country may rank current needs above economic growth.

POPULATION AND ECONOMIC GROWTH

13.5. The law of diminishing returns (see Chapter 16) refers to the falling incremental output resulting from the application of successive units of a variable economic resource to fixed quantities of other economic resources. The falling incremental output results in a non-proportional relationship between the variable input and total output; total output increases at a slower rate than the variable input. (a) From Table 3, find the incremental output resulting from the application of additional units of labor to fixed quantities of nonlabor economic resources. (b) At what quantity of labor do diminishing returns begin? (c) From Table 3 find average output per labor input. (d) What changes are there in technology and in the quantity of nonlabor economic resources in Table 3's schedule of output? (e) If column (1) represents the economy's total population and column (2) constant dollar GNP, what is happening to per capita income as the population expands?

(a) Total output increases from $800,000 to $809,000 as a result of increasing labor from 100 units to 101 units. By adding one labor input to 100 units of labor, output is increased by $9000. The incremental outputs from additional labor inputs are presented in column (3).

(b) Diminishing returns are evidenced throughout the production schedule since incremental output falls from $9000 to $3000.

(c) Average output per labor input is found by dividing total output by total labor inputs. The average output is $8,000 when 100 units of labor produce an $800,000 output. Average output per labor input is presented in column (4).

(d) Technology and nonlabor economic resources are assumed to be constant as labor units are added.

Table 3

(1) Variable Factor Labor (in man-years)	(2) Total Output (in constant $'s)	(3) Added Output from Additional Unit of Labor	(4) Average Output per Labor Input
100	$800,000		$8,000.00
101	809,000	$9,000	8,009.90
102	817,500	8,500	8,014.71
103	825,000	7,500	8,009.71
104	832,000	7,000	8,000.00
105	838,000	6,000	7,980.95
106	843,000	5,000	7,952.83
107	847,000	4,000	7,915.89
108	850,000	3,000	7,870.37

(e) Per capita income is falling.   If an economy's nonlabor economic resources remain constant and there is no technological advance, increases in population cause the standard of living of the country to fall.

13.6. In the early 19th century Thomas Malthus theorized that the population would grow at a rate faster than the rate at which the economy could increase its production of food.
(a) Use the law of diminishing returns to explain Malthus's position.
(b) What projections would one make about living standards if one accepted Malthus's theory of population and food production?
(c) Is it possible to postpone Malthus's dismal prediction?

(a) Malthus's theory of population and food production is simply an application of the law of diminishing returns to the production of food.   When labor inputs are continuously added to a fixed quantity of land, the incremental output of food will eventually fall.   If the marginal output of food is falling, the rate of population growth exceeds the rate of increase in the production of food, and the average output of food per unit of labor input falls.
(b) If the average output of food per unit of labor input falls, each household will possess decreasing quantities of food over time.   Lower income households will be pushed toward a subsistence diet; starvation will eventually check the population expansion and leave lower income households with a very low standard of living.
(c) Malthus's application of the law of diminishing returns to the production of food assumes a constant state of technology and no increases in economic resources other than labor.   If farmable land increases in proportion to the growth of population, food output should increase proportionately and there should be no decrease in average farm output.   On the other hand, new technology such as crop rotation, fertilizers, etc. should increase the productivity of land and raise the average output of food per unit of labor input.   Thus, the postponement of Malthus's dismal prediction depends upon technological advance outracing population growth.

13.7. In the average output curve in Fig. 13-4, technology and nonlabor economic resources are assumed to be constant.   (a) Why is OP the economy's optimum population?   (b) What should happen to the optimum population if there is technological advance and/or an increase in economic resources?

(a) OP is the optimum population because this population size maximizes output per person and the standard of living for individuals in the economy.   A population less or greater than OP results in a lower standard of living.
(b) As technological improvements are introduced and/or the quantity or quality of nonlabor economic resources expands, the output curve shifts upward and to the right.   The optimum population occurs at a population size greater than OP and output per person is greater than OS.

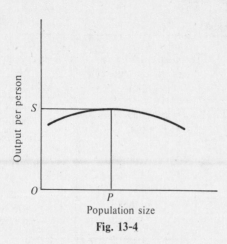

Fig. 13-4

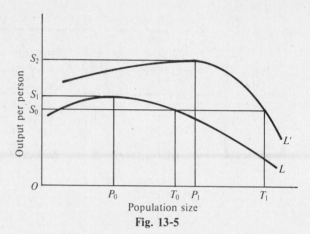

Fig. 13-5

13.8. Suppose an economy initially has a population of OT_0 and the average output curve is L in Fig. 13-5. (*a*) Comment on the economy's population size. (*b*) Suppose that through technological advance and an expansion of economic resources, the average output curve shifts upward to L' and population increases to OT_1. What has happened to the standard of living in this economy? (*c*) What might this country have done to raise its standard of living?

(*a*) The economy's population OT_0 is beyond the OP_0 optimum population and the law of diminishing returns has adversely affected output per person. Individuals in the economy have a standard of living which is lower than if population size had been limited to OP_0.

(*b*) With population expanding to OT_1, output per person has remained at OS_0. There is no change in the standard of living in this economy.

(*c*) There is a good reason to slow down the economy's rate of population growth. If the population expansion could have been limited to OP_1-OT_0, output per person and the standard of living would have risen from OS_0 to OS_2.

13.9. Why are high rates of population growth deterrents to economic growth in many underdeveloped countries?

Many underdeveloped countries can be characterized as follows: The country's economic resources are devoted primarily to the production of food; the quality of the labor force is generally poor and illiteracy is widespread; many families are near or at the subsistence standard of living; capital is scarce relative to labor; malnutrition, disease, and a high infant-mortality rate keep the population from increasing at even faster rates. Given these characteristics, rapid population growth combined with inefficient production techniques and a scarcity of capital prevent output per person from increasing and the average output curve of Problems 13.7 and 13.8 does not shift upward. If population increased more slowly, the capital/labor mix and the quality of the labor force would improve and the result would be more rapid increases in per capita output and the economy's standard of living.

FULL-EMPLOYMENT GROWTH

13.10. Suppose that (1) the increase in all economic resources is proportional, (2) technology is constant, and (3) aggregate spending consists only of consumption and investment.
(*a*) Referring to Fig. 13-6, explain what happens to the economy's potential output if capital increases from K_0 to $2K_0$ to $3K_0$.
(*b*) Net investment is one of the components of aggregate spending. With reference to Fig. 13-7, what effect does continuous net investment of I_0 have upon the full-employment level of income?

(*a*) By assumption, all economic resources increase proportionately and there is no change in technology. A doubling of the stock of capital (and, therefore of labor and natural resources) will

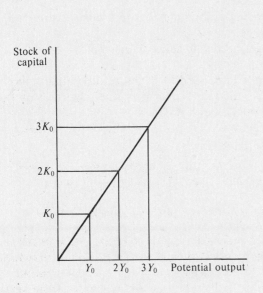

Fig. 13-6

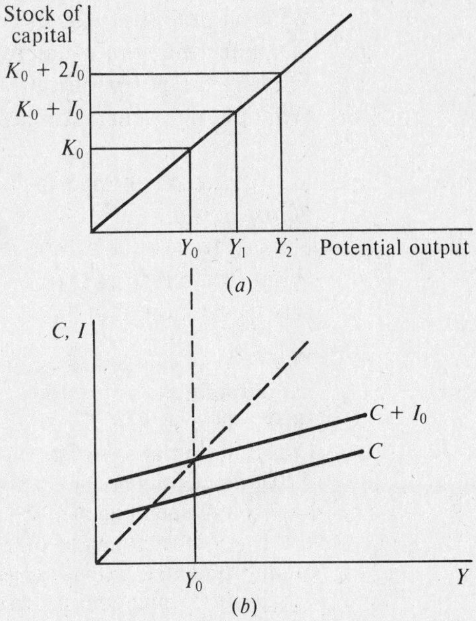

Stock of capital $K_0 + 2I_0$, $K_0 + I_0$, K_0 — Y_0 Y_1 Y_2 Potential output — (a)

C, I — $C + I_0$ — C — Y_0 — Y — (b)

Fig. 13-7

double potential output.   In Fig. 13-6, as capital increases from K_0 to $2K_0$ to $3K_0$, potential output increases from Y_0 to $2Y_0$ to $3Y_0$.

(b) Net investment expands the economy's productive capacity and raises the level of income at which there is full employment.   For example, suppose that in time period t productive capacity is Y_0 [Fig. 13-7(a)] and that the spending schedule $C + I_0$ given in Fig. 13-7(b) results in equilibrium at full employment.   Continuous net investment I_0 expands productive capacity to Y_1 in period $t + 1$ and to Y_2 in period $t + 2$ [Fig. 13-7(a)].   If the aggregate spending schedule ($C + I_0$) does not shift upward, the equilibrium level of income remains at Y_0 as the full-employment level of output increases to Y_1 during period $t + 1$ and to Y_2 in period $t + 2$.

13.11. Suppose that (1) the increase in all economic resources is proportional, (2) technology is constant, and (3) aggregate spending consists only of consumption and investment.
   (a) Assume that the stock of capital is initially $400 and potential output is $100.   What effect will increasing the stock of capital to the following amounts have upon potential output?   (1) $440, (2) $480, (3) $520.
   (b) From the data in part (a), find the economy's capital-output ratio and the average productivity of capital.

   (a) Given the assumption of proportional increases in all economic resources, a 10% increase in the stock of capital ($400 to $440) will increase potential output 10% ($100 to $110).   Since each situation represents a $40 increase in the stock of capital, productive capacity should increase $10 in each period.   Thus, potential output should increase from $100 to (1) $110 to (2) $120 to (3) $130.
   (b) By definition, the capital-output ratio is the relationship of the stock of capital to potential output (K/Y).   The capital-output ratio is 4 ($400/$100).   The average productivity of capital, by definition, is the ratio of potential output to the stock of capital (Y/K).   The average productivity of capital is 0.25 ($100/$400).

13.12. Suppose that (1) the increase in all economic resources is proportional, (2) technology is constant, (3) aggregate spending consists only of consumption and investment, (4) the marginal and average propensity to consume is 0.80, (5) the average and marginal productivity of capital is 0.25, and (6) during time period t the stock of capital is $800, consumption spending is $160 and net investment is $40.

(a)   What is potential output during period t?

(b)   Compare the sum of aggregate spending and potential output during period t.

(c)   What is the potential output during period $t + 1$?

(d)   What change in investment spending is needed to achieve full employment during period $t + 1$?

(e)   What rate of change in investment was needed to generate full employment during period $t + 1$?   Compare this rate to the rate found by multiplying the marginal propensity to save α by the marginal productivity of capital σ.

(f)   What is the rate of change in income from period t to $t + 1$?   What is the economy's rate of economic growth?

(a)   The stock of capital and marginal productivity of capital are $800 and 0.25, respectively.   Potential output equals the stock of capital times the average productivity of capital.   Thus, $Y_p = \$800 \times 0.25 = \$200$.

(b)   Consumption and investment spending are $160 and $40, respectively.   Aggregate spending ($200) equals the economy's potential output.

(c)   Investment spending of $40 during period t causes the capital stock to increase to $840 by period $t + 1$.   Since potential output equals the stock of capital times the average productivity of capital, potential output increases to $210 ($Y_p = \$840 \times 0.25$).

(d)   Aggregate spending must increase $10 during period $t + 1$.   The required change in investment is found by solving $\Delta Y = k_e \Delta I$ for ΔI.   (Review Chapter 5.)   Since $k_e = 5\,[k_e = 1/(1 - MPC)]$, investment spending must increase $2 to increase aggregate spending by $10 ($\Delta Y = k_e \Delta I = 5 \times \$2$).

(e)   The rate of change in investment spending is found by dividing the change in investment in period $t + 1$ by the amount of investment spending during period t.   Thus, $\Delta I/I = \$2/\$40 = 0.05 = 5\%$.   We also obtain a 5% rate by multiplying the marginal propensity to save α by the marginal productivity of capital σ ($0.20 \times 0.25 = 0.05 = 5\%$).

(f)   The rate of change in income is found by dividing the change in income in period $t + 1$ by the level of income during period t.   By dividing $10 by the $200 level of income during period t, we find that income increased at a 5% rate ($\Delta Y/Y = \$10/\$200 = 0.05 = 5\%$).

13.13.   An economy's rate of economic growth depends upon its marginal propensity to save α and marginal productivity of capital σ.   (a) What is an economy's rate of economic growth if (1) $\alpha = 0.10$ and $\sigma = 0.25$, (2) $\alpha = 0.20$ and $\sigma = 0.25$, (3) $\alpha = 0.20$ and $\sigma = .30$?   (b) What might an economy do to increase its rate of economic growth?

(a)   An economy's rate of economic growth is the product of α and σ.   Thus economic growth in situation (1) is 2.5% ($\alpha \cdot \sigma = 0.10 \times 0.25$); it is 5% in situation (2) and 6% in situation (3).

(b)   An economy's growth rate is increased by increasing the rate of saving and improving the productivity of capital.   While tax credits and low interest rates stimulate capital formation, technological advance is needed to make capital more productive.   Unfortunately, government does not have available measures that directly bear upon technological advance.   In a market economy, saving is encouraged by tax incentives that encourage postponement of consumption.

THE DESIRABILITY OF ECONOMIC GROWTH

13.14.   What are the principal objections to economic growth?

Some economists find economic growth objectionable because of its effect upon the quality of life, pollution of the environment, waste of natural resources, and its failure to resolve socioeconomic problems.   E. J. Mishan has been a leading critic of economic growth and contends that man has become enslaved by technology.   Rapid technological change has increased the rate of human obsolescence, brought with it new anxieties and insecurity, and has undermined the family structure.   Although attempts are being made to curb pollution, industrial waste is a by-product of production.   It therefore can be expected that water, land and air pollution will increase in magnitude over time.   Waste of economic resources is also a product of a high output economy where least-cost methods dictate current resource use and little attention is paid to the possible effect that current use may have upon future generations.   Antigrowth economists also argue that growth does not resolve such socio-economic problems as poverty.   The poverty level is relative to an economy's standard of living. Growth does not resolve the problem of relative poverty, which can be eliminated only by a redistribution of current income.

13.15.   What is the basis for the prediction that there may be a limit to economic growth?

Dire predictions for the 21st century are based upon a model of the world in which trends in world population, industrialization, food production, resource depletion, the supply of natural resources, capital per worker and technology are fixed.   The model predicts that if 20th century growth trends continue, the 21st century will be one of decline.   This fixed technology, resource availability model shows that output per person will peak during the early 21st century and then fall by the end of the century to a level equivalent to the one that existed in the early 20th century.   A model that allows for productivity increases and technological advance postpones the peaking of output per person but results in eventual economic collapse before the end of the 21st century.   These doomsday models suggest that one cannot postpone forever the eventual decline of the world's standard of living envisioned by Malthus.   Obviously, current living standards could be sustained if economies would adopt policies of zero economic and population growth.

Final Examination— Macroeconomics

1.   (a) What is the equation of exchange?   Why is it a tautology?
       (b) Explain how the quantity theory of money is developed from the equation of exchange.
       (c) Suppose the money supply is currently $200 and V is 5.   What is the nominal level of income?   What should be the effect of a 5% increase in the money supply according to the rigid and flexible versions of the quantity theory of money?

2.   (a) Explain the following terms: actual reserves, required reserves and excess reserves.
       (b) Suppose the actual reserves of a commercial bank total $200, the reserve requirement on demand deposits is 0.20 and the commercial bank's demand-deposit liability is $800.   Find the commercial bank's required reserves and excess reserves.   What is the potential expansion of demand deposits for this commercial bank?
       (c) Suppose the commercial banking system holds excess reserves of $40.   What is the banking system's potential for increasing demand deposits?   Why is there a difference in the demand-deposit expansion for a commercial bank and the commercial banking system?
       (d) Suppose the change in the money supply is specified as $\Delta M = \Delta B \left(\dfrac{1 + c}{r + c} \right)$ where c, the currency ratio, is 0.05 and r, the reserve requirement on demand deposits, is 0.20. What effect will a $100 increase in reserves have upon the money supply?   If people do not hold additional currency balances when demand deposits increase (i.e. $c = 0$), what effect will a $100 increase in reserves have upon the money supply?

3.   (a) Suppose the commercial banking system's reserve holdings total $250, loans are $750, demand deposits equal $1000, and the reserve requirement on demand deposits is 0.25.   Using "T" accounts for the commercial banking system and the Federal Reserve, show how the Federal Reserve can increase demand deposits $250 by (1) a change in the reserve requirement or (2) open-market operations.
       (b) Suppose the commercial banking system holds $300 in reserves, loans total $1200, demand deposits equal $1500, and the reserve requirement on demand deposits is 0.20.   Show the following events through "T" accounts for households and the commercial banking system: (1) Households increase their holding of currency $20 by withdrawing funds from their demand-deposit account.   (2) The commercial banking system retires loans to cover the reserve loss that results from transaction (1).
       (c) What is the difference between dynamic and defensive open-market operations?

4.   (a) What are the Keynesian and monetarist views on how money supply changes affect the level of nominal income?
       (b) What are the monetarist and Keynesian views on the demand for money and the predictability of changes in the money supply?
       (c) What other differences do monetarists and Keynesians have regarding the formulation of economic policy?

5.   (*a*) Suppose an economy's aggregate demand and aggregate supply schedules are D' and S'. Explain why successive rightward shifts of the aggregate demand schedule will cause the price level to rise prior to y_f, the full-employment level of income.

   (*b*) What is a Phillips curve? How has this curve influenced the formulation of economic policy?

   (*c*) Why do economists suggest that the long-run relationship between prices and unemployment is different from the one found in the short run? What is the nature of this long-run relationship?

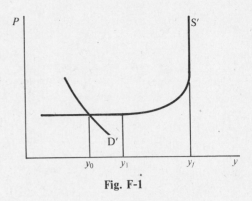

Fig. F-1

6.   (*a*) What was the basis for 19th century economists' predictions that population growth would lead to stagnation and economic decline? Why have their projections not been fulfilled in the industrialized nations of the world?

   (*b*) Why does net investment have both a capacity-creating effect and a demand effect? What determines an economy's potential rate of economic growth? How can this rate of economic growth be increased?

   (*c*) Why have some individuals viewed economic growth as undesirable?

Answers

1.   (*a*) The equation of exchange equates the quantity of M times its velocity V of circulation with the average price P of final goods and services times the quantity Q of final goods and services produced, i.e. $M \cdot V = P \cdot Q$ or $M \cdot V = Y$. This equation specifies that the amount spent on goods and services $(M \cdot V)$ is equal to the nominal value received from final output $(P \cdot Q)$. The equation of exchange is a tautology (a truism) as a result of the way the terms are defined since *ex post* the amount spent $(M \cdot V)$ must always equal the amount received $(P \cdot Q)$.

   (*b*) The quantity theory of money is developed from the equation of exchange by specifying behavior about the variables in the equation. For example, it could be assumed that V is constant, determined by the technical conditions of exchange and unrelated to money supply changes, and that Q is constant when the economy is at full employment. It is then possible to theorize about the effect of money supply changes.

   (*c*) When M is $200 and V is 5, the nominal level of income is $1000. The rigid version of the quantity theory of money asserts that money supply changes have a proportional effect upon the price level; the flexible version of the quantity theory of money does not assume full employment (a fixed Q) and thereby holds that money supply changes affect Y, the nominal value of final output. According to the rigid version of the quantity theory of money, then, a 5% increase in the money supply will cause a 5% increase in P, the average price of output; the flexible version predicts that the 5% increase in the money supply will cause the nominal value of final output to increase 5% (by $50) to a level of $1050.

2.   (*a*) Actual reserves equal a commercial bank's holdings of liquid assets that have been designated reserves by the central bank. Required reserves is the amount of reserves that the commercial bank is required to hold; this sum is found by multiplying the reserve requirement by the quantity of demand deposits issued by the commercial bank. Excess reserves is the difference between required and actual reserves and is found by subtracting a commercial bank's required reserves from its holdings of actual reserves.

   (*b*) With a demand-deposit liability of $800 and a 0.20 reserve requirement on demand deposits, the commercial bank's required reserves is $160. Excess reserves total $40, the difference between actual reserves ($200) and required reserves ($160).   Since a commercial bank will not expand loans and demand deposits by more than the quantity of excess reserves held, the commercial bank's potential for expanding demand deposits is $40.

(c)   A commercial banking system's potential expansion of demand deposits is the amount of excess reserves held divided by the reserve requirement.   If the commercial banking system is holding $40 in excess reserves, demand-deposit volume could increase $200 ($40/0.20).   A commercial bank will expand demand deposits by no more than the amount of excess reserves held because there is a high probability that newly created demand deposits will result in a loss of reserves to another commercial bank.   For example, a commercial bank that holds $40 in excess reserves is likely to lose these reserves to another commercial bank because a check may be issued to someone who has a demand-deposit account with another commercial bank.   If there is no reserve loss from the banking system and each bank expands demand deposits by the amount of its excess reserves, reserve changes will result in a multiple change in the quantity of demand deposits.

(d)   When $c = 0.05$, the change in the money supply is $420 [$\Delta M = \$100(1.05/0.25)$]. If $c = 0$, the change in the money supply would equal $500 [$\Delta M = \$100(1/0.20)$].   Thus, the effect that a change in reserves has upon the money supply depends upon the amount of additional currency balances households wish to hold as demand deposits expand; the larger the currency ratio, the smaller the effect that a given change in reserves has upon the quantity of money.

3.   (a)   (1) By reducing the reserve requirement on demand deposits from 0.25 to 0.20, the commercial banking system's excess reserve position changes from 0 when $r = 0.25$ (0.25 times a demand-deposit volume of $1000 equals $250 in required reserves) to $50 when $r = 0.20$ (0.20 times a demand-deposit volume of $1000 equals $200 in required reserves).   When the commercial banking system holds $50 in excess reserves, the potential increase in demand deposits is $250. A lowering of the reserve requirement from 0.25 to 0.20 can increase demand deposits $250; this is accomplished without a change in a Federal Reserve asset or liability account.
(2) Maintaining a reserve requirement of 0.25, the Federal Reserve can bring about a $250 increase in demand deposits by purchasing government securities valued at $62.50 from households.   The $62.50 purchase of government securities increases households' demand deposits at commercial banks, and increases the commercial banking system's excess reserves $46.875.   Potential loan and demand-deposit expansion is $187.50; this increase and the deposits created by purchase of government securities result in a $250 increase in the volume of demand deposits.

COMMERCIAL BANKING SYSTEM

	Assets		Liabilities		
(1)	Loans	+$250.00	Demand deposits	+$250.00	(1)
(2)	Reserve deposit at the Federal Reserve	+$ 62.50	Demand deposits of Households	+$ 62.50	(2)
	Loans	+$187.50	Demand deposits	+$187.50	

FEDERAL RESERVE

	Assets		Liabilities		
(2)	Government securities	+$ 62.50	Reserve deposit of commercial banks	+$ 62.50	(2)

(b)   (1) When households withdraw funds from their checking accounts to increase their currency holdings by $20, there is no net change in the asset and liability accounts of households but there is a $20 increase in the commercial banking system's reserve and demand-deposit accounts. The commercial banking system now has a $16 reserve deficiency, assuming that it previously held no excess reserves.   (Note that required reserves decrease $4 when the banking system's liability account decreases $20.   The $20 reserve loss less the $4 decrease in required reserves results in a $16 reserve deficiency.)
(2) Since the commercial banking system has a $16 reserve deficiency, it must contract loans and demand deposits by $80 to return its excess reserve position to 0.

HOUSEHOLDS

Assets		Liabilities
(1) { Demand Deposit	−$20	
Currency	+$20	

COMMERCIAL BANKING SYSTEM

Assets			Liabilities
(1)	Reserves (Currency)	−$20	Demand Deposits	−$20
(2)	Loans	−$80	Demand Deposits	−$80

(c) Defensive open-market operations are purchases or sales of government securities by the Federal Reserve to prevent factors such as an increase in currency in circulation from bringing about a decrease in commercial bank reserves. For example, in part (b), the Federal Reserve could have purchased government securities valued at $20 and thereby prevented commercial bank reserves from falling $20. Dynamic open-market operations are Federal Reserve purchases and sales of government securities to change the level of commercial bank reserves and thereby change the volume of demand deposits.

4. (a) In a Keynesian model, an increase in the money supply lowers the rate of interest; this reduced borrowing cost raises investment spending, which causes a multiple increase in the level of income. Monetarists view money as one of many assets households and businesses hold in a portfolio of assets. Any change in its quantity affects the demand for other assets in the portfolio. Thus, an increase in the money supply raises the demand for other assets; this increases the amount spent on capital investment, consumer durable goods, residential housing and a host of other private sector goods and services.

(b) Monetarists consider money unique and hold that its demand is stable and insensitive to the rate of interest. Keynesians contend that money has many close substitutes, and that the demand for money is variable. Given these views, monetarists argue that the velocity of money is stable and predictable; Keynesians believe that V is variable. Monetary policy has a predictable effect upon the nominal level of income according to the monetarists; Keynesians suggest that the effect of money supply changes is variable.

(c) The monetarists are politically "conservative" while the Keynesians are "liberal"; they also disagree about the strength and usefulness of fiscal policy and the impact of discretionary monetary management. Monetarists consider the market the best allocator of resources and output. Since monetary policy affects spending through the market, money supply changes are considered the best policy variable. Keynesians, however, see a need for government interference to overcome problems of social imbalance and the unequal distribution of income. Such objectives can be promoted by tax and/or government spending changes while the government is also trying to stabilize the level of income. Monetarists contend that fiscal measures are weak; they argue that stimulative fiscal measures force up the rate of interest and "crowd out" private investment. While objecting to the use of fiscal policy, monetarists do not advocate discretionary monetary management; their empirical studies have suggested that the Federal Reserve's discretionary management of the money supply has aggravated rather than moderated economic fluctuations.

5. (a) Beyond output level y_1, bottlenecks exist and further expansion of output is possible only if there is an increase in the average price of output. Bottlenecks represent inadequate supplies of specific resources and/or materials in a market economy that is below the full-employment level of income. Such shortages develop in a market economy as a result of specialized economic resources, geographical immobility of labor and/or the uneven distribution of increases in the demand for goods and services. For example, at output y_1, industry A may be operating at full capacity. Further increases in output are possible if additional workers who are less efficient are hired or if current workers work overtime; both measures would result in increased costs and necessitate that the good be sold at a higher price. Thus, an expansion of aggregate demand beyond y_1 necessitates price increases in some supply sectors because some producers are unable

to supply additional quantities without raising prices since labor and/or material shortages have developed in their industry.

(b) The Phillips curve is a line representing an economy's past relationship between the rate of change in prices and the rate of unemployment. Over time, the rate of inflation has had an inverse relationship with the rate of unemployment. Policy makers have inferred from this curve that there is a trade-off between full employment and price stability; in the 1960s they instituted expansionary policies that would lower the rate of unemployment but increase the rate of inflation. It was reasoned that the benefits of a higher rate of employment exceeded the costs of creeping inflation.

(c) Economists now recognize that the empirical relationship between the rate of inflation and the rate of unemployment is not immutable, and that the Phillips curve is subject to shifts over time. For example, if unexpected price increases occur, workers will seek to recover this lost purchasing power by raising their demand for nominal wages; such actions will shift the Phillips curve upward. If there is continuous inflation, some economists have argued that labor will base wage demands upon expected inflation rates which will probably coincide with the price expectations of businessmen; the result is that the rate of unemployment can no longer be pushed below a natural rate of unemployment and a vertical long-run Phillips curve evolves. Keynesians disagree with the contention that the Phillips curve is vertical in the long run. They argue that money-wage increases always lag and/or are below the inflation rate. Thus, while they admit that the Phillips curve is steeper in the long run than it is in the short run, they believe that a trade-off between inflation and unemployment exists even in the long run and that policy makers must weigh the benefits of maximum employment and the cost of inflation in formulating economic policy.

6. (a) Nineteenth-century economists analyzed population growth in terms of the law of diminishing returns. According to this law, the application of successive units of a variable economic resource to a fixed quantity of another resource causes total output to increase at a slower rate than the rate of increase of the variable input. Thus, with a fixed quantity of land, population growth would exceed the rate of increase in the production of food; the average output of food per unit of labor input would fall over time. The industrialized nations of the world have been able to escape these dire predictions by the introduction of new technology. Through hybrid seeds, crop rotation and fertilizers, industrialized nations have been able to expand food production to meet the demands of a growing population.

(b) Net investment is one of the components of aggregate demand in the Keynesian ($Y = C + I + G$) approach to income determination. Net investment, by definition, represents additions to the economy's stock of capital. Thus, net investment has a dual effect; it is a source of demand for output but in purchasing additional plant and equipment, net investment adds to the economy's stock of capital. Growth in productive capacity, therefore, depends upon additions to the economy's stock of capital (net investment) and the productivity of this capital. Since an economy must save, for net investment to occur, the economy's potential rate of growth depends upon the economy's rate of saving α and the productivity of capital additions σ, i.e. $\Delta Y/Y = \alpha\sigma$. An economy can increase its rate of economic growth by raising the rate of saving and/or by increasing the productivity of capital additions.

(c) Opponents of economic growth contend that the costs of economic growth exceed the benefits. They argue that the primacy of least-cost methods of production is harmful to workers, the environment and the conservation of resources in the long run. Rapid technological advances increase the rate of human obsolescence and generate anxiety and insecurity. Higher output levels generate greater quantities of industrial waste and more pollution. In using least-cost methods of production, businesses ignore the effect that current resource use has upon the availability of resources for future generations. It is also pointed out that the existence of poverty is not resolved by economic growth. An economy's poverty level is relative to the economy's standard of living; a redistribution of income must occur with economic growth if economic poverty is to be reduced.

Chapter 14

Demand, Supply and Elasticity

14.1 DEMAND, SUPPLY AND MARKET PRICE

In Section 2.1, we introduced the concepts of *demand schedule* and *demand curve,* and in Section 2.2, the *supply schedule* and *supply curve.* Then, in Section 2.3, we brought together demand and supply and showed how the *equilibrium market price and quantity* are determined in a free-enterprise system. After briefly reviewing these basic concepts, this chapter extends our discussion to the concept and measurement of elasticities of demand and supply and shows their usefulness with some applications.

EXAMPLE 1. Table 1 gives a hypothetical market demand and supply schedule for wheat; it shows whether a surplus or shortage occurs at each price and the pressure on price toward equilibrium.

Table 1

Price ($ per bu.)	Quantity Demanded in the Market (1000 bu. per mo.)	Quantity Supplied in the Market (1000 bu. per mo.)	Surplus (+) or Shortage (−)	Pressure on Price
$4	2.0	7.0	+5	downward
3	3.0	6.0	+3	downward
2	4.5	4.5	0	equilibrium
1	6.5	2.5	−4	upward

The market demand and supply schedules of Table 1 are plotted in Fig. 14-1. The figure shows that at the prices of $4 and $3, a surplus results which drives the price down. At the price of $1, a shortage results which drives the price up. Thus, the equilibrium price is $2 because the quantity demanded of 4500 bushels of wheat per month equals the quantity supplied.

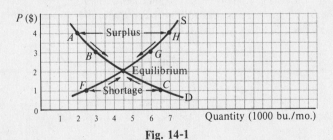

Fig. 14-1

14.2 ELASTICITY OF DEMAND

The *elasticity of demand* (E_D) measures the percentage change in the quantity demanded of a commodity as a result of a given percentage change in its price. The formula is

$$E_D = \frac{\text{percentage change in the quantity demanded}}{\text{percentage change in price}}$$

$$= \frac{\text{change in quantity demanded}}{\text{original quantity demanded}} \div \frac{\text{change in price}}{\text{original price}}$$

179

E_D can also be calculated in terms of the *new* quantity and *new* price; however, different results would then be obtained.   To avoid this problem, economists generally measure E_D in terms of the average quantity and the average price, as follows:

$$E_D = \frac{\text{change in quantity demanded}}{\text{sum of quantities demanded}/2} \div \frac{\text{change in price}}{\text{sum of prices}/2}$$

E_D is a pure number.   As such, it is a better measurement tool than the slope, which is always expressed in terms of the units of measurement [see Problem 14.3(*d*)].   Also, E_D is always expressed as a positive number, even though price and quantity demanded move in opposite directions.   The demand curve is said to be elastic if $E_D > 1$, unitary elastic if $E_D = 1$, and inelastic if $E_D < 1$.

EXAMPLE 2.   The elasticity between points A and B along the demand curve of Fig. 14-1 is calculated below, using the original, new and average quantities and prices.

$$E_D = \frac{\text{change in quantity}}{\text{original quantity}} \div \frac{\text{change in price}}{\text{original price}} = \frac{1}{2} \div \frac{1}{4} = \frac{1}{2} \times \frac{4}{1} = \frac{4}{2} = 2$$

$$= \frac{\text{change in quantity}}{\text{new quantity}} \div \frac{\text{change in price}}{\text{new price}} = \frac{1}{3} \div \frac{1}{3} = \frac{1}{3} \times \frac{3}{1} = \frac{3}{3} = 1$$

$$= \frac{\text{change in quantity}}{\text{sum of quantities}/2} \div \frac{\text{change in price}}{\text{sum of prices}/2} = \frac{1}{(2+3)/2} \div \frac{1}{(4+3)/2} = \frac{1}{2.5} \div \frac{1}{3.5} = \frac{1}{2.5} \times \frac{3.5}{1} = \frac{3.5}{2.5} = 1.4$$

By convention, we use the last result and say that this demand curve is elastic (on the average) between points A and B.   The student should check to see that between B and E, (average) $E_D = 1$.

14.3   ELASTICITY AND TOTAL REVENUE

When the price of a commodity falls, the total revenue of producers (price times quantity) increases if $E_D > 1$, remains unchanged if $E_D = 1$ and decreases if $E_D < 1$.   This is because when $E_D > 1$, the percentage increase in quantity exceeds the percentage *decline* in price and so total revenue (TR) increases.   When $E_D = 1$, the percentage increase in quantity equals the percentage decline in price and so TR remains unchanged.   Finally, when $E_D < 1$, the percentage increase in quantity is less than the percentage decline in price and so TR falls.

We can also say that as price falls, demand is elastic, unitary elastic or inelastic depending on whether total revenue rises, remains unchanged or declines, respectively.

EXAMPLE 3.   According to the total revenue rule, the market demand curve of Fig. 14-1 is shown in Table 2 to be elastic between points A and B, unitary elastic between B and E and inelastic between E and C (see also Example 2 and Review Question 5).

Table 2

Point	P (in \$)	QD (in thousands)	TR (in thousand \$)	E_D
A	\$4	2.0	\$8.0	elastic
B	3	3.0	9.0	unitary
E	2	4.5	9.0	inelastic
C	1	6.5	6.5	

The elasticity of demand is greater (1) the greater the number of good substitutes available, (2) the greater the proportion of income spent on the commodity, and (3) the longer the period of time considered.

14.4   ELASTICITY OF SUPPLY

The *elasticity of supply* (E_S) measures the percentage change in the quantity *supplied* of a commodity as a result of a given percentage change in its price.   As in the case of elasticity of demand, we get different values for the elasticity of supply if we use the original or the new price and quantity.   To avoid this problem, we again use the average quantity and price as follows:

$$E_S = \frac{\text{change in quantity supplied}}{\text{sum of quantities supplied}/2} \div \frac{\text{change in price}}{\text{sum of prices}/2}$$

E_S is a pure number and is positive because price and quantity move in the same direction.   Supply is said to be elastic if $E_S > 1$, unitary elastic if $E_S = 1$, and inelastic if $E_S < 1$.

EXAMPLE 4.   The (average) elasticity between points F and E along the supply curve of Fig. 14-1 is

$$E_S = \frac{2}{(2.5 + 4.5)/2} \div \frac{1}{(1 + 2)/2} = \frac{1}{3.5} \div \frac{1}{1.5} = \frac{1}{3.5} \times \frac{1.5}{1} = \frac{1.5}{3.5} \approx 0.43.$$

The student should check to see that between E and G, $E_S = \dfrac{3.75}{5.25} \approx 0.71$.   Thus, the supply curve of Fig. 14-1 is inelastic between F and G.   The supply curve becomes more elastic, the longer the time period under consideration (see Problem 14.13).

14.5   APPLICATIONS OF ELASTICITY

The concept of elasticity has many useful applications.   It tells us whether the price of a subway or taxi ride should be increased or decreased in order to increase total revenue, and it explains why farmers' income often rises in bad harvests (see Problem 14.14).   It shows that the more inelastic the demand for a commodity, the greater the burden (or incidence) on consumers of a per-unit tax collected from producers (see Problem 14.15).   On the other hand, for a given demand, the more elastic the supply, the greater the incidence of the tax on consumers (see Problem 14.16).   Elasticity can also help the government determine the relative cost of various alternative farm-aid programs (see Problem 14.17).

Important Economic Terms

Elasticity of demand (E_D).   The measurement of the (average) percentage change in the quantity demanded of a commodity as a result of a given (average) percentage change in its price, expressed as a positive pure number.   Demand is said to be elastic, unitary elastic and inelastic if $E_D > 1$, $E_D = 1$, $E_D < 1$, respectively.

Elasticity of supply (E_S).   The measurement of the (average) percentage change in the quantity supplied of a commodity as a result of a given (average) percentage change in its price, expressed as a positive pure number.   Supply is elastic, unitary elastic, or inelastic, if $E_S > 1$, $E_S = 1$, $E_S < 1$, respectively.

Equilibrium.   The market condition where the quantity of a commodity that consumers are *willing* and able to purchase equals the quantity producers are *willing* to supply.   Geometrically, equilibrium occurs at the intersection of the market demand and supply curves of the commodity.   The price and quantity at which equilibrium exists are known, respectively, as the equilibrium price and equilibrium quantity.

Incidence of a tax.   The burden or proportion of the tax paid.   The incidence on consumers of a per-unit tax collected by the government from producers gives the proportion of the tax burden that actually falls on consumers in the form of higher prices.   The more inelastic the demand and the more elastic the supply, the greater is the incidence of the tax on consumers.

Market demand curve.   A graphic representation showing the total quantity of a commodity that consumers are willing and able to purchase over a given period of time at various alternative commodity prices when everything else that affects demand is constant.   The market demand curve of a commodity is negatively sloped, because more of the commodity will be purchased at lower commodity prices.

Market supply curve.   A graphic representation showing the total quantity of a commodity that producers are willing to produce or sell over a given period of time at various alternative commodity prices when everything else that affects supply is constant.   The market supply curve for a commodity is usually positively sloped, because higher prices must be paid to induce producers to supply more of the commodity.

Shortage.   An excess in the quantity demanded over the quantity supplied of a commodity over a given period of time which leads to a pressure on the commodity price to rise.

Surplus.   The excess in the quantity supplied over the quantity demanded of a commodity over a given period of time which leads to a pressure on the commodity price to fall.

Total revenue (TR).   The total amount received in exchange for goods or services, which is equal to price times quantity.

Review Questions

1. The intersection of the market demand and supply curves for a commodity determines (*a*) the equilibrium price, (*b*) the equilibrium quantity, (*c*) the price at which there is neither a surplus nor a shortage of the commodity, (*d*) all of the above.
    Ans.   (*d*)

2. The elasticity of demand is measured by (*a*) the slope of the demand curve, (*b*) the inverse of the slope of the demand curve, (*c*) the percentage change in price for a given percentage change in quantity, (*d*) the percentage change in quantity for a given percentage change in price.
    Ans.   (*d*)

3. The elasticity between points *E* and *C* along the demand curve of Fig. 14-1, using the *original* quantity and price is (*a*) 2/4.5 or about 0.44, (*b*) 4/4.5 or about 0.89, (*c*) 4/6.5 or about 0.62, (*d*) 6/6.5 or about 0.92.
    Ans.   (*b*)

4. The elasticity between points *E* and *C* along the demand curve of Fig. 14-1, using the *new* quantity and price is (*a*) 2/6.5 or about 0.31, (*b*) 2/4.5 or about 0.44, (*c*) 1/6.5 or about 0.15, (*d*) 1/4.5 or about 0.22.
    Ans.   (*a*)

5. The (average) elasticity between points *E* and *C* along the demand curve in Fig. 14-1 is (*a*) 3/11 or about 0.27, (*b*) 2/11 or about 0.18, (*c*) 3/5.5 or about 0.55, (*d*) 2/5.5 or about 0.36.
    Ans.   (*c*)

6. If total revenue remains unchanged when price changes, the demand curve is (*a*) elastic, (*b*) unitary elastic, (*c*) inelastic, (*d*) any of the above.
    Ans.   (*b*)

7. If total revenue rises when price falls, the demand curve is (*a*) elastic, (*b*) unitary elastic, (*c*) inelastic, (*d*) any of the above.
    Ans.   (*a*)

8. If total revenue rises when price rises, the demand curve is (*a*) elastic, (*b*) unitary elastic, (*c*) inelastic, (*d*) any of the above.
    Ans.   (*c*)

9. The demand curve for a commodity is more elastic, (*a*) the greater the number of good substitutes available, (*b*) the greater the proportion of income spent on the commodity, (*c*) the longer the period of time considered, (*d*) all of the above.
    Ans.   (*d*)

10. The (average) elasticity between points *G* and *H* along the *supply* curve of Fig. 14-1 is (*a*) 3.5/13 or about 0.27, (*b*) 3.5/6.5 or about 0.54, (*c*) 4/13 or about 0.31, (*d*) 7/6.5 or about 1.08.
    Ans.   (*b*)

11. In bad harvests, (a) the supply of farm products decreases, (b) farm prices rise, (c) farmers' incomes usually rise, (d) all of the above.

Ans. (d)

12. The burden on consumers of a per-unit tax collected from producers is greater, (a) the more elastic the demand curve, (b) the more inelastic the demand curve, (c) the more inelastic the supply curve, (d) none of the above.

Ans. (b)

Solved Problems

DEMAND, SUPPLY AND MARKET PRICE

14.1. (a) What do a demand schedule and demand curve show? (b) What do a supply schedule and supply curve show? (c) How is the market price of a commodity determined in a free-enterprise system? (d) What is held constant in drawing a demand curve? What happens if there is change? (e) What is held constant in drawing a supply curve? What happens if there is change?

  (a) A *demand schedule* shows the quantity demanded of a commodity per unit of time at various alternative prices for the commodity, when everything else that affects demand is held constant. Plotting a demand schedule, we get a *demand curve*. This is negatively sloped because price and quantity are inversely related along a demand curve. See also Section 2.1.

  (b) A *supply schedule* shows the quantity supplied of a commodity per unit of time at various alternative prices for the commodity, when everything else that affects supply is held constant. Plotting a supply schedule, we get a *supply curve*. This is usually positively sloped because more of the commodity will be supplied at higher prices. See also Section 2.2.

  (c) In a free-enterprise system, the *market or equilibrium price* (and quantity) of a commodity is determined at the intersection of the market demand and supply curves for the commodity. This is the price at which the quantity of the commodity that consumers are willing to purchase over a given period of time exactly equals the quantity producers are willing to supply. At higher prices, the quantity demanded falls short of the quantity supplied and the resulting *surplus* will push the price down toward its equilibrium level. At prices below the equilibrium price, the quantity demanded exceeds the quantity supplied and the resulting *shortage* will drive the price up toward the equilibrium level. Thus, the equilibrium market price, once achieved, tends to persist. See also Section 2.3.

  (d) In defining the market demand curve for a commodity, it is assumed that the number of consumers, their tastes, money incomes and the price of related commodities remain constant. The market demand curve will *increase or shift up* if the number of consumers increases, if their money incomes rise, if the price of substitute commodities rises or if the price of complementary commodities falls. Opposite changes will cause a *decrease or downward shift* in demand. A commodity's equilibrium market price and quantity will both rise when its demand curve shifts up; both will fall when it shifts down. See also Section 2.4.

  (e) In defining the market supply curve of a commodity, technology, factor prices, and the price of other commodities related in production remain unchanged. If the number and size of producers of the commodity increase, technology improves, or the price of factors or other commodities (related in production) fall, then the entire market supply curve of the commodity will increase (i.e. shift down and to the right) leading to a lower equilibrium market price and higher quantity. See also Section 2.5.

14.2. A hypothetical market demand and supply schedule of wheat is given in Table 3. (a) Prepare a table showing the market equilibrium price and quantity. Show the surplus or shortage and the pressure on price at prices other than equilibrium. (b) Graph the results from part (a).

Table 3

Price ($ per bushel)	Quantity Demanded in the Market (billion bu. per yr.)	Quantity Supplied in the Market (billion bu. per yr.)
$5	2.5	5.7
4	3.5	5.5
3	5.0	5.0
2	7.0	4.0
1	10.0	2.5

(a) See Table 3A.

Table 3A

Price ($/bu.)	QD (billion bu./year)	QS (billion bu./year)	Surplus (+) or Shortage (−)	Pressure on Price
$5	2.5	5.7	+3.2	downward
4	3.5	5.5	+2.0	downward
3	5.0	5.0	0	equilibrium
2	7.0	4.0	−3.0	upward
1	10.0	2.5	−7.5	upward

(b) See Fig. 14-2.

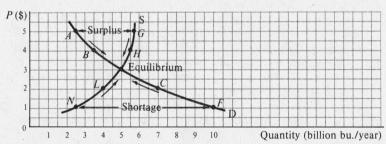

Fig. 14-2

ELASTICITY OF DEMAND

14.3.   (a) What happens to the quantity demanded of a commodity when its price falls?   How is the responsiveness in the quantity demanded of a commodity to a change in its price measured?   (b) Give the formula for the elasticity of demand.   How is the percentage change in quantity calculated?   The percentage change in price?   (c) How is the slope of the demand curve measured?   How is this different from the elasticity of demand? (d) Why is the slope of demand an unsatisfactory measure of the responsiveness in the quantity demanded of a commodity to a change in its price?   How does the elasticity of demand overcome these difficulties?

(a)   When the price of a commodity falls, the quantity demanded of the commodity per unit of time increases.   This is indicated by a downward movement along the negatively sloped demand curve for the commodity.   The responsiveness in the quantity demanded of a commodity per unit of time is measured by the elasticity of demand (E_D).

(b) $E_D = \dfrac{\text{the percentage change in the quantity demanded of the commodity}}{\text{the percentage change in the commodity price}}$

The percentage change in the quantity demanded is found by dividing the change in quantity by the original quantity or by the new quantity.   Because we get different results if we use the original or the new quantity, we divide the change in quantity by the *average* of the original and new quantities. Similarly, the percentage change in price is found by dividing the change in price by the original price or by the new price. But to avoid different results, we usually use the average price.

(c) The slope between any two points on a line is found by the vertical change divided by the horizontal change. Since we plot price on the vertical axis and quantity along the horizontal axis in drawing a demand curve, the slope of the demand curve is measured by the *change in price* divided by the change in quantity. This is different from the elasticity of demand which measures the *percentage change in quantity* divided by the percentage change in price.

(d) The slope of the demand curve cannot adequately measure the responsiveness in the quantity demanded of a commodity to a change in its price because the slope is expressed in specific units of measurement. By simply changing the units of measurement (i.e. dollars to cents, pounds to tons, etc.), we get a different slope for the same demand curve. In addition, since the slope is expressed in specific units of measurement, it cannot be used to compare the responsiveness of the demand of different commodities to changes in their prices. The elasticity of demand avoids these difficulties by comparing percentage changes which have no units attached to them.

14.4. Find the elasticity of the market demand curve in Problem 14.2, using the original, the new and the average quantity and price between points (a) A and B, (b) B and E, (c) E and C, and (d) C and F.

(a) The elasticity of demand between points A and B when the original quantity and price are used is

$$E_D = \frac{1}{2.5} \div \frac{1}{5} = \frac{1}{2.5} \times \frac{5}{1} = \frac{5}{2.5} = 2$$

Using the new quantity;

$$E_D = \frac{1}{3.5} \div \frac{1}{4} = \frac{1}{3.5} \times \frac{4}{1} = \frac{4}{3.5} \approx 1.14$$

Using the average quantity and price;

$$E_D = \frac{1}{(2.5 + 3.5)/2} \div \frac{1}{(5 + 4)/2} = \frac{1}{3} \div \frac{1}{4.5} = \frac{1}{3} \times \frac{4.5}{1} = \frac{4.5}{3} = 1.5$$

(b) Between points B and E when the original quantity and price are used,

$$E_D = \frac{1.5}{3.5} \div \frac{1}{4} = \frac{1.5}{3.5} \times \frac{4}{1} = \frac{6}{3.5} \approx 1.71$$

Using the new quantity and price,

$$E_D = \frac{1.5}{5} \div \frac{1}{3} = \frac{1.5}{5} \times \frac{3}{1} = \frac{4.5}{5} = 0.90$$

Using the average quantity and price,

$$E_D = \frac{1.5}{4.25} \div \frac{1}{3.5} = \frac{5.25}{4.25} \approx 1.24$$

(c) Between points E and C, in terms of the original quantity and price,

$$E_D = \frac{2}{5} \div \frac{1}{3} = \frac{2}{5} \times \frac{3}{1} = \frac{6}{5} = 1.20$$

Using the new quantity and price,

$$E_D = \frac{2}{7} \div \frac{1}{2} = \frac{2}{7} \times \frac{2}{1} = \frac{4}{7} \approx 0.57$$

Using the average quantity and price,

$$E_D = \frac{2}{6} \div \frac{1}{2.5} = \frac{2}{6} \times \frac{2.5}{1} = \frac{5}{6} \approx 0.83$$

(d) Between points C and F, using the original quantity and price,

$$E_D = \frac{3}{7} \div \frac{1}{2} = \frac{3}{7} \times \frac{2}{1} = \frac{6}{7} \approx 0.86$$

Using the new quantity and price,

$$E_D = \frac{3}{10} \div \frac{1}{1} = \frac{3}{10} \times \frac{1}{1} = 0.30$$

Using the average quantity and price,

$$E_D = \frac{3}{8.5} \div \frac{1}{1.5} = \frac{3}{8.5} \times \frac{1.5}{1} = \frac{4.5}{8.5} \approx 0.53$$

14.5. From the hypothetical market demand schedule in Table 4, find the elasticity of market demand between points (a) A' and B', (b) B' and E', (c) E' and C', and (d) C' and F'.

Table 4

Price ($ per bushel)	Quantity Demanded in the Market (billion bu. per year)	Alternative or Point
$5	3.5	A'
4	4.2	B'
3	5.0	E'
2	6.0	C'
1	7.5	F'

(a) Since nothing is specified to the contrary, we follow the convention of using the average quantity and price to measure the elasticity of the market demand schedule in Table 4.   Thus, between A' and B',

$$E_D = \frac{0.7}{(3.5 + 4.2)/2} \div \frac{1}{(4 + 5)/2} = \frac{0.7}{3.85} \div \frac{1}{4.5} = \frac{0.7}{3.85} \times \frac{4.5}{1} = \frac{3.15}{3.85} \approx 0.82$$

(b) Between B' and E',

$$E_D = \frac{0.8}{4.6} \div \frac{1}{3.5} = \frac{0.8}{4.6} \times \frac{3.5}{1} = \frac{2.8}{4.6} \approx 0.61$$

(c) Between E' and C',

$$E_D = \frac{1}{5.5} \div \frac{1}{2.5} = \frac{1}{5.5} \times \frac{2.5}{1} = \frac{2.5}{5.5} \approx 0.45$$

(d) Between C' and F',

$$E_D = \frac{1.5}{6.75} \div \frac{1}{1.5} = \frac{1.5}{6.75} \times \frac{1.5}{1} = \frac{2.25}{6.75} \approx 0.33$$

14.6. If we refer to the market demand of Table 3 as D_1 and that of Table 4 as D_2, (a) find the slope of D_1 between points A and B.   How does this compare with E_D between points A and B? (b) What is the relationship of E_D found by using the original, the new, and the average quantity and price for D_1? (c) What happens to E_D as we move down D_1 and D_2? (d) What is the relationship between E_D of D_1 and D_2? (e) Plot D_1 and D_2 on the same set of axes.   Can you explain the answer to part (d) by the slope of D_1 and D_2?

(a) The slope of D_1 between points A and B is equal to the change in price over the change in quantity, or $\frac{-1}{+1} = (-)1$. This is different from E_D [see the solution to Problem 14.4 (a)].

(b) For any movement along D_1, E_D is always largest when the original quantity and price are used; E_D is always smallest when the new quantity and price are used. E_D when the average quantity and price are used will always lie between the E_D found by using the original quantity and price and the E_D found by using the new quantity and price (see Problem 14.4).

(c) As we move down D_1 and D_2, E_D falls (see Problems 14.4 and 14.5). This is usually, but not always, the case.

(d) For corresponding changes in prices and movements along D_1 and D_2, (average) E_D is always greater on D_1 than on D_2.

(e) See Fig. 14-3.

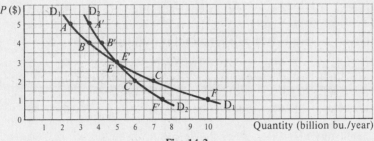

Fig. 14-3

Since D_2 is steeper or has a greater (absolute) slope than D_1, and E_D is always less on D_2 than on D_1, we might be tempted to say that the steeper the demand curve, the smaller its elasticity. While this is true here, it is not always the case—especially if the demand curves do not cross. We cannot (and should not) generally infer much about the elasticity of a demand curve by looking at its slope.

14.7. Find the elasticity of the market demand curve of Fig. 14-4 between points (a) A and C, (b) C and F, and (c) F and H.   (d) How do the results of parts (a), (b) and (c) compare with the slope of this demand curve?

(a) Between A and C, $E_D = \frac{2}{2} \div \frac{1}{3} = \frac{2}{2} \times \frac{3}{1} = \frac{6}{2} = 3$.   This is equivalent to finding E_D at point B (the midpoint between A and C) because we used the average quantity of 2 units and the average price of \$3 (point B).

(b) Between C and F, $E_D = \frac{2}{4} \div \frac{1}{2} = \frac{2}{4} \times \frac{2}{1} = \frac{4}{4} = 1$.   This is equivalent to finding E_D at point E (the midpoint between C and F).

(c) Between F and H, $E_D = \frac{2}{6} \div \frac{1}{1} = \frac{2}{6} \times \frac{1}{1} = \frac{2}{6} = \frac{1}{3}$.   This is equivalent to finding E_D at point G.

(d) Since the market demand curve of Fig. 14-4 is a straight line, its slope is constant at $(-)\frac{4}{8} = (-)\frac{1}{2}$.   Thus, while the slope of a straight-line demand curve is constant, $E_D > 1$ above the midpoint (E), $E_D = 1$ at E, and $E_D < 1$ below the midpoint.   This is always the case for a straight-line demand curve.

14.8. (a) On the same set of axes, draw a demand curve which is vertical (D_1), and one which is horizontal (D_2).   (b) What is the elasticity of D_1?   Why?   (c) What is the elasticity of D_2?   Why?

(a) See Fig. 14-5.

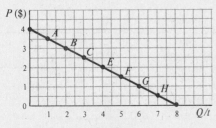

Fig. 14-4

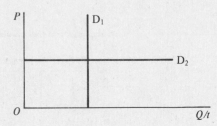

Fig. 14-5

(b) E_D of D_1 is always equal to zero because there is no percentage change in quantity, regardless of the change in price. Thus, when the slope of a demand curve is infinite, its elasticity is zero. This is always the case.

(c) E_D of D_2 is infinite because the percentage change in quantity is very large for an infinitesimally small percentage change in price. Thus, when the slope of D is zero, its elasticity is infinite. Note that vertical and horizontal demand curves are very rare occurrences, and it is only in these two cases that we can correctly infer the elasticity of demand by looking at the slope.

ELASTICITY AND TOTAL REVENUE

14.9. What is the relationship between total revenue and elasticity (a) if price declines? Why? (b) If price rises? Why? (c) What general conclusion can you reach with regard to the relationship between price, total revenue and elasticity?

(a) If TR rises as P falls, $E_D > 1$. The reason for this is that for TR to rise, the percentage increase in quantity must exceed the percentage decline in price. This is the definition of an elastic demand. If TR remains unchanged as P falls, $E_D = 1$ because for TR to remain unchanged, the percentage increase in quantity must be equal to the percentage decline in price (i.e. unitary elastic). Finally, if TR falls as P falls, $E_D < 1$ because for TR to fall, the percentage increase in quantity must be less than the percentage fall in price (i.e. demand is inelastic).

(b) If TR rises as P rises, $E_D < 1$ because for TR to rise, the percentage *decrease* in quantity (the numerator in the elasticity formula for a price increase) must be less than the percentage *increase* in price (the denominator). If TR is unchanged as P rises, $E_D = 1$ because for TR to remain unchanged, the percentage decrease in quantity must equal the percentage increase in price. Finally, if TR falls as P rises, $E_D > 1$ because for TR to fall, the percentage decrease in quantity must exceed the percentage increase in price.

(c) If P and TR move in the same direction, $E < 1$; if P and TR move in opposite directions, $E > 1$; if TR remains unchanged as P rises or falls, $E_D = 1$. This is a very handy rule for the student to remember.

14.10. Construct a table for each of the following, showing the relationship between price, quantity, total revenue and elasticity: (a) D_1 of Table 3 and Fig. 14-3, (b) D_2 of Table 4 and Fig. 14-3 and (c) the demand of Fig. 14-4.

(a) See Table 5.

Table 5

Point	P (in $)	QD (billion bu./year)	TR (billion $)	E_D
A	$5	2.5	$12.5	elastic
B	4	3.5	14.0	elastic
E	3	5.0	15.0	inelastic
C	2	7.0	14.0	inelastic
F	1	10.0	10.0	

Between points A and E in Table 5, D_1 is elastic because as P falls, TR rises; from E to F, D_1 is inelastic because as P falls, TR also falls (compare these results with those of Problem 14.4).

(b) See Table 6.

Table 6

Point	P (in $)	QD (billion bu./yr.)	TR (billion $)	E_D
A'	$5	3.5	$17.5	inelastic
B'	4	4.2	16.8	inelastic
E'	3	5.0	15.0	inelastic
C'	2	6.0	12.0	inelastic
F'	1	7.5	7.5	

Since in Table 6, TR falls continuously as P falls, D_2 is always inelastic (compare these elasticity results with those of Problem 14.5).

(c)   See Table 7.

Table 7

Point	P (in $)	QD (billion bu./yr.)	TR (billion $)	E_D
A	$3.5	1	$3.5	elastic
B	3.0	2	6.0	elastic
C	2.5	3	7.5	elastic
E	2.0	4	8.0	inelastic
F	1.5	5	7.5	inelastic
G	1.0	6	6.0	inelastic
H	0.5	7	3.5	inelastic

A straight-line demand curve extended to the axes is elastic above its geometric midpoint (E), inelastic below its midpoint, and unitary elastic at its midpoint (see Problem 14.7).

14.11.   Draw a demand curve which is unitary elastic throughout.

For a demand curve to be unitary elastic throughout, TR (or the area under the demand curve) must remain constant at every point.   D in Fig. 14-6 is a rectangular hyperbola with TR = 4 and $E_D = 1$ at every point.

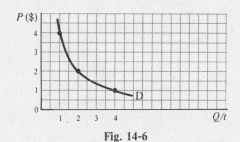

Fig. 14-6

14.12.   (a) Is the demand for table salt elastic or inelastic?   Why?   (b) Is the demand for stereos elastic or inelastic?   Why?

(a)   The demand for salt is inelastic because there are no good substitutes for salt and households spend only a very small proportion of their total income on this commodity.   Even if the price of salt were to rise substantially, households would reduce their purchases of salt minimally, and $E_D < 1$.

(b)   The demand for stereos is elastic because stereos are expensive and, as a luxury rather than a necessity, their purchase can be postponed or avoided when their price rises.   One could also use the radio as a partial substitute for a stereo.

ELASTICITY OF SUPPLY

14.13.   Find the elasticity of the market supply curve in Problem 14.2 between points (a) G and H, (b) H and E, (c) E and L, and (d) L and N.

(*a*) The elasticity of supply between points G and H is

$$E_S = \frac{\text{change in quantity supplied}}{\text{sum of quantities supplied}/2} \div \frac{\text{change in price}}{\text{sum of prices}/2}$$

$$= \frac{0.2}{(5.5 + 5.7)/2} \div \frac{1}{(5 + 4)/2} = \frac{0.2}{5.6} \div \frac{1}{45} = \frac{0.2}{5.6} \times \frac{4.5}{1} = \frac{0.9}{5.6} \simeq 0.16$$

(*b*) Between H and E,

$$E_S = \frac{0.5}{(5.5 + 5)/2} \div \frac{1}{(4 + 3)/2} = \frac{0.5}{5.25} \div \frac{1}{3.5} = \frac{0.5}{5.25} \times \frac{3.5}{1} = \frac{1.75}{5.25} \simeq 0.33$$

(*c*) Between E and L,

$$E_S = \frac{2.5}{4.5} \simeq 0.56$$

(*d*) Between L and N,

$$E_S = \frac{2.25}{3.25} \simeq 0.69$$

Thus, this supply curve is inelastic throughout.

14.14. With reference to Fig. 14-7, (*a*) explain the time relationship between S_1, S_2 and S_3. (*b*) What happens to equilibrium price and quantity if D increases to D' and S_1, S_2 or S_3, respectively, becomes the relevant supply curve?

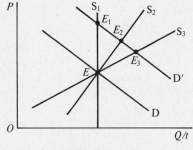

Fig. 14-7

(*a*) S_1 is vertical; that is, no matter what P is, Q remains unchanged. Thus, the elasticity of S_1 is zero and supply is said to be perfectly inelastic. This is called the *market period* or the very short run. For example, on any given day, the supply of fresh milk is given and fixed regardless of its price.

S_2 is positively sloped and shows that producers would be willing to supply more of the commodity at higher prices. Thus, the elasticity of S_2 is greater than zero. For example, this may represent the supply of fresh milk over a period of a month, or the *short run*. The quantity supplied responds positively to price because producers could redirect more of their milk to consumers and less to cheese makers.

S_3 could refer to the supply curve of milk over a still longer time period, say, one year or more. This longer period is referred to as the *long run*. In the long run, the quantity response for a given increase in price is even greater (i.e. the supply curve is even more elastic) because over a period of one or more years, farmers could raise more cattle, build more barns and hire more farmhands to produce more milk. Note that in the long run, S_3 could even be horizontal (constant costs); however, it is usually positively sloped because costs generally rise.

(*b*) With D and S_1 or S_2 or S_3, the equilibrium price and quantity is given by point E (see Fig. 14-7). If D shifts up to D', only P rises in the market period (point E_1 on S_1). In the short run and in the long run, both price and quantity increase but equilibrium output rises more and price less in the long run than in the short run (compare E_3 on S_3 in the long run with E_2 on S_2 in the short run).

APPLICATIONS OF ELASTICITY

14.15. (*a*) Should the price of a subway or bus ride be increased or decreased if total revenue needs to be increased? (*b*) What about the price of a taxi ride? (*c*) Why do farmers' incomes often rise in bad harvests and fall in good harvests?

(*a*)   To the extent that there are no inexpensive good substitutes for public transportation in metropolitan areas, the demand for subway and bus rides is inelastic.   Their prices should, therefore, be increased to increase total revenues.   In addition, unless the demand for public transportation has zero elasticity, some decrease in the quantity demanded is likely to occur when its price is increased.   This leads also to a reduction in operating costs.   With rising total revenues and falling operating costs, municipalities can reduce their deficits in public transportation.   However, this can be self-defeating.   Sharply increasing the price of public transportation will encourage people to use their cars and increase congestion and pollution.

(*b*)   For taxi rides, the case is likely to be different.   Taxi rides are relatively expensive; an increase in their price may encourage people to rely much more on their cars and public transportation. To the extent that this makes the demand for taxi rides elastic, total revenue will fall when the price of taxi rides is increased.   Since fewer people ride taxis when the price of taxi rides increases, total costs would also fall.   What happens to the total profits (or losses) of fleet owners depends on whether total revenue or total costs fall faster.   In the real world, a market study should be undertaken to estimate empirically the elasticity of demand before deciding to change prices.

(*c*)   A bad harvest is reflected in a decrease in supply (i.e. an upward shift in the market supply curve of agricultural commodities).   Given the market demand for agricultural commodities, this decrease in supply causes the equilibrium price to rise.   Since the demand for agricultural commodities is usually price inelastic, the total receipts of farmers as a group increase.   (When the demand for an agricultural commodity is price inelastic, the same result can be achieved by reducing the amount of land under cultivation for the commodity.   This is done in some farm-aid programs.)   In good harvests, the farmers' incomes usually fall for the opposite reason.

14.16.   Draw a figure showing that the more inelastic the market demand curve for a commodity, the greater the burden or incidence on the consumers of a per-unit tax collected from producers.

In Fig. 14-8, market demand D_1 is more elastic than its alternatives D_2 and D_3, while supply curve S' is parallel and above S by the amount of the per-unit tax collected by the government from producers.   (The supply curve shifts up by the amount of the per-unit tax in order to leave producers with the same *net* per-unit price for each quantity sold that they received before the imposition of the tax.)   With either D_1, D_2, *or* D_3 and S (i.e. in the absence of the per-unit tax), we have equilibrium at point E.   When the government imposes the per-unit tax on producers (i.e. with S'), the equilibrium point rises to E_1 with D_1 (the more elastic demand), to E_2 with D_2, and to E_3 (i.e. by the full amount of the vertical shift in S' or the per-unit tax) with D_3.   Thus, the more inelastic the market demand curve for a commodity, the more the equilibrium price will rise for a given per-unit tax collected from producers.   In other words, the more inelastic the demand, the more producers are able to shift the burden or incidence of the tax to consumers in the form of higher prices.

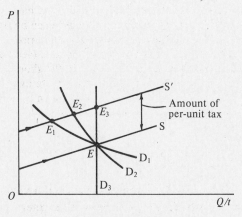

Fig. 14-8

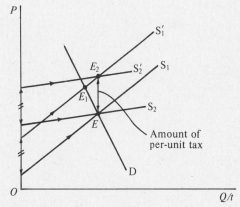

Fig. 14-9

14.17. Draw a figure showing that for a given demand, the more *elastic* the supply, the greater the incidence of the tax on consumers.

In Fig. 14-9, S_2 is more elastic than S_1 and equilibrium is at E without the tax. When a given per-unit tax is collected from producers, both S_1 and S_2 shift up vertically by the amount of the per-unit tax to S_1' and S_2', respectively. With S_1', the new equilibrium point (E_1) is lower than E_2 with S_2'. Thus, for a given demand, the more elastic the supply, the greater the incidence of the tax on (i.e. the greater the increase in price for) consumers and the smaller on producers or suppliers.

14.18. With reference to Fig. 14-10, consider the following two aid programs for wheat farmers: (1) The government sets the price of wheat at P_2 per bushel and purchases the resulting surplus of wheat at P_2. (2) The government allows wheat to be sold at the equilibrium price of P_1 and grants each farmer a cash subsidy of $P_2 - P_1$ for each bushel sold. Which of the two programs is more expensive to the government?

Regardless of the program, the total receipts of wheat farmers as a group are the same (OP_2 times OB). The greater the fraction of this total paid by the consumers of wheat, the smaller the cost to the government. Since the demand for wheat is likely to be inelastic (as reflected in the figure), consumers' expenditures on wheat would be greater under the first program, and so the first program would cost the government less. (Note that we have assumed no storage costs in this problem, nor have we considered what the government would do with the surplus wheat and what the effect of each of the two programs would be on the welfare of consumers.)

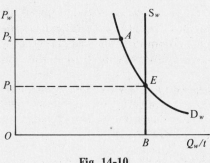

Fig. 14-10

Chapter 15

The Theory of Consumer Demand
and Utility

15.1 SUBSTITUTION AND INCOME EFFECTS AND THE DOWNSLOPING DEMAND

In Section 2.1, we saw that the market demand curve for a commodity is derived by adding the individuals' demand curves for the commodity.   We also said that each individual's (and thus the market) demand curve for a commodity is downward sloping because of the substitution and income effects.   The *substitution effect* refers to the fact that as the price of a commodity falls, we replace this for similar commodities in consumption.   The *income effect* refers to the fact that as the price of a commodity falls, a given money income allows the consumer to buy more of this and other commodities (because his or her purchasing power has increased).

EXAMPLE 1.   When the price of coffee falls, we substitute coffee for tea in consumption.   In addition, when the price of coffee falls, a consumer can buy more coffee (and other commodities) with a given money income.   Thus, the consumer's (and market) demand curve for coffee is downsloping because of this substitution and income effect. The better and the greater are the number of substitutes available for the commodity, the more elastic is its demand curve.   A complementary explanation of the law of downward-sloping demand rests on the law of diminishing marginal utility.

15.2 THE LAW OF DIMINISHING MARGINAL UTILITY

An individual demands a particular commodity because of the satisfaction or *utility* he receives from consuming it.   The more units of a commodity the individual consumes per unit of time, the greater is the *total utility* he receives.   Although total utility increases, the extra or *marginal utility* received from consuming each additional unit of the commodity decreases. This is referred to as the *law of diminishing marginal utility*.

EXAMPLE 2.   For purposes of illustration, we assume in Table 1 that satisfaction can actually be measured in terms of units of utility called *utils*.   The first two columns of Table 1 give an individual's hypothetical total utility (TU) schedule from consuming various quantities of commodity X (say oranges) per unit of time. Note that as the individual consumes more units of X, TU_x increases.

Columns (1) and (3) of the table give this individual's marginal utility (MU) schedule for commodity X. Each value of column (3) is obtained by subtracting two successive values of column (2).   For example, if the individual's consumption of X goes from zero units to 1, TU_x goes from zero utils to 10 utils and the MU of the first unit of X is 10 utils.   Similarly, if the consumption of X rises from 1 unit to 2 units, TU_x rises from 10 to 18, and the MU of the second unit of X is 8.

Table 1

(1) q_x	(2) TU_x	(3) MU_x
0	0	
		10
1	10	
		8
2	18	
		6
3	24	
		4
4	28	
		2
5	30	

EXAMPLE 3.   The total and marginal utility schedules of Table 1 give the total and marginal utility curves of Fig. 15-1.   Since marginal utility has been defined as the *change* in total utility from a one-unit change in consumption, each value of MU_x has been recorded midway between the two levels of consumption.   The falling MU_x curve illustrates the *law of diminishing marginal utility*.

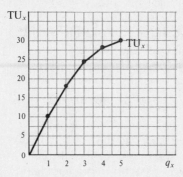 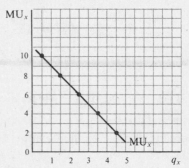

Fig. 15-1

15.3   UTILITY MAXIMIZATION AND CONSUMER EQUILIBRIUM

A consumer maximizes the total utility or satisfaction obtained from spending his or her income (and is said to be in equilibrium) when the marginal utility of the *last* dollar spent on each commodity is the same. This equilibrium condition for utility maximization can be restated as follows:

$$\frac{MU_x}{P_x} = \frac{MU_y}{P_y} = \ldots = \text{common MU of the } last \text{ \$ spent on each commodity}$$

EXAMPLE 4.   Table 2 shows the marginal utility that an individual receives from consuming various units of X and Y per unit of time.

Table 2

Units of commodities	MU_x	MU_y
1	10	6
2	8	5
3	6	4
4	4	3
5	2	2

Suppose that the consumer has \$7 to spend on X and Y, and that P_x (the price of X) = \$2 and P_y = \$1.   This consumer maximizes total utility and is in equilibrium by spending \$4 of his \$7 to buy $2X$ and the remaining \$3 to purchase $3Y$.   At this point, $\dfrac{MU_x \text{ of 8 utils}}{P_x \text{ of \$2}} = \dfrac{MU_y \text{ of 4 utils}}{P_y \text{ of \$1}}$ = MU of 4 utils from the *last* \$ spent on X and Y. By purchasing $2X$ and $3Y$, $TU_x = 18(10+8)$, $TU_y = 15(6+5+4)$ and TU from both is $33(18+15)$ utils. If this consumer had spent his \$7 in any other way, his TU would have been less.

15.4   DERIVATION OF AN INDIVIDUAL'S DEMAND CURVE

Starting with a consumer in equilibrium, we get one point on his demand curve.   At a lower commodity price, the consumer must purchase more of the commodity to be in equilibrium, and so we get another point on his demand curve.   From these and other points of consumer equilibrium, we can derive a downsloping demand curve because of diminishing MU.

EXAMPLE 5. In Example 4, we saw that the consumer was in equilibrium when he spent his income of $7 to purchase $2X$ and $3Y$, at $P_x = \$2$ and $P_y = \$1$.   Thus, $P_x = \$2$ and $q_x = 2$ is one point of consumer demand for X.   From Table 2, we see that at $P_x = \$1$, this consumer would be in equilibrium by purchasing $4X$ and $3Y$ because at that point

$$\frac{\text{MU}_x \text{ of 4 utils}}{P_x \text{ of } \$1} = \frac{\text{MU}_y \text{ of 4 utils}}{P_y \text{ of } \$1} = \text{MU of 4 utils for last \$ spent on } X \text{ and } Y$$

Table 3 gives two points on the consumer's demand schedule for commodity X.   Other points could be similarly obtained.   Note that because MU declines, P_x must fall to induce the individual to buy more of X.   Thus, a downsloping d_x can be explained in terms of diminishing MU_x.

Table 3

P_x	$2	$1
q_x	2	4

15.5   CONSUMER'S SURPLUS

Consumer's surplus refers to the difference between what the consumer would be willing to pay to purchase a given number of units of a commodity and what he actually pays for them.   It arises because the consumer pays for all units of the commodity the price he is just willing to pay for the last unit purchased, even though the MU on earlier units is greater.   Consumer surplus can be measured by the area under the consumer's demand curve and above the commodity price.

EXAMPLE 6. In Fig. 15-2, the consumer purchases AF units of the commodity at price AB and spends AB times AF (the area of the rectangle $ABCF$) on this commodity.   However, this consumer would have been willing to pay a higher price for all but the last unit of this commodity (as indicated by the height of his demand curve) because these previous units give him a greater MU than the last unit.   The difference between what he would be willing to pay for AF units of the commodity (the area of $AGCF$) and what he actually pays for them (the area of $ABCF$) is an estimate of this consumer's surplus (the area of triangle BGC).

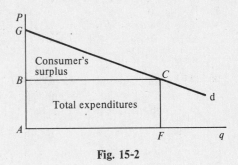

Fig. 15-2

Important Economic Terms

Consumer's equilibrium. The point at which the consumer maximizes the total utility of satisfaction from spending his income.

Consumer's surplus. Refers to the difference between what the consumer would be willing to pay for a given amount of a commodity and what he actually pays.

Diminishing marginal utility. A concept stating that as an individual consumes more units of a commodity per unit of time, the total utility he receives increases, but the extra or marginal utility decreases.

Income effect. The increase in the quantity purchased of a commodity with a given money income when the commodity price falls.

Paradox of value. The question of why some commodities which are essential to life cost much less than others which could be easily foregone.

Substitution effect. The increase in the quantity purchased of a commodity when its price falls (as a result of switching from the purchase of other similar commodities).

Utility. The property of a commodity that enables it to satisfy a want or a need.

Review Questions

1. The law of downward-sloping demand can be explained in terms of (a) the substitution effect, (b) the income effect, (c) both the substitution and income effects, (d) neither the substitution nor income effect.
   Ans. (c)

2. A complementary explanation of the downsloping demand curve is given by (a) diminishing returns, (b) diminishing marginal utility, (c) decreasing costs, (d) decreasing returns to scale.
   Ans. (b)

3. When total utility increases, marginal utility is (a) negative and increasing, (b) negative and declining, (c) zero, (d) positive and declining.
   Ans. (d)

4. If the consumer in Example 4 spent his $7 to purchase $3X$ and $1Y$, his TU would be (a) 35, (b) 33, (c) 30, (d) 27.
   Ans. (c)

5. If the consumer in Example 4 spent his $7 to purchase $1X$ and $5Y$, his TU would be (a) 35, (b) 33, (c) 30, (d) 27.
   Ans. (c)

6. At what combinations (other than $2X$ and $3Y$) is the condition $MU_x/P_x = MU_y/P_y$ satisfied in Table 2? (a) $1X$ and $2Y$, (b) $3X$ and $4Y$, (c) $4X$ and $5Y$, (d) all of the above.
   Ans. (d)

7. By purchasing $1X$ and $2Y$, the consumer in Example 4 is not in equilibrium because he (a) is not spending his entire income of $7 on X and Y, (b) does not have enough income to purchase $1X$ and $2Y$, (c) is not satisfied with $1X$ and $2Y$, (d) does not know P_x and P_y.
   Ans. (a)

8. With combinations $3X$ and $4Y$ or $4X$ and $5Y$, the consumer in Example 4 is not in equilibrium because he (a) is not spending his entire income of $7 on X and Y, (b) does not have enough income to purchase these combinations of X and Y, (c) does not want so much X and Y, (d) does not know P_x and P_y.
   Ans. (b)

9. d_x in Table 3 is downsloping because MU_x is (a) rising, (b) constant, (c) falling, (d) zero.
   Ans. (c)

10. d_x of Table 3 is unitary elastic (on the average) between $P_x = \$2$ and $P_x = \$1$ because (a) the consumer's total expenditure on X remains constant, (b) the consumer's total expenditure on X rises, (c) the slope of d_x is constant, (d) the slope of d_x is negative.
    Ans. (a) See Section 14.3.

11. Consumer's surplus is defined as
    (a) the difference between what the consumer actually pays and what he is willing to pay,
    (b) the difference between what the consumer is willing to pay and what he actually pays,
    (c) the sum of what the consumer pays and what he is willing to pay,
    (d) what the consumer is willing to pay divided by what he actually pays.
    Ans. (b)

12. From Fig. 15-2, we can see that at a commodity price lower than AB the consumer's surplus would (a) equal area BGC, (b) be smaller than area BGC, (c) be larger than area BGC, (d) any of the above.
    Ans. (c)

Solved Problems

SUBSTITUTION AND INCOME EFFECTS AND THE DOWNSLOPING DEMAND

15.1. (a) How is the market demand for a commodity derived?   (b) Why is the market demand curve for a commodity downsloping?   (c) Why is the individual's demand curve for a commodity downward or negatively sloped?   (d) How does the substitution effect contribute to the downward slope of the consumer's demand curve?   (e) How does the income effect contribute to the downward slope of the consumer's demand curve?

   (a) The market demand curve for a commodity is derived by the horizontal summation of all individuals' demand curves for the commodity (see Problems 2.2 and 2.3).

   (b) The market demand curve for a commodity is downsloping because the consumers' demand curves for the commodity (of which the market demand is the summation) are downward or negatively sloped.

   (c) The individual's demand for a commodity is downsloping (indicating that at lower prices the individual demands more of the commodity per unit of time) because of the substitution and the income effects.

   (d) The substitution effect refers to the fact that as the price of a commodity falls, consumers substitute this for similar commodities in consumption.   For example, if the price of wine falls, we substitute wine for beer in consumption.   On the other hand, if the price of wine rises, we consume less wine by substituting beer for wine.

   (e) The income effect refers to the fact that a reduction in the price of a commodity increases consumers' purchasing power or real income (from given and fixed money incomes) and this allows consumers to purchase more of this (and other) commodities.   For example, when the price of wine falls, a consumer can purchase more wine (and more of every other normal good) out of his given money income.   On the other hand, if the price of wine rises, the income effect is negative.

15.2. Suppose that $P_x = \$2$ and $P_y = \$1$, the consumer purchases $4X$ and $8Y$, and spends his entire income of $16.   Suppose now that P_x falls to $1.   (a) Explain how the income effect operates.   (b) Explain how the substitution effect operates.   (c) Explain why d_x is downward or negatively sloped.   How much of X and Y will this consumer purchase at $P_x = P_y = \$1$?

   (a) When P_x falls from $2 to $1, this consumer can purchase the same $4X$ and $8Y$ by spending only $12 of his fixed money income of $16.   Thus, the reduction in P_x increased his real income or purchasing power by $4.   Suppose that he uses this $4 to buy 2 additional units of X and Y. The additional $2X$ (and $2Y$) that the consumer is now able to purchase represents the income effect resulting from the fall in P_x.

   (b) When P_x falls from $2 to $1, commodity X becomes a better buy in relation to commodity Y. Thus, the consumer will purchase more X and less Y.   Suppose the consumer transfers 3 units of purchases from Y to X.   The substitution effect is 3 in this case and is independent of the above income effect.

   (c) When P_x falls from $2 to $1, this consumer purchases more of X because of the income and substitution effects.   This leads to a downward or negatively sloped demand curve for commodity X.   In part (a) we assumed that the income effect is $+2X$; in part (b) that the substitution effect is $+3X$.   This gives a total of $+5X$ for the income and substitution effects combined.   Thus, while at $P_x = \$2$, this consumer buys $4X$ (one point on d_x), at $P_x = \$1$, he purchases $9X$ (another point on d_x).   Note that at the unchanged $P_y = \$1$, there is an income effect of $+2Y$ but a substitution effect of $-3Y$, for a net change of $-1Y$.   Thus, d_y shifts leftward by one unit because of the fall in P_x, so that the consumer purchases $7Y$ at $P_y = P_x = \$1$.

THE LAW OF DIMINISHING MARGINAL UTILITY

15.3. (a) With what is consumer demand theory concerned?   Why do we study it?   (b) What do we mean by "utility"?   What does a utility schedule show?   (c) What happens to the total utility that a consumer receives from consuming increasing quantities of a commodity per unit of time?   (*d*) What is "marginal utility"?   What happens to marginal utility as an individual consumes more units of the commodity per unit of time?

(*a*)   Consumer demand theory is concerned with the individual's demand curve for a commodity, how it is derived, and the reasons for its location and shape.   We study consumer demand theory in order to learn more about the market demand curve for a commodity (which, as shown in Section 2.1, is obtained by the horizontal summation of all individuals' demand curves for the commodity).

(*b*)   Utility refers to the property of a commodity that enables it to satisfy a want.   Without this property, there would be no demand for the commodity.   For purposes of illustration, we assume that utility can be measured in terms of "utils."   A utility schedule shows the number of utils that an individual receives from consuming various quantities of the commodity per unit of time.   Thus, a utility schedule shows the tastes of an individual for the commodity.   Different individuals usually have different tastes for the commodity and therefore have different utility schedules.   When the tastes of an individual change, his utility schedule also changes (shifts).

(*c*)   As an individual consumes more units of a commodity per unit of time, the total utility (TU) he receives increases.   However, if an individual continued to consume more and more units of a commodity, a point would be reached where his total utility would stop increasing.   This is called the *saturation point*.   Consuming still more units of the commodity would cause his TU to fall (because of storage or disposal problems).

(*d*)   Marginal utility (MU) refers to the change in TU as an individual consumes each additional unit of the commodity.   MU is positive but declining as long as TU rises.   MU is zero at the saturation point (where TU is maximum and is neither rising nor falling).   Past the saturation point, TU falls and MU is negative.   Note that up to a point, MU may be rising.   For example, the second cigarette may give more satisfaction than the first.   But as the individual smokes more and more cigarettes per day, MU will eventually begin to decline.

15.4.   (*a*) From the TU_x schedule in Table 4, derive the MU_x schedule.   (*b*) Graph the two schedules.

Table 4

q_x	0	1	2	3	4	5	6	7	8	9	10
TU_x	0	14	26	37	47	56	64	70	74	77	78

(*a*)   See Table 5.

Table 5

q_x	0	1	2	3	4	5	6	7	8	9	10
TU_x	0	14	26	37	47	56	64	70	74	77	78
MU_x		14	12	11	10	9	8	6	4	3	1

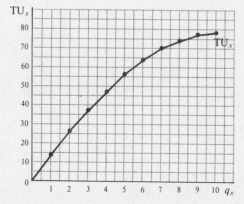
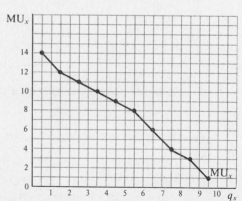

Fig. 15-3

(*b*) See Fig. 15-3. Note that MU_x is plotted at the midpoints.   The decline in MU_x is referred to as the *law of diminishing marginal utility*.

15.5.   (*a*) From the TU_y schedule in Table 6, derive the MU_y schedule. (*b*) Graph the two schedules. (*c*) Where is this individual's saturation point for commodity Y?

Table 6

q_y	0	1	2	3	4	5	6	7	8	9	10
TU_y	0	13	24	34	42	49	55	58	60	60	55

(*a*)   In Table 7, note that the sum of all MU_y up to a particular q_y equals TU_y at that q_y.

Table 7

q_y	0	1	2	3	4	5	6	7	8	9	10
TU_y	0	13	24	34	42	49	55	58	60	60	55
MU_y		13	11	10	8	7	6	3	2	0	−5

(*b*) See Fig. 15-4.

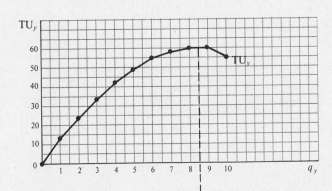

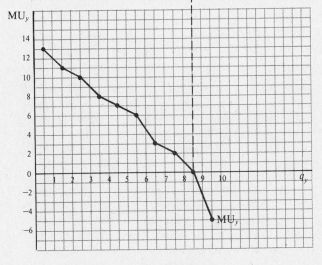

Fig. 15-4

(c) The saturation point is reached when this individual increases his consumption of Y from 8 to 9 units.   At that point TU_y is maximum (and constant) and $MU_y = 0$.   This individual would not want to consume more units of Y even if they were free.   More than $9Y$ would cause TU_y to fall and MU_y to be negative.   While MU_y could rise up to a point and be negative past the saturation point, the economically relevant portion of the MU_y function is positive but declining.

UTILITY MAXIMIZATION AND CONSUMER EQUILIBRIUM

15.6. (a) What is meant by "consumer equilibrium"?   (b) State the condition for consumer equilibrium.   (c) If MU_x/P_x of the last dollar spent on commodity X exceeds MU_y/P_x of the last dollar spent on Y, how can the consumer reach equilibrium?

(a) Given his tastes (from MU schedules), his income and commodity prices, a rational consumer is in equilibrium when he spends his income in such a way as to maximize the total utility or satisfaction that he receives from spending his income.

(b) A consumer maximizes the total utility or satisfaction from spending his income (and is said to be in equilibrium) when the marginal utility of the *last* dollar spent on each commodity is the same.   This equilibrium condition for utility maximization can be stated mathematically as follows:

$$\frac{MU_x}{P_x} = \frac{MU_y}{P_y} = \text{common MU of the } last \text{ \$ spent on each commodity}$$

where P_x and P_y refer to the price of X and the price of Y, respectively.   The equilibrium condition can also be restated as $\frac{MU_x}{P_x} = \frac{MU_y}{P_y}$ at the point where $(p_x)(q_x) + (p_y)(q_y) = M$ (the consumer's money income). $MU_x/P_x = MU_y/P_y = ...$, by itself, is a necessary but not sufficient condition for consumer equilibrium.   There may be other levels of consumption at which $MU_x/P_x = MU_y/P_y = ...$, but only the one at which the consumer is exactly spending his total income is *the* (single) point of consumer equilibrium or utility maximization.

(c) If MU_x/P_x exceeds MU_y/P_y, the last dollar spent on commodity X gives this consumer more utility than the last dollar spent on Y.   This consumer would increase his total utility from his given and fixed level of expenditures by purchasing more of X and less of Y.   As he purchases *more* of X, the consumer moves *down* his diminishing MU_x schedule.   As he purchases *less* of Y, he moves *up* his diminishing MU_y schedule.   This should continue until $MU_x/P_x = MU_y/P_y$ for the last dollar spent on X and Y.   Note that the consumer can reach the equilibrium position of utility maximization because of the law of diminishing MU_x and MU_y.   The consumer should follow exactly the same process to reach equilibrium if he spends his income on more than two commodities.

15.7. Suppose that a consumer has the MU_x of Table 5 and the MU_y of Table 7.   Suppose also that his money income is \$10, $P_x = \$2$ and $P_y = \$1$.   (a) Describe how this consumer should spend *each* of his \$10 to purchase *each unit* of X and Y so as to maximize his total utility or satisfaction.   (b) Show that his TU would be less if he bought one more unit of either X or Y.   (c) Find the TU of this consumer if he spent all of his income (1) on X (2) on Y.

(a) Because $P_x = \$2$, if this consumer spent his first \$2 to buy the first unit of X, he would receive a MU_x of only 14 or 7 utils per dollar spent on X.   On the other hand, if this consumer spent his first dollar to purchase the first unit of Y, he would receive a MU_y of 13 or 13 utils per dollar.   Thus, he should spend his first dollar to purchase the first unit of Y and receive 13 utils of satisfaction.   Similarly, this consumer should spend his second, third and fourth dollars to purchase the second, third and fourth units of Y and receive 11, 10 and 8 utils, respectively.   This consumer is indifferent between purchasing the fifth unit of Y or the first unit of X because he receives 7 utils *per dollar* spent on each.   Suppose that he purchases both and spends his fifth, sixth and seventh dollars to purchase the fifth Y and the first X (remember, $P_x = \$2$).   Similarly, the consumer should spend his eighth, ninth and tenth (or last) dollar to purchase the sixth Y (and receive 6 utils) and the second X (and receive 12 utils or 6 utils per dollar—the same as for the sixth Y).   By purchasing $2X$ and $6Y$, this consumer is receiving 81 utils (14 + 12 from

X and $13 + 11 + 10 + 8 + 7 + 6$ from Y).   This is the maximum TU he can receive by spending his total income of $10 on X and Y when $P_x = \$2$ and $P_y = \$1$.   Thus, the consumer is in equilibrium by purchasing $2X$ and $6Y$.

(b)   To buy the third unit of X (at $P_x = \$2$), this consumer would have had to give up the fifth and sixth units of Y (at $P_y = \$1$).   He would gain 11 utils by purchasing the third unit of X but lose 13 utils $(7 + 6)$ by giving up his sixth and fifth Y, with a net loss of 2 utils.   The TU of this consumer would be only 79 utils if he purchased $3X$ and $4Y$ (compared with a TU of 81 utils with $2X$ and $6Y$) and he would not be maximizing the TU from spending his $10 of income.   On the other hand, by giving up his second X (thus losing 12 utils), this consumer could purchase his seventh and eighth Y (gaining only a total of 5 utils), with a net loss of 7 utils.   Purchasing $1X$ and $8Y$, this consumer would receive a total of 74 utils $(81 - 7)$ and would not be in equilibrium.

(c)   If this consumer spent his $10 on X only, he could purchase $5X$ (at $P_x = \$2$) and receive a TU $= 56$ utils $(14 + 12 + 11 + 10 + 9)$.   If, instead, he spent his $10 on Y only, he could purchase $10Y$ (at $P_y = \$1$) and receive a TU $= 55$ utils $(13 + 11 + 10 + 8 + 7 + 6 + 3 + 2 + 0 - 5)$. From the above, we can conclude that any combination of X and Y (other than $2X$ and $6Y$) that this consumer could purchase with his income of $10 would give him a smaller TU than the 81 utils he receives from purchasing $2X$ and $6Y$.

15.8.   (a) Show that the equilibrium condition for utility maximization given in Problem 15.6(b) is satisfied when the consumer in Problem 15.7 purchases $2X$ and $6Y$.   (b) Why is $1X$ and $5Y$ not equilibrium?   (c) Why are $7X$ and $7Y$ or $8X$ and $8Y$ not equilibrium?

(a)   With $2X$ and $6Y$, the consumer is in equilibrium because

$$\frac{MU_x \text{ of 12 utils}}{P_x \text{ of } \$2} = \frac{MU_y \text{ of 6 utils}}{P_y \text{ of } \$1} = MU \text{ of 6 utils from the last } \$ \text{ spent on } X \text{ and } Y$$

Another way of showing that this consumer is in equilibrium by purchasing $2X$ and $6Y$ is

$$\frac{MU_x}{P_x} = \frac{MU_y}{P_y} \qquad \text{and} \qquad (P_x)(q_x) + (P_y)(q_y) = M \text{ (the consumer's money income)}$$

Substituting the values of the problem into the above expression for consumer equilibrium, we get

$$\frac{12 \text{ utils}}{\$2} = \frac{6 \text{ utils}}{\$1} \qquad \text{and} \qquad (\$2)(2) + (\$1)(6) = \$10$$

In order to be in equilibrium, not only must the MU per dollar spent on each commodity be the same, but the consumer's income must just be exhausted.

(b)   If the consumer purchases $1X$ and $5Y$,

$$\frac{MU_x \text{ of 14 utils}}{P_x \text{ of } \$2} = \frac{MU_y \text{ of 7 utils}}{P_y \text{ of } \$1}$$

but the consumer spends only $7 of his income of $10.   The consumer is not in equilibrium because he can increase his TU by spending his remaining $3 on X and Y.

(c)   With $7X$ and $7Y$ or $8X$ and $8Y$, $MU_x/P_x = MU_y/P_y$ but the consumer does not have enough income to purchase these combinations of X and Y and is not in equilibrium.   Note that if in part (a), MU_x had been 11 utils instead of 12, the equilibrium condition would hold only approximately (unless X and Y were perfectly divisible, in which case the consumer should purchase a little less than $2X$ and a little more than $6Y$ until MU_x/P_x exactly equaled MU_y/P_y).

15.9.   Why is water, which is essential to life, so cheap while diamonds, which are not essential to life, so expensive?

Because water is essential to life, the TU received from water exceeds the TU received from diamonds.   However, the price we are willing to pay for each unit of a commodity depends not on the TU but on the MU.   We consume so much water that the MU of the last unit of water consumed is very low.   Therefore, we are willing to pay only a very low price for the last unit of water consumed.   Since all units of water consumed are identical we pay the same low price on all other units of water consumed.

On the other hand, we purchase so few diamonds that the MU of the last diamond purchased is very high.   Therefore, we are willing to pay a high price for this last diamond and for all the other diamonds purchased.   Classical economists did not distinguish TU from MU and thus they were unable to resolve this so-called "water-diamond paradox."

DERIVATION OF AN INDIVIDUAL'S DEMAND CURVE

15.10.   (a) Explain, on the basis of diminishing MU, why an individual purchases more of a commodity per unit of time when the commodity price falls.   (b) How do we get one point on the consumer's demand schedule and curve for a commodity?   (c) How are other points found?   (d) Explain the process by which the consumer in Examples 4 and 5 moves from the first to the second equilibrium point as P_x falls from \$2 to \$1.

(a)   Because each additional unit of the commodity gives the individual less extra or marginal utility, he will purchase more units of the commodity only at lower commodity prices.   Thus, a downsloping demand can be explained in terms of diminishing MU.   This is a complementary explanation to the substitution and income effects for a downsloping demand curve.

(b)   Given an individual's MU schedules, income and the commodity prices, we can find the point of consumer equilibrium.   This gives the quantity of the commodity that the individual would purchase at the given commodity price in order to maximize the TU from spending his income. This defines one point on the consumer's demand schedule and demand curve for the commodity.

(c)   In order to find other points on the consumer's demand schedule and demand curve for the commodity, we must use alternative commodity prices.   At each alternative commodity price, the consumer will have to purchase a different quantity of the commodity in order to be in equilibrium.   These alternative price-quantity relationships at consumer equilibrium points give other points of consumer demand for the commodity.   Since the MU of the commodity falls, lower commodity prices will be associated with greater quantity purchases of the commodity (and the demand curve will be downsloping).

(d)   In Example 4, the individual was in equilibrium when he purchased $2X$ and $3Y$ (at $P_x = \$2$ and $P_y = \$1$ respectively) with an income of \$7.   When P_x fell to \$1 in Example 5, the individual's equilibrium condition was no longer satisfied by the continued purchase of $2X$ and $3Y$ because $\dfrac{MU_x \text{ of 8 utils}}{P_x \text{ of \$1}} > \dfrac{MU_y \text{ of 4 utils}}{P_y \text{ of \$1}}$ and the individual was spending only \$5 of his \$7 income.   In order to reach equilibrium when $P_x = \$1$, this consumer must spend his sixth and seventh dollars of income to purchase the third and fourth units of X so that his MU_x falls to 4 utils (the same as MU_y at $P_x = P_y = \$1$) and his entire income of \$7 is spent.

15.11.   Table 7 is repeated below as Table 8.   With income of \$10, $P_x = \$2$, and $P_y = \$1$, the consumer is in equilibrium by purchasing $2X$ and $6Y$.   (a) Find the point of consumer equilibrium with $P_x = \$1$.   (b) How is this consumer's demand schedule for commodity X derived?

Table 8

Units	1	2	3	4	5	6	7	8	9	10
MU_x	14	⑫	11	10	9	8	6	4	3	1
MU_y	13	11	10	8	7	⑥	3	2	0	-5

(a)   If P_x falls to \$1, the consumer cannot maintain his equilibrium position by continuing to purchase $2X$ and $6Y$ because

$$\frac{MU_x \text{ of 12 utils}}{P_x \text{ of \$1}} > \frac{MU_y \text{ of 6 utils}}{P_y \text{ of \$1}}$$

and he is spending only $8 of his income of $10.   Compare this with Problem 15.8(*a*).   Since the second dollar spent to purchase the second unit of X (at $P_x = \$1$) gives this individual more (marginal) utility than the sixth dollar spent to purchase the sixth unit of Y, the individual should spend more on X and less on Y.   As he buys more X, the consumer moves down his diminishing MU_x schedule.   As he buys less of Y, he moves up his diminishing MU_y.   The consumer will be in equilibrium when the MU of the last dollar spent on X equals the MU of the last dollar spent on Y.   This occurs when this consumer spends his $10 to purchase $6X$ and $4Y$ because

$$\frac{MU_x \text{ of 8 utils}}{P_x \text{ of \$1}} = \frac{MU_y \text{ of 8 utils}}{P_y \text{ of \$1}} = \text{MU of 8 utils from the last \$ spent on } X \text{ and } Y$$

Note that as P_x fell from $2 to $1 in Example 5, the consumer bought more X *but the same amount of* Y to reach a new equilibrium point.   Here, the consumer buys more X but *less* Y.

(*b*) When $P_x = \$2$, this consumer purchases $2X$ in order to be in equilibrium.   This gives one point of his demand schedule for commodity X.   Other points on the consumer's demand schedule for X can be similarly obtained by allowing P_x to change again and recording q_x at equilibrium. Since the total expenditures of this consumer on commodity X rise as P_x falls, d_x is price elastic between $P_x = \$2$ and $P_x = \$1$.

CONSUMER'S SURPLUS

15.12. (*a*) How does the consumer's surplus arise?   How can it be measured?   (*b*) What is the consumer's surplus in Fig. 15-5 when price is AF? AC? AB?   How is the size of the consumer's surplus related to the commodity price?

(*a*) The price that a consumer is willing to pay for each unit of the commodity is given by the height of his demand curve.   Since each additional unit of the commodity gives him less MU, he is willing to pay less for each additional unit (i.e. his demand curve is downsloping).   The consumer ends up with a surplus because he pays for all units the price that he is willing to pay for the last unit, even though the MU on previous units is greater.   When, as in Fig. 15-5, the commodity is perfectly divisible, the consumer's surplus can be measured by the area under the consumer's demand curve and above the commodity price.

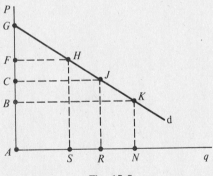

Fig. 15-5

(*b*) At the price of AF, the consumer purchases AS of the commodity and spends $AFHS$.   Because he would be willing to pay $AGHS$ for AS of the commodity but pays only $AFHS$, he receives a consumer surplus of FGH.   At price of AC, the consumer's surplus is CGJ.   At price AB, the consumer's surplus is BGK.   Given the individual's demand curve for a commodity, the lower the commodity price, the greater the consumer's surplus.

15.13. Given the consumer's demand schedule for commodity X in Table 9, (*a*) indicate how much this consumer would be willing to pay for each unit of commodity X.   (*b*) If the *market* demand and supply curves for commodity X intersect to give a market equilibrium $P_x = \$1$, what is this consumer's surplus from commodity X?   (*c*) How could the producer of commodity X extract from this consumer the entire consumer surplus?   (*d*) Draw a figure that would allow you to measure this consumer's surplus graphically.

Table 9

P_x	$2.50	$2.00	$1.50	$1.00
q_x	1	2	3	4

(a) The demand schedule of Table 9 shows that this consumer would be willing to pay $2.50 for the first unit of X, $2.00 for the second, $1.50 for the third and $1.00 for the fourth.

(b) If the market demand curve for commodity X intersects the market supply at $P_x = \$1$, this consumer will purchase $4X$ at $P_x = \$1$. Since he would be willing to pay $7 ($2.50 + $2.00 + $1.50 + $1.00) for these $4X$, but instead pays only $4, he receives a surplus of $3 ($1.50 on the first unit of X, $1.00 on the second, $0.50 on the third, and nothing on the fourth).

(c) The producer of commodity X could extract the entire surplus from the consumer by offering to sell these $4X$ for a total price of $7—take it or leave it. Since to the consumer, $4X$ are "worth" $7, he will pay the $7 and lose his entire consumer's surplus. Note that this implies that the producer has the economic and legal power to do this and knows precisely the consumer's demand schedule for commodity X. These conditions do not generally hold in the real world and the consumer in general retains his surplus.

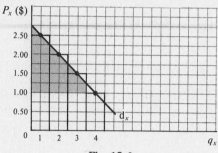

Fig. 15-6

(d) In Fig. 15-6, the consumer's surplus of $3 is given by the shaded area. This figure is different from Fig. 15-5 because we are here dealing with discrete rather than perfectly divisible units of the commodity.

Chapter 16

Costs of Production

16.1 EXPLICIT COSTS, IMPLICIT COSTS AND ECONOMIC PROFIT

In this chapter, we concentrate on the firm's production costs—or what lies behind its supply curve. *Explicit costs* are the actual, out-of-pocket expenditures of the firm to purchase or hire the services of the factors of production it needs. *Implicit costs* are the costs of the factors owned by the firm and used in its own production processes. These costs should be imputed or estimated from what these factors could earn in their best alternative employment. In economics, costs include both explicit and implicit costs. *Profit* is the excess of revenues over these costs.

EXAMPLE 1. The explicit costs of a firm are the wages it must pay to hire labor, the interest to borrow money capital, and the rent on land and buildings used in the production process. To these, the firm must add such implicit costs as the wage that the entrepreneur would earn working as a manager for somebody else; the interest he would get by supplying his money capital (if any) to someone else in a similarly risky business; and the rent on his owned land and buildings, if he were not using them himself. Only if the total revenue received from selling the output exceeds both its explicit and implicit costs is the firm making an economic or pure profit.

16.2 THE LAW OF DIMINISHING RETURNS

The law of diminishing returns is one of the most important and unchallenged laws of production. This law states that as we use more and more units of some factors of production to work with one or more fixed factors, after a point, we get less and less extra or marginal output or product from each additional unit of the variable factors used. The time period when at least one factor of production is fixed in quantity (i.e. cannot be varied) is referred to as the *short run*. Thus, the law of diminishing returns is a short-run law. In the *long run*, all factors are variable.

EXAMPLE 2. Table 1 shows the total and marginal product of using each additional unit of labor on the same (say, one acre of) land. Note that with zero labor, TP = O. By adding the first unit of labor, TP = 3 and MP (i.e. the change in TP) = 3. By adding the second unit of labor, TP = 8 and MP = 5. The third unit of labor leads to a TP of 12 and an MP of 4, etc. The law of diminishing returns begins to operate in this example with the addition of the third unit of labor.

Table 1

Inputs of the Variable Factor (labor, in man-years)	Total Product (TP, in bushels per year)	Extra or Marginal Product (MP)
0	0	3
1	3	5
2	8	4
3	12	3
4	15	2
5	17	

16.3 SHORT-RUN TOTAL COSTS

In the short run, there are total fixed costs, total variable costs and total costs. *Total fixed costs* (TFC) are the costs which the firm incurs in the short run for its fixed inputs; these are constant regardless of the level of output and of whether it produces or not.   An example of TFC is the rent which a producer must pay for the factory building over the life of a lease.   *Total variable costs* (TVC) are costs incurred by the firm for the variable inputs it uses.   These vary directly with the level of output produced.   Examples of TVC are raw material costs and some labor costs.   *Total costs* (TC) are equal to the sum of total fixed costs and total variable costs.

EXAMPLE 3.   Table 2 presents hypothetical TFC, TVC and TC schedules for various levels of output (Q).   These schedules are graphed in Fig. 16-1.

Table 2

Q	TFC ($)	TVC ($)	TC ($)
0	60	0	60
1	60	30	90
2	60	40	100
3	60	45	105
4	60	55	115
5	60	75	135
6	60	120	180

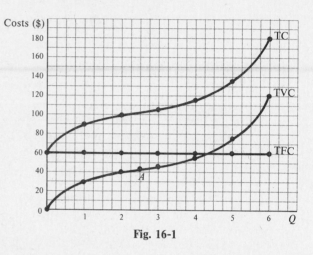

Fig. 16-1

From Table 2, we see that TFC are $60 regardless of the level of output.   This is reflected in Fig. 16-1 in a TFC curve which is parallel to the quantity axis and $60 above it.   TVC are zero when output is zero and rise as output rises.   The particular shape of the TVC curve follows directly from the law of diminishing returns.   Up to point A (about 2.5 units of output), the firm is using so few of the variable inputs together with its fixed inputs that the law of diminishing returns is not yet operating.   Therefore, TVC increase at a decreasing rate and the TVC curve faces down.   Past point A, the law of diminishing returns begins to operate so that TVC increase at an increasing rate and the TVC curve faces up.   At every output level, TC equals TFC plus TVC.   For this reason, the TC curve has the same shape as the TVC curve and, in this case, is everywhere $60 above it.

16.4 SHORT-RUN PER UNIT COSTS

Though total costs are very important, per-unit or average costs are even more important in the short-run analysis of the firm.   The short-run per-unit costs that we consider are the average fixed cost, the average variable cost, the average cost and the marginal cost.   *Average fixed cost* (AFC) equals total fixed costs divided by output.   *Average variable cost* (AVC) equals total variable costs divided by output.   *Average cost* (AC) equals total costs divided by output; AC also equals AFC plus AVC.   *Marginal cost* (MC) equals the change in TC or the change in TVC per unit change in output.

EXAMPLE 4.   Table 3 presents the AFC, AVC, AC and MC schedules derived from the TFC, TVC and TC schedules of Table 2 (repeated in the left portion of Table 3).   The AFC schedule (column 5) is obtained by dividing TFC (column 2) by the corresponding quantities of output produced (Q in column 1).   The AVC schedule (column 6) is obtained by dividing TVC (column 3) by Q.   The AC schedule (column 7) is obtained by dividing TC (column 4) by Q.   AC at every output level also equals AFC (column 5) plus AVC (column 6).   The MC schedule (column 8) is obtained by subtracting successive values of TC (column 4) or TVC (column 5).   Thus, MC does not depend on the level of TFC.

EXAMPLE 5.   The AFC, AVC, AC and MC schedules of Table 3 are graphed in Fig. 16-2.   Note that the values of the MC schedule (from column 8) are plotted halfway between successive levels of output.   Also note that while the AFC curve falls continuously as output is expanded, the AVC, the AC and the MC curves are U-shaped.   The MC curve reaches its lowest point at a lower level of output than either the AVC curve or the AC curve.   Also, the rising portion of the MC curve intersects the AVC and AC curves at their lowest points.   This is always the case (see Problem 16.11).

Table 3

(1) Q	(2) TFC ($)	(3) TVC ($)	(4) TC ($)	(5) AFC ($)	(6) AVC ($)	(7) AC ($)	(8) MC ($)
1	60	30	90	60	30	90	
2	60	40	100	30	20	50	10
3	60	45	105	20	15	35	5
4	60	55	115	15	13.75	28.75	10
5	60	75	135	12	15	27	20
6	60	120	180	10	20	30	45

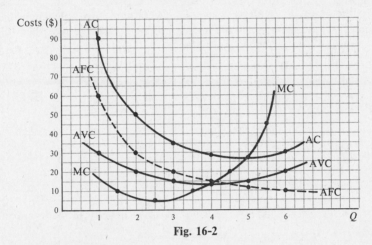

Fig. 16-2

16.5   LONG-RUN PRODUCTION COSTS

In the long run, there are no fixed factors, and the firm can build a plant of any size.   Once a firm has constructed a particular plant, it operates in the short run.   A plant size can be represented by its short-run average cost curve (SAC).   Larger plants can be represented by SAC curves which lie further to the right.   The long-run average cost (LAC) curve shows the minimum per-unit cost of producing each level of output when any desired size of plant can be built.   The LAC curve is thus formed from the relevant segment of the SAC curves.

EXAMPLE 6.   Fig. 16-3 shows four hypothetical plant sizes that the firm could build in the long run.   Each plant is shown by a SAC curve.   To produce up to 300 units of output, the firm should build and utilize plant 1 (given by SAC_1).   From 300 to 550 units of output, it should build the larger plant given by SAC_2.   From 550 to 1050, it should operate on SAC_3, etc.   Note that the firm could produce an output of 400 with plant 1, but only at a higher cost than with plant 2.   The irrelevant portions of the SAC curves are dashed.   The remaining (undashed) portions form the LAC curve.   By drawing many more SAC curves, we would get a smoother LAC curve.

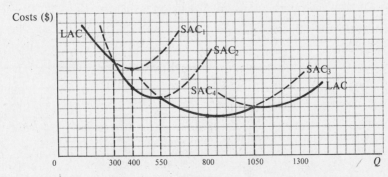

Fig. 16-3

16.6   CONSTANT, INCREASING AND DECREASING RETURNS TO SCALE

If in the long run we increase all factors used in production by a given proportion, there are three possible outcomes: (1) output increases in the same proportion, so that there are *constant returns to scale* or constant costs; (2) output increases by a greater proportion, giving *increasing returns to scale* or decreasing costs; and (3) output increases in a smaller proportion, giving *decreasing returns to scale* or increasing costs.   Increasing returns to scale or economies of mass production may result because of division of labor and specialization in production.   Beyond a certain size, however, management problems resulting in decreasing returns to scale may arise.

EXAMPLE 7.   The LAC curve of Fig. 16-3 at first shows increasing returns to scale or decreasing costs.   Then for a small range of outputs (around 800 units), it shows constant returns to scale (constant costs).   For larger outputs, we have decreasing returns to scale (increasing costs).   Whether and when this occurs in the real world depend on the firm and industry under consideration.

Important Economic Terms

Average cost (AC).   Total costs divided by output, or average fixed cost plus average variable cost.

Average fixed cost (AFC).   Total fixed costs divided by output.

Average variable cost (AVC).   Total variable costs divided by output.

Constant returns to scale (or constant costs).   The long-run situation when increasing all inputs by a given proportion results in output increasing in the same proportion.

Decreasing returns to scale (or increasing costs).   The long-run situation when output increases proportionately less then inputs.

Explicit costs.   The actual, out-of-pocket expenditures made by the firm to purchase or hire the services of the factors of production it needs.

Implicit costs.   The estimated values (in their best alternative employment) of the factors owned by the firm and used in its own production processes.

Increasing returns to scale (or decreasing costs).   The long-run situation when output increases proportionately more than inputs.

Law of diminishing returns.   Refers to the falling marginal product resulting from using more variable factors with some other fixed factor(s).

Long run.   The time period when all factors of production are variable.

Long-run average cost (LAC).   The minimum per-unit cost of producing a level of output when any desired scale of plant can be built.

Long-run marginal cost (LMC).   The change in total costs per unit change in output when any desired scale of plant can be built.

Marginal cost (MC).   The change in total costs and the change in total variable costs per unit change in output.

Opportunity cost.   The amount of a commodity that society must give up in order to release just enough (scarce) resources to produce one more unit of a second commodity.

Profit.   The excess of total revenue over all explicit costs and implicit costs.

Short run.   The time period in which at least one factor of production is fixed in quantity.

Total costs (TC).   The sum of total fixed costs and total variable costs.

Total fixed costs (TFC).   The costs which the firm incurs in the short run for all fixed inputs, regardless of the level of output.

Total variable costs (TVC).   The costs incurred by the firm for all variable inputs.   TVC change as the firm changes its level of output.

Review Questions

1. The interest paid by a firm to borrow money capital represents an (a) explicit cost, (b) implicit cost, (c) opportunity cost, (d) all of the above.

   Ans. (a)

2. The wage that an entrepreneur would earn if he worked instead as a manager for someone else in his best alternative employment represents a(n) (a) profit, (b) explicit cost, (c) implicit cost, (d) opportunity cost.

   Ans. (c)

3. The law of diminishing returns is a (a) monetary relationship between inputs and output, (b) short-run law, (c) long-run law, (d) questionable production relationship.

   Ans. (b)

4. The law of diminishing returns begins to operate when the (a) total product begins to rise, (b) total product begins to fall, (c) marginal product begins to rise, (d) marginal product begins to fall.

   Ans. (d)

5. If only part of the labor force employed by a firm can be dismissed at any time and without pay, the total wages and salaries paid out by the firm must be considered (a) a fixed cost, (b) a variable cost, (c) partly a fixed and partly a variable cost, (d) any of the above.

   Ans. (c)

6. When the law of diminishing returns begins to operate, the TVC curve begins to (a) fall at an increasing rate, (b) rise at a decreasing rate, (c) fall at a decreasing rate, (d) rise at an increasing rate.

   Ans. (d)

7. All of the following cost curves are U-shaped except the (a) AVC curve, (b) AFC curve, (c) AC curve, (d) MC curve.

   Ans. (b)

8. AFC equals the vertical distance between the (a) AC curve and the AVC curve, (b) AC curve and the MC curve, (c) AVC curve and the MC curve, (d) all of the above.

   Ans. (a) See Fig. 16-2.

9. The MC schedule is obtained by subtracting successive values of (a) TC, (b) TVC, (c) either TC or TVC, (d) none of the above.

   Ans. (c) See Table 3.

10. The LAC curve shows the
    (a)   minimum cost of producing various levels of output within a particular plant,
    (b)   minimum cost of producing various levels of output when plant size can be varied,
    (c)   profit-maximizing level of output,
    (d)   change in TC of producing various levels of output when all inputs can be varied.

    Ans. (b)

11. A firm's declining LAC curve over some ranges of output can be explained by (a) diminishing returns, (b) decreasing returns to scale, (c) increasing returns to scale, (d) increasing costs.

    Ans. (c)

12. If a firm doubles all inputs in the long run and total output less than doubles, we have a case of (a) diminishing returns, (b) constant returns to scale, (c) increasing returns to scale, (d) decreasing returns to scale.

   Ans. (d)

Solved Problems

ECONOMIC COSTS AND PROFITS

16.1. (a) Why do we study a firm's costs of production?   (b) Distinguish among opportunity costs, explicit costs and implicit costs.

   (a) We study a firm's costs of production to learn more about the firm's supply curve.   It is by adding individual firms' supply curves for a commodity that we get the market supply curve of the commodity.   This, together with the market demand curve, determines the equilibrium price and quantity of the commodity in a free-enterprise economy (see Sections 2.2 and 2.3).

   (b) Opportunity costs refer to the fact that as *society* uses more of its scarce resources to produce some goods and services, fewer resources are available to produce other goods and services. In Example 3 in Section 1.3, we saw that the (opportunity) cost of producing each additional unit of cloth equalled the amount of food that *society* had to give up to release just enough (scarce) resources to produce each of the additional units of cloth.   Explicit costs are the actual out-of-pocket expenditures of the *firm* to purchase or hire the services of the factors of production it needs.   Implicit costs are the costs of the services of the factors owned and used by the *firm* in its own production process.

16.2. (a) Distinguish between cost and profit in economics.
   (b) How do these concepts differ from the everyday usage of these terms?

   (a) In economics, costs include both explicit and implicit costs.   The resources that a firm owns and uses in production are not free.   They involve costs which can be estimated by what these same resources would earn in their best alternative employment.   If we say that the firm is making zero profit, it must be remembered that the firm is already receiving a "normal" return on its owned factors.   When we speak of profits in economics, we mean above-normal returns.

   (b) The everyday usage of the term "cost" refers only to the out-of-pocket expenditures of the firm to purchase or hire the services of factors of production (what economists call explicit costs). The man in the street calls profit all the excess of the firm's revenue over these out-of-pocket expenditures.   For the economist, part or all of this revenue represents the "normal return" on the firm's owned factors or implicit costs.   This normal return on owned factors must be included in order for the firm to justify the continued use of its owned factors (i.e. to bid its owned factors away from their best alternative employments).

16.3. A firm pays $200,000 in wages, $50,000 in interest on borrowed money capital, and $70,000 for the yearly rental of its factory building.   If the entrepreneur worked for somebody else as a manager he would earn at most $40,000 per year, and if he lent out his money capital to somebody else in a similarly risky business, he would at most receive $10,000 per year. He owns no land or building.   (a) Calculate the entrepreneur's profit if he received $400,000 from selling his year's output.   (b) How much profit is the entrepreneur earning from the point of view of the man in the street?   To what is the difference in the results due?   (c) What would happen if the entrepreneur's total revenue were $360,000 instead?

   (a) The explicit costs of this entrepreneur are $320,000 ($200,000 in wages plus $50,000 in interest plus $70,000 in rents).   His implicit costs are $50,000 ($40,000 in wages in his best alternative employment plus $10,000 interest on his money capital).   Thus, his total costs (explicit plus implicit) are $370,000.   Since the total revenue from selling the year's output is $400,000, this entrepreneur earns a (pure or economic) profit of $30,000 for the year.

(b) The man in the street would instead say that this entrepreneur's profit is $80,000 (the total revenue of $400,000 minus the out-of-pocket expenditures or explicit costs of $320,000).   However, $50,000 of this $80,000 represents the normal return on the entrepreneur's owned factors and is appropriately considered a cost by the economist.

(c) If the entrepreneur's total revenue were $360,000, he would earn less than a normal return on his owned factors (his wage and interest in the best alternative employment) and it would pay for him (eventually) to go out of business and work as a manager for and lend his money to someone else.   This clearly shows that implicit costs are indeed part of costs of production because they must be covered in order for the firm to remain in business and continue indefinitely to supply the goods or services it produces.

THE LAW OF DIMINISHING RETURNS

16.4.   (a) Distinguish between the short run and the long run.   (b) How long is the long run?

(a) The short run refers to the time period during which at least one factor of production, such as plant, is fixed in size and there is not sufficient time to change it.   Thus, in the short run, the firm can increase its output by hiring more labor and using more raw materials within its existing plant.   The time period sufficiently long for the firm to be able to change all of its factors of production, such as enlarging its plant or building a larger plant, is defined as the long run.

(b) The length of the long run depends on the industry under consideration.   For some firms producing services, the long run may be only a few weeks.   For others in basic industries, such as steel, it may be several years.   It all depends on how long it takes for the particular industry to be able to change all of its factors of production, including its plant size.

16.5.   (a) State the law of diminishing returns in terms of labor and land.   (b) When does the law of diminishing returns begin to operate?   What is its cause?   Why may it start only after some quantity of labor is employed?

(a) As more units of labor per unit of time are used to cultivate a fixed amount of land, after a point the extra or marginal output or product (MP) will *necessarily* decline.   This is one of the most important laws of production and is referred to as the law of diminishing returns.   Note that to observe the law of diminishing returns, at least one factor of production or input must be fixed.   Technology is also assumed to remain constant.

(b) The law of diminishing returns begins to operate when the marginal product resulting from an additional unit of a variable factor begins to decline.   Up to that point, the variable factor(s) have been used so sparsely with the fixed factors that we (may) get increasing rather than diminishing returns.   However, as we use more and more of the variable factors with some fixed factor(s), each unit of the variable factor will have less and less of the fixed factor(s) to work with, and diminishing returns will eventually result.

16.6.   Suppose that a tailor working alone can make 2 suits per month; 2 tailors working in the same shop can produce 5 suits; 3 tailors, 10 suits; 4 tailors, 14 suits; 5 tailors, 17 suits; and 6 tailors, 19 suits.   (a) Find the marginal product of labor (MP$_L$).   (b) When does the law of diminishing returns begin to operate?   Why do you have increasing returns up to that point?   (c) Why do diminishing returns eventually set in?

(a) See Table 5.

(b) The law of diminishing returns begins to operate with the addition of the fourth tailor.   Up to that point, the shop is underutilized.   Since a single tailor could either be taking measurements, cutting the fabric, or sewing the suit together, most of the equipment in the shop is idle most of the time.   As we go from one to two and then to three tailors, one tailor could be taking measurements most of the time, a second cutting the fabric, and the third sewing so that the men and equipment are in use almost constantly.   In addition, each tailor can now specialize and become more productive by performing only one specific routine.

Table 5

Number of Tailors	Number of Suits (TP per month)	Extra or Marginal Suits per Additional Tailor (MP_L)
0	0	
1	2	2
2	5	3
3	10	5
4	14	4
5	17	3
6	19	2

(c) Adding the fourth tailor to the same shop does not increase the number of suits proportionately (i.e. by one-quarter) but by less.   There is now not enough equipment in the shop to keep all four tailors fully occupied all the time.   The shop is also becoming ''too crowded'' and too much ''conversation'' may start going on.   Diminishing returns have set in and they become even smaller as still more tailors are added to the same shop.

SHORT-RUN TOTAL COSTS

16.7. (a) On the same set of axes, plot the TFC, TVC and TC schedules in Table 6. (b) Explain the reason for the shape of the curves.

Table 6

Q	TFC ($)	TVC ($)	TC ($)
0	120	0	120
1	120	60	180
2	120	80	200
3	120	90	210
4	120	105	225
5	120	140	260
6	120	210	330

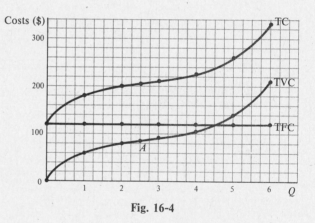

Fig. 16-4

(a) See Fig. 16-4.

(b) Since TFC are $120 per time period at all levels of output, the TFC curve is parallel to the horizontal axis and $120 above it.   TVC are zero when output is zero and rise as output rises. Up to about 2.5 units of output (point A), the law of diminishing returns does not operate and TVC increase at a decreasing rate.   Past 2.5 units of output, the law of diminishing returns operates and TVC increase at an increasing rate.   Thus, the TVC curve begins at the origin and is positively sloped.   It faces downward up to point A and faces upward thereafter.   Since TC equal TFC plus TVC, the TC curve has exactly the same shape as the TVC curve but is at all outputs $120 above it.

16.8. (a) Give some examples of fixed and variable factors in the short run.   (b) What is the relationship between the quantity of fixed inputs used and the short-run level of output?

(a) Fixed factors in the short run include payments for renting land and buildings, at least part of depreciation and maintenance expenditures, most kinds of insurance, property taxes, and some salaries such as those of top management, which are fixed by contract and may have to be paid over the life of the contract whether the firm produces or not.   Variable factors include raw materials, fuels, most types of labor, excise taxes, and interest on short-run loans.

(b) The quantity of fixed inputs used determines the size or the *scale of plant* which the firm operates in the short run.   Within the limits imposed by its scale of plant, the firm can vary its output in the short run by varying the quantity of variable inputs used per unit of time.

SHORT-RUN PER UNIT COSTS

16.9.   From Table 6, (a) find the AFC, the AVC and the AC schedules and (b) plot the AFC, AVC and AC on the same set of axes.   (c) Why does the AFC curve fall continuously?   What is the relationship between AFC, on the one hand, and the AC and AVC on the other?

(a)   See Table 7.   AFC equals TFC divided by output.   AVC equals TVC divided by output. AC equals TC divided by output.   AC also equals AFC plus AVC.

Table 7

Q	TFC ($)	TVC ($)	TC ($)	AFC ($)	AVC ($)	AC ($)
0	120	0	120			
1	120	60	180	120	60	180
2	120	80	200	60	40	100
3	120	90	210	40	30	70
4	120	105	225	30	26.25	56.25
5	120	140	260	24	28	52
6	120	210	330	20	35	55

(b)   See Fig. 16-5.

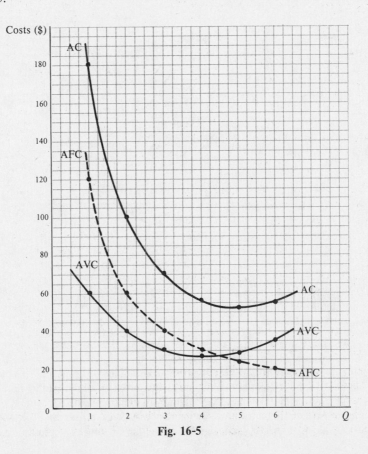

Fig. 16-5

(c) AFC in Table 7 declines continuously as output expands as TFC are spread over more and more units of output.   This is reflected in the continuously falling AFC curve of Fig. 16-5.   Since AC equals AFC plus AVC (see Table 7), the vertical distance between the AC curve and the AVC curve at each level of output in Fig. 16-5 represents AFC.   Thus, as output increases, the vertical distance between the AC curve and the AVC curve decreases, reflecting the continuously falling AFC.   For this reason, the AFC curve will be omitted in subsequent figures and chapters (and was dashed in Figs. 16-2 and 16-5).

16.10. Refer to Table 7.   (a) Find the MC schedule, and (b) on the same set of axes, plot the MC, AVC, and AC schedules.

(a) See Table 8.   MC equals the change in either TVC or TC per unit change in output.   Since TVC and TC differ only by TFC, *the change* in TVC and TC per unit change in output (MC) are the same.

Table 8

Q	TVC ($)	TC ($)	MC ($)
1	60	180	
2	80	200	20
3	90	210	10
4	105	225	15
5	140	260	35
6	210	330	70

(b) See Fig. 16-6.   Note once again that MC is recorded in Table 8 and plotted in Fig. 16-6 *between* the various levels of output

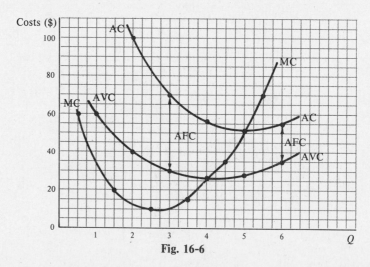

Fig. 16-6

16.11. (a) Why are the MC, AVC and AC curves U-shaped?   (b) Why does the AC curve reach its lowest point to the right of the point at which the AVC curve is lowest?   (c) Why does the MC curve intersect the AVC and the AC curves at their respective lowest points?

(a) As we start using variable factors with some fixed factors, we may first obtain increasing returns, but eventually diminishing returns will set in.   As a result, the MC, AVC and AC curves first fall but eventually rise, giving them their U shapes.

(b) The reason the AC curve reaches its lowest point at a higher level of output than the AVC curve is that for a while, the falling AFC (as output expands) more than counterbalances the rising AVC, and AC will continue to fall.   Because the AC curve does and the AVC curve does not include this falling AFC, the AC curve falls over a larger range of outputs than does the AVC curve.

(c) The MC curve always intersects the AVC and the AC curves at their respective lowest points because as long as MC is below AC, it pulls the average down.   When MC is above AC, it pulls the average up.   Only when MC equals AC, is AC neither falling nor rising (i.e. AC is at its lowest point).   This is logical.   For example, if your grade on the next quiz is lower than your previous average, your average will fall.   If your grade on the next quiz is higher than your previous average, your new average will be higher.   If your grade is equal to your previous average, the average will remain unchanged.

LONG-RUN PRODUCTION COSTS

16.12. Suppose that five of the alternative scales of plant that a firm can build in the long run are shown by the SAC schedules in Table 9.   (a) Sketch these five SAC curves on the same graph, and (b) show the firm's LAC curve if these five plants are the only ones that are feasible technologically.   Which plant would the firm use in the long run if it wanted to produce three units of output?   (c) Define the firm's LAC curve if the firm could build an infinite (or a very large) number of plants.

Table 9

SAC_1		SAC_2		SAC_3		SAC_4		SAC_5	
Q	SAC ($)	Q	SAC ($)	Q	SAC ($)	Q	SAC ($)	Q	SAC ($)
1	15.50	2	15.50	5	10.00	8	10.00	9	12.00
2	13.00	3	12.00	6	8.50	9	9.50	10	11.00
3	12.00	4	10.00	7	8.00	10	10.00	11	11.50
4	11.75	5	9.50	8	8.50	11	12.00	12	13.00
5	13.00	6	11.00	9	10.00	12	15.00	13	16.00

(a) See Fig. 16-7.

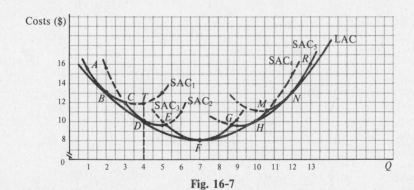

Fig. 16-7

(b) The firm's LAC curve is the solid portions of the SAC curves in Fig. 16-7.   That is, the LAC curve for the firm is given by the solid line joining points A, B, C, D, E, F, G, H, M, N and R. The dashed portions of the SAC curves are irrelevant since they represent higher-than-necessary AC for the firm in the long run.   If the firm wanted to produce three units of output per time period, the firm would utilize either plant 1 or plant 2 and the firm would be at point C.   In either case the SAC for the firm would be $12.

(c) If the firm could build an infinite (or a very large) number of alternative plants, in the long run, there would be a very large number of SAC curves.   By drawing a curve tangent to all these SAC curves we get the curve labeled LAC in Fig. 16-7.   This curve is the "envelope" of all the SAC curves and shows the minimum per-unit cost of producing each output when the firm can build any desired scale of plant.

16.13. From the LAC schedule in Table 10 (which corresponds to the LAC curve in Fig. 16-7), (*a*) find the long-run total costs (LTC) schedule, and (*b*) derive the long-run marginal costs (LMC) schedule.   What do these measure?   (*c*) What is the relationship between LAC and LMC?

Table 10

Q	1	2	3	4	5	6	7	8	9	10	11	12
LAC ($)	15	13	11.30	10	9	8.30	8	8.20	8.90	10	11.30	13

(*a*) The LTC for any level of output can be obtained by multiplying output by the LAC at that level of output.   LTC show the minimum total costs of producing various levels of output when any scale of plant can be built.   LMC equals the change in LTC per unit change in output.   The LTC and LMC are calculated in Table 11.   Note that the LMC is entered *between* the various levels of output.

Table 11

Q	1	2	3	4	5	6	7	8	9	10	11	12
LAC ($)	15	13	11.30	10	9	8.30	8	8.20	8.90	10	11.30	13
LTC ($)	15	26	33.90	40	45	49.80	56	65.60	80.10	100	124.30	156
LMC ($)	11		7.90	6.10	5	4.80	6.20	9.40	14.50	19.90	24.30	31.70

(*b*) In Fig. 16-8, the LMC values are plotted between the various levels of output.

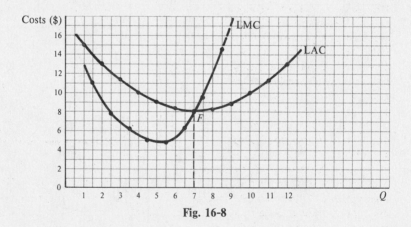

Fig. 16-8

(*c*) The relationship between LMC and LAC is the same as between SAC and SMC.   That is, when the LAC curve is falling, the LMC curve is below it; LMC = LAC when LAC is lowest; and when the LAC curve is rising, the LMC curve is above it.

CONSTANT, INCREASING AND DECREASING RETURNS TO SCALE

16.14. Explain (*a*) constant returns to scale, (*b*) increasing returns to scale and (*c*) decreasing returns to scale.   Give examples.

(*a*) *Constant returns to scale* occurs when all factors of production are increased in a given proportion and the output produced increases in the *same* proportion.   If, for example, the quantities of labor and capital used per unit of time are both increased by 10%, output will also increase by 10%; if labor and capital are doubled, output doubles.   This makes sense: if we use two workers of the same type and two identical machines, we expect twice as much output as with one worker with one machine.   Similarly, if all inputs are reduced by a given proportion, output is reduced by the same proportion.   As a result, long-run average cost (LAC) is constant.

(b) *Increasing returns to scale* occurs when all factors are increased in a given proportion and output increases in a *greater* proportion.   If labor and capital are increased by 10%, output rises by more than 10%; if labor and capital are doubled, output more than doubles.   As a result, LAC declines.   Increasing returns to scale may occur because by increasing the scale of operation, greater division of labor and specialization becomes possible.   That is, each worker can specialize in performing a simple repetitive task rather than many different tasks.   As a result, labor productivity increases.   Time is also not wasted by workers going from one machine to another. In addition, a larger scale of operation may permit the use of more productive, specialized machinery which was not feasible at a lower scale of operation.   A great part of our high productivity and standard of living is due to these *economies of mass production*.

(c) If output increases in a *smaller* proportion than the increase in all inputs, we have decreasing returns to scale and increasing LAC.   For example, an increase in the scale of operation may cause communications problems which make it more and more difficult for the entrepreneur to operate effectively.   It is generally believed that at very small scales of operation, the firm encounters increasing returns to scale.   As the scale of operation rises, increasing returns give way to constant returns to scale and eventually to decreasing returns to scale.   Whether this is the case for a particular firm is an empirical question.

16.15. (a) Draw an LAC curve showing increasing returns to scale in the first small range of outputs, constant returns to scale in the ensuing "large range" of outputs, and decreasing returns to scale thereafter.   (b) What does this LAC curve imply for the sizes of the firms in the same industry?

(a) In Fig. 16-9, we have increasing returns to scale and decreasing LAC up to output *OA*; we have constant returns to scale and constant LAC between the output levels *OA* and *OB*; past output *OB*, we have decreasing returns to scale and increasing LAC.   LAC and returns to scale are opposite sides of the same coin.   Note that economies and diseconomies of scale may both operate in the same range of outputs.   When economies of scale overwhelm diseconomies of scale, the LAC curve falls; otherwise the LAC is either constant or rising. The actual output level at which the LAC stops falling or starts rising depends, of course, on the industry.

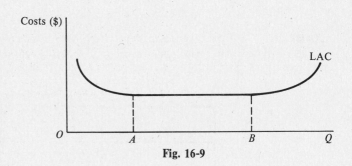

Fig. 16-9

(b) An LAC curve with a flat bottom, showing constant returns to scale over a wide range of outputs, implies that small firms may coexist side by side with larger firms in the same industry.   If increasing returns to scale operated over a very wide range of outputs, large firms (operating large plants) would have much lower LAC than small firms and would drive the latter out of business.   Many economists and businessmen believe (and some empirical studies indicate) that the LAC curve in many industries has a flat bottom, as shown in Fig. 16-9.   In such cases, the flat portion of the LAC curve is formed by the lowest point of a number of SAC curves.

Chapter 17

Price and Output: Perfect Competition

17.1 PERFECT COMPETITION DEFINED

An industry is said to be *perfectly competitive* if (1) it is composed of a large number of independent sellers of a commodity, each too small to affect the commodity price; (2) all firms in the industry sell homogeneous (identical) products; and (3) there is perfect mobility of resources, and firms can enter or leave the industry in the long run without much difficulty. As a result, the perfectly competitive firm is a "price taker" and can sell any amount of the commodity at the prevailing market price.

EXAMPLE 1. Perhaps the closest we have ever come to perfect competition is in the market for such agricultural commodities as wheat, corn and cotton. There, we may have a large number of producers each too small to affect commodity price. The output of each farmer (say wheat of a given grade) is identical, and it is rather easy to enter or leave this industry. The perfectly competitive model is used to analyze markets, such as these, that approximate perfect competition. It is also used to evaluate the efficiency of the other forms of market organization (see Chapters 18 and 19).

17.2 PROFIT MAXIMIZATION IN THE SHORT RUN: THE TOTAL APPROACH

A firm maximizes total profits in the short run when the (positive) difference between total revenue (TR) and total costs (TC) is greatest. TR equals price times quantity. TC were examined in Section 16.3.

EXAMPLE 2. In Table 1, quantity (column 1) times price (column 2) equals TR (column 3). TR minus TC (column 4) equals total profits (column 5). Total profits are maximized (at $16.90) when the firm sells 6.5 units of output (if we assume that fractional units, such as parts of a bushel of wheat, can be produced and sold).

Table 1

(1) Q	(2) P ($)	(3) TR ($)	(4) TC ($)	(5) Total Profits ($)
0	8	0	8	− 8
1	8	8	20	−12
2	8	16	23	− 7
3	8	24	24	0
4	8	32	25.40	+ 6.60
5	8	40	28	+12
6	8	48	32	+16
*6.5	8	52	35.10	+16.90*
7	8	56	40	+16
8	8	64	64	0

EXAMPLE 3. The profit-maximizing level of output for this firm can be seen graphically in Fig. 17-1 (obtained by plotting the values of columns 3 and 4 of Table 1). TR is a positively sloped straight line through the origin because P is constant at $8. At outputs smaller than 3 and larger than 8, TC exceeds TR and the firm incurs losses. At the outputs of 3 and 8 (points A and B), TR = TC and the firm breaks even. Between A and B, TR exceeds TC and the firm makes a profit. Total profits are maximized at 6.5 units of output when TR exceeds TC by the greatest amount ($16.90).

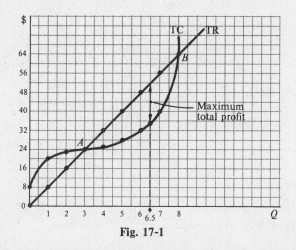

Fig. 17-1

17.3   PROFIT MAXIMIZATION IN THE SHORT RUN: MARGINAL APPROACH

In general, it is more useful to analyze the short-run behavior of the firm by using the marginal-revenue-marginal-cost approach.   Marginal revenue (MR) is the change in TR per unit change in the quantity sold.   Since the perfectly competitive firm can sell any quantity of the commodity at the prevailing price, its MR = P, and the demand curve it faces is horizontal at that price.   The perfectly competitive firm maximizes its short-run total profits at the output at which *MR or P equals MC* (and MC is rising).

EXAMPLE 4. In Table 2, MR (column 4) is the change in TR and is recorded *between* the various quantities sold.   MC (column 7) is the change in TVC and in TC and is also entered *between* the various levels of output.   AVC (column 8) equals TVC/Q.   AC (column 9) equals TC/Q.   Profit per unit (column 10) equals $P - $ AC.   Total profits (column 11) equal profits per unit times the quantities sold (and are the same as in column 5 of Table 1, except for rounding).   Note that total profits are maximized at $16.90 when the firm produces and sells 6.5 units of output (as in the total approach of Table 1).   At that level of output, MR or $P = $ MC and MC is rising.

Table 2

(1) Q	(2) P ($)	(3) TR ($)	(4) MR ($)	(5) TVC ($)	(6) TC ($)	(7) MC ($)	(8) AVC ($)	(9) AC ($)	(10) Profit per unit ($)	(11) Total Profits ($)
0	8	0		0	8		—	—	—	− 8
			8			12				
1	8	8		12	20		12	20	−12	−12
			8			3				
2	8	16		15	23		7.5	11.50	− 3.50	− 7
			8			1				
3	8	24		16	24		5.33	8	0	0
			8			1.40				
4	8	32		17.40	25.40		4.35	6.35	+ 1.65	+ 6.60
			8			2.60				
5	8	40		20	28		4	5.60	+ 2.40	+12
			8			4				
6	8	48		24	32		4	5.33	+ 2.67	+16.02
			8			8				
*6.5	8	52		27.10	35.10		4.17	5.40	+ 2.60	+16.90*
			8			24				
7	8	56		32	40		4.57	5.71	+ 2.29	+16.03
8	8	64		56	64		7	8	0	0

EXAMPLE 5.   The profit-maximizing (or best) level of output of this firm can also be viewed in Fig. 17-2. The MC and AC values are from Table 2.   The demand curve facing the firm is horizontal at $P = $8 = $ MR. As long as MR exceeds MC, it pays for the firm to expand output.   The firm would be adding more to its TR

than to its TC and so its total profits would rise.   It does not pay for the firm to produce past point C since MC exceeds MR.   The firm would add more to its TC than to its TR and so its total profits would fall.   Thus, the firm maximizes its total profits at the output level of 6.5 units (given by point C where P or MR equals MC and MC is rising).   The profit per unit at this level of output is CF or $2.60 (see Table 2) and total profit is given by the area of rectangle $CFGH$ which equals $16.90.

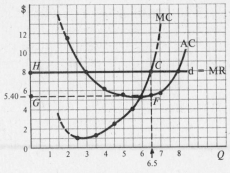

Fig. 17-2

17.4   SHORT-RUN PROFIT OR LOSS

If, at the point wher MR $= P =$ rising MC, P exceeds AC, the firm is maximizing its total profits.   If $P =$ AC, the firm is breaking even.   If P is larger than AVC but smaller than AC, the firm minimizes total losses.   If P is smaller than AVC, the firm minimizes its total losses by shutting down.   Thus, $P =$ AVC is the *shut-down point* for the firm.

EXAMPLE 6.   In Fig. 17-3, the AVC curve (from column 8 of Table 2) and three *alternative* demand and MR curves that the firm might face are shown with the MC and AC curves of Fig. 17-2.   With d_3, the firm produces at C and $Q = 6.5$, profit per unit equals $2.60 and total profits $= 16.90 (as in Example 5).   With d_2, the firm produces at J and breaks even (since $P =$ AC).   With d_1, $P =$ AVC (point T) and the firm incurs a loss per unit equal to its AFC and a total loss equal to its TFC, whether it produces or not.   Thus, T is the shut-down point.   Below $P = 4$, the firm minimizes its total losses (equal to its TFC) by shutting down.   Between the prices of $4 and $5.33, P exceeds AVC so that the firm is also covering part of its AFC.   In this case, the firm minimizes its total losses by staying in business.

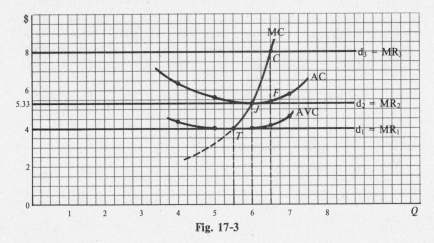

Fig. 17-3

17.5   FIRM'S SHORT-RUN SUPPLY CURVE

Since the perfectly competitive firm always produces where MR $= P =$ rising MC (as long as P exceeds AVC), the firm's short-run supply curve is given by the rising portion of its MC curve over and above its AVC or shut-down point.

EXAMPLE 7.   The short-run supply curve of the firm of Fig. 17-3 is the rising portion of its MC curve above T (shut-down point).   If factor prices remain constant, the short-run supply curve of the competitive *industry* is obtained by adding the individual firms' supply curves (see Problem 17.11).   The (equilibrium) price at which all firms in this competitive industry sell their output is determined by the intersection of this industry supply curve and the market demand curve (see Problem 17.12).

17.6   LONG-RUN EQUILIBRIUM OF THE COMPETITIVE FIRM

If the firms in a perfectly competitive industry are making short-run profits, more firms will enter the industry in the long run.   This increases the market supply of the commodity and reduces the market price until all profits are competed away and all firms just break even.   The exact opposite occurs if we start with firms with short-run losses.   As a result, all firms in a perfectly competitive industry with long-run equilibrium produce where P = lowest LAC.   Resources are utilized in the most efficient way to produce the goods and services most wanted by society, and consumers pay the lowest possible price.

EXAMPLE 8.   Figure 17-4 shows that each firm in a perfectly competitive industry at long-run equilibrium produces at point E, where P = SAC = SMC = lowest LAC.   The forces that inevitably lead to point E are explained in Problem 17.13.   Some shortcomings of perfect competition are discussed in Problem 17.15.

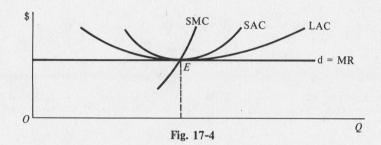

Fig. 17-4

17.7   CONSTANT, INCREASING AND DECREASING COST INDUSTRIES

When industry output expands as more firms enter the industry and more factors of production are demanded in the long run, factor prices might remain constant, rise, or fall.   This leads to a constant, increasing or decreasing cost industry, respectively.   The long-run supply curve of a *constant-cost industry* is horizontal.   It rises in an *increasing-cost industry* and falls in a *decreasing-cost industry* (see Problems 17.16 and 17.17).   Of the three, increasing-cost industries are the most common.

Important Economic Terms

Break-even point.   The output level at which the firm's total revenue equals its total costs and its total profits are zero.

Constant-cost industry.   An industry whose long-run supply curve is horizontal because factor prices remain constant as industry output expands.

Decreasing-cost industry.   An industry whose long-run supply curve is negatively sloped because factor prices fall as industry output expands.

External diseconomy.   An upward shift in a firm's cost curves as industry output expands.

External economy.   The downward shift in a firm's cost curves as industry output expands.

Increasing-cost industry.   An industry whose long-run supply curve is positively sloped because factor prices rise as industry output expands.

Marginal revenue (MR).   The change in TR for a unit change in the quantity sold.   With perfect competition, P is constant, and MR = P.

Perfect competition.   The form of market organization in which (1) there are a large number of sellers, each too small to affect the commodity price, (2) all firms in the industry produce homogeneous (identical) products, and (3) there is perfect mobility of resources, and firms can enter or leave the industry in the long run without difficulty.

Perfectly competitive firm's short-run supply curve.   The rising portion of the firm's MC curve above its AVC or shut-down point.

Shut-down point.   The output level at which P = AVC which involves a loss equal to TFC, whether the firm produces or not.

Review Questions

1. In perfect competition, (a) there are a large number of independent sellers, each too small to affect the commodity price, (b) the product of all firms is homogeneous or identical, (c) firms can easily enter or leave the industry, (d) all of the above.

    Ans.   (d)

2. A firm maximizes its total profits when (a) TR = TC, (b) TC exceeds TR by the greatest amount, (c) TR exceeds TC by the greatest amount, (d) it is at the break-even point.

    Ans.   (c)

3. The demand curve faced by a perfectly competitive firm is (a) negatively sloped, (b) positively sloped, (c) horizontal, (d) any of the above.

    Ans.   (c)

4. MR for the perfectly competitive firm (a) is equal to the change in TR per unit change in the quantity sold, (b) equals P, (c) is constant, (d) all of the above.

    Ans.   (d)

5. In the marginal approach, the best level of output for a perfectly competitive firm is the output at which (a) MR or P = rising MC, (b) MR or P = falling MC, (c) AC is lowest, (d) AVC is lowest,

    Ans.   (a)

6. If at the output at which MC or P = rising MC, P = AC, the firm is (a) making a profit, (b) breaking even, (c) minimizing losses, (d) at its shut-down point.

    Ans.   (b)

7. If at the best level of output, P is smaller than AC but higher than AVC, the firm (a) shuts down, (b) breaks even, (c) minimizes total losses, (d) maximizes total profits.

    Ans.   (c)

8. If at the best level of output, P is smaller than AC but higher than AVC, the firm (a) incurs total losses greater than its TFC, (b) incurs total losses equal to its TFC, (c) incurs total losses smaller than its TFC, (d) makes a profit.

    Ans.   (c)

9. The shut-down point for the firm is the output of lowest (a) AC, (b) AVC, (c) MC, (d) P.

    Ans.   (b)

10. The competitive firm's short-run supply curve is the rising portion of the (a) MC curve above AVC, (b) MC curve above AC, (c) AC curve above AVC, (d) AVC curve above MC.

    Ans.   (a)

11. A perfectly competitive firm in long-run equilibrium produces the output at which (a) P = lowest SAC, (b) P = lowest LAC, (c) P = SMC, (d) all of the above.

    Ans.   (d)

12. If factor prices rise as industry output expands in the long run, we have (a) a constant-cost industry, (b) a decreasing-cost industry, (c) an increasing-cost industry, (d) any of the above.

    Ans.   (c)

Solved Problems

PERFECT COMPETITION DEFINED

17.1. Explain each of the three component parts of the definition of perfect competition given in Section 17.1.

  (1) There are a large number of independent sellers of the commodity, each too small in relation to the market to be able to affect the price of the commodity by its own actions. This means that a change in the output of a single firm will not *perceptibly* affect the market price of the commodity.

  (2) The products of the firms in the market are homogeneous, identical or perfectly standardized. As a result, the buyer cannot distinguish between the product of one firm and that of another, and so he is indifferent as to the particular firm from which he buys. This refers not only to the physical characteristics of the commodity but also to the "environment" (such as the location and pleasantness of the seller, etc.) in which the purchase is made.

  (3) There is perfect mobility of resources. That is, workers and other inputs can easily move geographically and from one job to another, and respond very quickly to monetary incentives. In the long run, firms (entrepreneurs) can enter or leave the industry without much difficulty. That is, the products are not patented or copyrighted, vast amounts of capital are not necessary to enter the industry, and already-established firms do not have any lasting cost advantages based on experience over new entrants.

17.2. (*a*) Does perfect competition, as defined above, exist in the real world? (*b*) Why do we study the perfectly competitive model?

  (*a*) Perfect competition, as defined above, has never existed. Perhaps the closest we may have come to satisfying the three assumptions is in the market for certain agricultural commodities such as wheat and corn.

  (*b*) The fact that perfect competition has never existed in the real world does not reduce the usefulness of the perfectly competitive model. The perfectly competitive model does give us some very useful (if at times rough) explanations and predictions of many real-world economic phenomena when assumptions are only approximately (rather than exactly) satisfied. In addition, this model helps us evaluate and compare the *efficiency* with which resources are used under different forms of market organization.

17.3. A car manufacturer may regard his business as highly competitive because he is keenly aware of his rivalry with the few other car manufacturers in the market. Each car manufacturer undertakes vigorous advertising campaigns seeking to convince potential buyers of the superior quality and better style of his automobiles and reacts very quickly to claims of superiority by his rivals. Is this the meaning of perfect competition from the economist's point of view? Explain.

  The above market is diametrically opposed to the economist's view of perfect competition. It describes a market which stresses the rivalry among firms. The economist's view stresses the *impersonality* of a perfectly competitive market. According to the economist, in a perfectly competitive market there are so many independent sellers of the commodity, each so small in relation to the market, that no seller regards others as competitors or rivals. The products of all firms in the market are homogeneous and so there is no rivalry among firms based on advertising, quality and style differences.

PROFIT MAXIMIZATION IN THE SHORT RUN: TOTAL APPROACH

17.4. (*a*) How can the firm increase its output in the short run? (*b*) How many units of the commodity can the firm sell in the short run at the prevailing commodity price? (*c*) What is the shape of the total revenue curve of a perfectly competitive firm?   Why?   (*d*) What is the shape of the short-run total cost curve of the firm?   Why?   (*e*) When is the firm in short-run equilibrium?

(*a*)   Within the limitations imposed by its given scale of plant, the firm can vary the amount of the commodity produced in the short run by varying its use of the variable inputs.

(*b*)   The perfectly competitive firm is too small to affect market price and can sell any amount of the commodity at the prevailing market price.

(*c*)   The TR of a perfectly competitive firm is shown by a positively sloped straight line through the origin.   This is the case whenever commodity price is constant.

(*d*)   The short-run total cost of the firm is equal to its fixed costs at zero output.   It rises at a decreasing rate (faces down) as output rises, before the law of diminishing returns begins to operate, and it rises at an increasing rate (faces up) thereafter.

(*e*)   The firm is in short-run equilibrium when it maximizes its total profits or minimizes its total losses.   It should be noted that not all firms seek to maximize total profits (or minimize total losses) at all times.   However, the assumption of profit maximization is essential if we are to have a general theory of the firm.   The short-run equilibrium of the firm can be looked at from a total revenue-total cost approach or from a marginal revenue-marginal cost approach.

17.5.   If short-run TVC and TC of a firm at various outputs are the values in Table 3 and $P = \$4$, (*a*) determine the output and dollar amount at which the firm maximizes total profits.   At what two levels of output does the firm break even?   (*b*) Plot the TR and TC schedules on one set of axes and indicate the point of profit maximization.

Table 3

Q	0	10	20	30	40	50	60	65	70	75	80	85	90
TVC	0	35	65	85	95	105	120	131	145	162	185	225	295
TC	65	100	130	150	160	170	185	196	210	227	250	290	360

(*a*)   Table 4 shows that this firm maximizes its total profits of $73 at 75 units of output, and breaks even at 40 and 90 units of output.

Table 4

(1) Q	(2) P ($)	(3) TR ($)	(4) TVC ($)	(5) TC ($)	(6) Total Profits ($)	(7) Position
0	4	0	0	65	−65	Losses
10	4	40	35	100	−60	Losses
20	4	80	65	130	−50	Losses
30	4	120	85	150	−30	Losses
40	4	160	95	160	0	Break-even Point
50	4	200	105	170	+30	Profits
60	4	240	120	185	+55	Profits
65	4	260	131	196	+64	Profits
70	4	280	145	210	+70	Profits
75	4	300	162	227	+73	Total Profits Maximized
80	4	320	185	250	+70	Profits
85	4	340	225	290	+50	Profits
90		360	295	360	0	Break-even Point

(*b*) See Fig. 17-5.

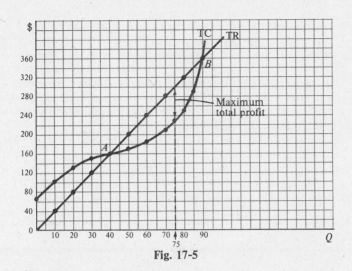

Fig. 17-5

PROFIT MAXIMIZATION IN THE SHORT RUN: MARGINAL APPROACH

17.6. (*a*) Define marginal revenue.   How is it calculated?   Why is marginal revenue constant and equal to price under perfect competition?   (*b*) What is the shape and elasticity of the demand curve facing a perfectly competitive firm?   Why?   (*c*) What is the shape of and relationship among the firm's MC, AVC and AC curves?   Why?   (*d*) How does the firm determine how much to produce in the short run?

  (*a*)   MR is defined as and is equal to the change in TR for a 1-unit change in the quantity sold.   Since the perfectly competitive firm can sell any amount of the commodity at the prevailing market price, its MR = P = constant.   For example, if P = \$4, TR = \$4 when the firm sells 1 unit and TR = \$8 for 2 units.   Thus, MR = change in TR = \$4 = P.

  (*b*)   Since the perfectly competitive firm can sell any amount at the prevailing market price, the demand curve it faces is *horizontal* or *infinitely elastic* at the prevailing market price.   With a horizontal demand curve, an infinitely *small* fall in price causes an infinitely *large* increase in sales.   As the denominator of the elasticity formula (the percentage change in price) approaches zero and the numerator (the percentage change in quantity) becomes very large, the value of the fraction and elasticity (E_d) approaches infinity (see Section 14.2).

  (*c*)   The MC, AVC and AC curves of the firm are usually U-shaped.   MC, AVC and AC eventually rise because of diminishing returns.   The rising portion of the MC curve intersects the AVC and AC curves at their lowest points.   AC − AVC = AFC.   Since AFC declines continuously as output expands, the AC curve reaches its minimum point at a higher level of output than the AVC curve.

  (*d*)   We can determine how much a firm produces in the short run by making the reasonable assumption that the firm wants to maximize its total profits or minimize its total losses.   The general rule is that the firm should expand its output until MR = rising MC (as long as *P* exceeds AVC).   Total profits are maximized when the (positive) difference between TR and TC is greatest.   A firm should expand its output as long as the addition to TR from an additional unit sold (its MR) exceeds the addition to TC to produce this extra unit (its MC).   As long as MR exceeds (>) MC, and up to the point where MR = MC, the firm can increase its total profits by expanding output. The firm should not produce any unit for which MC > MR.   If it did, it would be adding more to its TC than to its TR and its total profits would fall.

17.7. From Table 4, construct a table similar to Table 2 showing MR, MC, AVC, AC, profit per unit, total profits and the profit-maximizing level of output.

  In Table 5, MR (column 4) equals the change in TR per unit change in sales.   For example, as the quantity sold rises from zero to 10, TR rises from zero to \$40, giving an average change in TR per additional unit sold of \$40/10 = \$4 = MR (entered *between* Q = 0 and Q = 10).   Similarly, MC equals the change in TVC or TC per unit change in output.   For example, as Q rises from 0 to 10, TC rises from \$65 to \$100, giving an MC of \$35/10 = \$3.50 for each of the additional 10 units produced (entered *between* Q = 0 and Q = 10). Note that the MR and MC between Q = 60 and 70, Q = 70 and 80 and Q = 80 and 90, are entered *alongside* the midvalues of 65, 75 and 85, respectively. AVC (column 8) equals TVC/Q. AC (column 9) equals TC/Q. Profit per unit (column 10) equals P − AC. Total profits (column 11) equal profit per unit times the units produced (and equal the values in Table 4, except for rounding). As in the case of the total approach, the marginal approach indicates that this firm maximizes its total profits when it produces and sells 75 units of output, given by the point where MR or P = rising MC (and P > AVC).

Table 5

(1) Q	(2) P (\$)	(3) TR (\$)	(4) MR (\$)	(5) TVC (\$)	(6) TC (\$)	(7) MC (\$)	(8) AVC (\$)	(9) AC (\$)	(10) Profit per Unit (\$)	(11) Total Profit (\$)
0	4	0		0	65		—	—	—	−65
			4			3.50				
10	4	40		35	100		3.50	10	−6	−60
			4			3				
20	4	80		65	130		3.25	6.50	−2.50	−50
			4			2				
30	4	120		85	150		2.83	5	−1	−30
			4			1				
40	4	160		95	160		2.38	4	0	0
			4			1				
50	4	200		105	170		2.10	3.40	+0.60	+30
			4			1.50				
60	4	240		120	185		2	3.08	+0.92	+55.20
65	4	260	4	131	196	2.50	2.02	3.02	+0.98	+63.70
70	4	280		145	210		2.07	3	+1	+70
*75	4	300	4	162	227	4	2.16	3.03	+0.97	+72.75
80	4	320		185	250		2.31	3.13	+0.87	+69.60
85	4	340	4	225	290	11	2.65	3.41	+0.59	+50.15
90	4	360		295	360		3.28	4	0	0

17.8. (*a*) On the same set of axes, plot the firm's demand curve and its MC and AC curves from Table 5. Indicate the output at which the firm maximizes its total profits. (*b*) At what output level is profit per unit greatest? Why does the firm not produce at this output?

(*a*) In Fig. 17-6, the best level of output is 75 units (indicated by point *C*, where MR = rising MC). Since at *C*, P = \$4 while AC = \$3.03, the firm is earning a profit per unit (P − AC) of \$0.97 (*CF* in Fig. 17-6) and a total profit of \$72.75 (\$0.97 times 75 units) which equals the area of rectangle *CFGH*.

(*b*) Profit *per unit* is maximized at the lowest point on the AC curve, where Q = 70 (see Fig. 17-6 and Table 5). At that point AC = \$3, so that a price of \$4 gives

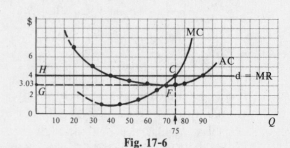

Fig. 17-6

a profit per unit of $1. However, total profit at that point is $70 as opposed to $73 (rounded to the nearest dollar) at point C, and the firm wants to maximize total profits—not profit per unit.

PROFIT OR LOSS

17.9. From Table 5, (a) plot the AC and AVC curves and the rising portion of the firm's MC curve. On the same figure, draw five alternative demand curves that the firm might face: d_5 at $P = \$4$, d_4 at $P = \$3$, d_3 at $P = \$2.50$, d_2 at $P = \$2$ and d_1 at $P = \$1.50$. (b) Set up a table indicating for each alternative demand curve, the best level of output, AC, profit per unit, total profits, whether the firm produces or not, and whether it makes profits or losses.

(a) See Fig. 17-7.

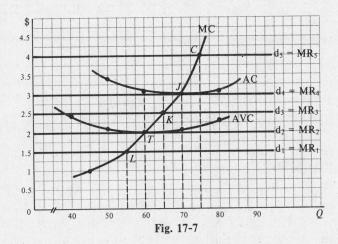

Fig. 17-7

(b) Table 6 shows that with d_5, the firm maximizes total profits. With d_4, $P = AC$ and $TR = TC$ so that the firm breaks even. With d_3, the firm minimizes total losses at $33.80 by producing 65 units of output. If the firm stopped producing, it would incur losses equal to its TFC of $65. Thus, by producing, the firm recovers all of its TVC plus part of TFC. With d_2, the firm's total losses equal $65 (rounded to the nearest dollar) whether it produces or not. This is the shut-down point for the firm. With d_1, the best level of output is 55 units (at which MR = rising MC). However, at this output, the firm's total losses would equal $92.40. But by stopping production altogether and going out of business, the firm would limit its total losses to only $65 (its TFC). Thus, the firm would not produce at $P = \$1.50$.

Table 6

Demand	Q	AC ($)	Profit per Unit ($)	Total Profits ($)	Result
d_5 ($P=\$4$)	75 (point C)	3.03	0.97	+72.75	Total profits maximized
d_4 ($P=\$3$)	70 (point J)	3	0	0	Break-even point
d_3 ($P=\$2.50$)	65 (point K)	3.02	−0.52	−33.80	Total losses minimized
d_2 ($P=\$2$)	60 (point T)	3.08	−1.08	−64.80	Shut-down point
d_1 ($P=\$1.50$)	55 (point L)	3.18	−1.68	−92.40	Firm does not produce

17.10. On a set of axes, draw typical AC, AVC and MC curves and five alternative demand curves that the perfectly competitive firm might face. Draw d_5 such that the firm makes a profit and indicate by point A where the firm produces and by AB the profit per unit. Draw d_4 so that the firm breaks even and indicate by point C where the firm produces. Draw d_3 such that the firm minimizes its total losses and indicate by point D where the firm produces and by *DE* the losses per unit.   Draw d₂ such that the firm is at its shut-down point and indicate by point *F* where the firm would produce (if it chose to) and by *FG* the losses per unit.   Draw d₁ such that the firm would prefer to shut down rather than produce at point *H*.

See Fig. 17-8.

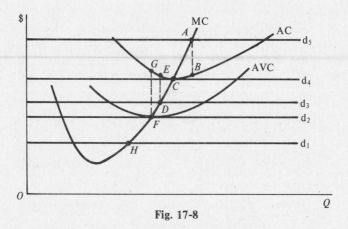

Fig. 17-8

FIRM'S SHORT-RUN SUPPLY CURVE

17.11. (*a*) What gives the firm's short-run supply curve?   Why?   (*b*) Draw the short-run supply curve of the perfectly competitive firm of Problem 17.9, and a short-run *industry* supply curve on the assumption that there are 100 identical firms in this perfectly competitive industry (and factor prices remain constant).

(*a*) The best level of output for any firm is the output at which MR = rising MC.   Since under perfect competition, MR = P, the firm should produce the output at which P = rising MC, as long as P > AVC.   Given the market price, we can read off the MC curve how much the perfectly competitive firm would produce and sell at that price.   This unique price-quantity relationship is nothing more than the firm's supply curve.   Therefore, we can say that the firm's MC curve above its AVC or shut-down point is the competitive firm's short-run supply curve.

(*b*) Panel A of Fig. 17-9 shows the short-run supply curve of the competitive firm.   Note that at prices below $2, the firm supplies zero units of the commodity.   Panel B shows the industry's short-run supply curve (S).   Note that the quantity supplied by the industry at each price is 100 times greater than the quantity supplied by a single firm and reflects the assumption that there are 100 identical firms in the industry (the symbol "Σ" stands for the summation of).   This conclusion is based on the assumption that as the commodity price rises and each firm in the industry expands its output (and demands more factors), *factor prices* remain constant.

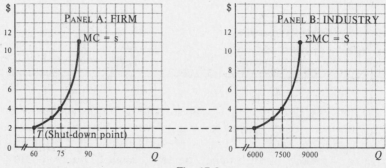

Fig. 17-9

17.12. (*a*) Redraw Fig. 17-9.   Add to Panel B a typical market demand curve for the commodity intersecting the industry supply curve at P = $4.   Add to Panel A the firm's demand curve and its AC and AVC curves (from Problem 17.9).   (*b*) Explain the sequence of events shown by this figure.

(*a*) See Fig. 17-10.

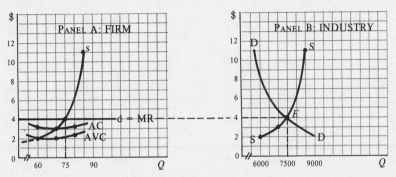

Fig. 17-10

(*b*) The sequence of events shown in Fig. 17-10 is as follows.   We start in Panel A with the firm's MC curve above its AVC or shut-down point.   This is the competitive firm's short-run supply curve (s).   By multiplying this by 100, we get the competitive industry short-run supply curve (S, in Panel B).   At the intersection of the market demand (D) and supply (S) curves, we find the equilibrium market price of $4 (point *E* in Panel B).   Each competitive firm is too small to affect the commodity price (i.e. each firm is a "price taker") and can sell any quantity at that price.   Thus, each firm's demand curve is horizontal or infinitely elastic at the equilibrium market price of $4.   Since *P* is constant, *P* = MR and d = MR (in Panel A).   Given the firm's MC curve, the firm produces where MR = *P* = rising MC (75 units in Panel A).   Since there are 100 identical firms in the industry, the equilibrium market quantity is 7500 units (in Panel B).   At 75 units of output, each firm makes a profit per unit equal to the excess of *P* over AC ($0.97, from Table 5) and maximizes its total profits at $73 (rounded to the nearest dollar) by multiplying the per-unit profit of $0.97 times *Q* = 75.

LONG-RUN EQUILIBRIUM OF THE FIRM

17.13. Starting at point *E* in Fig. 17-4, show what happens if the equilibrium market price (*a*) rises and (*b*) falls.

(*a*) Figure 17-11 shows that as the equilibrium market price rises, d shifts up, say, to d'.   Each firm then produces at point *A* in the short run, where MR or *P* = rising MC, and makes a profit per unit of *AB*.   Profits attract new firms into this industry in the long run.   This will increase industry output and reduce market price until all firms (old and new) produce at point *E*, where *P* = SAC = SMC = lowest LAC and are in long-run equilibrium.   Industry output is now larger

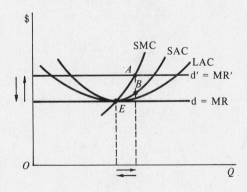

Fig. 17-11

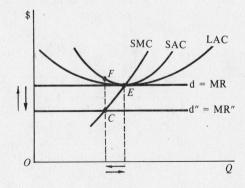

Fig. 17-12

because there are more firms in the industry.   The market price is the same as the original long-run equilibrium price, if factor prices are assumed to remain constant.

(b)   Figure 17-12 shows that as the equilibrium market price falls, d shifts down, say, to d″.   Each firm then produces at point C in the short run, where MR or P = rising MC (as long as P > AVC) and incurs a loss per unit of CF.   As a result, some firms leave the industry in the long run. This will lower the industry output and increase market price until all the remaining firms produce at point E, where P = SAC = SMC = lowest LAC, and are once again in long-run equilibrium. This conclusion is also based on the assumption that factor prices remain constant as fewer factors are demanded to produce the smaller industry output.

17.14.   Discuss the advantages of perfect competition.

The most important advantages of the perfectly competitive form of market organization are that resources are utilized in the most efficient way to produce the goods and services most wanted by society and that consumers pay the lowest possible prices.   In long-run equilibrium, each perfectly competitive firm operates the *optimum scale of plant* at the *optimum level of output*.   This is given by the lowest point of the SAC curve, which generates the lowest point of the LAC curve.   Resources could not possibly be arranged more efficiently.   Furthermore, since the forces of competition eliminate all profits in the long run, consumers get the good or service at P = lowest LAC.   Finally, since the commodity price measures the utility or satisfaction that the last unit of the commodity produced gives the consumer, and this is equated to the MC of producing this unit, there is no better use of these resources.   That is, the same resources could not possibly be used to produce goods and services which give greater utility or satisfaction to consumers.   As a result, perfect competition is used as the standard against which the efficiency of other forms of market organization (discussed in Chapters 18 and 19) is compared.

17.15.   What are the major shortcomings of the perfectly competitive market organization?

First, some economists believe that while perfect competition may be the most efficient form of market organization *at one point in time,* it might not be the most efficient *over time*.   The perfectly competitive firm is generally small and makes no profit (aside from normal returns on its investment) in the long run.   It is thus not able to undertake "sufficient" research and development (R & D), which perhaps more than anything else is responsible for today's high standard of living.   Profits resulting from the introduction of a new technique by a firm are easily and quickly competed away by other firms that copy the new technique.

Second, perfect competition is most efficient only if commodity prices and costs truly and accurately reflect social benefits and costs.   This is often not the case.   For example, social costs (i.e. the cost to society as a whole) when a producer pollutes exceed the producer's private costs. Since a producer equates his private costs to his MC in determining his best level of output, too much of this commodity is produced from society's point of view.

Third, the distribution of income resulting from the perfectly competitive form of market organization may leave some people very rich while leaving others very poor (even though not less "deserving").   Thus, there is the need for the government to step in and with "appropriate" taxes and subsidies provide a more "equitable and fair" distribution of income and try to reconcile social costs and benefits with private costs and benefits.   There are also some goods and services, such as police protection, which are best provided by government rather than by the free market.

CONSTANT, INCREASING AND DECREASING COST INDUSTRIES

17.16.   Draw a two-panel figure showing (A) one of a large number of identical perfectly competitive firms and (B) the industry.   Start with a particular industry demand curve (D) and supply curve (S) and assume that the firm is originally in long-run equilibrium.   Suppose that the industry demand then increases to D′.   Discuss the sequence of events whereby industry and firm achieve short-run and long-run equilibrium.   (Assume that factor prices remain constant.)   Draw the industry long-run supply curve.

Point E_1 in Panel B of Fig. 17-13 shows the original equilibrium market price at which the perfectly competitive firm is in long-run equilibrium (point E in Panel A).   Suppose that now, for some reason (such as a change in tastes), the industry demand curve increases to D'.   A new market equilibrium price is determined at E_2.   Each firm will be in short-run equilibrium by producing at point A, where d' = MR' = rising MC and will have a profit per unit of AB.   These profits attract more firms to the industry until the industry supply curve increases from S to S', giving the new equilibrium point E_3. The firm now returns to its original long-run equilibrium point E.   Industry output is greater because new firms entered the industry in the long run.   The equilibrium prices at E_1 and E_3 are the same because we have assumed that factor prices remained constant.   By joining E_1 to E_3, we get this industry's horizontal long-run supply curve.   This is a constant-cost industry.

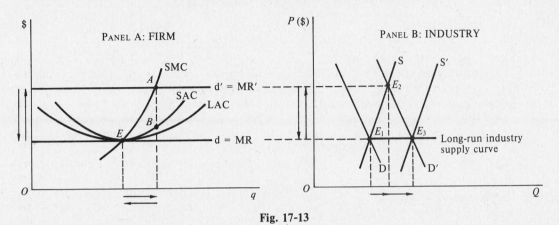

Fig. 17-13

17.17.   (*a*) Draw two figures similar to Panel B of Fig. 17-13 that show an increasing-cost and a decreasing-cost industry.   (*b*) Explain, using examples, why there are increasing-cost and decreasing-cost industries.

(*a*)   See Fig. 17-14.

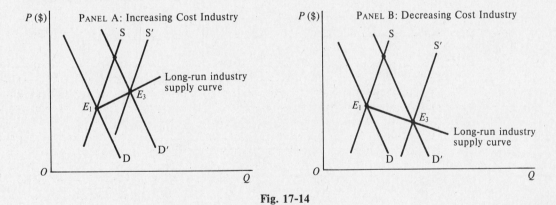

Fig. 17-14

(*b*)   If an industry uses very specialized resources (rather than resources used by many other industries and widely available in the economy) it is likely to be an increasing-cost industry.   That is, when the demand for these specialized resources increases in order to expand this industry's output, resource prices are likely to rise and cause an upward shift in all firms' cost curves.   For example, if there is a change in tastes in favor of more beef, of more single-family homes or almost anything else, more output and higher prices usually result (see Panel A).   This is often referred to as an "external diseconomy."   On the other hand, in some rare instances, as industry output expands, factor prices might fall.   This would lower all firms' cost curves and lead to a negatively sloped, long-run industry supply curve (see Panel B).   For example, as more firms are established in a given locality, improvements in transportation may become feasible and lead to lower costs for all firms in the industry.   This is referred to as an "external economy."

Midterm Examination—
Microeconomics

1. Suppose that the quantity demanded of a commodity increases from 10 to 30 units per month as a result of a reduction in its price from $20 to $10 per unit. (a) What is the elasticity of demand? How does this differ from the change in Q divided by the change in P? Which is better? Why? (b) What happens to the total revenue of producers of this commodity as its price falls? Will the increase in total revenue increase the total profits of producers?

2. From the total utility schedules of commodities X and Y in Table 1, (a) derive MU_x and MU_y, (b) find the point of consumer's equilibrium if the consumer's income is $5 and $P_x = P_y = 1, (c) find a new point of consumer's equilibrium if P_x falls to $0.50, and (d) identify two points on this consumer's demand schedule for commodity X. (e) Explain the fact that the consumer buys more of a commodity at lower prices.

Table 1

Units of commodity	0	1	2	3	4	5
TU_x	0	5	9	12	14	15
TU_y	0	6	11	15	18	20

3. Given the data in Table 2, (a) find the AFC, AVC, AC and MC schedules. (b) On one set of axes, plot the schedules of part (a). (c) Explain the shape of each curve and the relationship among them.

Table 2

Quantity Produced	TFC	TVC	TC
0	$100	$ 0	$100
1	100	100	200
2	100	150	250
3	100	250	350
4	100	400	500
5	100	600	600

4. Given: Figure M-1, for a perfectly competitive firm. (a) What level of output will the firm produce when faced with demand curve d_3? Why? Is the firm making a profit or loss? How much is this per unit? In total? (b) Redo part (a) for d_2. (c) Redo part (a) for d_1. (d) What is this firm's short-run supply curve? Why? (e) What adjustment can the firm make in the long run? Where will it produce? (f) What are some of the advantages and shortcomings of perfect competition? Why?

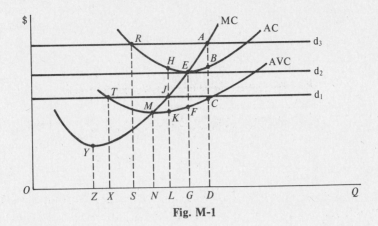

Fig. M-1

Answers

1. (a)

$$E_D = \frac{\text{percentage change in quantity demanded}}{\text{percentage change in price}}$$

$$= \frac{\text{change in quantity demanded}}{\text{sum of quantities}/2} \div \frac{\text{change in price}}{\text{sum of prices}/2}$$

$$= \frac{20}{(10 + 30)/2} \div \frac{10}{(20 + 10)/2} = \frac{20}{40/2} \div \frac{10}{30/2} = \frac{20}{20} \times \frac{1.5}{1} = \frac{30}{20} = \frac{3}{2} = 1.5$$

The change in Q divided by the change in P or $\Delta Q/\Delta P = 20/(-)10 = (-)2$. This is the inverse of the slope of the demand curve. It indicates that for every \$1 reduction in the price of the commodity, the quantity demanded increases by 2 units per month. By defining E_D in terms of percentages, the units of measurement cancel out and so E_D is a pure number. Also, if we measured prices in cents rather than dollars, E_D would remain unchanged at 1.5 but $\Delta Q/\Delta P = 20/(-)1000 = (-)1/50$.

(b) Before the reduction in the commodity price, with $P = \$20$ and $Q = 10$ units per month, TR = \$200. At $P = \$10$ and $Q = 30$, TR = \$300. Thus, when P falls, TR of producers increases and demand is elastic. However, there is not much we can say (without additional information) about the total profits of producers. The reason for this is that as P falls and Q rises, total production costs (TC) will also rise. Total profits (which equal TR $-$ TC) will rise, remain unchanged or fall depending on whether TR rises more, the same or less than TC, respectively.

2. (a) See Table 3.

Table 3

Units of commodity	1	2	3	4	5
MU_x	5	4	3	2	1
MU_y	6	5	4	3	2

(b) With income of \$5 and $P_x = P_y = \$1$, the consumer is in equilibrium when he purchases $2X$ and $3Y$ because

$$\frac{MU_x \text{ of 4 utils}}{P_x \text{ of \$1}} = \frac{MU_y \text{ of 4 utils}}{P_y \text{ of \$1}} = \text{MU of 4 utils for the last \$ spent on } X \text{ and } Y$$

(c) When $P_x = \$0.50$, this consumer is in equilibrium when he purchases $4X$ and $3Y$ because

$$\frac{MU_x \text{ of 2 utils}}{P_x \text{ of \$0.50}} = \frac{MU_y \text{ of 4 utils}}{P_y \text{ of \$1}} = \text{MU of 4 utils for the last \$ spent on } X \text{ and } Y$$

(d) From the consumer equilibrium points in parts (b) and (c) we get the following two points on this consumer's demand schedule for commodity X: at $P_x = \$1.00, q_x = 2$; at $P_x = \$0.50, q_x = 4$.

(e) The consumer buys more of a commodity only at lower commodity prices (i.e. his d_x is down-sloping) because MU_x declines. This is a complementary explanation to the substitution and income effects for a downsloping demand.

3.

(a) $\text{AFC} = \dfrac{\text{TFC}}{Q}$; $\text{AVC} = \dfrac{\text{TVC}}{Q}$; $\text{AC} = \dfrac{\text{TC}}{Q}$; $\text{MC} = \dfrac{\Delta \text{TC}}{\Delta Q} = \dfrac{\Delta \text{TVC}}{\Delta Q}$ ("Δ" equals change in).
See Table 4.

Table 4

Q	AFC	AVC	AC	MC
0	—	0	—	$100
1	$100	$100	$200	50
2	50	75	125	100
3	$33\frac{1}{3}$	$83\frac{1}{3}$	$116\frac{2}{3}$	150
4	25	100	125	200
5	20	120	140	

(b) In Fig. M-2, MC, defined as $\Delta \text{TC}/\Delta Q$ or $\Delta \text{TVC}/\Delta Q$, is plotted between successive levels of outputs.

(c) AFC declines continuously as output expands because TFC is spread over more units of output.   AFC also equals the declining distance between AC and AVC in Fig. M-2.   The MC, AVC and AC curves are U-shaped.   They eventually rise because of the law of diminishing returns.   The AC and AVC fall as long as MC is below them.   AC and AVC rise when MC is above them.   MC = AC and MC = AVC at the lowest AC and AVC, respectively.   AC falls over a greater level of output than AVC because, for a while, the falling AFC included in AC but not AVC, overwhelms the law of diminishing returns.

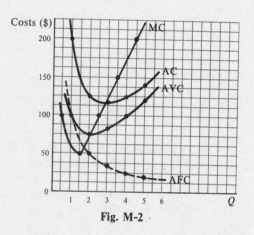

Fig. M-2

4.   (a) With d_3, the firm produces at point A where MR or P = rising MC.   Up to that point, MR > MC and total profits increase.   Past that point, MR < MC and total profits fall.   The firm makes a profit per unit equal to AB and a maximum total profit of AB per unit times OD units by producing at point A.

(b) With d_2, the firm produces at E and breaks even because P = AC.

(c) With d_1, the firm produces at J.   Since P < AC, the firm incurs a loss per unit of HJ and a total loss of HJ times the OK units produced.   If the firm discontinued production, it would incur the greater loss per unit of HK = AFC and a total loss of HK times OK units = TFC.   Thus, the firm minimizes its total losses by producing OK units.

(d) Since the perfectly competitive firm always produces where P = rising MC (as long as P > AVC), the rising portion of its MC curve over and above AVC or shut-down point represents the firm's short-run supply curve (*MJEA* in Fig. M-1).

(e) In the long run, the firm can leave the industry or construct the optimum scale of plant and operate it at the optimum level of output.   This is given by the lowest point on the SAC curve which forms the lowest point of the LAC curve.   The forces of competition will push each firm in the industry to produce at P = lowest LAC.

(f) In long-run perfectly competitive equilibrium, the firm produces at the lowest possible LAC the goods and services most wanted by society, and consumers pay the lowest possible price. Against these impressive advantages are the following shortcomings.   Perfect competition may not lead to "adequate" research and development (technological progress).   When social costs and benefits do not correspond to private costs and benefits, efficiency is hampered.   Perfect competition may not lead to an "equitable" distribution of income, making some very rich and others very poor.

Chapter 18

Price and Output:
Monopoly

18.1 PURE MONOPOLY DEFINED

Pure monopoly is the form of market organization in which there is a single seller of a commodity for which there are no close substitutes.   Thus, it is at the opposite extreme from perfect competition.   Pure monopoly may be the result of (1) increasing returns to scale, (2) control over the supply of raw materials, (3) patents, or (4) government franchise.

EXAMPLE 1. Electrical companies, telephone companies and other "public utilities" usually have increasing returns to scale (i.e. falling long-run average costs) over a sufficient range of outputs as to enable a single firm to satisfy the entire market at a lower per-unit cost than two or more firms could.   These *natural monopolies* usually operate under a government franchise and are subject to government regulation.   Up to World War II, Alcoa (the Aluminum Corporation of America) had a virtual monopoly over the production of aluminum in the U.S. by controlling the entire supply of bauxite (the raw material required to produce aluminum).   A monopoly may also arise because a firm may own a patent which precludes other firms from producing the same commodity.

18.2 DEMAND AND MARGINAL REVENUE

Under pure monopoly, the firm *is* the industry and faces the negatively sloped industry demand curve for the commodity.   As a result, if the monopolist wants to sell more of the commodity, it must lower its price.   Thus, for a monopolist, MR is less than P and its MR curve lies below its D curve.

EXAMPLE 2. In Table 1, columns (1) and (2) give the demand schedule faced by a monopolist.   The TR values of column (3) are obtained by multiplying each value of column (1) by the corresponding value in column (2).   The MR values of column (4) are the differences between successive TR values and are recorded between successive levels of TR and sales.   The MR of $3 recorded *at* the sales level of 2.5 units is the change in TR resulting from the increase in sales from 2 to 3 units (this will be needed later to find the equilibrium level of output for the monopolist).   D and MR are graphed in Fig. 18-1.   Note that the MR values are plotted *between* successive levels of sales.

Table 1

(1) P ($)	(2) Q	(3) TR ($)	(4) MR ($)
8.00	0	0	
7.00	1	7.00	7
6.00	2	12.00	5
*5.50	2.5	13.75	3
5.00	3	15.00	1
4.00	4	16.00	−1
3.00	5	15.00	−3
2.00	6	12.00	−5
1.00	7	7.00	−7
0	8	0	

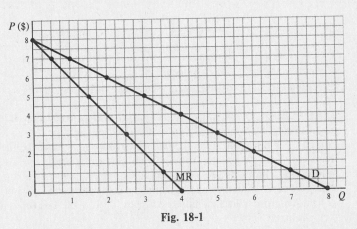

Fig. 18-1

18.3   PROFIT MAXIMIZATION

The profit-maximizing or best level of output for the monopolist is given at the output at which MR = MC.   Price is then read off the demand curve.   Depending on the level of AC at this output, the monopolist can have profits (see Example 3), break even or minimize the short-run total losses (see Problem 18.11).

EXAMPLE 3.   In Table 2, the values in columns (1) through (4) come from Table 1.   Columns (2) and (5) give a typical TC schedule.   The other values in this table are derived from the values given in columns (1), (2), (3) and (5).   The monopolist maximizes total profits at $3.75 when it produces and sells 2.5 units of output at the price of $5.50.   At this output, MR = MC = $3.   As long as MR exceeds MC, the monopolist will expand output and sales because doing so adds more to TR than to TC (and profits rise).   The opposite is true when MR is less than MC (see Table 2).   Thus total profits are maximized where MR = MC.   The same conclusion can be reached with the "total-revenue-total-cost approach" (see Problem 18.8).

Table 2

(1) P ($)	(2) Q	(3) TR ($)	(4) MR ($)	(5) TC ($)	(6) MC ($)	(7) AC ($)	(8) Profit/unit ($)	(9) Total Profit ($)
8.00	0	0		6		. . .	. . .	− 6.00
7.00	1	7.00	7	8	2	8.00	−1.00	− 1.00
6.00	2	12.00	5	9	1	4.50	+1.50	+ 3.00
*5.50	2.5	13.75	3	10	3	4.00	+1.50	+ 3.75*
5.00	3	15.00		12		4.00	+1.00	+ 3.00
4.00	4	16.00	1	20	8	5.00	−1.00	− 4.00
3.00	5	15.00	−1	35	15	7.00	−4.00	−20.00

EXAMPLE 4.   The profit-maximizing or best level of output for this monopolist can also be seen in Fig. 18-2 (obtained by plotting the value of columns 1, 2, 4, 6 and 7 of Table 2).   In Fig. 18-2, the best level of output is at the point where MR = (rising) MC.   At this best output level of 2.5 units, the monopolist makes a profit of $1.50 per unit (the vertical distance between D and AC at 2.5 units of output) and $3.75 in total (2.5 units of output times the $1.50 profit per unit).   Note that since P exceeds MR where MR = MC, the rising portion of the MC above AVC does not represent the monopolist supply curve (see Problem 18.12).   In the long run, the monopolist can adjust the scale of plant and profits may persist because of blocked or restricted entry.

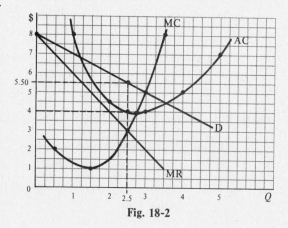

Fig. 18-2

18.4   PRICE DISCRIMINATION

A monopolist can increase TR and profits at a given level of output and TC by practicing *price discrimination*.   This involves charging different prices for the commodity (1) for different quantities purchased, (2) to different classes of consumers, or (3) in different markets.

EXAMPLE 5.   A telephone company may charge individuals 15 cents for each of the first 50 telephone calls made during each month, 10 cents for each of the next 100 calls, and so on.   Electrical companies usually charge less per kilowatt-hour to industrial users than to households because industrial users have more substitutes available (such as generating their own electricity) and thus have a more elastic demand curve than households.   The markets are kept separate or segmented by meters whereby industrial users are unable to buy more electricity than they need and undersell the monopolist to households.   The monopolist reaps the maximum benefit from price discrimination when the MR of the last unit sold to different buyers or markets is the same (see Problem 18.15).

18.5   EFFICIENCY CONSIDERATIONS

Since the monopolist produces the output at which MR = MC and P exceeds MR, the monopolist produces less and charges a higher price than a perfect competitor with the same cost curves.   For example, if Fig. 18-2 referred to a perfectly competitive *industry*, output would be 3 units and price $5 (given where P = MC), rather than Q = 2.5 and P = $5.50 for the monopolist.   Thus, monopoly leads to a misallocation of resources.   Monopoly profits may also persist in the long run because of blocked or restricted entry.   Since corporate stocks are owned mostly by high-income groups, monopoly profits lead to greater income inequality.   Finally, the monopolist may feel secure and have no great incentive to make technological advances.

18.6   REGULATION OF MONOPOLY

For efficiency considerations, a government (Federal, state or local) often allows natural monopolies (such as public utilities) to operate but subjects them to regulation.   This usually takes the form of setting a price which allows the monopolist only the "normal or fair" return of about 10% to 14% on its investment.   However, this only partially corrects the more serious problem of misallocation of resources.

EXAMPLE 6.   In Fig. 18-3, the unregulated monopolist would produce 400 units (shown by the point where MR = MC), sell them at P = $12 (on D), and receive a profit of $1 per unit ($P$ − AC at Q = 400) and $400 in total.   The government could set P = $9 (where P = AC) so that the monopolist would break even and earn only a normal or fair return at Q = 600 units.   However, at this point, P still exceeds MC and there still remains some misallocation of resources.   At P = MC (where D crosses MC), P exceeds AC.   In this case, this monopolist would incur a loss and would not produce in the long run without a government subsidy.

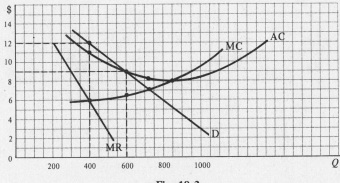

Fig. 18-3

Important Economic Terms

Natural monopoly.   A firm that experiences increasing returns to scale (i.e. falling long-run average cost) and is able to supply the entire market at a lower per-unit cost than two or more firms could.

Price discrimination.   The practice of charging different prices for a commodity (1) for different quantities purchased, (2) to different classes of consumers, or (3) in different markets.

Pure monopoly.   The form of market organization characterized by a single seller of a commodity for which there are no close substitutes.

Review Questions

1. In pure monopoly, (a) there is a single seller of a commodity for which there are no close substitutes, (b) there is a single seller of a commodity for which there are close substitutes, (c) there are few sellers of a commodity for which there are no close substitutes, (d) firms can enter or leave the industry in the long run without much difficulty.

   Ans. (a)

2. Pure monopoly may be based on (a) increasing returns to scale, (b) control over the supply of raw materials, (c) patent or government franchise, (d) all of the above.

   Ans. (d)

3. The demand curve facing the pure monopolist is (a) negatively sloped, (b) horizontal, (c) positively sloped, (d) any of the above are possible.

   Ans. (a)

4. The MR of the monopolist is (a) larger than P, (b) equal to P, (c) smaller than P, (d) any of the above is possible.

   Ans. (c)

5. The best level of output for the monopolist is the output at which (a) MR = AC, (b) MR = MC, (c) MR exceeds MC, (d) MR is less than MC.

   Ans. (b)

6. In the short run, the monopolist (a) makes a profit, (b) breaks even, (c) incurs a loss, (d) any of the above are possible.

   Ans. (d)

7. The short-run supply curve of the monopolist is (a) the rising portion of the MC curve, (b) the rising portion of the MC curve above AVC, (c) the rising portion of the MC curve above AC, (d) none of the above.

   Ans. (d)

8. In the long run, the monopolist
   (a) can incur losses,
   (b) breaks even because other firms enter the industry and compete away profits,
   (c) can continue to make profits because entry into the industry is blocked or restricted,
   (d) always produces at the lowest point on the LAC curve.

   Ans. (c)

9. Price discrimination involves charging different prices for a commodity (a) for different quantities purchased, (b) to different classes of customers, (c) in different markets, (d) all of the above.

   Ans. (d)

10. With respect to a perfectly competitive industry with identical cost conditions, a monopolist (a) produces a larger quantity, (b) produces a smaller quantity, (c) charges the same price, (d) charges a lower price.

    Ans. (b)

11. Government can eliminate all monopoly profits by setting a price equal to (a) AC, (b) AVC, (c) AFC, (d) MC.

    Ans. (a)

12. A regulated monopolist would *not* misallocate resources only if the government regulatory agency set the price equal to (a) AC, (b) AVC, (c) AFC, (d) MC.

    Ans. (d)

Solved Problems

PURE MONOPOLY DEFINED

18.1. Define pure monopoly.   What is the relationship between pure monopoly and perfect competition?

Pure monopoly occurs when (1) there is a single firm selling the commodity, (2) there are no close substitutes for the commodity and (3) entry into the industry is very difficult or impossible (see Problem 18.2).   Pure monopoly is at the opposite extreme from perfect competition.   See Chapter 17.   Instead of an industry composed of numerous firms, in pure monopoly there is only a single firm.   Instead of many firms producing a homogeneous, identical or perfectly standardized product, there are no close substitutes or similar commodities for the monopolist's product.   Instead of firms being easily able to enter or leave the industry in the long run, entry under pure monopoly is blocked or very difficult (otherwise the monopolist would not remain a monopolist in the long run).

18.2. What conditions might give rise to monopoly?

(1)   Increasing returns to scale may operate over a sufficiently large range of outputs as to leave only one firm to produce the industry output.   These are called "natural monopolies" and are fairly common in industries such as public utilities and transportation.   What the government usually does in these cases is to allow the monopolist to operate but subjects it to government control. For example, electricity rates in New York City are set so as to leave Con Edison with only a "normal rate of return" of say 10% to 14% on its investment.

(2)   A firm may control the entire supply of raw materials required to produce the commodity.   For example, up to World War II, Alcoa owned or controlled almost every source of bauxite (the raw material necessary to produce aluminum) in the U.S. and had a complete monopoly over the production of aluminum in the U.S.

(3)   A firm may own a patent which precludes other firms from producing the same commodity.   For example, when cellophane was first introduced, Du Pont had monopoly power based on its patents.

(4)   A monopoly may be established by a government franchise.   In this case, the firm is set up to be the sole producer and distributor of a good or service but is subjected to governmental control in certain aspects of its operation.   For efficiency considerations, this is fairly common in public utilities [see (1), above].

18.3. (*a*) Are cases of pure monopoly common in the U.S. today?   (*b*) What forces limit the pure monopolist's market power?

(*a*)   Aside from regulated monopolies, cases of pure monopoly have been rare in the past and are prohibited today by antitrust laws.   Even so, the pure monopoly model is often useful in explaining observed business behavior in cases approximating pure monopoly, and also gives us insights into the operation of the other types of imperfectly competitive markets discussed in Chapter 19.

(*b*)   A pure monopolist does not have unlimited market power.   He faces indirect competition for the consumer's dollar from all other commodities.   Even though there are no *close* substitutes for the commodity sold by the monopolist, substitutes may nevertheless exist, as for example, plastic for aluminum, aluminum for steel, etc.   Fear of government prosecution and the threat of potential competition also act as a check on the monopolist's market power.

DEMAND AND MARGINAL REVENUE FACING THE MONOPOLIST

18.4. (*a*) What type of demand curve does the monopolist face?   Why?   How does this differ from perfect competition?   Why?   (*b*) Why is MR less than *P* for the monopolist?   How does this differ from perfect competition?   Why?

(*a*)   Since the monopolist is the only seller of a commodity for which there are no good substitutes, it *is* the industry and faces the negatively sloped industry demand curve for the commodity.

The market demand curve facing a perfectly competitive *industry* is also negatively sloped. However, in a perfectly competitive industry there are a very large number of firms, each supplying only a very small fraction of the total market.   As a result each competitive firm, being so small in relation to the market, does not affect market price and faces a horizontal or infinitely elastic demand curve at the prevailing market price.

(b)   Since the monopolist faces the negatively sloped industry demand curve, it must lower its price if it wants to sell more.   Because it must also lower its price on *all* units sold, the MR (i.e. the change in TR from selling one more unit) is less than P.   For example, when the monopolist of Table 1 sells 3 units at $P = \$5$, its TR $= \$15$.   To sell 4 units, it must lower its price *on all units* to $4 each.   Thus, TR $= \$16$ and MR $= \$1$, while $P = \$4$.   A perfectly competitive firm, on the other hand, can sell any quantity at the prevailing market price; thus the change in TR in selling one more unit (i.e. its MR) is constant and equals P.

18.5.   For the monopolist demand schedule of Table 3, (a) find TR and MR and (b) graph D and MR.

Table 3

P ($)	12	11	10	9	8	7	6	5	4	3	2	1	0
Q	0	1	2	3	4	5	6	7	8	9	10	11	12

(a)   Note that in Table 4 MR is obtained by subtracting successive TR and is recorded *between* various levels of sales.

Table 4

P ($)	12	11	10	9	8	7	6	5	4	3	2	1	0
Q	0	1	2	3	4	5	6	7	8	9	10	11	12
TR ($)	0	11	20	27	32	35	36	35	32	27	20	11	0
MR ($)		11	9	7	5	3	1	−1	−3	−5	−7	−9	−11

(b)   In Fig. 18-4, MR is plotted *between* various levels of sales and lies below D.

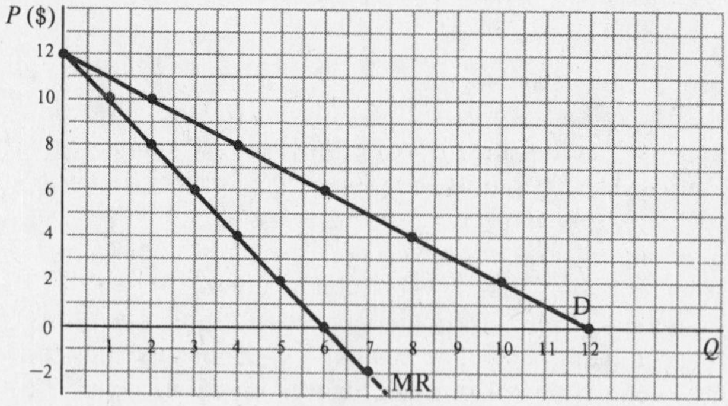

Fig. 18-4

18.6.   (a) From the relationship between P and TR in Table 4, determine if and when the D of Fig. 18-4 is elastic, inelastic and unitary elastic.   (b) What can you say in general about the relationship among E_D, TR and MR?   Why?

(a)   In Section 14.3, we saw that when P falls, D is elastic if TR rises, unitary elastic if TR remains unchanged, and inelastic if TR falls.   The D of Table 4 is elastic up to $P = \$6$, inelastic at P lower than $6 and unitary elastic at $P = \$6$.

(b)   From Table 4 and Fig. 18-4, we see that as long as $E_D > 1$, a fall in P increases TR and MR is positive.   When $E_D < 1$, a fall in P reduces TR and so MR is negative.   When $E_D = 1$, TR does not change (and is maximum) and MR = 0.

PROFIT MAXIMIZATION

18.7.   (a) What is the basic difference between the pure monopolist and the perfectly competitive firm, if the monopolist does not affect *factor* prices?   (b) What basic assumption do we make in order to determine the pure monopolist's best level of output?

(a)   If the monopolist does not affect factor prices (i.e. if it is a perfect competitor in the factor markets), then its cost curves are similar to those developed in Chapter 16 and need not be different from those used in Chapter 17 for the analysis of perfect competition.   Thus, the basic difference between the perfectly competitive firm and the monopolist lies on the selling or demand side rather than on the production or cost side.

(b)   In order to determine the pure monopolist's best level of output, we assume (as in the case of perfect competition) that the monopolist wants to maximize total profits.   We can look at this either from the total-revenue-total-cost approach or from the marginal-revenue-marginal-cost approach.

18.8.   Referring to Table 5, (a) find the profit-maximizing or best level of output for this monopolist by using the TR and TC approach, and (b) graph the results.

Table 5

P ($)	12	11	10	9	8	7
Q	0	1	2	3	4	5
TC	10	17	18	21	30	48

(a)   Table 6 shows that the best level of output for this monopolist is three units per time period.   At this output, the monopolist charges a price of $9 and has the maximum total profit of $6 per time period.

Table 6

P ($)	Q	TR ($)	TC ($)	Total Profits ($)
12	0	0	10	−10
11	1	11	17	− 6
10	2	20	18	+ 2
*9	3	27	21	+ 6
8	4	32	30	+ 2
7	5	35	48	−13

(b)   Note that the monopolist's TR curve in Fig. 18-5 is not a (positively sloped) straight line through the origin as it was in the case of perfect competition.   Total profits are maximized at $Q = 3$, where TR exceeds TC by the greatest amount ($27 − $21).

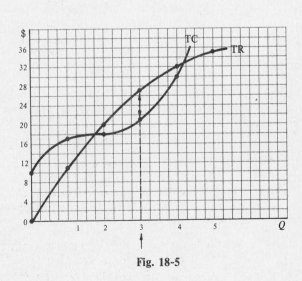

Fig. 18-5

18.9. In terms of the marginal-revenue-marginal-cost approach, (*a*) state and explain the condition for profit maximization. (*b*) At what price does the monopolist sell? How does this differ from perfect competition? (*c*) Can the monopolist incur short-run losses?

(*a*) The profit-maximizing or best level of output for the monopolist is the output at which MR = MC. The reason for this is that as long as MR exceeds MC, the monopolist expands output, adding more to total revenue than to total cost, and so total profits rise. On the other hand, it does not pay for the monopolist to produce where MR is smaller than MC because it would be adding more to TC than to TR and the total profits would fall. This leaves the output at which MR = MC as the profit-maximizing or best level of output for the monopolist.

(*b*) The price charged is read from the demand curve facing the monopolist at the sales level at which MR = MC. Because the demand curve is negatively sloped, P exceeds MR. This differs from the perfectly competitive case where (because the demand facing each firm is horizontal or infinitely elastic) P = MR. Note that the monopolist neither charges the highest possible price ($12 in Table 5 at which the monopolist would incur a loss of $10), nor sells the output at which TR is maximum ($36 at Q = 6 in Table 4).

(*c*) The monopolist can incur losses, break even or make a profit in the short run. If P = AC, it breaks even. If P is lower than AC (as long as P exceeds AVC), the monopolist minimizes total losses by staying in business in the short run.

18.10. (*a*) Using Table 5, find this monopolist's MR, MC and AC. (*b*) Show graphically the profit-maximizing level of output. How much profit per unit and in total does the monopolist make?

(*a*) See Table 7.

Table 7

P ($)	Q	TR ($)	MR ($)	TC ($)	MC ($)	AC ($)
12	0	0		10		—
11	1	11	11	17	7	17
10	2	20	9	18	1	9
9	3	27	7	21	3	7
8	4	32	5	30	9	7.50
7	5	35	3	48	18	9.60

(*b*) From Fig. 18-6, we can see that this monopolist should produce 3 units of output (shown by the point where MR = MC) and charge P = $9 (on D). Since P = $9 and AC = $7 at Q = 3, the monopolist makes a profit per unit of $2, and a total profit of $6 (the same as when the total approach was used in Problem 18.8). Note that from Q = 2 to Q = 4, MR = (32 − 20)/2 = $6 and equals MC = (30 − 18)/2 = $6 at Q = 3.

18.11. (*a*) Draw a figure showing, for a monopolist, the best level of output. Include three alternative AC curves, showing that the monopolist (1) makes a profit, (2) breaks even, and (3) incurs a loss. (*b*) What would happen to this monopolist in the long run if it incurs short-run losses? Short-run profits?

(*a*) In Fig. 18-7, the best level of output of the monopolist is *OB*, given by point *C* where MR = MC. With AC₁, the monopolist makes a per-unit profit of *GF* and a total profit of *GF* times *OB*. With AC₂, P = AC and TR = TC; thus, the monopolist breaks even. With AC₃, the monopolist incurs a per-unit loss of *HG* and a total loss of *HG* times *OB*. Only if P exceeds AVC (so that TR exceeds TVC) will the monopolist stay in business and minimize short-run total losses by producing *OB*.

(*b*) If the monopolist has short-run losses, it could, in the long run, build the most appropriate scale of plant to produce the best long-run level of output. The monopolist might also advertise in an attempt to cause an upward shift in the D curve it faces. (This, however, will also shift cost

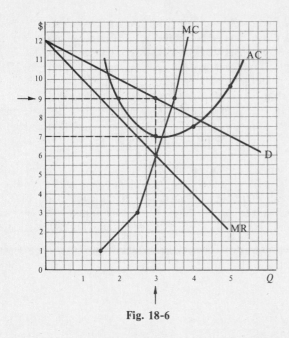

Fig. 18-6

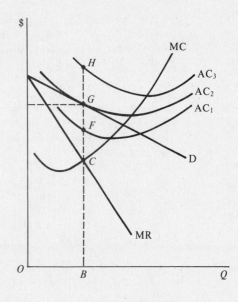

Fig. 18-7

curves up.)   If this monopolist would still incur a loss after having considered all of these long-run possibilities, it will stop producing the commodity in the long run.   If the monopolist was already making short-run profits, it will still build the most appropriate plant in the long run and increase total profits (if entry into the industry continues to be blocked and the monopolist does not fear government action).

18.12. Can we derive the monopolist's supply curve from the MC curve?   Why?

In Chapter 17, we saw that the perfectly competitive firm always produces where MR = P = rising MC (as long as P exceeds AVC).   As a result, given P, we can read from the MC curve the quantity supplied by the firm at that price.   Thus, the rising portion of the firm's MC above AVC or shut-down point is the firm's supply curve.   On the other hand, the monopolist produces where MR = MC but P exceeds MR.   As a result, the monopolist's MC curve does not give a unique price-quantity relationship as required along a supply curve.   All we can say is that for the monopolist, costs are related to supply but the MC curve does not itself represent the supply curve.   In the next chapter, we will see that this is the case whenever the demand curve faced by the firm is negatively sloped, as in all forms of imperfect competition.

PRICE DISCRIMINATION

18.13. (*a*) What is price discrimination?   Why does a monopolist want to practice it?   (*b*) What are the conditions necessary for the monopolist to be able to practice price discrimination? (*c*) Give an example of each of the three types of price discrimination.

(*a*) Price discrimination involves charging different prices for the commodity (1) for different quantities purchased, (2) to different classes of customers, or (3) in different markets.   By practicing price discrimination, the monopolist can increase TR and total profits from any given level of output and TC.

(*b*) In order for the monopolist to practice and benefit from price discrimination, (1) it must have knowledge of the demand for its commodity by different classes of customers or in different markets, (2) these demand curves must have different elasticities, and (3) the monopolist must be able to separate (or segment) the two or more markets and keep them separate.

(*c*) An example of price discrimination which involves charging a different price for different quantities purchased by customers is the practice of telephone companies.   These may charge 15 cents each for the first 50 calls per month and 10 cents for each additional call.

An example of price discrimination which involves charging different prices to each class of customers is the prevailing practice of electrical power companies. They charge a lower rate to industrial users of electricity than to households because the former have a more elastic demand for electricity because there are more substitutes, such as generating their own electricity, available to them. The markets are kept separate by different meters. If the two markets were not kept separate, industrial users of electricity would buy more electricity than they use and would undersell the monopolist in supplying electricity to household and other private users until the price of electricity in the two markets were completely equalized. We will see later that if the demands in the two markets have the same price elasticity, the monopolist could not benefit from price discrimination.

Finally, an example of charging different prices in different markets is found in international trade when a nation sells a commodity abroad at a lower price than in its home market. This is referred to as "dumping." The reason for dumping is that the demand for the monopolist's product is more elastic abroad (because substitutes are available from other nations) than in the domestic market (where imports from other nations may be kept out and the markets kept separate by import restrictions).

18.14. Refer to Fig. 18-8, which contains the market demand curve facing a monopolist. (*a*) What price should the monopolist charge without price discrimination if its best level of output (given by the point where MR = MC) is *OB*? What would the TR be? How much is the consumers' surplus? (*b*) Suppose the monopolist sold *OA* units at price *OF* and in order to induce consumers to buy *AB* additional units, it lowered its price to *OC* only on *AB* units. How much would TR be now? How much of the consumers' surplus remains? If the monopolist was already making profits without price discrimination, why would the total profits now be higher? (*c*) Could the monopolist completely take away all of the consumers' surplus?

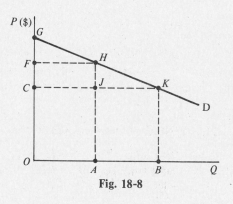

Fig. 18-8

(*a*) The highest price the monopolist can charge (without price discrimination) to sell *OB* units is *OC* (*BK* in Fig. 18-8). The TR would then equal the area of rectangle *OCKB*. Consumers' surplus is *CGK* (see Section 15.5).

(*b*) TR is *OFHA* (for *OA* units) plus *AJKB* (for *AB* units). Note that price discrimination has increased TR by *CFHJ* (and this is the amount by which the consumers' surplus declined). Consumers' surplus is now only *FGH* plus *HKJ*. The monopolist's total profits are now higher because TR has increased for unchanged TC (for the same *OB* units produced).

(*c*) The monopolist could completely take away the consumers' surplus by demanding to sell *OB* units *as a whole* for TR = *OGKB*, take it or leave it (see Problem 15.13). This is rare in the real world.

18.15. Figure 18-9 shows a monopolist selling output in market 1 (with its more inelastic D_1 and MR_1) and in market 2 (with D_2 and MR_2). The monopolist is able to keep these two markets separate. (*a*) What is this monopolist's best *total* level of output? How is it determined? (*b*) What part of total output should the monopolist sell in each market in order to maximize TR and total profits? Why? (*c*) What price should the monopolist charge in each market? How is the price charged in each market related to price elasticity of demand? (*d*) What price would the monopolist charge without price discrimination?

(*a*) The profit-maximizing or best level of output for the monopolist is *OC* in Panel C. This is at the point where the horizontal sum of MR_1 and MR_2 equals MC in Panel C.

(*b*) The monopolist should sell *OA* in market 1 and *OB* in market 2 (*OA* + *OB* = *OC*). This is at the point where $MR_1 = MR_2 = MC$ for the entire output. If MR were different in the two markets, the monopolist would not be maximizing TR for given TC. For example, if from the

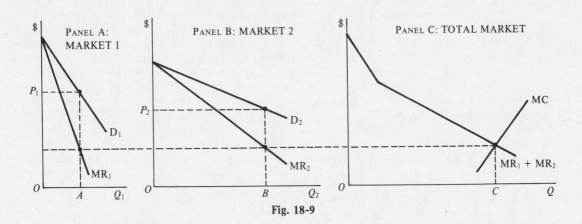

Fig. 18-9

last unit sold, MR = $10 in market 1 and $8 in market 2, the monopolist would gain $10 and lose $8 in revenue (for a net gain of $2) by transferring one unit of sales from market 2 to market 1. The possibility of further gain would be exhausted only when $MR_1 = MR_2$.

(c) The monopolist should charge P_1 for OA units sold in market 1 and P_2 for OB units sold in market 2. Since D_1 is more inelastic than D_2, P_1 exceeds P_2.

(d) Without price discrimination, the monopolist would charge a price (the same in both markets) between P_1 and P_2 such that the total sold in both markets equaled OC units. However, at this price, TR and total profits from OC units of output would be less than with price discrimination.

EFFICIENCY CONSIDERATIONS

18.16. (a) If Fig. 18-6 referred to a perfectly competitive industry instead of to a monopolist, what would the output and price be? Why? How does this compare with the monopolist's price and output? (b) How does monopoly affect the distribution of income? Why?

(a) If Fig. 18-6 referred to a perfectly competitive industry, output would be about 3.40 units and price about $8.60 because this is where D crosses MC. MC would in this case represent the perfectly competitive industry's supply curve if factor prices are constant (see Section 17.5). Therefore, the equilibrium price and quantity would be determined where D crosses MC or S. This compares with the monopolist's $Q = 3$ and $P = $9, determined where MR = MC. Thus, monopoly involves a misallocation (specifically, an underallocation) of resources.

(b) Since long-run profits may persist in monopoly because of blocked or restricted entry into the industry and corporate stocks are owned mostly by high-income groups, monopoly tends to increase income inequality.

18.17. (a) Should the government break up a monopoly into a large number of perfectly competitive firms? Why? (b) Does monopoly lead to more technological progress than perfect competition? Why?

(a) *In industries operating under cost and technological conditions (such as constant returns to scale) that make the existence of perfect competition feasible,* the dissolution of a monopoly (by government antitrust action) into a large number of perfectly competitive firms will result in a greater long-run equilibrium output for the industry, a lower commodity price and usually a lower LAC than under monopoly. However, because of cost and technological conditions, it is not desirable to break up a *natural* monopoly into a large number of perfectly competitive firms. In such cases, comparison of the long-run equilibrium position of the monopolist with that of the perfectly competitive industry is meaningless. In dealing with natural monopolies, the government usually chooses to regulate them rather than break them up.

(b) There is a great deal of disagreement on whether monopoly or perfect competition leads to more technological progress. Since a monopolist usually makes long-run profits while perfect competitors do not, the monopolist has more resources to devote to research and development

(R & D).   The monopolist is also more likely to retain the benefits of the technological advance it introduces.   A technological advance introduced by a perfect competitor which leads to lower costs and short-run profits is easily and quickly copied by other firms and eliminates the profits of the firm that introduced it.   On the other hand, a monopolist may feel very secure in his position and have no incentive to engage in research and development and to innovate.

REGULATION OF MONOPOLY

18.18.   Evaluate setting (a) $P = AC$ and (b) $P = MC$ as choices that government can employ to regulate a public utility which is a natural monopoly.

By setting $P = AC$ for the monopolist's service, the government can eliminate all of the monopolist's profits so that it receives only a normal or fair return on investment.   However, at $P = AC$, P still exceeds MC and some misallocation of resources remains (see Fig. 18-3).   If the governmental regulatory agency set $P = MC$, the misallocation of resources would be eliminated.   If the monopolist still makes a profit at $P = MC$, those profits can be completely eliminated by also imposing a flat (or lump-sum) tax on the monopolist equal to total profits (see Problem 18.19).   However, at $P = MC$, P may be smaller than AC (see Fig. 18-3) so that the monopolist would incur a loss and not supply the service in the long run without a government subsidy.   This, together with the great difficulties in estimating MC, usually leads the government to set $P = AC$ for regulated public utilities.

18.19.   With reference to Fig. 18-10, (a) determine the output, P, and profit for the unregulated monopolist.   (b) What happens if the government sets $P = AC$? (c) What happens if the government sets $P = MC$?

(a)   The unregulated monopolist would produce OA (at which MR $=$ MC), sell at $P = AF$ (on D), receive a profit of FC per unit, and FC times OA in total.

(b)   If the government set $P = AC$, the monopolist would produce OK, sell at $P = (AC =) KL$, and break even.   However, P is smaller than MC and resources are misallocated (too much of this product or service is produced).

(c)   If the government set $P = MC$, the monopolist would produce OG, sell at $P = GJ$, and obtain a profit per unit of JH.   However, the government could also impose a flat or lump-sum tax on the monopolist equal to JH times OG and so tax away all of the monopolist's total profits.   In this way there would be no misallocation of resources and no profits.   However, it is often the case that at $P = MC$, P is less than AC.   In this case, the monopolist would incur a loss and could not continue to supply this service in the long run without a government subsidy.   This, together with the fact that MC is much more difficult to estimate than AC, leads the government to set $P = AC$ for public utilities.

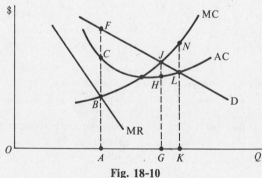

Fig. 18-10

Chapter 19

Price and Output:
Monopolistic Competition and Oligopoly

19.1 MONOPOLISTIC COMPETITION DEFINED

In *monopolistic competition* there are many firms selling a *differentiated* product or service. It is a blending of competition and monopoly. The competitive elements result from the large number of firms and the easy entry. The monopoly element results from differentiated (i.e. similar but not identical) products or services. Product differentiation may be real or imaginary and can be created through advertising. However, the availability of close substitutes severely limits the ''monopoly'' power of each firm.

EXAMPLE 1. Monopolistic competition is the most prevalent form of market organization in retailing. The numerous grocery stores, gasoline stations, dry cleaners, etc. within close proximity of each other are good examples. Examples of differentiated products include the numerous brands of headache remedies (e.g. aspirin, Bufferin, Anacin, Excedrin, etc.), soaps, detergents, breakfast cereals and cigarettes. Even if the differences are imaginary (as in the case of the various brands of aspirin), they are economically important if the consumer is willing to pay a few pennies more or walk a few blocks more for a preferred brand.

19.2 PROFIT MAXIMIZATION

The monopolistic competitor faces a demand curve which is negatively sloped (because of product differentiation) but highly elastic (because of the availability of close subsitutes). His profit-maximizing or best level of output is the output at which MR = MC, provided P exceeds AVC. At that output, the firm can make a profit, break even or minimize losses in the short run. In the long run, firms are either attracted into an industry by short-run profits or leave an industry if faced with long-run losses until the demand curve (d) facing each remaining firm is tangent to its AC curve, and the firm breaks even (P = AC).

EXAMPLE 2. Panel A of Fig. 19-1 shows a monopolistic competitor producing 550 units of output (given where MR = MC), selling it at $10.50 (on d), and making a profit of $3.50 per unit and $1925 in total. These profits attract more firms into the industry. This causes a downward (leftward) shift in this firm's demand curve to d′ (in Panel B), at which the firm sells 400 units at $8 and breaks even. Since P exceeds MR where MR = MC, the rising portion of the MC curve above AVC does not represent the firm's supply curve. Because of product differentiation, our analysis is confined to the ''typical'' or ''representative'' firm and we do not have a single equilibrium price and quantity but a cluster of prices and quantities.

19.3 LONG-RUN EFFICIENCY IMPLICATIONS
OF MONOPOLISTIC COMPETITION

The monopolistically competitive firm misallocates resources because it produces where P exceeds MC (see Fig. 19-1). It does not, in addition, produce at the lowest point on its LAC curve as the perfect competitor does. However, these inefficiencies are usually not great because of the highly elastic demand faced by monopolistic competitors.

In contrast to the perfect competitor, the monopolistic competitor engages in *nonprice competition*, which takes the form of advertising and product differentiation. Such tactics are intended to increase the firm's share of the market and shift its demand curve upward (to the right). However,

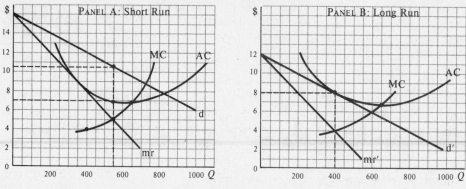

Fig. 19-1

they also increase the firm's costs and shift the firm's cost curves upward.   While some advertising informs the consumer and product differentiation satisfies the consumers' desire for variety, both may be excessive and wasteful (see Problem 19.8).

19.4 OLIGOPOLY DEFINED

Oligopoly is the form of market organization in which there are few sellers of a product.   If the product is homogeneous, there is a *pure (or standardized) oligopoly*.   If the product is differentiated, there is a *differentiated oligopoly*.   Since there are only few large sellers of a product, the action of each seller affects the others and vice versa.   That is, the firms are *mutually interdependent*. As a result, oligopolists usually engage in nonprice rather than price competition.

EXAMPLE 3.   Pure oligopoly is found in the production by few firms of cement, steel, copper, aluminum, and many other industrial products which are sold according to precise specifications and are virtually standardized.   Examples of differentiated oligopolies are industries producing automobiles, cigarettes, typewriters and most electrical appliances, where three or four large firms dominate the market.   Because of mutual interdependence, if one firm lowered its price, it could take most of the sales away from the other firms.   Other firms are then likely to retaliate and possibly start a price war.   As a result, there is a strong compulsion for oligopolists not to change prices but, rather, to compete on the basis of quality, product design, customer service and advertising.

19.5 THE KINKED-DEMAND CURVE AND PRICE RIGIDITY

The kinked-demand curve model seeks to explain the observed existence of price rigidity or inflexibility in oligopolistic markets.   It postulates that the demand curve facing each oligopolist has a "kink" or is bent at the prevailing market price.   The demand curve is much more elastic above the kink than below because other oligopolists will not match price increases but will match price cuts.   As a result, the MR curve has a discontinuous vertical section directly below the kink.   As long as the MC curve shifts within the vertical section of the MR curve, the oligopolist keeps his price unchanged or rigid.

EXAMPLE 4.   In Fig. 19-2, the demand curve facing the oligopolist is *CEJ* and has a "kink" at the prevailing price of $4 per unit and quantity of 200.   Note that demand curve *CEJ* is much more elastic above the kink than below, illustrating the assumption that other oligopolists will not match price increases but will match price cuts. The corresponding marginal revenue curve is *CFGN; CF* is the segment corresponding to the *CE* portion of the demand curve; *GN* corresponds to the *EJ* portion of the demand curve.   The kink at point *E* on the demand curve causes the discontinuity between *F* and *G* in the marginal revenue curve.   The oligopolist's marginal cost

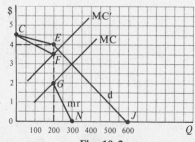

Fig. 19-2

curve can rise or fall anywhere within the vertical (discontinuous) portion of the MR curve (from MC to MC', in Fig. 19-2) without inducing the oligopolist to change the sales level and the price of $4 it charges.   Note that once again, P exceeds MR where MR $=$ MC, and so the rising portion of the MC curve above AVC does not represent the oligopolist's supply curve.

19.6   COLLUSION

An orderly price change (i.e. without starting a price war) is usually accomplished by *collusion* when changed cost conditions make such a price change inevitable.   Collusion can be overt or tacit.   The most extreme form of *overt collusion* is the *centralized cartel*, where the oligopolists produce the monopoly output, charge the monopoly price and somehow allocate production and profits among the cartel members (see Problem 19.14).   Antitrust laws make overt collusion illegal in the U.S.   In *tacit collusion,* the oligopolists, informally and without even meeting, follow a recognized *price leader* in their pricing policies or agree on how to share the market.

EXAMPLE 5. As the dominant steel producer, U.S. Steel is the recognized price leader.   When rising production costs require it, U.S. Steel raises its price on some of its products with the tacit understanding that other domestic steel producers will match the price within a few days.   An orderly price increase is thus achieved without exposing steel producers to government antitrust action or the danger of a price war.

Recently, the pattern has become more complex.   Other companies may initiate the price rise.   For example, suppose that Bethlehem Steel announces a price rise of say 10%, when 6% would do, and then "voluntarily" rolls the price back to 6% when the President of the United States complains that it is inflationary. A few days later, other steel companies, including U.S. Steel, increase their prices from 5.5 to 6.5%.   If the rise in domestic steel price stimulates more imports from other nations, domestic steel producers then lobby in Congress for import restrictions.

19.7   LONG-RUN EFFICIENCY IMPLICATIONS OF OLIGOPOLY

While the oligopolist can make profits, break even or incur losses in the short run, in the long run the firm will leave the industry rather than incur losses.   Oligopolists underallocate resources and can earn long-run profits because of restricted entry.   Usually they also engage in excessive advertising and product differentiation.   However, efficiency considerations may allow only few firms in the industry, and oligopolists may use their profits for research and development (R & D). See Problem 19.17.

The great economic power of large oligopolistic corporations may have stimulated the growth of powerful labor unions and large organizations of buyers from and sellers to these large corporations.   The function of these unions and organizations is to protect themselves from and check the power of the large corporation ("countervailing power").   This, and the fear of antitrust prosecution, has resulted in a degree of "workable competition" or a balancing of the efficiency requirements of large-scale production with some protection from the abuses of oligopoly power.

Important Economic Terms

Antitrust laws. Legislation which prohibits unregulated monopoly and overt collusion, and tries to achieve "workable competition."

Centralized cartel. A formal organization of oligopolists which achieves the monopoly solution and is the most extreme form of overt collusion.

Collusion.   A formal or informal agreement among oligopolists on what prices to charge and how to divide the market.

Countervailing power. The powerful labor unions, organizations of suppliers to and buyers from large corporations which often arise to protect themselves from and check the power of the large corporation.

Differentiated oligopoly.   The form of market organization in which there are few sellers of a differentiated product.

Differentiated products.   Similar but not identical products, having real or imaginary differences which can be created by advertising.

Kinked-demand curve.   A demand curve with a kink or bend at the prevailing market price, which is used to rationalize the price rigidity often observed in oligopolistic markets.

Mark-up pricing.   The prevalent real-world policy of setting product prices by adding a specific percentage to estimated average costs.

Monopolistic competition.   The form of market organization in which there are many sellers of a differentiated product.

Mutual interdependence.   The relationship among the few large sellers of a product in oligopoly which causes the actions of each to affect the others and vice versa.

Nonprice competition.   The competitive techniques of advertising, sales promotion, customer service, and product differentiation often found in monopolistically competitive and oligopolistic markets.

Oligopoly.   The form of market organization in which there are few interdependent sellers of a homogeneous or differentiated product.

Overt collusion.   A *formal* agreement among oligopolists (as in a cartel) on what price to charge, what output to produce and how to divide the market.

Price leadership.   A form of tacit collusion by which oligopolists achieve an orderly price change and match the price changes initiated by the dominant or most efficient firm, recognized as the price leader of the industry.

Price rigidity.   The inflexible or unchanging prices often observed in oligopolistic markets during relatively long periods of time and in the face of widely changing cost conditions.

Pure oligopoly.   The form of market organization in which there are few sellers of a homogeneous product.

Tacit collusion.   An informal understanding among oligopolists, even without explicitly meeting for that purpose, for setting commodity prices and/or dividing the market.

Workable competition.   The balancing of the efficiency requirements of large-scale production with protection from the abuses of monopoly or oligopoly power.

Review Questions

1. Monopolistic competition refers to the form of market organization in which there are (a) many sellers of a homogeneous product, (b) many sellers of a differentiated product, (c) few sellers of a homogeneous product, (d) few sellers of a differentiated product.
   Ans.   (b)

2. The demand curve facing the monopolistic competitor is (a) negatively sloped and highly elastic, (b) negatively sloped and highly inelastic, (c) horizontal, (d) infinitely elastic.
   Ans.   (a)

3. The best level of output for the monopolistic competitor is the output at which (a) MR = AC, (b) MR = MC, (c) MR exceeds MC, (d) MR is less than MC.
   Ans.   (b)

4. In the short run, the monopolistic competitor (a) breaks even, (b) makes a profit, (c) incurs a loss, (d) any of the above is possible.
   Ans.   (d)

5. In the long run, a monopolistic competitor (a) incurs a loss, (b) breaks even, (c) makes a profit, (d) any of the above is possible.

    Ans. (b)

6. A monopolistic competitor, in the long run, (a) produces where P exceeds MC, (b) does not produce at the lowest point on its AC curve, (c) engages in nonprice competition, (d) all of the above.

    Ans. (d)

7. Which of the following most closely approximates an oligopoly? (a) the cigarette industry, (b) the barber shops in a city, (c) the gasoline stations in a city, (d) wheat farmers in the Midwest.

    Ans. (a)

8. The short-run supply curve of the oligopolist is (a) the rising portion of the MC curve, (b) the rising portion of the MC curve above AVC, (c) the rising portion of the MC curve above AC, (d) none of the above.

    Ans. (d)

9. The kinked-demand curve is used to rationalize (a) collusion, (b) price competition, (c) price rigidity, (d) price leadership.

    Ans. (c)

10. Price leadership is (a) a form of overt collusion, (b) a form of tacit collusion, (c) illegal in U.S., (d) used to explain price rigidity.

    Ans. (b)

11. If an oligopolist incurs losses in the short run, then in the long run, (a) it will go out of business, (b) it will stay in business, (c) it will break even, (d) any of the above is possible.

    Ans. (a)

12. The oligopolist (a) produces where P exceeds MC, (b) usually produces at the lowest point on the AC curve, (c) breaks even in the long run, (d) does not engage in nonprice competition.

    Ans. (a)

Solved Problems

MONOPOLISTIC COMPETITION DEFINED

19.1.   (a) Define monopolistic competition, giving a few examples, and (b) identify its competitive and monopolistic elements.

   (a)   Monopolistic competition is the market organization in which there are many sellers of a differentiated product.   Monopolistic competition is common in the retail and service sectors of our economy.   Examples are the barber shops, gasoline stations, grocery stores, liquor stores, drug stores, etc. located in close proximity to one another.

   (b)   The competitive element results from the fact that in a monopolistically competitive industry (as in a perfectly competitive industry) there are so many firms that the activities of each have no perceptible effect on the other firms in the industry.   The monopoly element results because the monopolistic competitors sell a differentiated rather than a homogeneous product.

PROFIT MAXIMIZATION

19.2.   (a) What is the shape of the demand curve facing a monopolistic competitor?   Why? (b) How does the monopolistic competitor decide what output to produce?   (c) Can the monopolistic competitor incur short-run losses?   (d) Can we derive the monopolistic competitor's supply curve from its MC curve?   Why?   (*e*) What happens in the long run if the monopolist competitor is making short-run profits?   Incurring short-run losses?

(*a*)   The demand curve facing a monopolistic competitor is negatively sloped because of product differentiation, but it is highly elastic because of the availability of close substitutes.

(*b*)   The best level of output of the monopolistic competitor is the output at which MR = MC, provided that *P* exceeds AVC.

(*c*)   The monopolistic competitor can make a profit, break even or incur a loss in the short run.   It all depends on the level of its AC in relation to *P* at the output level at which MR = MC.

(*d*)   Because the demand curve facing the monopolistic competitor is negatively sloped, *P* exceeds MR at the output level at which MR = MC.   As a result, the MC curve does not give the unique price-quantity relationship required along a supply curve.   All we can say is that costs are related to supply but the MC curve does not itself represent the supply curve.

(*e*)   Short-run profits attract more firms in the long run.   As more firms share the market, each competitor's demand shifts down until it is tangent to the AC curve and each firm just about breaks even.   On the other hand, short-run losses cause some firms to shut down in the long run.   This causes the demand curves of the remaining firms to shift up until they are tangent to their respective AC curves and each firm just breaks even.

19.3.   Draw a figure showing, in Panel A, a monopolistic competitor making short-run profits, and, in Panel B, the same monopolistic competitor breaking even in the long run.

In Panel A of Fig. 19-3, the monopolistic competitor produces 800 units (at which MR = MC) at AC = $6.25, sells them at *P* = $8 (on d), and makes a per-unit profit of $1.75 and a total profit of $1,400.   In the long run, more firms are attracted into the industry and cause the firm's demand curve to shift down to d' (in Panel B), where it is tangent to the AC curve and the firm breaks even by producing 700 units and selling them at *P* = $6.50.

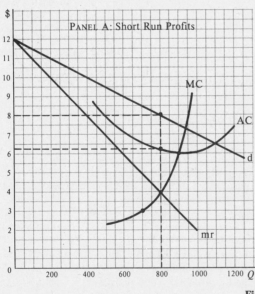 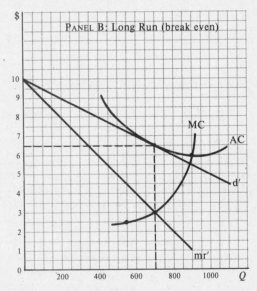

Fig. 19-3

19.4.   Draw a figure showing, in Panel A, a monopolistic competitor incurring short-run losses, and, in Panel B, the same monopolistic competitor breaking even in the long run.

The AC and MC curves in Fig. 19-4 are the same as in Fig. 19-3, but the demand curve facing the firm in Panel A is lower (d'').   With d'', the monopolistic competitor produces 550 units at AC = $7.50, sells them at *P* = $5.25, incurs a loss of $2.25 per unit and $1237.50 in total.   In the long run, some firms shut down and cause the firm's demand curve to shift up to d' (in Panel B, the same as in Fig. 19-3), where it is tangent to the AC curve and the firm breaks even by producing 700 units and selling them at P = $6.50.   Note that the end result is the same as in Problem 19.3.

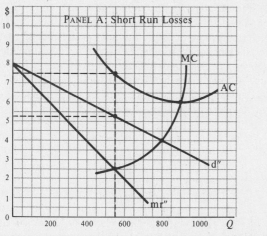
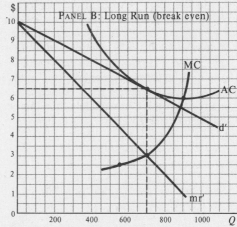

Fig. 19-4

19.5.   (a) Why does a prospective monopolistic competitor find it relatively easy to start production in the long run?   (b) Why does the demand curve of a monopolistic competitor shift down when more firms start production?   (c) Why is it difficult or impossible to define the industry under monopolistic competition?   (d) Why is there a cluster of prices rather than a single equilibrium price in this kind of industry?

  (a)   A prospective monopolistic competitor usually finds it relatively easy to start production because very little capital and no great technical know-how are required to open a small gasoline station, grocery store, country store, barber shop, etc.

  (b)   When more firms start producing a differentiated product, the demand curve of previously existing monopolistic competitors shifts down because each firm now supplies a smaller portion of the entire market.

  (c)   Technically speaking, we cannot define the monopolistically competitive industry because each firm produces a somewhat different product.   We simply cannot add together aspirins, Bufferins, Anacins, Excedrins, etc. to get the market demand and supply curves because they are very similar, but not identical, products.   Thus, our graphical analysis must be confined to the "typical" or "representative" firm.

  (d)   Slightly differentiated products also permit and cause slightly different prices.   That is, even in long-run equilibrium, there will be a cluster of equilibrium prices, one for each differentiated product, rather than a single, industry-wide equilibrium price.

LONG-RUN EFFICIENCY IMPLICATIONS OF MONOPOLISTIC COMPETITION

19.6.   Discuss the long-run efficiency implications of monopolistic competition with respect to (a) resource allocation (b) size of plant and plant utilization.

  (a)   The price charged by the monopolistic competitor when in long-run equilibrium exceeds the MC of the last unit produced.   As a result resources are misallocated.   However, this misallocation of resources is usually not great because the demand curve facing the monopolistically competitive firm, though negatively sloped, is highly elastic.

  (b)   We saw before that in long-run equilibrium the demand curve facing each firm is tangent to its AC curve and each firm breaks even.   Since the demand curve is negatively sloped, the tangency point will always occur to the left of the lowest point on the firm's AC curve (see Figs. 19-3 and 19-4).   Thus, the firm underutilizes a smaller than optimum scale of plant when in long-run equilibrium.   This allows the existence of more firms in the industry than otherwise (see Problem 19.7).   An example of this is the "overcrowding" of gasoline stations, barber shops, grocery stores, etc., each of which is idle some of the time.

19.7.   Compare the long-run equilibrium position of the firm of Problems 19.3 and 19.4 to the long-run equilibrium position of a perfectly competitive firm with the same AC curve.

In Fig. 19-5, point E' is the long-run equilibrium point for the monopolistically competitive firm of Problems 19.3 and 19.4.   If this had been a perfectly competitive firm with the same AC curve, it would have produced at point E in long-run equilibrium.   Thus, the cost of production and price of the monopolistically competitive firm is $6.50 rather than $6 and its output is 700 rather than 900 units.   As a result, the monopolistically competitive firm underallocates resources.   The smaller output of each firm in monopolistic competition allows more firms to exist and results in excessive capacity and overcrowding.   Sometimes, losses even persist in the long run because as soon as some firms leave, others immediately take their place because of ignorance or misplaced hope.   These are sometimes referred to as "sick industries."

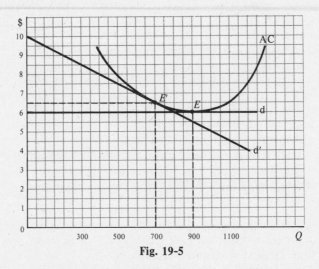

Fig. 19-5

19.8.   (*a*) What is meant by nonprice competition?   Why do monopolistic competitors engage in it while perfectly competitive firms do not?   (*b*) What is the effect of advertising and product differentiation on the firm's demand and cost curves?   (*c*) What are the benefits and costs of advertising and product differentiation?

(*a*)   Nonprice competition refers to advertising, sales promotion, customer services and product differentiation.   A monopolistic competitor engages in it in order to convince customers that its product or service is unique and superior.   The perfect competitor does not engage in nonprice competition because he can sell any quantity at the prevailing market price and the product is homogeneous or perfectly standardized.

(*b*)   Advertising and product differentiation, when successful, can shift the demand curve of the monopolistic competitor up, allowing him to charge a slightly higher price and/or capture a bigger share of the market.   However, they also add to the firm's costs and cause an upward shift in its AC and MC curves.   Advertising and product differentiation should be undertaken as long as they add more to TR than TC.   By doing this, the firm would increase its total profits.   However, it is often difficult to anticipate the exact effect of advertising and product differentiation on the firm's TR and profits.

(*c*)   Some advertising is useful, particularly in a dynamic world, because it educates consumers and informs them of new products and their usefulness.   Some product differentiation, such as different qualities, design, color, etc., is also useful since it satisfies the different tastes of consumers and their desires for variety.   However, these practices are often thought to be excessive in monopolistic competition.   "Excessive" advertising adds only to costs and is passed on to consumers in the form of higher prices.   In addition, an excessive number of brands, styles, designs, etc. confuses consumers and also adds to costs and prices.   For example, consider the number of detergents on the market today.

OLIGOPOLY DEFINED

19.9.   (*a*) Define oligopoly.   (*b*) What is the single most important characteristic of oligopolistic markets?   (*c*) Do oligopolists engage in price or nonprice competition?   Why?

(a)   Oligopoly is the form of market organization in which there are few sellers of a commodity. If there are only two sellers, we have a duopoly.   If the product is homogeneous (e.g. steel, cement, copper) we have a pure oligopoly.   If the product is differentiated (e.g. cars, cigarettes), we have a differentiated oligopoly.   Oligopoly seems to be the most prevalent form of market organization in the manufacturing sector of modern economies and arises for the same general reasons as monopoly (i.e. economies of scale, control over the source of raw materials, patents and government franchise).

(b)   The interdependence among the firms in the industry is the single most important characteristic of oligopoly and sets it apart from other market structures.   This interdependence is the natural result of fewness.   That is, since there are few firms in an oligopolistic industry, when one of them lowers its price, undertakes a successful advertising campaign, or introduces a better model, the demand curve faced by other oligopolists will shift down.   So the other oligopolists react. How they react will vary from one oligopolist to another; there is no general theory of oligopoly. All we have are specific cases or models.

(c)   Oligopolists usually compete on the basis of quality, product design, customer service and advertising (i.e. nonprice competition).   The reason that they do not usually engage in price competition is their fear of triggering a price war.   Specifically, by lowering its price, an oligopolist could significantly reduce the sales of the other firms in the industry and prompt them to retaliate with an even greater price reduction of their own.   Thus, to a great extent, the decision context in oligopoly resembles chess or poker-playing and military strategy.

19.10.   (a) What four different types of market organization do economists usually identify?   (b) Why do we study the two extreme and less realistic forms of market organization first?

(a)   The four different types of market organization usually identified by economists are perfect competition, monopolistic competition, oligopoly and pure monopoly.   The last three forms of market organization fall into the realm of imperfect competition.   Economists identify these four types of market organization in order to organize their analysis.

(b)   We examined first the two extreme forms of market organization (i.e. perfect competition and pure monopoly) because historically, these are the models that were first developed.   More importantly, these are the models that are more fully and satisfactorily developed.   The monopolistic competition and oligopoly models, though more realistic in terms of actual forms of business organization in our economy (and, in general, in most other economies), are not very satisfactory and leave much to be desired from a theoretical point of view.

THE KINKED-DEMAND CURVE AND PRICE RIGIDITY

19.11.   (a) Draw a figure showing a kinked-demand curve, its corresponding MR curve, and an MC curve that shows the oligopolist selling at the price at which the demand curve is kinked. (b) How can you explain the shape of a kinked-demand curve?   Of the corresponding MR curve?   Over what range of MC will the oligopolist sell at the same price?

(a)   In Fig. 19-6, CEJ (with kink at E) is the demand curve facing the oligopolist. CFGN is its MR curve.   The oligopolist produces 300 units (at which its MR curve crosses its MC curve) and sells them at P = $6 (shown on d).

(b)   The demand curve facing the oligopolist is drawn with a kink at the prevailing market price at the quantity sold.   It is very elastic above the kink because if an oligopolist increases his price, others in the industry will not raise theirs and so he would lose most of his customers.   On the other hand, d is much less elastic below the kink because if the oligopolist lowers his price, the others will match the price reduction and he only

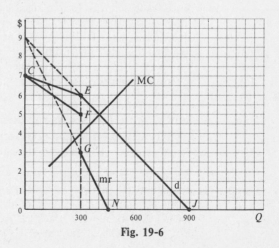

Fig. 19-6

retains his approximate share of the market. The *CF* portion of the MR curve is derived from the *CE* portion of d, and *GN* from *EJ*. The MR curve is discontinuous directly below (and caused by) the kink at point *E* on d. MC can vary from \$3 to \$5 and still intersect MR at $Q = 300$ with $P = \$6$.

19.12. (*a*) What does the kinked-demand curve model accomplish?   (*b*) What would happen if a new and higher MC curve were to intersect the MR curve to the left of and above its vertical portion?   (*c*) Does this rising portion of the oligopolist's MC over and above AVC represent his supply curve?   Why?

   (*a*)   The kinked-demand curve model can *rationalize* the price rigidity in oligopolistic markets, when there are widespread changes in cost conditions.   It is of no use, however, in *explaining* how the prevailing prices were originally determined.

   (*b*)   If a new and higher MC curve intersects the MR curve to the left and above its vertical portion, this and other firms would want to increase prices.   An orderly price increase is then usually accomplished through collusion (see Section 19.6).

   (*c*)   In oligopoly, as in other forms of imperfect competition where the firm faces a negatively sloped demand curve, *P* exceeds MR at the output at which MR = MC.   As a result, the rising portion of the oligopolist's MC curve above AVC does not represent his supply curve.   Once again, we must conclude that MC is related to supply but the MC curve is not the oligopolist's supply curve.

COLLUSION

19.13. (*a*) What is meant by collusion?   By tacit collusion?   By overt collusion?   (*b*) What are the forces which lead to collusion?   What are the obstacles to it?   (*c*) What is a cartel? How does it operate?   (*d*) What is price leadership?   How does it operate?

   (*a*)   Collusion refers to a formal or informal agreement among oligopolists on what prices to charge and/or on how to divide the market.   Overt collusion refers to a formal agreement, such as a cartel, and it is illegal under our antitrust laws.   Tacit collusion is an informal agreement, such as price leadership, and is not illegal.

   (*b*)   Collusion is the natural result of the mutual interdependence of firms in oligopolistic markets. It can serve to avert price wars and to increase industry profits.   The greatest obstacle to collusion is antitrust laws.   But the greater the number of firms and the extent of product differentiation, the more difficult collusion becomes.   Poor economic conditions, as in a recession, and cheating by the member firms are other obstacles to effective collusion.

   (*c*)   A cartel is a formal organization of producers for the purpose of setting prices and/or dividing the market so as to maximize industry profits and/or block entry into the industry.   The most extreme form is the centralized cartel, which behaves as a monopolist.   Cartels are illegal in the U.S. today, but they nevertheless help us understand some oligopolistic practices and tendencies.

   (*d*)   Price leadership is a form of tacit collusion often practiced in oligopolistic markets.   It is not illegal in the U.S. today.   When changed cost conditions make a price change inevitable, the dominant or most efficient firm in the industry usually starts a price increase on the tacit understanding that the other firms in the industry will more or less match the price increase within a few days.   This averts the danger of a price war without exposing the oligopolists to possible government antitrust action.

19.14. (*a*) Draw a figure that shows the demand, marginal revenue and marginal cost curves of a centralized cartel producing a homogeneous product, and use them to determine the industry output and price.   (*b*) How can the cartel allocate production and profits among its members?

   (*a*)   Since the centralized cartel behaves as a monopolist, it faces the market demand curve for the commodity (D, in Fig. 19-7) and the related marginal revenue curve (MR). Σ MC is the summation of the MC curves above AVC of all the cartel members, if factor prices remain constant.   Behaving as a monopolist, the cartel produces 300 units of output (where MR $= \Sigma$ MC) and sets $P = \$4.50$ (on D).   The cartel's profits depend on the AC of producing $Q = 300$.

(b) The cartel's total output of 300 units can then be obtained by allowing each member to produce up to the point where its MC equals \$3 (MR = Σ MC in Fig. 19-7).   This may involve the shutting down of the most inefficient plants (while still sharing the profits).   The cartel profits can then be shared among its members equally, according to the amount produced, or through bargaining.

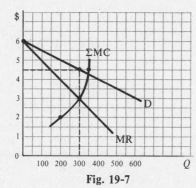

Fig. 19-7   Fig. 19-8

19.15. Suppose that there are only two identical firms in a particular *pure* oligopolistic industry (duopoly) facing a total market demand curve identical to that of Fig. 19-7.   Suppose also that *each* duopolist has an MC curve identical to that of the entire cartel of Fig. 19-7.   Draw a figure showing how much each duopolist would produce and what price each would charge in the absence of collusion.

In Fig. 19-8, D is the market demand shared equally by the duopolists.   Each duopolist will produce 200 units (given where MR = MC) and charge $P = \$4$ (on d).   Thus, 400 units of output are sold to the market as a whole at $P = \$4$ (on D).

19.16. Suppose that in Problem 19.15, the second duopolist has a lower MC, which intersects mr_2 at \$1.   (a) Draw a figure showing how much each duopolist would like to produce and the price he would like to charge in order to maximize total profits.   (b) What must the final result be without collusion?   How is this related to price leadership?

(a) In Fig. 19-9, duopolist 1 would like to produce 200 units and charge $P = \$4$ (as in Problem 19.15 and Fig. 19-8).   However, duopolist 2 would like to produce 250 units ($mr_2 = MC_2$) and charge $P = \$3.50$ (on d_2).

(b) Since the product is homogeneous (we assumed a pure duopoly in Problem 19.15), the more *in*efficient duopolist 1 will also be forced to sell 250 units at $P = \$3.50$, and so will not maximize total profits (since mr_1 is smaller than MC_1 at $Q = 250$).   The larger and more efficient duopolist may then assume the natural role of price leader and set a price which will allow the other to stay in business and earn some profits even if this means not maximizing his own total profits.   (If the less efficient duopolist went out of business, duopolist 2 could be prosecuted for monopolizing the market.)

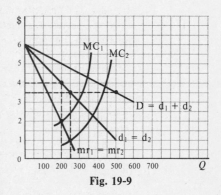

Fig. 19-9

LONG-RUN EFFICIENCY IMPLICATIONS OF OLIGOPOLY

19.17. (a) What are some of the natural and artificial barriers to entry into oligopolistic industries?   (b) What are the possible harmful effects of oligopoly?   (c) What are the possible beneficial effects of oligopoly?

(a) The natural barriers to entry into such oligopolistic industries as the automobile, aluminum, and steel industries are the smallness of the markets in relation to efficient operation and the huge amounts of capital and specialized inputs required to start efficient operation.   Some of the artificial barriers to entry are control over sources of raw materials, patents and government franchise.   When entry is blocked or at least restricted (the usual case), the firms in an oligopolistic industry can earn long-run profits.

(b) In the long run, oligopoly may lead to the following harmful effects: (1) P exceeds MC and so there is an underallocation of the economy's resources to the firms in the oligopolistic industry, (2) price usually exceeds LAC in oligopolistic markets, (3) the oligopolist usually does not produce at the lowest point on its LAC curve, and (4) when oligopolists produce a differentiated product, too much may be spent on advertising and model changes.

(c) For technological reasons, many products (such as automobiles, steel, aluminum, etc.) cannot possibly be produced under conditions of perfect competition (because their cost of production would be prohibitively high).   In addition, oligopolists spend a great deal of their profits on research and development, and some believe that this leads to faster technological advance and a higher standard of living than if the industry were organized along more competitive lines. Finally, some advertising is useful since it informs customers, and some product differentiation has the economic value of satisfying the different tastes of different consumers.

19.18. Compare the efficiency implications in long-run equilibrium of the four different forms of market organization with respect to (a) total profits, (b) allocation of resources, (c) LAC, and (d) sales promotion.

(a) It is difficult to interpret and answer this question since cost curves may differ under various forms of market organization.   A few generalizations can nevertheless be made, if they are interpreted with caution.   First, the perfectly competitive firm and the monopolistically competitive firm break even in long-run equilibrium.   Thus, consumers get the commodity at cost of production.   On the other hand, the monopolist and the oligopolist can and usually do make profits in the long run.   These profits, however, may lead to more research and development and to faster technological progress and a rising standard of living in the long run.

(b) While the perfectly competitive firm in long-run equilibrium produces the output at which $P = $ MC, the imperfectly competitive firm produces the output at which P exceeds MC.   Thus there is an underallocation of resources in these imperfectly competitive industries and a misallocation of resources in the economy.   That is, under any form of imperfect competition, the firm is likely to produce less and charge a higher price than in perfect competition.   This difference is greater in pure monopoly and oligopoly than in monopolistic competition because of the greater elasticity of demand in monopolistic competition.

(c) While the perfectly competitive firm produces at the lowest point on its LAC curve in long-run equilibrium, the monopolist and the oligopolist are very unlikely to do so, and the monopolistic competitor never does.   However, the size of efficient operation is often so large in relation to the market that only a few firms are required in the industry.   Perfect competition under such circumstances would either be impossible or lead to prohibitively high costs.

(d) Finally, the waste resulting from excessive sales promotion is likely to be zero in perfect competition, and greater in oligopoly and monopolistic competition.

19.19. (a) Explain the term "countervailing power."   What is its function and usefulness in modern economies?   (b) What is meant by "workable competition"?

(a) Countervailing power refers to the rise in powerful labor unions and large organizations of buyers from and sellers to large corporations in response to and in order to protect themselves from and check the great power of the giant corporation.   Thus, the giant GM faces the powerful United Automobile Workers Union.   The big three of the auto industry purchase steel from the big four or five of the steel industry.   Large agricultural cooperatives sell their produce to large food processors.   This limits the power and the possible abuses of such power in oligopolistic markets and makes the economy more competitive.   However, countervailing power does not work in the same or in a sufficient degree in all oligopolistic markets.   For example, GM dealers are not in a position to check the great power of GM.

(b)   Workable competition refers to the balancing of the efficiency requirements of large-scale production with protection from the abuses of monopoly and oligopoly power.   Those who agree
that workable competition is desirable acknowledge that perfect competition is often impossible
or would lead to prohibitive costs.   However, they also see the need to check the great economic
power often associated with large corporations.   Workable competition would result in government regulation of public utilities, antitrust action against overt collusion, and the encour-
agement of the development of countervailing power.

19.20.   It is often asserted that businessmen usually set prices by adding a specific "markup" to
their estimated average costs of production because they do not know the exact shape of
the demand curve and cost curves that they face.   Therefore, most of microeconomics is
"academic" and irrelevant.   How would you counter such charges?

It is true that business people often do not know the shape of the demand curve and cost curves
that they face.   It is also true that in the real world many businessmen in imperfectly competitive
markets set prices at the level of their estimated average cost plus a certain percentage, or "markup,"
of costs.   However, those firms who constantly set their prices at levels far different from those
consistent with the MR = MC condition are likely to go out of business in the long run.   On the other
hand, those firms which, by a process of trial and error, correctly estimate the "best" price to charge
are more likely to make profits, to remain in business in the long run, and to expand.

The study of the general principles of demand, production and cost can be very useful in providing
guidelines in this estimation process.   They are also a rational and logical way for the firm to think
when selecting production and pricing policies.   In addition, they will surely stimulate the alert
manager to collect pertinent data.   Note, however, that sometimes the firm may purposely not want
to charge the price that would lead to profit maximization, even if it knew exactly what that price
should be.   One reason for this was given in Problem 19.16 (b).   Another reason might be to limit
profits voluntarily to discourage potential entry into the industry.

Chapter 20

Production and the Demand for Economic Resources

20.1 INTRODUCTION TO RESOURCE PRICING

We now begin to examine how the prices of productive resources such as *wages, rents, interests* and *profits* are determined in a mixed economy such as our own.   Resource prices are a major determinant of money incomes and of the allocation of resources to various uses and firms.

Broadly speaking, the price of a resource is determined by its market demand and supply.   Firms demand resources in order to produce commodities.   The demand for resources is a *derived demand*—derived from the commodities which require the resources in production.   The greater the demand for the commodity and the more productive the resource, the greater the price that firms are willing to pay for the resource.

EXAMPLE 1.   As a result of consumers' demand for a final commodity, say shoes, firms hire labor and other resources in order to produce shoes.   The greater the demand for shoes and the more productive labor in shoe production, the greater the firms' demands for labor.   In the absence of market imperfections, minimum wage laws, union power, etc., the wage rate of labor is determined exclusively by the market demand and supply of labor.   The wage rate is the major determinant of the money income of labor and of how labor is allocated to various firms and users in the economy.

20.2 MARGINAL REVENUE PRODUCT UNDER PERFECT COMPETITION

In order to derive a firm's demand for a resource, we must first define the *marginal revenue product (MRP).   MRP measures the increase in the firm's total revenue from selling the extra product that results from employing one additional unit of the resource*.   If the firm is a perfect competitor in the commodity market, it can sell this extra output at the given market price for the commodity (see Section 17.3).   However, as additional units of the variable resource are used together with fixed resources, after a point, the extra output or *marginal physical product (MPP)* declines because of the operation of the law of diminishing returns (see Section 16.2).   Because of the declining MPP, MRP also declines.

EXAMPLE 2.   In Table 1, column (1) refers to units of a variable resource, say labor employed in a given plant.   Column (2) gives the total product produced.   Column (3) gives the marginal physical product or the change in total product per unit change in the use of the resource.

Table 1

(1) Units of Resource	(2) Total Product	(3) MPP or $\Delta(2)$	(4) Product Price	(5) Total Revenue $(2) \times (4)$	(6) MRP or $\Delta(5)$
0	0		$10	$ 0	
1	5	5	10	50	$50
2	9	4	10	90	40
3	12	3	10	120	30
4	14	2	10	140	20
5	15	1	10	150	10

MPP declines because of the law of diminishing returns (assumed here for simplicity to begin operating with the first unit of resource hired).   Column (4) shows the commodity price.   It is constant because of perfect competition in the product market.   Column (5) gives the total revenue obtained by multiplying the commodity price by the total product.   Column (6) gives the marginal revenue product, measured as the increase in the total revenue in Column (5).   MRP declines because MPP declines.

20.3   PROFIT MAXIMIZATION AND RESOURCE DEMAND UNDER PERFECT COMPETITION

In order to maximize total profits, a firm should hire additional units of a resource as long as each adds more to the firm's total revenue than to its total costs.   The increase in total revenue was defined in Section 20.2 as the marginal revenue product (MRP).   The increase in total cost gives the *marginal resource cost* (MRC) of the resource.   If the firm is a perfect competitor in the resource market, it can hire any quantity of the variable resource at the given resource price, and MRC equals the resource price.   Thus to maximize total profits, the firm should hire the resource until MRP equals the resource price.   The declining MRP schedule then represents the firm's demand schedule for the variable resource.

EXAMPLE 3.   If the firm of Table 1 is also a perfect competitor in the resource market and the resource price is $50, the firm will hire only one unit of the resource (say one worker) given where the MRP of $50 (column 6 in Table 1) equals the resource price of $50.   If the resource price were $40, the firm would hire two units of the resource.   At the price of $30, the firm would hire 3 units, and so on.   The declining MRP schedule [columns (6) and (1) in Table 1] gives the firm's demand schedule for this resource and is graphed in Fig. 20-1.

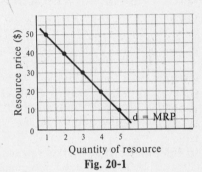

Fig. 20-1

20.4   MARGINAL PRODUCTIVITY AND RESOURCE DEMAND UNDER IMPERFECT COMPETITION

If the firm is an imperfect competitor in the commodity market, the MRP declines both because the MPP declines and because the firm must lower the commodity price in order to sell more units. If the firm remains a perfect competitor in the resource market, the firm again maximizes total profits when it hires the resource until MRP equals the resource price.   The declining MRP schedule then represents the firm's demand schedule for the variable resource.

EXAMPLE 4.   The first three columns of Table 2 are the same as in Table 1.   Commodity price (column 4) declines because of imperfect competition in the commodity market.   Total revenue (column 5) is obtained by multiplying commodity price by total product.   Column (6) gives the MRP, measured as the change in total revenue in column (5).   MRP declines both because MPP declines (column 3) and the product price declines (column 4).   A firm which is a perfect competitor in the resource market would maximize its total profits by employing the resource (say workers) until their MRP equals the resource price.

Table 2

(1) Units of Resource	(2) Total Product	(3) MPP of Δ(2)	(4) Product Price	(5) Total Revenue (2) × (4)	(6) MRP or Δ(5)
0	0		$11	$ 0	
		5			50
1	5		10	50	
		4			31
2	9		9	81	
		3			15
3	12		8	96	
		2			2
4	14		7	98	
		1			− 8
5	15		6	90	

The MRP schedule of columns (6) and (1) in Table 2 is the firm's demand schedule for the resource and is graphed as d' in Fig. 20-2.   At the resource price of $50, the firm will hire one unit of the resource.   At the resource price of $31, the firm will hire two units of the resource, and so on.   Note that d' is less elastic than d in Fig. 20-1.

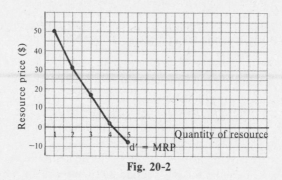

Fig. 20-2

20.5   CHANGES IN RESOURCE DEMAND AND ELASTICITY

A firm's demand for a productive resource will increase (i.e. shift up) if: (1) the product demand increases, (2) the productivity of the resource rises, (3) the prices of substitute resources rise, or (4) the prices of complementary resources fall.

On the other hand, the elasticity of the resource's demand is greater: (1) the greater the elasticity of the product demand, (2) the smaller the rate of decline of the resource's MPP, (3) the easier it is to substitute this resource for other resources in production (as the resource price falls), and (4) the larger the proportion of the cost of this resource to the total costs of production.

EXAMPLE 5.   If the market demand for shoes rises and if the firm provides each worker with better but more expensive equipment, the firm's demand for labor will also rise (i.e. shift up).   That is, to produce more shoes requires more labor; better equipment makes labor more productive and so the demand for labor increases; an increase in the price of capital equipment encourages the substitution of labor for capital in production.   On the other hand, the firm's demand for labor is very elastic if consumers' demand for shoes is very elastic, if the MPP of labor in shoe production falls very slowly, if the firm can easily substitute labor for capital equipment when the price of labor falls, or if the cost of labor in relation to total costs is high.

20.6   A FIRM'S DEMAND FOR SEVERAL RESOURCES

If a firm uses more than one variable resource, say labor (L) and capital (K), the firm will maximize total profits when it uses labor and capital until the marginal revenue product of each resource equals the resource price (if the firm is a perfect competitor in the resource markets).   That is, the firm will maximize total profits when $MRP_L = P_L$ or wage rate, and $MRP_K = P_K$ or the rate of interest. This can be rewritten as $MRP_L/P_L = MRP_K/P_K = 1$ and can be generalized to any number of resources.   If the firm is an imperfect competitor in the resource markets, the profit maximization condition is generalized to $MPP_L = MRC_L$ and $MPP_K = MRC_K$ or $MPP_L/MRC_L = MPP_K/MRC_K = 1$ (where MRC refers to the marginal resource cost—see Sections 20.3 and 21.3).

Important Economic Terms

Derived demand.   The demand for productive resources which arises because resources are needed to produce final commodities that consumers demand.

Firm's demand schedule for a resource.   The MRP schedule of the resource (when the firm is a perfect competitor in the resource market), reflecting the profit-maximization rule that the firm should continue to hire a resource until MRP equals the resource price.

Marginal physical product (MPP). The change in total product that results from employing one additional unit of a variable resource together with other fixed resources.

Marginal revenue product (MRP). A measurement of the change in the firm's total revenue from selling the extra or marginal physical product that results from employing one additional unit of a resource together with other fixed resources.

Perfectly competitive firm in the factor market. A firm that is too small to affect the price of the resource it purchases and can hire any quantity of the resource at the prevailing market price.

Perfectly competitive firm in the product market. A firm that is too small to affect the price of the product it sells and can sell any quantity of the product at the prevailing market price.

Resource pricing. The manner in which wages for various kinds of labor, rents for various types of land and other natural resources, interests on capital assets, and profits on entrepreneurship are determined in a mixed economy such as our own.

Total revenue (TR). The product price times the total product sold.

Review Questions

1. Wages, rents, interests and profits are a major determinant of (a) the money incomes of resource owners, (b) the relative shares of national income going to various kinds of resource owners, (c) how resources are allocated to various uses and firms, (d) all of the above.

    Ans. (d)

2. Which of the following statements is *incorrect?*
    (a) Consumers demand final commodities because of the utility or satisfaction they get from them.
    (b) Firms demand resources in order to produce goods and services demanded by consumers.
    (c) Firms demand resources because of the utility or satisfaction they get from them.
    (d) The more productive a resource in producing a commodity, the greater the resource price.

    Ans. (c)

3. The extra product generated by adding one unit of a resource to the other fixed resources is called (a) marginal physical product (MPP), (b) marginal revenue product (MRP), (c) marginal resource cost (MRC), (d) marginal revenue (MR).

    Ans. (a)

4. When the firm is a perfect competitor in the product market, its MRP declines because of declining (a) MPP only, (b) commodity price only, (c) marginal revenue only, (d) MPP and the commodity price.

    Ans. (a)

5. Which of the following statements is *incorrect?*
    (a) The increase in the firm's total costs in hiring one more unit of the variable resource is called the marginal resource cost (MRC).
    (b) When the firm is a perfect competitor in the resource market, the marginal resource cost equals the resource price.
    (c) Total revenue equals product price times MPP.
    (d) To maximize total profits, a firm should hire the variable resource until MRP = MRC.

    Ans. (c)

6. When the firm is a perfect competitor in the resource market, its demand for the variable resource is the schedule of (a) MRP, (b) MPP, (c) MRC, (d) MR.

    Ans. (a)

7. When the firm is an imperfect competitor in the product market, its MRP declines because of declining (a) MPP only, (b) commodity price only, (c) marginal revenue only, (d) MPP and commodity price.

    Ans. (d)

8. When the firm is an imperfect competitor rather than a perfect competitor in the product market, its demand for the variable resource (other things being equal) is (a) more elastic, (b) less elastic, (c) infinitely elastic, (d) unitary elastic.

   Ans.   (b)

9. A firm's demand for a productive resource increases (i.e. shifts up) when (a) the product demand increases, (b) the productivity of the resource rises, (c) the prices of substitute resources rise or the prices of complementary resources fall, (d) all of the above.

   Ans.   (d)

10. Which of the following is *incorrect?*   A firm's demand for a resource is *more elastic*, (a) the more elastic the product demand, (b) the greater the rate of decline of the resource's MPP, (c) the easier it is to substitute this for other resources in production when the price of the resource falls, (d) the larger the proportion of the resource's cost to total production costs.

    Ans.   (b)

11. When a perfectly competitive firm in the labor and capital markets is maximizing its total profits, (a) $\text{MRP}_L = P_L$, (b) $\text{MRP}_K = P_K$, (c) $\text{MRP}_L/P_L = \text{MRP}_K/P_K = 1$, (d) all of the above.

    Ans.   (d)

12. When an imperfectly competitive firm in the labor and capital markets is maximizing profits, (a) $\text{MRP}_L = P_L$ and $\text{MRP}_K = P_K$, (b) $\text{MRP}_L/P_L = \text{MRP}_K/P_K = 1$, (c) $\text{MRP}_L/\text{MRC}_L = \text{MRP}_K/\text{MRC}_K = 1$, (d) none of the above.

    Ans.   (c)

Solved Problems

INTRODUCTION TO RESOURCE PRICING

20.1.   (a) What is resource pricing?   (b) Why is it important?   (c) How is the price of resources determined in a mixed economy such as our own?

   (a)   Resource pricing examines or studies the determination of (1) the wages of various kinds of labor, (2) the rents of various types of land and other natural resources, (3) the interest rates on capital assets, and (4) profits from various forms of entrepreneurial activity.   This chapter deals with resource pricing in general.   Chapter 21 deals with wage determination; and Chapter 22 covers the determination of rents, interests and profits.

   (b)   Wages, rents, interests and profits are major determinants of the money income of resource owners and of the inequality in the personal distribution of income.   Thus, the prices of resources help determine the answer to the fundamental economic question of "for whom to produce" (see Section 1.4) and refer to the bottom loop in Fig. 1–5.   The prices of resources also help to determine which commodities will be produced and how firms will combine various resources to minimize the costs of production and to maximize profits.

   (c)   Broadly speaking, the price of a resource is determined, just as the price of a final commodity is determined, by the interaction of the market supply and demand.   The interaction of the forces of market demand and supply for each kind of labor time determines the wage rate of various kinds of labor.   The interaction of the forces of market demand and supply for each type of land or other natural resource determines the rent of each of these natural resources.   The same is true for interest on various kinds of capital and profit on various forms of entrepreneurship.   However, in a mixed economy such as our own, the operation of the forces of market demand and supply is often modified by such market imperfections as union power and minimum wage legislation.   See Section 21.3.

20.2.   (a) Why do firms demand resources?   In what way is a firm's demand for a resource a derived demand?   How does this differ from consumers' demand for final commodities? (b) What determines the strength of a firm's demand for a productive resource?

(*a*) Firms demand resources in order to produce final commodities.   However, resources may first
be utilized to produce capital equipment that would then facilitate the production of final commodities.   It is the consumers' demand for final commodities that ultimately gives rise to the
firm's demand for productive resources.   Because of this, the demand for a resource is referred
to as a "derived demand."   It is derived from the demand for the final commodities which
require the resource in production.   While consumers demand final commodities because of the
direct utility or satisfaction that they get from consuming commodities, producers demand resources only because the resource can be used to produce the commodities that consumers
demand.

(*b*) The strength of a firm's demand for a resource depends on (1) the strength of the demand for the
commodity that the resource is used to produce, (2) the productivity of the resource in producing
the final commodity, and (3) the prices of other related (i.e. substitute and complementary)
resources.   The higher the demand for the final commodity, the more productive is the resource.   The higher the price of substitute resources and the lower the price of complementary
resources, the greater the firm's demand for the resource.

MARGINAL REVENUE PRODUCT UNDER PERFECT COMPETITION

20.3.   (*a*) When is a firm a perfect competitor in the product market?   (*b*) When is a firm a perfect
competitor in the resource market?

(*a*) A firm is a perfect competitor in the product market if it is one of a large number of sellers of
a homogeneous commodity and can sell any quantity of the commodity without affecting the
market price.   The perfectly competitive firm is a price taker.   That is, it faces an infinitely
elastic demand for the commodity it sells at the prevailing market price (see Sections 17.1 and
17.3).

(*b*) A firm is a perfect competitor in the resource market if it is one of a large number of buyers of
the resource, each too small to affect the resource price.   Thus, the firm faces an infinitely elastic
supply of the resource and can purchase any quantity of the resource at its prevailing market
price (see Section 21.1).

20.4.   From Table 4, (*a*) find the marginal physical product (MPP), total revenue and the marginal
revenue product (MRP) schedules.   (*b*) Why does the MPP decline?   Why does the MRP
decline?   How can you tell that this firm is a perfect competitor in the product market?

Table 4

Units of Resource	Total Product	Product Price
0	0	
1	10	$1
2	18	1
3	24	1
4	28	1
5	30	1

(*a*) Column (3) in Table 5 gives the MPP.   It is obtained from the change in total product per unit
change in the use of the variable resource.   Column (5) gives the total revenue of the firm.
It is obtained by multiplying the product price (column 4) by the total product (column 2).
Column (6) gives the marginal revenue product.   It is obtained from the increase in the total
revenue in column (5).

(*b*) The MPP that results from employing each additional unit of the variable resource (together with
fixed amounts of other resources) declines because of the law of diminishing returns (see Section
16.2).   For simplicity, it is here assumed that the law of diminishing returns begins to operate
with the first unit of the variable resource hired.   The marginal revenue product declines because
MPP declines.   We know that this firm is a perfect competitor in the product market because

Table 5

(1) Units of Resource	(2) Total Product	(3) MPP or Δ(2)	(4) Product Price	(5) Total Revenue (2) × (4)	(6) MRP or Δ(5)
0	0			$ 0	
		10			$10
1	10		$1	10	
		8			8
2	18		1	18	
		6			6
3	24		1	24	
		4			4
4	28		1	28	
		2			2
5	30		1	30	

product price remains constant at $1 per unit regardless of the quantity of the product sold by the firm.

PROFIT MAXIMIZATION AND RESOURCE DEMAND UNDER PERFECT COMPETITION

20.5. (a) What general rule should a firm follow in hiring a resource in order to maximize total profits?   Explain marginal resource cost (MRC).   (b) What is MRC when the firm is a perfect competitor in the resource market?   How does this affect the rule that the firm should follow in hiring a resource in order to maximize its total profits?

(a) In order to maximize total profits, a firm should hire additional units of a resource as long as each adds more to the firm's total revenue than to its total costs.   The increase in total revenue is called the marginal revenue product (MRP).   The increase in total costs (from hiring one additional unit of a resource to be used with other fixed resources) is called the marginal resource cost (MRC).   Thus, to maximize total profits a firm should hire a resource as long as MRP exceeds MRC and until MRP = MRC.   Note the similarity between this and the condition for profit maximization (MR = MC) in Section 17.3.   The only difference is that our main focus is now the resource market rather than the product market.

(b) If the firm is a perfect competitor in the resource market (so that it can hire any quantity of the resource at the prevailing market price of the resource), the change in its total costs in hiring one more unit of the resource (i.e. its MRC) equals the resource price.   The rule for profit maximization when the firm is a perfect competitor in the resource market is to hire a resource as long as MRP exceeds the resource price and up to the point when they are equal.   (The case where the firm is an imperfect competitor in the resource market is discussed in detail in Section 21.3.)

20.6. (a) Following the profit maximization rule for the firm of Problem 20.4, how many units of the variable resource should the firm hire if the resource price is $10, $8, $6, $4, $2?   (b) Draw this firm's demand curve for the variable resource.

(a) Since the firm is a perfect competitor in the resource market, it will maximize its total profits by hiring the variable resource as long as MRP exceeds the resource price and until they are equal.   Thus, at the resource price of $10, the firm will hire one unit of the resource. At the resource price of $8, the firm will hire two units of the resource.   The firm will hire three units of the resource at the price of $6, four units at the price of $4, and five at the price of $2.   Thus, columns (6) and (1) of Table 5 give the firm's demand schedule for the variable resource.

(b) Graphing the firm's demand schedule, we get the firm's demand curve (d) for the resource.   Note that the MRP is plotted at the midpoint of each resource unit.

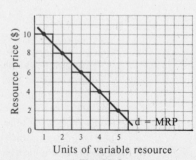

Fig. 20-3

MARGINAL PRODUCTIVITY AND RESOURCE DEMAND
UNDER IMPERFECT COMPETITION

20.7. Suppose that the product price in Table 4, instead of remaining at $1, declined to $0.90 when two units of the product sold, to $0.80 for three units sold, $0.70 for four, and to $0.60 for five units of the product sold.   (a) Find the MPP, the total revenue, and the MRP schedules.   (b) Why does the MRP decline?   How can you tell that this firm is an imperfect competitor in the product market?

  (a) Column (3) in Table 6 gives the MPP (the same as in Table 5).   Column (5) gives the total revenue of the firm (obtained by multiplying total product by product price).   Column (6) gives the MRP, measured as the change in total revenue.

  (b) The MRP declines because both (1) MPP declines (due to the operation of the law of diminishing returns) and (2) product price declines.   The firm of Table 6 is an imperfect competitor in the product market because it must lower the product price in order to sell more units of the product. (In order to distinguish it from this case, the MRP when the firm is a perfect competitor in the product market is sometimes referred to as "the value of the marginal product" or the VMP.)

Table 6

(1) Units of Resource	(2) Total Product	(3) MPP or Δ(2)	(4) Product Price	(5) Total Revenue (2) × (4)	(6) MRP or Δ(5)
0	0			$ 0.00	
1	10	10	$1.00	10.00	$10.00
2	18	8	0.90	16.20	6.20
3	24	6	0.80	19.20	3.00
4	28	4	0.70	19.60	0.40
5	30	2	0.60	18.00	−1.60

20.8. If the firm in Problem 20.7 is a perfect competitor in the resource market, (a) how many units of the variable resource should this firm hire at the resource price of $10, $6.20, $3.00 and $0.40?   Why will the firm not hire the fifth unit of the resource even if it were free? (b) Draw this firm's demand curve for the variable resource.

  (a) The firm will hire one unit of the variable resource at the resource price of $10, (where MRP equals the resource price), two units at the resource price of $6.20, three at the price of $3 and four at the resource price of $0.40 per unit.   The firm would not employ the fifth unit of the resource even if it were free because the MRP of this fifth unit is negative (−$1.60).   That is, by lowering the product price in order to sell the MPP of the fifth unit of the variable resource, the total revenue of the firm will decline.   Because the firm hires a resource up to the point where MRP equals the resource price, this is referred to as the "marginal productivity theory."

  (b) Columns (6) and (1) of Table 6 give the firm's demand schedule for the variable resource.   This is plotted as (d') in Fig. 20-4.   Note that d' is less elastic than d in Fig. 20-2.

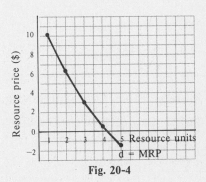

Fig. 20-4

CHANGES IN RESOURCE DEMAND AND ELASTICITY

20.9. Explain what can cause an increase or upward shift in a firm's demand for a productive resource.

When the market demand for a product increases, firms will purchase more resources in order to increase their output of the product.   For example, when the demand for housing rises, construction firms tend to hire more electricians, plumbers, construction workers and to purchase or rent more construction equipment and land in order to build more homes.   As workers are supplied with better equipment, the productivity and demand for labor increase still further.   If the price of capital equipment subsequently rose in relation to wages, firms would increase their demand for labor as they substituted labor for capital in production.   On the other hand, when the wage rate of electricians falls, (so that more electricians are employed), the demand for plumbers (the complementary labor to build houses) also increases.

20.10. Explain what determines the elasticity of demand for a resource.

The elasticity of resource demand depends on several conditions:

(1)   The greater the elasticity of the product demand, the greater the elasticity of resource demand. When the firm is a perfect competitor in the product market and faces an infinitely elastic product demand, the firm's resource demand is more elastic than when the firm is an imperfect competitor in the product market (compare d in Fig. 20-3 to d' in Fig. 20-4).

(2)   Since a resource demand schedule is given by its MRP schedule and the MRP depends on the resource MPP schedule (and the commodity price), the smaller (i.e. the flatter) the rate of decline in the resource MPP schedule, the more elastic the MRP or the resource demand curve (everything else being held constant).

(3)   If a resource can easily be substituted for others as the resource's price falls, the percentage increase in the quantity demanded of the resource will be large in relation to the percentage decline in the resource's price and result in an elastic resource demand.

(4)   If the resource's cost is large in relation to the firm's total costs, an increase in the resource's price will cause a relatively large increase in costs of production, leading to a relatively large decline in production and, hence, in the quantity of the resource demanded.

20.11. (*a*) How do we get the total market demand for a resource?   (*b*) Why is this important?

(*a*)   The total market demand (i.e. the demand of all firms) for a resource is obtained by summing the quantity demanded of the resource by each firm at each resource price.   In a more advanced course, you will see that this is not as straightforward and simple as obtaining the market demand for a *product* by totaling *individual* demands for the product (see Section 2.1).   This happens because as a resource price falls, firms will hire more of the resource and produce more of the commodities which require that resource in production.   This increase in the product-market supplies will reduce product prices and cause a downward shift in the resource MRP and the demand curve.

(*b*)   The resource-market demand is important because, together with the resource-market supply, it determines the resource-market equilibrium price.   This is the price which the perfectly competitive firm in the resource market uses to determine how much of the resource to employ (see Section 21.1).

A FIRM'S DEMAND FOR SEVERAL RESOURCES

20.12. Explain how much of each variable resource a firm should hire in order to maximize total profits, if the firm is a perfect competitor in the resource markets.

We saw in Section 20.3 that in order to maximize total profits, a firm which is a perfect competitor in the resource market should hire the variable resource as long as its MRP exceeds its price and until they are equal.   In the usual case, the firm employs more than one variable resource, say labor (L) and capital (K), but the same rule applies.   That is, in order to maximize total profits, the firm should hire labor and capital as long as the MRP_L exceeds P_L or wage rate (W) and until $MRP_L = P_L$ or W. Similarly, the firm should employ capital as long as the MRP_K exceeds P_K or rate of interest and until $MRP_K = P_K$.   When $MRP_L = P_L$, $MRP_L/P_L = 1$.   Similarly, when $MRP_K = P_K$, $MRP_K/P_K = 1$. Thus, the condition for profit maximization for a firm employing labor and capital can be rewritten as $MRP_L/P_L = MRP_K/P_K = 1$.   This is a *special rule* for the firm which is a *perfect competitor* in the resource markets, and can be extended to any number of variable resources.   See Problem 20.13.

20.13. Explain how much of each variable resource a firm should hire in order to maximize total profits, if the firm is an imperfect competitor in the resource markets.

When a firm which is an imperfect competitor in the resource markets wants to hire more of a resource, it will have to pay a higher price, not only on the additional units of the resource but also on all previous units of the resource hired.   Thus, the increase in the total costs of hiring an additional unit of the resource or marginal resource cost (MRC) exceeds the resource price (see Section 21.2). The firm will maximize total profits when it hires variable resources as long as each resource MRP exceeds its MRC and until they are equal.   With variable resources labor (L) and capital (K), the firm maximizes total profits when $MRP_L = MRC_L$ and $MRP_K = MRC_K$ or $MRP_L/MRC_L = MRP_K/MRC_K = 1$.   This is the *general rule* of which $MRP_L/P_L = MRP_K/P_K = 1$ is the special case for the firm in a perfectly competitive resource market.   Another way of stating the profit maximization condition is to say that a firm should hire resources until the MRP per dollar spent on each resource is the same and equal to 1.   Once again, this rule can be extended to any number of variable resources.

Chapter 21

Wage Determination

21.1 GENERAL LEVEL OF WAGES

The wage rate (or money-wage rate) refers to the earnings per hour of labor. The money-wage rate divided by the price index gives the *real wage rate* or actual "purchasing power" of money wages. We are primarily concerned with real wages.

The level of real wages depends on the productivity of labor. Real wages are higher (1) the greater the amount of capital available per worker, (2) the more advanced the technology of production, and (3) the greater the availability of natural resources such as fertile land, mineral deposits, etc.

EXAMPLE 1. If the average U.S. *money-wage index* doubled (from 100 to 200) between 1970 and 1980 but the general price index rose by 60 percent (from 100 to 160), the real-wage index increased by only one-quarter or 25 percent (i.e. $200/160 = 1\frac{1}{4}$).

Real wages are generally higher in the U.S. than in Europe because (1) capital equipment per worker is higher in the U.S., (2) the technology of production is more advanced, and (3) the relationship between workers and natural resources is more favorable. On the other hand, real wages in Europe are higher than in developing nations for generally the same reasons.

21.2 WAGE DETERMINATION UNDER PERFECT COMPETITION

In the preceding chapter, we saw that firms demand labor (and other resources) in order to produce the products demanded by customers. By adding each firm's demand for labor, we get the *market demand* for labor. On the other hand, the *market supply* of labor depends on the population size, the proportion of the population in the labor force, the state of the economy (such as boom or recession), and the level of real wages (see Problem 21.5).

The *competitive equilibrium real-wage rate* is determined at the intersection of the market demand and supply of labor curves. The firm then hires labor until the marginal revenue product of labor (MRP_L) or its demand for labor (d_L) equals the wage rate.

EXAMPLE 2. In Panel B of Fig. 21-1, the competitive equilibrium real-wage rate of $6 per hour is determined at the intersection of the market demand and supply of labor. The supply of labor to the competitive firm of Panel A (s_L) is horizontal at the wage rate of $6. This means that the firm is so small (say, 1 of 1,000 identical firms in the market) that it can hire any quantity of labor at the equilibrium market wage rate without affecting

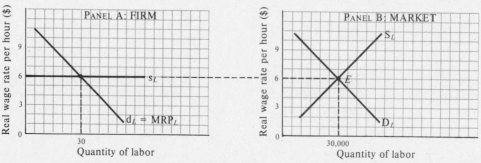

Fig. 21-1

that wage rate.   To maximize total profits the firm hires 30 units of labor because $MRP_L = W = \$6$ at 30 units of labor (see Section 20.3).

21.3 WAGE DETERMINATION WITH IMPERFECT COMPETITION

Workers are often not hired competitively.   In a company town, a firm that is the only or dominant employer has monopoly power in the local labor market and is referred to as a *monopsonist*.   A monopsonist faces the rising *market* supply curve of labor which indicates that it must pay higher wages to hire more workers.   As a result, the change in the total cost of hiring an additional unit of labor or *marginal resource cost of labor* (MRC_L) exceeds the wage rate.   To maximize total profits, the firm hires labor until $MRP_L = MRC_L$ and pays the wage indicated on the supply curve of labor for that quantity of labor.

EXAMPLE 3. In Table 1, columns (1) and (2) are the market supply schedule of labor facing the monopsonist.   Column (1) times column (2) gives column (3) which measures the total cost of hiring various quantities of labor.   Column (4) shows the change in total costs in hiring each additional unit of labor or MRC_L.   Note that MRC_L exceeds W.   Plotting columns (1) and (2) as S_L and columns (2) and (4) as MRC_L in Fig. 21-2 and superimposing the firm's MRP_L on the same graph, we see that the monopsonist will hire 3 units of labor (given by point E where $MRP_L = MRC_L$) and pay the wage of \$3 (on S_L at $Q_L = 3$).

Table 1

(1) Wage Rate ($)	(2) Quantity of Labor	(3) Total Cost of Labor	(4) Marginal Cost of Labor
1	1	1	3
2	2	4	5
3	3	9	7
4	4	16	9
5	5	25	

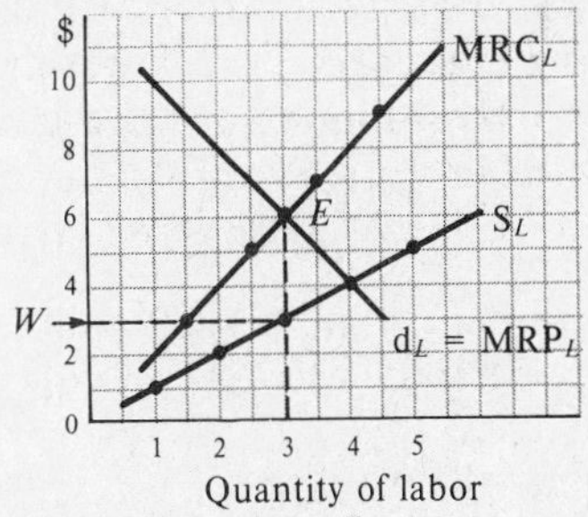

Fig. 21-2

21.4 THE EFFECT OF UNIONS ON WAGES

Labor unions attempt to increase wages in three ways.   *First,* unions attempt to increase the demand for labor by increasing labor productivity, by financing advertising of union-made products and by lobbying to restrict imports.   This is the most desirable but also the least effective method.   *Second,* unions attempt to raise wages by restricting the supply of labor through the imposition of high initiation fees and long apprenticeships and requirements that employers hire only union members.   This is done primarily by *craft unions* (i.e. unions of such skilled workers as electricians).   *Third,* unions attempt to raise wage rates directly by bargaining with employers, under the threat of a strike.   This is the most common method and is used primarily by *industrial unions* (i.e. unions of all the workers of a particular industry, such as automobile workers).   Empirical studies seem to indicate that in general, unions in the U.S. have raised real wages for their members by only about 10 to 15 percent.

EXAMPLE 4. In Panel A of Fig. 21-3, the equilibrium real-wage rate is \$4 and employment is 3000 workers (at point E where D_L intersects S_L).   If the union can successfully increase D_L to D'_L, $W = \$6$ and employment rises to 4000.   Starting from the same original equilibrium point E in Panel B, a craft union could instead attempt to reduce S_L to S'_L so that $W = \$6$ but only 2000 are employed.   In Panel C, an industrial union could attempt to negotiate $W = \$6$ at which 2000 workers are employed and another 2000 workers $(E'A)$ are unable to find jobs.   The result would be the same without a union if the government set the minimum wage at \$6. A union or a government minimum-wage requirement could also overcome the tendency of a monopsonist to pay wages below the marginal revenue product of labor [see Problem 21.13 (a)].

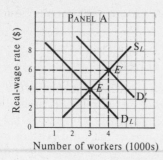
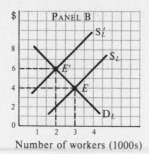
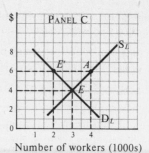

Fig. 21-3

21.5   WAGE DIFFERENTIALS

If all jobs and individuals were exactly alike and all markets perfectly competitive, there would be a single wage for all jobs and all workers.   However, jobs requiring equal qualifications may differ in attractiveness, and higher wages must be paid to attract and retain workers in more unpleasant jobs.   Thus, garbage collectors receive higher wages than porters.   Such wage differentials are known as *equalizing differences*.   Even if all jobs were equally attractive, wage differences would persist because individuals such as doctors, accountants, clerks, etc. differ widely in capacities, skills, training and education.   Thus, labor falls into many *noncompeting groups*, each requiring different training and receiving different wages.   Finally, some wage differences are the result of *imperfect markets*.   Market imperfections include lack of information, unwillingness to move, union power, minimum-wage laws and monopsony power.   The wide wage differences actually observed in the real world among different categories of people and jobs are in general the result of a combination of these three factors.

Important Economic Terms

Bilateral monopoly.   The market in which a union (a monopolist in selling labor services) faces a monopsonist (a monopolist buyer of labor services).

Competitive equilibrium real-wage rate.   The wage rate at which the quantity of labor demanded equals the quantity of labor supplied.

Craft union.   A union in which all members have a particular type of skill (e.g. printers, electricians, plumbers, etc.).

Equalizing differences.   The wage differences resulting from the varying attractiveness of different jobs. For the same level of capacity and training, the more unpleasant a job, the higher the wage rate.

Industrial union.   A union whose membership is comprised of workers (skilled and unskilled) employed in a given industry.   Examples are the United Mine Workers (UMW) and the United Auto Workers (UAW) of America.

Marginal resource cost (MRC).   A measurement of the change in total cost of hiring an additional unit of the resource.   MRC exceeds the resource price in imperfectly competitive resource markets.

Market demand for labor.   The total quantity of labor demanded at various alternative wage rates.   It is obtained by summing all firms' demands for labor.

Market supply of labor.   The total quantity of labor supplied at various alternative wage rates.   It depends on the population size, the proportion of the population in the labor force and the state of the economy.

Money wage.   The dollar payment received for one hour, day, week, etc. of labor.

Money-wage index.   An economic indicator that measures the percentage change in the money-wage rate with respect to a base year taken as 100.

Monopsony.   A market in which there is a single buyer of a resource.   The monopsonist has a monopoly power in the purchase of the resource.

Noncompeting groups.   Occupations requiring different capacities, skills and training and, therefore, receiving different wages.

Price index.   An indicator which measures the percentage change in the general price level with respect to a base year taken as 100.

Real wage.   The actual purchasing power of the money wage.

Real-wage index.   The money-wage index divided by the price index and multiplied by 100, which measures the percentage change in actual purchasing power associated with a given percentage change in money wages.

Review Questions

1. If the money wage index were to rise by 50% between 1980 and 1985 and the price index were to rise by 20% over the same period, then the real wage index would rise by (*a*) 35%, (*b*) 30%, (*c*) 25%, (*d*) 20%.

   Ans.   (*c*) $150/120 = 1\frac{1}{4}$ or 25%.

2. Real wages are higher, (*a*) the greater the amount of capital available per worker, (*b*) the more advanced the technology of production, (*c*) the greater the availability of natural resources such as fertile land, mineral deposits, etc., (*d*) all of the above.

   Ans.   (*d*)

3. Which of the following statements is *incorrect?*
   (*a*)   Firms demand labor and other resources in order to produce the products demanded by consumers.
   (*b*)   A perfectly competitive firm's demand for labor is its marginal revenue product of labor schedule or curve.
   (*c*)   Another name for the marginal revenue product of labor is the marginal resource cost of labor.
   (*d*)   The market demand for labor is obtained by adding each firm's demand for labor.

   Ans.   (*c*)

4. The market supply of labor depends on (*a*) the population size, (*b*) the proportion of the population in the labor force, (*c*) the state of the economy, (*d*) all of the above.

   Ans.   (*d*)

5. Which of the following statements is *incorrect?*
   (*a*)   The competitive equilibrium wage rate is determined at the intersection of the market demand and supply curve of labor.
   (*b*)   In order to hire more labor, the perfectly competitive firm must pay a higher wage rate.
   (*c*)   The perfectly competitive firm hires labor until the marginal revenue product of labor equals the wage rate.
   (*d*)   If the market demand for labor increases, the equilibrium wage rate rises.

   Ans.   (*b*)

6. A firm which is the only buyer of or has monopoly power in the labor (or other resource) market is called a (an) (*a*) monopolist, (*b*) monopsonist, (*c*) oligopolist, (*d*) oligopsonist.

   Ans.   (*b*)

7. Which of the following statements about a monopsonist in the labor market is *incorrect?*
   (*a*)   It faces a rising market supply curve of labor.
   (*b*)   The marginal resource cost of labor is rising.
   (*c*)   The wage rate exceeds the marginal resource cost of labor.
   (*d*)   The marginal resource cost of labor curve is above the market supply curve of labor.

   Ans.   (*c*)

8. Which of the following statements about a monopsonist is *not* correct?
   (*a*) To maximize total profits, it hires labor up to the point where $MRP_L = MRC_L$.
   (*b*) The wage that it pays is read from the labor supply curve.
   (*c*) W is smaller than MRP_L.
   (*d*) $W = MRC_L$.

   Ans. (*d*)

9. If a union is successful in increasing the demand for labor, (*a*) the wage rate rises but employment falls, (*b*) the wage rate falls but employment rises, (*c*) both the wage rate and employment will rise, (*d*) all of the above are possible.

   Ans. (*c*)

10. The attempt of industrial unions to raise wage rates usually results in (*a*) higher wages and more employment, (*b*) higher wages and less employment, (*c*) higher wages without affecting employment, (*d*) actually lower wages but more employment.

    Ans. (*b*)

11. The reason for wage differentials is (*a*) the different attractiveness of different jobs, (*b*) the different skills and training required for different jobs, (*c*) imperfect labor markets, (*d*) all of the above.
    Ans. (*d*)

12. Noncompeting groups refer to workers (*a*) in jobs of different attractiveness, (*b*) with different capacities, skills and training, (*c*) in imperfect labor markets, (*d*) all of the above.
    Ans. (*b*)

Solved Problems

GENERAL LEVEL OF WAGES

21.1. (*a*) In what sense is labor the "most important" resource? (*b*) What is the relationship between the discussion of resource pricing in Chapter 20 and wage determination? (*c*) Why are wage rates important? (*d*) What is the distinction between money wages and real wages?

   (*a*) Labor is the most important resource because, first and foremost, labor refers to human beings rather than to machines or objects. Secondly, labor receives between 75 and 80 percent of the national income.

   (*b*) The discussion of resource pricing in Chapter 20 was general and referred to any factor of production (labor, land, capital and entrepreneurship). Wage determination refers particularly to the price of labor services. What we said in Chapter 20 is entirely relevant, but we now extend that discussion to those things which are unique to labor resources.

   (*c*) Wage rates are the most important determinant of individuals' incomes and of the distribution of incomes in society. Individuals' incomes depend for the most part on the wage rate they receive and the number of hours they work. The different wages for different types of jobs also determine to a large extent the income inequalities among different occupations and individuals.

   (*d*) The money wage is the *dollar* payment that a worker receives for work. This can be expressed in so many dollars per hour, day, week or year; but is most usually dollars per hour. However, the actual *real* or *purchasing power* of the money wage depends also on the general price level. The higher the price level, the lower the real wage or purchasing power of a given money wage.

21.2. Explain the terms (*a*) money-wage index, (*b*) price-level index, and (*c*) real-wage index. (*d*) If the money-wage rate were $5 per hour in 1976 and $6.50 per hour in 1980, and the price index rose from 100 in 1976 to 120 by 1980, what is the real-wage index in 1980 in terms of 1976 prices?

(a) The money-wage index refers to the dollar money wage in one year, say, in 1980, in terms of the money wage in a previous (base) year, say, 1976, when the money wage in 1976 is taken as 100. When we say that the money wage index in 1980 is 130 relative to 1976 = 100, this means that the money wage rose by 30% between 1976 and 1980.

(b) The price-level index expresses the general level of prices in one year, say, in 1980, in terms of the price level in a previous (base) year, say, in 1976, when the price level in 1976 is taken as 100. When we say that the price level index in 1980 is 120 relative to 1976 = 100, this means that the price level rose by 20% between 1976 and 1980. The government regularly publishes several price indexes. The consumer price index gives the price in terms of a "representative basket" of goods purchased by the "average" family.

(c) The real-wage index equals the money-wage index deflated or divided by the price index and then multiplied by 100. That is,

$$\text{Real-wage index} = \frac{\text{money-wage index}}{\text{price index}} \times 100$$

The real-wage index measures the change in the purchasing power of a given change in money wages.

(d) If we take the $5 wage per hour in 1976 as 100, we can then express the 1980 wage of $6.50 as 130. This is calculated by setting up the following proportion: $5/100 = 6.5/W$, and cross multiplying, so that $5W = 650$ and $W = 130$.

This says that the money-wage index rose by 30 percent between 1976 and 1980. However, since the price index was 120 in 1980, the real-wage index in 1980 is $130/120 \times 100 = 1.0833 \times 100 = 108.33$. This means that the purchasing power of wages rose by only 8.33 percent between 1976 and 1980.

21.3.   Why have real wages risen in the U.S. over time?

Real wages have risen historically in the U.S. (and in most other nations) because the productivity of labor has increased. The productivity of labor increased as labor became more skilled and better trained, as technology improved, and as more capital and natural resources were made available to each worker. Over the past century or so, labor productivity in the U.S. rose on the average between 2 and 2.5 percent per year, and doubled real wages every 30–35 years. The larger part of this increase resulted from an increase in the level of skills and training of the labor force and from technological progress. The growth of real wages seems to have slowed down a bit in recent years as a result of a greater social awareness of the environment (pollution control is expensive) and in the attempt to achieve greater income equality (more progressive income taxes tend to reduce the efforts of workers somewhat).

WAGE DETERMINATION UNDER PERFECT COMPETITION

21.4.   (a) Why do firms demand labor?   (b) What is the firm's demand for labor?   Why does it slope downward?   (c) What determines the strength of a firm's demand for labor?   (d) How is the market demand curve of labor determined?

(a) Firms demand labor (and other resources) in order to produce the products demanded by customers. Thus, the demand for labor as well as the demand for any productive resource is a derived demand—derived from the demand for *final* commodities that require labor and other resources in production.

(b) The firm's demand for labor is its marginal revenue product (MRP) of labor schedule or curve. A perfectly competitive firm's MRP or demand for labor curve slopes downward because the returns from each additional unit of labor, when used with other fixed resources, diminish.

(c) A firm's demand for labor is greater: (1) the greater the demand for the commodity that uses labor in production, (2) the greater the productivity of labor and (3) the higher the price of substitute resources, say, capital equipment, and the lower the price of complementary resources (say land, used with labor and capital to produce the final commodity).

(d) The market demand for labor is obtained by summing all firms' demands for labor. The greater the number of firms demanding labor and the greater the demand of each firm, the greater the market demand for labor.

21.5. (a) On what does the market supply of labor depend? (b) How does the state of the economy affect the market supply of labor? (c) What is the effect of the real-wage rate level on the quantity of labor supplied in the market?

(a) The market supply of labor depends on the population size, the proportion of the population in the labor force, and the state of the economy. In general, the larger the population and the greater the participation rate of the population in the labor force, the greater the market supply of labor.

(b) The state of the economy (boom or recession) affects the market supply of labor. When the economy is booming, many people not previously employed or seeking work may, attracted by the availability of high-paying jobs, decide to enter the labor force. On the other hand, a homemaker or college student who felt the need to look for a job under less prosperous conditions, may leave the labor force when the husband or father gets a high-paying job in a booming economy. Thus, the supply of labor may increase, decrease or remain unchanged depending on the net effect of these two opposing forces. The opposite is true in a recession.

(c) The level of real wages also gives rise to two opposing forces affecting the quantity of labor supplied. On the one hand, a high level of real wages induces workers to substitute work for leisure and work more hours per week to take advantage of the high real wages. On the other hand, a high real wage (and income) results in workers demanding more of every normal commodity, including leisure, and working fewer hours per week. Once again, the quantity of labor supplied may increase, decrease or remain unchanged, depending on the net effect of these two opposing forces.

21.6. Suppose that the marginal revenue product schedule or demand for labor for one of 100 identical and perfectly competitive *firms* is given by columns (1) and (2) of Table 2, and the market supply schedule of labor is given by columns (1) and (3). (a) Find the market demand schedule for labor and the equilibrium wage rate. (b) How much labor should the firm hire to maximize its total profits? (c) Graph the results to parts (a) and (b).

Table 2

(1) Wage Rate ($)	(2) Quantity of Labor Demanded by One Firm	(3) Total Quantity of Labor Supplied
12	40	12,000
10	60	10,000
8	80	8,000
6	100	6,000
4	120	4,000

(a) Since there are 100 identical firms, the market demand schedule for labor is 100 times the firm's demand schedule for labor and is given by columns (1) and (2A) of Table 3. The competitive equilibrium wage rate is $8 per hour, at which the market quantity of labor demanded matches the market quantity supplied of 8000 hours. At higher wages, the quantity of labor supplied in the market exceeds the quantity of labor demanded. The resulting surplus of labor (involuntary unemployment) puts pressure on the wage rate to move downward toward the equilibrium level. At wages below the equilibrium wage rate, the resulting shortage of labor causes wages to rise toward the equilibrium level of $8 per hour.

(b) Since the firm is a perfect competitor in the labor market, it can hire any amount of labor at the $8 per hour market equilibrium wage rate. This means that the supply curve of labor to the firm

Table 3

(1) Wage Rate ($)	(2) Quantity of Labor Demanded by One Firm	(2A) Market Demand of Labor	(3) Total Quantity of Labor Supplied
12	40	4,000	12,000
10	60	6,000	10,000
8	80	8,000	8,000
6	100	10,000	6,000
4	120	12,000	4,000

(s_L) is horizontal or infinitely elastic at the competitive market equilibrium price [see Problem 21.3 (b)]. To maximize total profits, each firm should hire 80 hours of labor, at which the firm's marginal revenue product of labor equals the $8 per hour equilibrium market-wage rate.

(c) The solutions to parts (a) and (b) are shown graphically in Fig. 21-4.

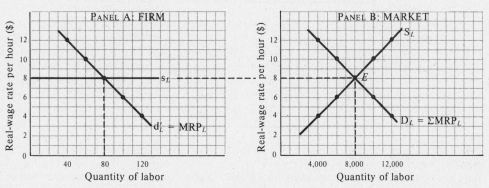

Fig. 21-4

WAGE DETERMINATION WITH IMPERFECT COMPETITION

21.7. (a) What is monopsony?   (b) How does monopsony arise?   (c) What are oligopsony and monopsonistic competition?

(a) Monopsony is the form of market organization where there is a single buyer of a particular resource. An example of monopsony is the "mining towns" of yesteryear in the U.S., where the mining company was the sole employer of labor in town (often these mining companies even owned and operated the few stores in town).

(b) Monopsony arises when a resource is specialized and is thus much more productive to a particular firm than to any other firm or use. Because of the greater resource productivity, this firm can pay a higher price for the resource and so become a monopsonist. Monopsony can also occur when resources lack geographical and occupational mobility.

(c) Oligopsony and monopsonistic competition are two other forms of imperfect competition in resource markets. An oligopsonist is one of few buyers of a homogeneous or differentiated resource. A monopsonistic competitor is one of many buyers of a differentiated resource.

21.8. Given the labor market supply schedule of Table 4, (a) derive the monopsonist marginal resource cost of labor schedule. Why does MRC_L exceed W? (b) Graph the labor supply and marginal resource cost schedules faced by the monopsonist. (c) How would these schedules look if we were dealing instead with an oligopsonist or monopsonistic competitor? A perfect competitor?

Table 4

Wage rate per day ($)	10	15	20	25	30	35	40	45
Number of workers	0	1	2	3	4	5	6	7

(a) In Table 5, column (1) times column (2) gives column (3) which measures the total cost of hiring various numbers of workers. Column (4) shows the changes in total costs from hiring each additional worker or MRC_L. MRC_L exceeds W because in order to hire more workers, the monopsonist must pay a higher wage not only to the additional workers hired but also to all previously hired workers.

Table 5

(1) Wage Rate per Day ($)	(2) Number of Workers	(3) Total Cost of Labor ($)	(4) Marginal Cost of Labor ($)
10	0	0	
			15
15	1	15	
			25
20	2	40	
			35
25	3	75	
			45
30	4	120	
			55
35	5	175	
			65
40	6	240	
			75
45	7	315	

(b) See Fig. 21-5.

(c) As imperfect competitors in the labor market, oligopsonists and monopsonistic competitors also face rising supply curves of labor (i.e. they must pay higher wages to hire more workers). Thus, MRC_L exceeds W and their MRC_L curve also lies above the supply of labor curve that they face. This is to be contrasted with perfect competition in the labor market, where even though the market supply curve of labor is positively sloped, each buyer is so small that he can purchase all the labor time he wants at the given market wage rate (i.e. he faces an infinitely elastic supply curve of the labor). Thus, for the perfectly competitive employer, the MRC_L curve coincides with the horizontal supply curve of labor at the market equilibrium wage rate.

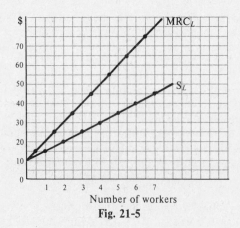

Fig. 21-5

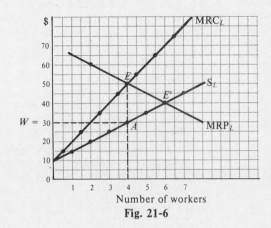

Fig. 21-6

21.9. Given the S_L and MRC_L curves of Fig. 21-5, if labor is the monopsonist's only variable factor and $MRP_L = \$60$ at $Q_L = 2$ (i.e. with 2 workers), $\$50$ with 4 workers, and $\$40$ with 6 workers, (*a*) draw a figure showing how many workers this monopsonist employs to maximize its total profits and what wage it pays.   Why is this the profit-maximizing point?   (*b*) How many workers would have been hired and what wage would have been paid if this labor market had been perfectly competitive?

(*a*)   In Fig. 21-6, the monopsonist hires 4 workers because $MRP_L = MRC_L$ at $Q_L = 4$, and pays a wage of \$30 (point *A* on S_L).   With 3 workers, MRP_L exceeds MRC_L and the monopsonist's total profits would increase by hiring more workers.   However, the monopsonist would not hire the fifth worker because its MRP_L is smaller than MRC_L and total profits would be lower.   Thus, the monopsonist maximizes its total profits when it hires 4 workers.

(*b*)   If the labor market had been perfectly competitive, all firms together would have hired a total of 6 workers and paid a wage of \$40 per worker (shown at point *E'* where $MRP_L = S_L$).   Because of its monopoly power in hiring labor, the monopsonist hires fewer workers and pays a lower wage rate than if the labor market had been perfectly competitive.   The same is generally true with oligopsony and monopsonistic competition [see Problem 21.8 (*c*)].

THE EFFECT OF UNIONS ON WAGES

21.10.   (*a*) What is a craft union?   What is its primary method of attempting to increase wages?   (*b*) What is an industrial union?   What is its primary method of attempting to increase wages?

(*a*)   A craft union is one which includes only workers having a particular skill.   For example, there are separate craft unions for electricians, plumbers, printers, etc.   Such unions attempt to increase the real wages of their members primarily by restricting the supply of labor (i.e. by causing an upward and leftward shift in the supply curve of labor with this skill).   Craft unions do this by forcing firms to hire only union members and then limiting the number of union members by imposing high initiation fees, long apprenticeships, etc.

(*b*)   An industrial union is one which includes *all* workers, skilled and unskilled, of a particular industry.   Examples are the United Automobile Workers (UAW), the United Steel Workers (USW), and the United Mine Workers (UMW) of America.   Industrial unions attempt to increase wage rates directly by bargaining with employers and threatening to strike.   The ability and willingness of such unions to negotiate wage increases is limited not only by the bargaining strength of employers but also because the larger the negotiated wage increase, the smaller the number of union members who will actually remain employed (see Panel C of Fig. 21-3).

21.11.   (*a*) What is another (third) general method that unions can use to raise wages?   Why is this the best method of raising wages?   What is its feasibility?   (*b*) Have unions raised real wage in the U.S.?

(*a*)   Another general method by which any union can attempt to increase wages is by increasing the (derived) demand for union labor by (1) raising the productivity of labor, (2) lobbying to restrict imports, and (3) financing such advertising campaigns for union-made products as the "buy a union label" of the International Ladies' Garment Workers Union (ILGWU).   This is the "best" method of increasing wages because it also increases the level of employment.   However, it offers only limited possibilities because labor productivity and the derived demand for union labor is largely outside the unions' control.   The most widely used method of increasing wages by unions today is by collective bargaining with employers under the threat of a strike.

(*b*)   The ability of unions to increase wages is a controversial subject.   Union labor does receive wages that are about 20 percent higher than nonunion labor wages in the U.S. today.   However, unionized industries are generally large-scale industries that employ more skilled labor and paid higher wages before unionization.   On the other hand, wage differences between unionized and nonunionized labor may underestimate the effectiveness of unions in raising wages because nonunionized firms may more or less match union wages in order to retain their workers and to keep unions out.   Most economists who have studied this question tentatively concluded that unions in the U.S. increased the wages of their members by about 10 to 15 percent.

21.12. (*a*) Sketch a graph showing the three main methods that unions can use to raise wages. (*b*) To which of these methods is the imposition of a minimum wage by the government most similar?   What are the pros and cons of having minimum-wage laws?

(*a*)   Panel A of Fig. 21-7 shows that a union can increase wages from W to W' and employment from OA to OB by increasing D_L to D'_L.   This is the most desirable but also the least effective method.   Panel B shows that a (craft) union can increase wages from W to W' by reducing S_L to S'_L.   However, employment falls from OA to OC.   Panel C shows that an (industrial) union might increase the wage from W to W' by direct bargaining with employers.   However, employment falls from OA to OG and GH ($= E'\ F$) workers are unable to find jobs.   The actual loss of employment resulting from a given rise in wages depends on the elasticity of D_L (see Section 20.5).

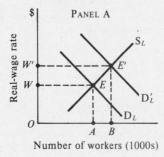
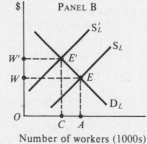
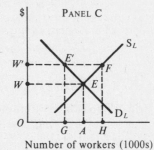

Fig. 21-7

(*b*)   If government imposed a minimum wage of W', the result would be the same as the union negotiating a wage of W' shown in Panel C.   This is particularly beneficial to previously low-paid workers near the poverty level.   With higher wages and incomes, the health and vigor of these workers may increase and result in greater productivity.   Imposing or raising a minimum wage can also have a "shock effect" on business and induce lethargic employers to introduce more productive techniques.   However, the imposition of a minimum wage also tends to reduce the level of employment.   Therefore, while those remaining employed are better off, others find themselves jobless.   Training programs for the unemployed might then help them find jobs.   However, this is not easy to accomplish.   The U.S. has had a minimum wage since 1938.   In 1979, its level was $2.90 per hour.

21.13. (*a*) What would happen if a strong union forced the monopsonist of Fig. 21-6 to pay a wage of $40 per day?   How does this compare with the profit-maximizing position of the monopsonist in the absence of the union?   (*b*) How are the wage rate and employment level determined in the real world when a powerful labor union faces a monopsonist?

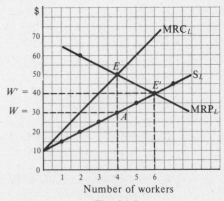

Fig. 21-8

(*a*)   When a union forces a wage of $40 per day upon the monopsonist of Fig. 21-6 (repeated as Fig. 21-8 for ease of reference), the monopsonist will behave as a perfect competitor in the labor market and hire 6 workers (at which $MRP_L = W = \$40$) instead of 4 workers at $W = \$30$.   Thus, both the wage rate and the level of employment are higher.   A minimum wage set by the government at $40 per day would have exactly the same effect in curbing monopsony power.

(*b*)   When a powerful labor union (a monopoly in supplying labor) faces a monopsonist (a monopolist buyer of labor time), we have a so-called *bilateral monopoly*.   With a bilateral monopoly, wages and employment are *theoretically* indeterminate.   That is, economic theory cannot tell us what wage rate and level of employment will actually be established.   The result depends on the relative bargaining strength of the union and the employer.   In general, the final result of the bargaining process is somewhere between what the two sides originally wanted.   Thus, big labor (e.g., U.A.W., U.S.W., etc.) to some extent checks the power of big business (e.g. G.M., U.S. Steel, etc.), and *vice versa*.   This is an example of countervailing power (see Section 19.7).

WAGE DIFFERENTIALS

21.14. (*a*) What causes wage differences?   (*b*) What are equalizing differences?   How do these give rise to wage differences?   (*c*) What are noncompeting groups?   How do they give rise to wage differences?   (*d*) What are imperfect labor markets?   How do they give rise to wage differences?

    (*a*)   Wages differ among different categories of people and jobs because of (1) equalizing differences, (2) the existence of noncompeting occupational groups and (3) imperfections in labor markets.

    (*b*)   Equalizing differences are wage differences that serve to compensate workers for nonmonetary differences among jobs.   That is, jobs requiring equal qualifications may differ in attractiveness and higher wages must be paid to attract and retain workers in the more unpleasant jobs.   For example, garbage collectors receive higher wages than porters.

    (*c*)   Noncompeting groups are occupations which require different capacities, skills, training and education and, therefore, receive different wages.   That is, labor is not a single productive resource but many different resources, each not in direct competition with others.   Thus, doctors form one group which is not in direct competition with other groups of workers.   Lawyers, accountants, electricians, bus drivers, etc. belong to other separate, noncompeting groups. There is a particular wage rate structure for each of these noncompeting groups, depending on the abilities, skills and training required for each occupation.   To be noted is that some job mobility among competing groups may be possible (for example, when an electrician becomes an electronics engineer by going to night school).   However, mobility is generally limited.

    (*d*)   An imperfect labor market is one in which there is some lack of information on job opportunities and wages, where some workers are unwilling to move to other areas and jobs in order to take advantage of higher wages and where union power, and minimum-wage laws and monopsony power exist.   Any of these circumstances causes some differences in wages for jobs which are exactly alike and require equal capacities and skills.

21.15. Getting an education and training is sometimes referred to as an "investment in human capital."   (*a*) In what ways is this similar to any other investment?   (*b*) Why is treating education and training as investments in human capital useful?   (*c*) What are its shortcomings?   Are there any objections to this point of view?

    (*a*)   Getting an education and training can be considered an investment in human capital because, as any other investment, it involves a cost and entails a return.   The cost of getting an education and training involves such explicit expenses as tuition, books, etc. and such opportunity cost as the foregone wages while in school or the lower wages received while in training.   The return on education and training takes the form of the *higher* wages and salaries received over the individual's working life.   By discounting all costs and extra income to the present and comparing returns to costs, we can calculate the rate of return on the investment in human capital and compare it to the returns from other investments.

    (*b*)   Viewing education and training as investments in human capital is useful in explaining many otherwise unexplainable real world occurrences such as why we educate and train the young more than the old, why young people migrate more readily than old, etc.   The answer is that young people have a longer working time over which to receive the benefits of education, training and migration.

    (*c*)   Some shortcomings of this line of thinking are as follows: (1) Not all expenses for education and training represent costs.   Some of these expenses should be regarded as consumption since they do not contribute to subsequent higher earnings (for example, when an engineering student takes a course in poetry).   (2) Higher subsequent earnings may be as much the result of innate ability and greater intelligence and effort as it is of training.   (3) The antipoverty programs of the 1960s to improve the health of and to train low-income people failed to reduce income inequalities.

        Besides these shortcomings, there is the objection that education and training deal with human beings and should not be compared or analyzed with the same tools used to analyze investment in machinery, factories, etc.

Chapter 22

Rent, Interest and Profits

22.1 RENT

Rent is the price for the use of land and other natural resources which are given and fixed in total supply. If we assume for simplicity that all land is alike and has only one competitive use (say, the growing of wheat), then rent is determined at the intersection of the market demand curve with the *vertical* market supply curve of land. Regardless of the height of the market demand and the rent paid, the same amount of land remains available. As a result, rent could be taxed away entirely without affecting the supply of land. In contrast, *variable* resources of labor and capital are supplied in reduced quantities when taxed. This concept was the basis for Henry George's proposal for a *single tax* on land in the late 19th century (see Problem 22.3).

EXAMPLE 1. With the supply of land fixed (S) in Fig. 22-1, rent is equal to r when the market demand curve for land is D and r' when it is D'. If from the equilibrium rent of r', the government imposed a tax of $r'r$ on rental incomes, land users would continue to pay r' but landowners would retain only r. The quantity of land supplied, however, would remain unchanged (see Section 14.5). In the real world, we have different types and uses of land with different rental values. The supply of land can also be increased somewhat (by drainage, reclamation, etc.) or reduced (by improper use). On the other hand, the quantities of certain kinds of labor and capital resources may not be entirely variable and part of their return may thus be in the nature of a rent (see Problem 22.4).

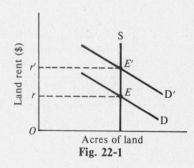

Fig. 22-1

22.2 INTEREST

Interest is the price paid for the use of money or *loanable funds*, expressed as a percentage of the amount borrowed. If the rate of interest is 8 percent per year, this means that for $100 borrowed today, $108 will have to be repaid a year from today. For simplicity, we will discuss the *pure rate of interest*. This is the interest on a riskless loan (as on a U.S. government bond). Other interest rates are higher depending on the risk, maturity, administrative cost and the competitiveness of the loanable-fund market (see Problem 22.5).

The equilibrium interest rate is determined at the intersection of the market demand and supply curves of loanable funds. The *demand for loanable funds* comes from the borrowing of firms, consumers and government, and is negatively sloped. To maximize profits, a firm will borrow in order to invest in machinery, inventory, etc., as long as the return, or marginal productivity, of the investment exceeds the rate of interest on borrowed funds. Thus, interest rates allocate the scarce loanable funds to the most productive uses. The *supply of loanable funds* stems from the past and current savings of individuals and firms. It is upward sloped, and is greatly affected by monetary policy [see Problem 22.8 (*b*)].

EXAMPLE 2. In Fig. 22-2, the intersection of the market demand and supply curves of loanable funds determines the equilibrium interest rate of 8 percent. Related to this is the *liquidity-preference theory*, which states that the interest rate is determined at the intersection of the demand curve for *all money* (not just loanable funds) and the supply curve of *all money*. The demand for money or *liquidity preference* arises in order to carry out everyday transactions (the transactions motive), to meet unforeseen conditions (the precautionary motive), and from the expectation of higher interest rates in the future (the speculative motive).   At lower interest rates, it is cheaper (in terms of the earnings foregone) to hold idle money and thus the quantity demanded for money (or liquidity preference) is greater.   The supply of money is determined or controlled by the Federal government (through the Federal Reserve Banks) and is fixed at any time [see Problem 22.8 (*b*)].

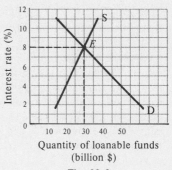

Quantity of loanable funds
(billion $)

Fig. 22-2

22.3   PROFITS

Profits are the excess of total revenue over total costs, where total costs include both explicit and implicit costs.   This differs from the everyday usage of the term profit, which refers to total revenue minus the explicit or out-of-pocket expenses only (see Problem 22.9).

Profits stem from the introduction of a successful innovation, as a reward for uninsurable risk-bearing or uncertainty, and as a result of monopoly power.   They serve as incentives for innovation, to shift resources to the production of those commodities that society wants most, and as a reward for efficiency.

EXAMPLE 3.   Firms introduce new products and new production methods in the expectation of profits.   If successful, other firms will imitate the successful innovator and compete those profits away.   But in the meantime other innovations are introduced.   Similarly, more risky ventures (such as petroleum exploration) require the expectation of a higher profit to induce investments.   Finally, monopoly power allows a firm to restrict output artificially, keep competitors out, and charge a price that allows profits to persist.

22.4   INCOME SHARES

In 1978, the breakdown of U.S. national income was as follows: wages and salaries, 76%; proprietors' incomes, 7%; corporate profits, 8%; interest, 7%; and rents, 2%.   However, this classification does not precisely fit the economist's definitions.   For example, much of proprietors' incomes represent the implicit wages and salaries of the persons owning and running businesses (e.g. the corner drugstore).

Since 1900, wages and salaries have increased relatively and proprietors' incomes have fallen relatively.   This is due to the increase in the importance of corporations relative to individual-owned businesses and similarly, of manufacturing and services relative to agriculture.   As a result, the share of wages, salaries and proprietors' incomes combined remained fairly stable at about 80% of national income.   This has left a fairly constant share of about 20% for rent, interest and corporate profits combined.

22.5   EPILOGUE ON COMMODITY AND RESOURCE PRICING

In a free-enterprise economy, commodity and factor prices are determined by their respective demands and supplies.   Firms demand resources owned by households in order to produce the goods and services demanded by households.   Households then use the income they receive to purchase the goods and services produced by firms.   This circular flow of economic activity determines what, how and for whom to produce.   It is a *general equilibrium system* because a change in any part of the economy affects every other part of the economy (see Sections 1.5 and 2.6 and Problem 22.15).

When markets are perfectly competitive and are in long-run equilibrium, resources are allocated most efficiently and the economy's output of goods and services is maximized.   In the real world, however, this most efficient resource allocation is interfered with by market imperfections, by the existence of social goods, and by divergencies between social and private benefits and costs (see

Problem 22.16). Government may seek to overcome these complications and achieve a more equal distribution of income through a system of taxes and subsidies (see Problem 22.17).

EXAMPLE 4. The top loop in Fig. 22-3 shows that households purchase goods and services from business firms. Thus, what is a cost of consumption expenditure from the households' point of view represents the income or the money receipts of business firms. On the other hand, the bottom loop shows that business firms purchase the services of economic resources from households. What is a cost of production from the viewpoint of business firms also represents the money income of households. This circular flow of economic activity represents a vast and interdependent general equilibrium system. The operation of this system is modified by government measures aimed at maximizing social welfare.

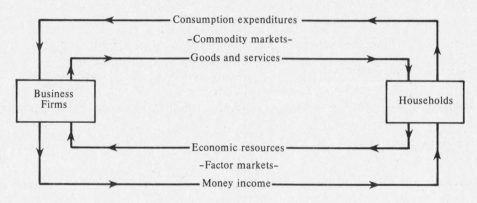

Fig. 22-3

Important Economic Terms

Circular flow of economic activity. The flow of resources from households to firms and goods and services from firms to households.

Demand for loanable funds. The demand for borrowed funds of firms, consumers and governments.

Entrepreneur or innovator. An individual or firm who introduces a new product or a new production technique in hopes of making a profit.

General equilibrium system. The vast and interdependent system of markets of which the economy is composed and such that a change in any market affects every other market.

Income shares. The proportion of national income going for (1) wages and salaries, (2) proprietors' incomes, (3) corporate profits, (4) interest and (5) rent.

Interest. The price for the use of money or loanable funds, expressed as a percentage of the amount borrowed.

Liquidity-preference theory of interest. States that the competitive equilibrium market rate of interest is determined by the market demand curve for money (or liquidity) and the supply of money.

Loanable-funds theory of interest. States that the competitive equilibrium market rate of interest is determined by the market demand and supply of loanable funds.

Partial equilibrium analysis. The study of one market in isolation by abstracting all the interconnections existing between this and other markets.

Precautionary demand for money. The demand for money needed to make unforeseen payments. It varies directly with national income.

Private benefits and costs. The benefits and costs to the individual or household.

Profits.   The excess of total revenue over total explicit and implicit costs.

Pure rate of interest.   The rate of interest on a riskless loan (such as on a U.S. government bond).

Rent.   The price paid for the use of land (and other natural resources).

Risk.   The probability of incurring an extra cost (such as the breakdown of a machine) or a loss (such as from fire or theft) against which the firm can insure itself.

Single-tax movement.   A proposal introduced by Henry George in the late 1800s aimed at raising government revenue by taxing only rental incomes since the amount of land available is fixed and would not be reduced by the tax.

Social benefits and costs.   The benefits and costs to society as a whole.

Social or public goods.   Such goods and services as public schools, public transportation, etc., which can be used by more than one person at the same time.

Social welfare.   The common good or well-being of society.

Speculative demand for money.   The demand for money in the expectation of higher interest rates in the future.   It is inversely related to the rate of interest.

Supply of loanable funds.   The supply of loanable funds saved by individuals and firms and available for borrowing.

Transaction demand for money.   The demand for money needed to make everyday payments.   It depends on the level of national income.

Uncertainty.   The possibility of a fall in revenue or increase in costs due to cyclical and structural changes which are uninsurable.

Review Questions

1.   When the amount of land is fixed, (a) the supply curve for land is vertical and has zero elasticity, (b) the rent on land is actively determined by the demand for land, (c) the higher the demand for land, the greater the rent, (d) all of the above.
   Ans.   (d)

2.   A tax on land falls (a) entirely on land users, (b) entirely on landowners, (c) partly on land users and partly on land owners, (d) any of the above is possible.
   Ans.   (b)

3.   The interest rate is (a) the price of using money or loanable funds, (b) expressed in percentage terms, (c) determined by the demand for and the supply of loanable funds, (d) all of the above.
   Ans.   (d)

4.   In order to maximize profits, a firm borrows until the return on investment (a) equals the rate of interest, (b) exceeds the rate of interest, (c) is smaller than the rate of interest, (d) any of the above.
   Ans.   (a)

5.   The interest rate serves to allocate the scarce loanable funds to (a) the most needed uses, (b) the most productive uses, (c) the most liquid uses, (d) none of the above.
   Ans.   (b)

6.   The interest rate charged on a loan depends on (a) the risk of the loan, (b) the maturity of the loan, (c) the administrative cost and competitive conditions of the loan, (d) all of the above.
   Ans.   (d)

7. Profit is equal to total revenue minus (*a*) explicit costs, (*b*) implicit costs, (*c*) implicit and explicit costs, (*d*) wages and rents.

    Ans. (*c*)

8. Which of the following statements is *not* true with regard to profit? (*a*) It may arise from diminishing returns. (*b*) It may arise from introducing an innovation. (*c*) It may be the reward for uncertainty. (*d*) It may arise from monopoly power.

    Ans. (*a*)

9. Which is *not* a function of profits? (*a*) To encourage innovations. (*b*) To shift resources to the production of those commodities that society wants most. (*c*) To increase costs of production. (*d*) To reward efficiency.

    Ans. (*c*)

10. The share of 1978 U.S. national income going for wages and salaries, and for wages, salaries and proprietors' income combined were, respectively, (*a*) 76% and 83%, (*b*) 70% and 93%, (*c*) 85% and about 93%, (*d*) 66% and about 73%.

    Ans. (*a*)

11. Which of the following is *not true* with regard to the functioning of a free-enterprise economy? (*a*) It is a vast and interdependent system. (*b*) It is a partial equilibrium system. (*c*) The questions of what, how and for whom to produce are answered simultaneously. (*d*) It is a general equilibrium system.

    Ans. (*b*)

12. The most efficient allocation of resources is prevented in the real world by (*a*) imperfect competition, (*b*) the existence of social goods, (*c*) divergencies between social and private benefits and costs, (*d*) all of the above.

    Ans. (*d*)

Solved Problems

RENT

22.1. (*a*) What is rent? How is it determined? (*b*) What determines the demand for land? (*c*) How is the supply of land different from the supply of other resources?

    (*a*) Rent is the price for the use of land and other natural resources which are fixed in total supply. The rent on land, as the price of any other resource, is determined by the market demand for and the market supply of land.

    (*b*) The demand for land, like the demand for any other resource, is a derived demand. It is derived from demand for the commodities that require land (and other resources) in production. The demand for land is greater: (1) the greater the demand for the commodities that use land in production, (2) the greater the productivity of land, and (3) the higher the price of substitute resources and the lower the price of complementary resources.

    (*c*) Land and other natural resources are usually taken as fixed in total supply while the supply of other factors (labor and capital) is usually regarded as variable. Thus, while the supply curve of land is taken as vertical or having zero price elasticity, the supply of other factors is taken as upward sloping, indicating that at higher resource prices more will be supplied to the market. However, in the real world, land and other natural resources are not completely fixed. Thus, the supply of land can be increased somewhat by drainage, reclamation, clearing, etc., and can be reduced by soil erosion, improper use, etc. Similarly, natural resources such as mineral deposits can be depleted and new ones discovered. On the other hand, the supply of other resources may not be completely variable. For example, even with proper training, not everyone could become a heart surgeon, an electrical engineer, or an accomplished violinist.

22.2. (*a*) Draw a figure showing the level of rent with three alternative demand curves D_1, D_2 and D_3. (*b*) How is the determination of rent different from the determination of the price of other resources?

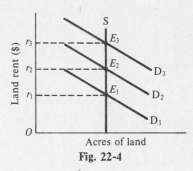

Fig. 22-4

  (*a*) Given the fixed supply of land (S) in Fig. 22-4, rent is equal to r_1 with D_1, r_2 with D_2 and r_3 with D_3.

  (*b*) In general, demand and supply are equally important in determining resource prices. But because the quantity of land available is fixed, only the height of the demand curve actively determines the rent of land.

22.3. (*a*) What is the incidence of (i.e. who actually ends up paying) a tax on rental income? Why? (*b*) What is the economic significance of this? (*c*) How is it related to the single-tax movement? (*d*) What are the criticisms of the single-tax movement?

  (*a*) The incidence of a tax on rents falls entirely on landowners if the total quantity of land is fixed. The general rule stated in Section 14.5 is that for a given demand, the more inelastic supply, the greater the incidence of the tax on suppliers. Therefore, with the supply of land having zero price elasticity, all of the tax burden falls on landowners.

  (*b*) The economic significance of this is that a tax on rental income does not reduce the availability of land and other natural resources in fixed supply. On the other hand, a tax on wages, salaries or interest income causes an upward shift in and a reduced supply of labor and capital. (With the supply curve of land vertical, an upward shift, due to the tax, leaves the supply curve of land unchanged.)

  (*c*) A tax on land and other natural resources in fixed supply is in a sense an ideal tax since the tax does not reduce the availability of land and other natural resources. This gave impetus to the single-tax movement promoted by Henry George in the late 1880s. The thrust of this movement was that since a tax on variable resources of labor and capital reduces the supply of these resources while a tax on land does not, all taxes should be raised by taxing only rental incomes.

  (*d*) There are three basic criticisms of a single tax on land. First, the rental value of land is the return to land itself as well as on costly land improvements such as drainage, reclamation or irrigation. Therefore it may be difficult in practice to isolate the purely rental elements. Second, rents in the U.S. today amount to just about 2% of GNP while taxes are above 25% of GNP. Third, the price of labor and capital also may contain some purely rental elements (see Problem 22.4), so that taxing only landowners may be an unfair and discriminatory practice.

22.4. (*a*) Describe some of the different uses to which land can be put. How do these affect the rental value of land? (*b*) How is the large salary paid to a star baseball player similar to rent on land?

  (*a*) Land, like labor and capital, is not homogeneous. It has many different uses, each with a different productivity and each commanding a different rent. Each of the large number of rents paid on land of different quality and uses is determined by the market demand and supply of land for the particular type and location. For example, rents are high in the center of the city and they are lower in areas of urban decay and remote, barren land. Note, however, that since the same land can have many alternative uses, the supply of land for any of these uses is not fixed but can be bid away for other uses (e.g. urban renewal). Thus, while the return on land is a rent from the point of view of society as a whole, it is a cost of production from the viewpoint of a firm using the land.

  (*b*) The difference between what the star baseball player earns in playing baseball and what he would earn in the best alternative occupation (say, by being a baseball coach) is a rent in the sense that the large salary need not be paid to keep him playing baseball. Of the $150,000 paid to the player per year, $120,000 is a rent if he would earn only $30,000 in his best alternative occupation. The government could tax the player $120,000 and he would probably continue to play baseball.   To be sure, the $150,000 is a cost to the team's front office because if one team does not pay, another would, but most of it ($120,000) is a rent from society's point of view.

INTEREST

22.5. (*a*) What is the interest rate?   Loanable funds?   (*b*) On what does the demand for loanable funds depend?   (*c*) How does a firm determine how much to borrow at various interest rates?   (*d*) On what does the supply of loanable funds depend?   (*e*) Draw a figure showing how the rate of interest is determined according to the loanable-funds theory.

(*a*)   The interest rate (given in percentage terms) is the price paid for the use of money or loanable funds.   For example, if the interest rate is 10 percent per year and a firm borrows $1000 today for one year, it will have to repay $1100 a year from today.   Loanable funds is the total amount of money available for borrowing.

(*b*)   The demand for loanable funds arises from (1) firms that want to invest in machinery, inventory and buildings; (2) consumers who want to finance the purchase of homes, automobiles, washing machines, vacations, etc. and (3) governments in order to finance budgets to construct highways, schools and other public projects.   In general, the quantity demanded of loanable funds is greater at lower than at higher interest rates.

(*c*)   Firms borrow funds in order to make productive investments.   The net productivity of various investments varies and the firm seeking maximum profits first makes those investments with the highest return.   A firm should continue to borrow and invest as long as the rate of return on investment exceeds the rate of interest on borrowed funds, and until they are equal.   New technological advances, by opening new investment opportunities, cause the firm's investment schedule to shift upward.

(*d*)   The supply of loanable funds stems from the past and current savings of households and businesses and from money created by commercial banks (see Section 9.3).   Broadly speaking, the supply of loanable funds is greater at higher rates of interest.   However, it is greatly affected by monetary policies (the control which government exerts over the nation's money supply) designed to regulate the level of business activity [see Problem 22.8 (*b*) and Chapter 10].

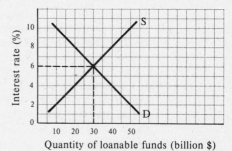

Quantity of loanable funds (billion $)

Fig. 22-5

(*e*)   In Fig. 22-5, the competitive equilibrium market rate of interest is 6 percent, at which the quantity demanded of loanable funds of $30 billion matches the quantity supplied.

22.6.   How many rates of interest do we have?   On what do they depend?

In the real world, we do not have a single rate of interest but a whole structure of many different rates of interest.   Each of these rates depends on the risk, maturity, administrative cost of the loan and on the competitiveness of the loanable-fund market.   In general, the interest rate on a loan is higher, (1) the greater the risk of borrower default, (2) the longer the term of the loan, (3) the smaller the amount of the loan (i.e. administering many small loans costs much more than administering one larger loan, everything else remaining the same) and (4) the less competitive the financial system (i.e. a single financial institution in an isolated locality can charge higher interest rates on loans than if there were several such lenders).

When we speak of the rate of interest, we usually refer to the *pure* rate of interest.   This is the rate of interest on riskless loans and is roughly equal to the interest rate on long-term government bonds which will almost certainly be repaid.   Other interest rates are higher and depend on the four factors listed above.   Generally, when the pure rate of interest rises, the whole structure of interest rates also rises.

22.7. (*a*) What are the "transaction, precautionary and speculative demands for money?" On what do they depend? (*b*) On what does the supply of money depend? (*c*) How is the rate of interest determined according to the liquidity-preference theory of interest? What is its relationship to the loanable-funds theory of interest?

    (*a*)   The *transaction demand for money* refers to the demand of households and businesses to hold money balances rather than bonds, stocks, etc. in order to carry on their everyday purchases and payments. This does not depend on the rate of interest but varies directly with the level of national income only.

           The *precautionary demand for money* refers to the demand for money in order to make any unforeseen payments. This too depends only on the level of national income.

           The *speculative demand for money* refers to the demand for money in the expectation of higher interest rates in the future. That is, people hold larger money balances if they expect interest rates to rise in the future, rather than tying this money up in bonds now. This speculative demand for money is inversely related to the interest rate. As a result, the *total* demand curve for *money* or liquidity is also downward sloped when plotted against interest rates.

    (*b*)   The total supply of money is determined or controlled by the Federal government and is given and fixed at any time. That is, the U.S. government regulates the creation of demand deposits by the banking system, and changes the money supply in the conduct of monetary policy.

    (*c*)   According to the liquidity-preference theory of interest, the interest rate is determined at the intersection of the demand for *all money* or the liquidity-preference curve and the supply curve of *all money*. On the other hand, according to the loanable-funds theory, the rate of interest is determined by the intersection of the market demand and supply curves of *loanable funds* only. These two theories are complementary rather than conflicting. However, their relationship is rather intricate and is discussed in more advanced courses and books.

22.8. (*a*) What is the function of the rate of interest? (*b*) How and why does the Federal government influence the rate of interest?

    (*a*)   The function of the rate of interest, like the price of other resources, is to allocate the scarce supply of loanable funds to the most productive uses (i.e., to those uses where the net productivity or rate of return on investment are greatest). This is accomplished because firms borrow and invest as long as the rate of return on investments exceeds the interest rate and up to the level at which they are equal. However, the government directly allocates some public investments to highways, schools, hospitals and other public projects without regard to their profitability. In addition, the greater bargaining power of larger firms may allow them to borrow at lower rates than smaller firms and thus make some investments that are less productive than those that could be made by smaller firms.

    (*b*)   The Federal government influences the rate of interest or interest rate structure by changing the nation's money supply, and through it, the supply of loanable funds. The government may want to increase the money supply (i.e. conduct an easy monetary policy) in order to reduce the rate of interest and stimulate investment (which would then cause a multiple expansion in GNP) if the economy is operating at less than full employment. The opposite is true when the economy faces demand-pull inflation (see Chapter 10).

PROFITS

22.9. (*a*) Distinguish between cost and profit in economics. (*b*) How do these concepts differ from the everyday usage of these terms?

    (*a*)   In economics, costs include both explicit and implicit costs. The resources that a firm owns and uses in production are not free. They involve an element of cost which can be estimated by what these same resources would earn in their best (most rewarding) alternative employment. Thus, if we say that the firm is making zero profit, it means that the firm is already receiving a "normal" return on its owned factors. When we speak of profits in economics, we mean above-normal returns (see also Chapter 16).

    (*b*)   The everyday usage of the term "cost" refers only to the out-of-pocket expenditures of the firm made to hire factors of production (what economists call explicit costs). The man-in-the street calls profit the excess of the firm's revenue over these out-of-pocket expenditures. For the economist, part or all of this revenue represents the "normal return" on the firm's owned factors (i.e. what its owned factors would earn in their best alternative employments). Thus, for the economist, profit refers to total revenue minus all explicit and implicit costs.

22.10. From what do economic profits arise?

Profits can be regarded as the reward for a successful innovation, as a reward for bearing uncertainty, and as a result of monopoly power. We saw in Section 17.6 that in a long-run and perfectly competitive equilibrium, all firms make zero profits. In the short run, a firm may make profits by introducing such a successful innovation as a new product or a cost-reducing production technique. However, in the long run other firms will imitate the innovation until all profits are competed away. In the meantime, other innovations may be introduced. The expectation of higher profits is also necessary to induce investments in more uncertain ventures. For example, petroleum exploration and the introduction of new products face greater uncertainties and possibilities of losses than entering established industries to produce traditional products. Investments will flow into new ventures facing greater uncertainties only in the expectation of higher profits. Similarly, buying a stock may give a greater but more uncertain return than putting the money in a savings account. Finally, monopolists and oligopolists produce at a price which exceeds marginal cost, and by keeping competitors out, they can continue to make profits in the long run.

22.11. (*a*) What is meant by invention? An innovation? (*b*) What is the difference between risk and uncertainty?

(*a*) An invention refers to a new process, a new technique or a new product. An innovation is the commercial introduction of an invention. For example, the discovery of radio waves led to the introduction of radios. Not all inventions lead to innovations. The invention may involve a new product that society does not want or a new process or technique which at present may be more costly than existing processes and techniques. Thousands of inventions patented each year in the U.S. are never introduced or applied commercially, giving only delusions to the inventors. It is to stimulate inventions by offering a temporary monopoly and possibility of profit to the inventor that most nations allow inventions to be patented. In this context it is important to distinguish an entrepreneur or innovator from a manager. The entrepreneur or innovator, if successful, makes profits. The manager only earns wages.

(*b*) A risk refers to the probability of incurring an extra cost (such as the breakdown of a machine) or a loss (such as from a fire or theft) against which the firm can insure itself. For example, if experience indicates that 3 out of 100 machines break down in the course of production each year, the firm can include the cost of repairs and of lost production into its estimates of future production costs. Similarly, firms can buy insurance against the hazards of fire and theft. Uncertainty, on the other hand, refers to the possiblity of a fall in revenue or increase in costs due to cyclical and structural changes in the economy. Against these uncertainties, firms cannot buy insurance.

22.12. (*a*) What are the functions of profits? (*b*) What are some objections to profits?

(*a*) Profits serve as incentives for innovators to shift resources to the production of those commodities that society wants most, and as a reward for efficiency. The introduction of an innovation involves uncertainty and may result in financial loss if it is not successful. The expectation of a financial reward in the form of profits is required to induce innovations. Similarly, profit in some industries and losses in others is the indication that society wants more commodities from the former and less from the latter. This is the signal for resources to shift from the industries incurring losses into those making a profit. Related to this is the fact that more efficient firms in a given industry are rewarded with profits which they can then use to expand, while less efficient firms incur losses and have to contract operations or go out of business.

(*b*) Among the objections to profits are the following: (1) Profits arising from monopoly serve no socially useful purpose (except when they lead to more innovations). Therefore, such profits should be taxed away or the monopoly should be regulated (if it is not feasible to break it up).

(2) Profits may lead to an excessively unequal distribution of income. This, too, can be corrected by progressive taxation.

However, a general attack on all profits is not justified, because profits, as we have seen before, do perform socially useful functions. Thus, the sharp criticism of Marxists that all profits represent exploitation of labor by the capitalist class and should therefore be entirely eliminated is invalid.

INCOME SHARES

22.13. (*a*) What was the distribution of 1978 U.S. national income among the owners of the various resources? What definitional problems arise? (*b*) How have these relative shares changed over time?

(*a*) In 1978, U.S. national income was distributed as follows: wages and salaries, 76%; proprietors' incomes, 7%; corporate profits, 8%; interest, 7%; and rents, 2%. However, these are for the most part accounting definitions and differ somewhat from the economist's concept of wages, profit, interest and rent. For example, most of proprietors' incomes were implicit wages and salaries, interest and rent from owned resources rather than profits in the economist's sense. As such, most of proprietors' incomes should be added to wages and salaries, giving a combined total of 83% of U.S. national income in 1978.

(*b*) Since 1900, the share of U.S. national income that was wages and salaries rose from about 55% to 76% in 1978. On the other hand, proprietors' incomes have fallen from about 24% in 1900 to 7% in 1978. The fall in proprietors' income resulted from the reduction in the number and relative importance of individual-owned-and-run small businesses (unincorporated sole proprietorships and partnerships) since 1900 and the growing importance of corporations. Another reason has been the exodus of small independent farmers from agriculture and the growth in the relative importance of manufacturing and services. As the number of self-employed declined, so did the share of proprietors' incomes. However, most of proprietors' income represents their implicit wages and salaries and should thus be added to wages and salaries. As a result, the share going to labor remained fairly constant over time at about 80%. This left the relatively constant share (of about 20%) for corporate profits, interest and rent combined. Within this 20%, interest remained fairly stable, rents declined sharply while corporate profits, as it might well have been expected, fluctuated greatly over time, depending on the state of the economy.

EPILOGUE ON COMMODITY AND RESOURCE PRICING

22.14. (*a*) How are commodity prices determined in a free-enterprise economy? What are the shapes of the market demand curves and market supply curves for commodities? (*b*) How are resource prices determined in a free-enterprise economy? What are the shapes of the market demand curves and market supply curves for resources? (*c*) How does the circular flow of economic activity solve the basic economic problems in a free-enterprise economy?

(*a*) In a free-enterprise economy, commodity prices (and outputs) are determined at the intersections of the market demand curve and the market supply curve for the commodity. The market demand curves are downward sloped because of diminishing marginal utilities. The market supply curves are usually upward sloped because of increasing marginal costs.

(*b*) In a free-enterprise economy, resource prices (i.e. wages, rents, interest and profits) are determined at the intersections of the market demand curve and the market supply curve for the resource. The market demand curves are downward sloped because of diminishing marginal productivities. The market supply curves are usually upward sloped (except for land where it is vertical) indicating that higher resource prices are usually required to make larger quantities of the resource available.

(*c*) In a free-enterprise economy, households use the income received from selling the use of their resources to business firms to purchase the goods and services produced by business firms. In this circular flow of economic activity, the market demand and supply curves for commodities determine commodity prices. These prices help determine *how* businessmen should combine resources to minimize costs of production. In addition, resource prices together with inheritance, luck, etc., determine the distribution of income in society. This distribution in turn determines *for whom* goods and services are produced.

22.15. (*a*) What is meant when we say that the economy is a general equilibrium system?   (*b*) How can we study only one market or justify partial equilibrium analysis?

   (*a*)   As indicated by the circular flow of economic activity, the economy is a vast and interdependent system of markets in which a change in any market affects every other market.   It is to stress the fact that all markets in the economy are interrelated that the economy is often referred to as a general equilibrium system.   For example, an increase in gasoline prices affects primarily the petroleum and automobile industries, but through them, practically every other market in the economy is also affected.   The demand for large cars decreases relative to small cars and public transportation.   Resources shift to the production of more small cars and public transportation.   This shift affects the distribution of income and thus other commodity and factor markets.

   (*b*)   In economics, we usually study one market in isolation and initially abstract from the interconnections existing between this and other markets.   This is referred to as *partial equilibrium analysis*.   This differs from general equilibrium analysis which studies all markets of the economy and their interconnections at the same time or *simultaneously*.   The justification for partial equilibrium analysis is that by focusing on a single market at a time, the analysis is more manageable and does give, in most instances, a sufficiently close first approximation to the solution sought. For example, suppose we want to study the effect of the increase in gasoline prices on the automobile industry.   To do so, we might initially disregard the effect of the auto industry on related industries (steel, rubber, glass, etc.) and the repercussions which then might affect the auto industry itself.   The smaller these repercussions are, the more accurate and justified is partial equilibrium analysis.

22.16. (*a*) Why is a perfectly competitive system of markets the most efficient system in the long run?   (*b*) How do market imperfections, the existence of social goods and divergencies between social and private benefits and costs interfere with the most efficient allocation of resources?

   (*a*)   A perfectly competitive system is the most efficient system in the long run because (1) consumers purchase commodities in such a way as to maximize the total utilities from spending their incomes, and (2) firms produce the goods and services most wanted by consumers with the most efficient methods.   That is, firms produce goods and services at the lowest possible long-run average cost and up to the point where the commodity price equals its marginal cost.   Firms hire resources in quantities at which the marginal revenue product of each resource equals its price or marginal cost.   As a result, there is *economic efficiency* in consumption because no transfer of commodities among consumers would make anyone better off without at the same time making someone else worse off.   Similarly, there is *technical efficiency* in production because no reallocation of resources would increase the output of some commodities without reducing the output of others (i.e. society is on its production-possibilities curve; see Section 1.4).

   (*b*)   If we have imperfect competition in some commodity markets, the output of those commodities is artificially restricted because the firm produces where MR = MC but MC falls short of the commodity price.   Similarly, in imperfectly competitive resource markets, the use of resources is artificially restricted because the firm uses resources only in the quantity at which MRP = MRC but MRP exceeds the resource price.

   Even a perfectly competitive system will not allocate resources most efficiently when there are social goods and when social and private benefits and costs diverge.   Without government intervention, there would be a tendency to underproduce and underconsume social or public goods (i.e. such goods and services as public schools, public transportation, etc., which can be used by more than one individual at a time).   Similarly, there might be underinvestment in education when the social benefits (i.e. the benefits to society as a whole) exceed the private benefit (i.e. the benefit to the individuals paying for their education).   At the same time, there is overproduction of such goods as automobiles which pollute the air, resulting in social costs which exceed the private costs of buying and operating the car.

22.17. (*a*) How does the government seek to overcome market imperfections, provide adequate social or public goods, and reconcile social and private benefits and costs?   (*b*) Why and how does the government redistribute income from the rich to the poor?   Why is it important to define objectively the maximum social welfare?

(*a*)   The government seeks to overcome the distortions resulting from market imperfections with a system of taxes and controls.   For example, controls and taxes are imposed on monopolists in an attempt to overcome the artificial restrictions that they would otherwise place on production in their effort to maximize total profits.   Governments use most of their tax revenues to provide such essential social or public goods as education, transportation, law and order, defense, etc. Similarly, they subsidize private education and basic research and tax and control pollutants in the effort to reconcile social with private benefits and costs.

(*b*)   In the name of fairness and equity, the government redistributes income from the rich to the poor (through a system of progressive taxation and subsidies) in order to reduce the income inequality that results from the operation of the market mechanism.   However, since it is impossible to make interpersonal comparisons of utility, governments do not generally know how far this redistribution should be pursued in order to maximize social welfare.   Indeed, it is impossible even to know objectively whether social welfare increases when, in order to make someone better off, we make someone else worse off.

Chapter 23

International Trade and Finance

23.1 THE IMPORTANCE OF INTERNATIONAL TRADE

Thus far, we have assumed a *closed economy,* or an economy completely isolated from the rest of the world.   In reality, most nations are *open economies*.   That is, they are connected to other nations through a network of trade and financial relationships.   These relationships have great advantages but they may also result in problems.

Even though trade is generally more important to small than to large developed nations, the welfare of the latter is also greatly dependent on trade.   See Problem 23.2.

EXAMPLE 1.   In Table 1, we see that exports as a percentage of GNP for the U.S. in 1977 are lower than for most other nations but are the highest in dollar amount.   The earnings from these exports helped the U.S. finance imports of petroleum, automobiles, machinery, steel, coffee, metals, etc.

Table 1

Country	Exports as a Percentage of GNP	Total Value of Exports in 1977 (in billion $)
The Netherlands	58	53
Belgium	46	37
Switzerland	35	22
United Kingdom	31	75
W. Germany	29	142
Italy	26	51
France	22	76
Japan	14	95
United States	8	151
Soviet Union	4	39

Source: *International Financial Statistics,* Nov. 1978.

23.2 THE BASIS AND THE GAINS FROM TRADE: COMPARATIVE ADVANTAGE

Since the availability of resources differs among nations, the opportunity cost of producing more of one commodity (in terms of the amount of a second commodity that would not be produced) also usually differs among nations.   In a two-nation, two-commodity world, each nation should specialize in the production of the commodity with the lower opportunity cost; this is the commodity in which the nation has a *comparative advantage*.   The nation should trade part of its output (with the other nation) for the commodity with the higher opportunity cost; this is the commodity in which the nation has a *comparative disadvantage*.   Doing this results in a larger *combined* output of both commodities than would occur in the absence of specialization in production and trade.

EXAMPLE 2.   Figure 23-1 shows a hypothetical production-possibilities curve for cloth (C) and food (F) for the U.S. and U.K. under constant costs (the solid lines).   It shows that the U.S. could produce $40C$ and $0F$, $30C$ and $20F$, $20C$ and $40F$, $10C$ and $60F$, or $0C$ and $80F$.   For each unit of cloth the U.S. gives up, it releases resources to produce two additional units of food.   The *domestic exchange ratio* or *cost ratio* is $1C = 2F$ or

$\frac{1}{2}C = 1F$ and is constant in the U.S.   In the U.K., $2C = 1F$.   Since the opportunity cost of F is $\frac{1}{2}C$ in the U.S. and $2C$ in the U.K., the U.S. has a comparative advantage in F.   Similarly, the U.K. has a comparative advantage in C.   Suppose that in the absence of trade, the U.S. and U.K. produced and consumed at points A ($20C$ and $40F$) and A' ($20C$ and $20F$) respectively.   With trade, the U.S. should specialize in the production of F and produce at B ($80F$ and $0C$) and the U.K. should specialize in C and produce at B' ($60C$ and $0F$). By then exchanging, say, $30F$ for $30C$ with the U.K., the U.S. would end up consuming at E ($30C$ and $50F$) and the U.K. would consume at E' ($30C$ and $30F$).   Thus, both the U.S. and the U.K. end up consuming $10C$ and $10F$ more than without specialization and trade (compare E with A and E' with A').   With increasing costs, the production-possibilities curves are concave or bulge outward and there would be incomplete specialization in production (see Problem 23.7).   Besides comparative advantage, trade could also be based on economies of scale and differences in tastes (see Problem 23.8).

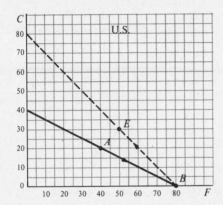 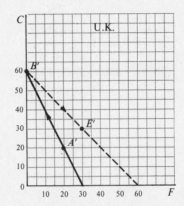

Fig. 23-1

23.3   OBSTACLES TO THE FLOW OF TRADE: TARIFFS AND QUOTAS

Even though trade can be the source of major gains, most nations restrict the free flow of trade by imposing tariffs, quotas and other obstructions.   An *import tariff* is a tax on the imported commodity.   An *import quota* is a quantitative restriction on the amount of a good that may be imported during a year.   Trade restrictions are advocated by labor and firms in some industries as a protection against foreign competition.   This, however, generally imposes a burden on society as a whole because it reduces the availability of goods and increases their prices.   Some of the specific arguments advanced for trade restrictions are (1) to protect domestic labor against cheap foreign labor, (2) to reduce domestic unemployment, (3) to protect young or "infant" industries, and (4) to protect industries important for national defense.   Most of the arguments are invalid and are based on misconceptions (see Problem 23.10).

EXAMPLE 3. Protection is advocated by labor and firms in those industries in which the U.S. has lost or is losing its comparative advantage.   Some of these industries are textiles, shoes, bicycles and perhaps even steel and automobiles.   Protection generally reduces the range of goods available and raises prices for U.S. consumers.

23.4   THE BALANCE OF PAYMENTS

The balance of payments is a summary statement of a nation's transactions with the rest of the world during a year.   The balance of payments is divided into three major sections: I. The Current Account, which shows flows of goods and services and government grants.   II. The Capital Account, which shows flows of investments and loans.   (A statistical discrepancy may also be included here since it refers mostly to unreported capital transactions.)   III. The Official Reserve Account, which shows the change in the nation's official (i.e. government) reserves and liabilities to balance the current and capital accounts.

The nation earns foreign currencies by exporting goods and services and receiving capital inflows (i.e. investments and loans) from abroad.   All of these are credits and are entered with a plus sign.   The nation spends these foreign currencies to import goods and services and to invest and lend abroad.   These are debits and are shown with a minus sign.   When the sum of all these debits (−) exceeds the sum of all the credits (+) *in the current and capital accounts,* the nation has a deficit in its balance of payments equal to the difference.   The deficit is settled by a reduction in the nation's reserves of foreign currency or by an increase in the foreign monetary authorities' holdings of the deficit nation's currency.   The opposite is true for a balance-of-payments surplus.

EXAMPLE 4.   Table 2 is a simplified version of the U.S. Balance of Payments for the year 1977.

Table 2
The U.S. Balance of Payments, 1977
(in billions of dollars)

I.	Current Account		
	Exports of Goods and Services	+141	
	Imports of Goods and Services	−153	
	U.S. Government Grants	− 3	
	Balance on Current Account		−15
II.	Capital Account		
	Capital Inflow	+ 14	
	Capital Outflow	− 35	
	Discrepancy	+ 1	
	Balance on Capital Account		−20
	*Deficit in 1977 U.S. Balance of Payments		−35
III.	Official Reserve Account		
	Increase in Foreign Official Holdings of U.S. Dollars		+35
			0

Source: *Survey of Current Business,* Oct. 1978.

23.5   FLEXIBLE-EXCHANGE-RATE SYSTEM OF ADJUSTMENT

A nation generates a supply of foreign currencies or monies in the process of exporting goods and services to and receiving grants, investments and loans from abroad.   On the other hand, the nation uses foreign currencies to import goods and services and to make grants, investments and loans abroad.   When foreign currencies can be freely bought and sold, the rate of exchange between the domestic and a foreign currency is determined by the market demand for and the supply of the foreign currency.   If the demand for the foreign currency increases, the rate of exchange rises. That is, more domestic currency is required to purchase one unit of the foreign currency (so that the domestic currency depreciates).

EXAMPLE 5.   In Fig. 23-2, D is the U.S. demand curve for and S is the U.S. supply curve for pounds (£, the currency of the United Kingdom). D is downsloping because at *lower* dollar prices for pounds it is cheaper for the U.S. to import from, invest in and extend loans to the U.K.   S is upward sloping because at *higher* dollar prices for pounds, it is cheaper for the U.K. to import from, invest in and extend loans to the U.S.   D and S intersect at the equilibrium rate of exchange of $2 = £1 and the equilibrium quantity of £300 million.   If D shifts up to D′, the rate of exchange rises to $3 = £1.   If, on the other hand, the rate of exchange is not allowed to rise (as under the fixed-exchange-rate system), the U.S. would have a deficit (with the U.K.) of *EF* = £200 = $400 million in its balance of payments (see Fig. 23-2).   This deficit could only be corrected by reducing the level of national income, by allowing domestic prices to rise less than abroad, or by government control of trade and payments (see Problem 23.15).

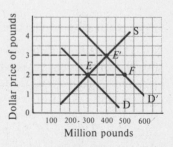

Fig. 23-2

23.6 CURRENT INTERNATIONAL ECONOMIC PROBLEMS

From the end of World War II until 1971, the world operated under a fixed-exchange rate-system, known as the Bretton Woods System.   Under this system, the U.S. faced large and chronic deficits, which it was justifiably unwilling to correct by domestic deflation or direct controls on trade and payments.   The resulting lack of adjustment forced the abandonment of the fixed—and the establishment of a flexible-exchange rate system in 1973.   However, the system that is in operation today is not freely flexible or completely floating because national monetary authorities intervene in foreign exchange markets to prevent erratic and unwanted fluctuations in exchange rates.   This is referred to as "managed" or "dirty floating."   Today, there is a need to make such an arrangement more formal by devising acceptable rules for intervening in foreign exchange markets.   Other current and related international economic problems are the worldwide inflation and possible recession, the sharp rise in petroleum prices since 1973, the great economic power of multinational corporations, and the slow rate of economic development in most poor nations of the world.

Important Economic Terms

Appreciation of the domestic currency. A decrease in the domestic currency price of one unit of the foreign currency. (This is the same as a depreciation of the *foreign* currency.)

Balance of payments. A summary statement of all the transactions of a nation with the rest of the world during a year. It includes the current, capital and official reserve accounts.

Bases for trade. The forces that give rise to trade. These are: comparative advantage, increasing returns to scale or decreasing costs and differences in tastes.

Capital account. The balance-of-payments section that includes the flows of investments and loans between the nation and the rest of the world.

Closed economy. An economy which has no trade and financial relationships with and is completely isolated from the rest of the world.

Comparative advantage. The ability of a nation to produce a commodity at a relatively lower cost or at a lower opportunity cost than another nation.

Complete specialization. A nation which produces only one of the two commodities with trade. This generally occurring under constant costs.

Constant opportunity costs. The *constant* amounts of a commodity that must be given up in order to release just enough resources to produce each additional unit of a second commodity.

Credit (+). A transaction that results from a payment *from* foreigners. This includes exports of goods and services, and capital inflows (i.e. investments and loans received from abroad).

Current account. A balance-of-payments section that includes the flow of goods, services and government grants between the nation and the rest of the world.

Debit (−). A transaction that results in a payment *to* foreigners. This includes imports of goods and services, government grants to foreigners and capital outflows (i.e. investments and loans made abroad).

Deficit in balance of payments. The excess of debits (−) over credits (+) in the nation's current and capital accounts.

Depreciation of the domestic currency. An increase in the domestic currency price of one unit of the foreign currency. (This is the same as the appreciation of the *foreign* currency.)

Fixed-exchange-rate system. The system in which the rates of exchange between the domestic and foreign currencies are fixed.

Flexible-exchange-rate system.   A system in which the rate of exchange floats freely to find its equilibrium level at the intersection of the market demand and supply curves of the foreign currency.

Gains from trade.   The increases in the consumption of both commodities that result from specialization in production and trade.

Import quota.   A restriction on the quantity of a good that is allowed to be imported into a nation during a year.

Import tariff.   A tax on imports.

Increasing opportunity costs.   The increasing amounts of a commodity that must be given up in order to release just enough resources to produce each additional unit of a second commodity.

Infant-industry argument for protection.   States that a newly established industry requires protection until it can grow in size and efficiency and be able to face foreign competition.

Official reserve account.   The balance-of-payments section that shows the change in the nation's official (i.e. government) reserves and liabilities required to balance its current and capital accounts.

Open economy.   An economy which is connected with the rest of the world through trade and financial relationships.

Production-possibilities or transformation curve.   The graphic representation of the various alternative combinations of two commodities that a society can produce by fully utilizing all of its resources and the best available technology.

Rate of exchange or exchange rate.   The domestic currency price of one unit of the foreign currency.

Surplus in the balance of payments.   The excess of credits (+) over debits (−) in the nation's current and capital accounts.

Terms of trade.   The trade exchange ratio or the rate at which one commodity is exchanged for another.

Review Questions

1. Most nations of the world are (a) closed economies, (b) open economies, (c) self-sufficient, (d) nontrading nations.
   Ans. (b)

2. The production-possibilities (or transformation) curves of two nations usually differ because of (a) a difference of tastes between the two nations, (b) a difference in the availability of resources, (c) constant costs, (d) increasing costs.
   Ans. (b)

3. Which of the following statements is *incorrect?*
   (a) A straight-line transformation curve indicates constant opportunity costs.
   (b) The *flatter* transformation curve for the U.S. in Fig. 23-1 indicates that the U.S. has lower opportunity costs or a comparative advantage in *food* (measured along the horizontal axis).
   (c) The *steeper* transformation curve for the U.K. in Fig. 23-1 indicates that the U.K. has a comparative advantage in *cloth* (measured along the vertical axis).
   (d) In the absence of trade, the U.S. is likely to produce only food and the U.K. only cloth.
   Ans. (d)

4. Which of the following statements is *incorrect* with regard to Example 1 and Fig. 23-1?
   (a) In the absence of specialization in production and trade, the combined U.S. and U.K. output of food is 60.
   (b) In the absence of specialization in production and trade, the combined U.S. and U.K. output of cloth is 40.

(c) With specialization in production and trade, the total output of food is 50.

(d) With specialization in production and trade, the total output of cloth is 60.

Ans. (c)

5. In Example 1 and Fig. 23-1, trade takes place at the exchange ratio (or terms of trade) of (a) $1F = 1C$, (b) $\frac{1}{2}F = 1C$, (c) $2F = 1C$, (d) $1\frac{1}{2}F = 1C$.

Ans. (a)

6. A specific argument advanced for protection is (a) to protect domestic labor against cheap foreign labor, (b) to reduce domestic unemployment, (c) to protect infant industries and industries important for national defense, (d) all of the above.

Ans. (d)

7. Which of the following is *not* included in the current account section of the balance of payments? (a) The exports of goods and services, (b) the import of goods and services, (c) capital inflows, (d) government grants.

Ans. (c)

8. A deficit or surplus in a nation's balance of payments is measured by subtracting all the debits from all the credits in the (a) current account, (b) current and capital accounts, (c) current, capital and official reserve accounts, (d) capital and official reserve accounts.

Ans. (b)

9. Which of the following statements is *not* true with respect to the 1977 U.S. balance of payments?   (a) Exports exceeded imports.   (b) Capital outflows exceeded capital inflows.   (c) The U.S. had a deficit. (d) The foreign official holdings of U.S. dollars increased.

Ans. (a)

10. The rate of exchange between the domestic and a foreign currency is defined as the (a) foreign currency price of a unit of the domestic currency, (b) domestic currency price of a unit of the foreign currency, (c) foreign currency price of gold, (d) domestic currency price of gold.

Ans. (b)

11. Under a freely flexible exchange rate system, a deficit in a nation's balance of payments is corrected by (a) a decrease in the domestic currency price of the foreign currency, (b) an appreciation of domestic currency, (c) a depreciation of the domestic currency, (d) a depreciation of the foreign currency.

Ans. (c)

12. A serious current international economic problem is (a) the lack of generally acceptable rules for intervention in foreign exchange markets, (b) worldwide inflation, (c) the sharp rise in petroleum prices and the slow rate of economic development, (d) all of the above.

Ans. (d)

Solved Problems

THE IMPORTANCE OF INTERNATIONAL TRADE

23.1.   (a) What is an "open economy"?   (b) Why does our study of economics include international trade and finance?   (c) How do the economic relationships among nations differ from the economic relationships among various parts or regions of a nation?

(a) An open economy is one which is connected to other nations through a network of trade and financial relationships.   Most, if not all, nations of the world are open economies in various degrees.

(b) We want to analyze the international flow of goods, services, resources and payments because they can greatly affect the nation's welfare.

(c) Nations usually impose restrictions on the free international flow of goods, services, resources and payments.   Differences in language, customs and laws also hamper these international flows.   In addition, international flows involve receipts and payments in different currencies which usually change in value in relation to one another through time.   This is to be contrasted with the interregional flows of goods, services, resources and payments within the same nation.   These flows face no such restrictions as tariffs and quotas.   They are conducted in the same currency and usually in the same language, customs and laws.

23.2. (a) How can we measure a nation's degree of economic interdependence with the rest of the world?   (b) Why does the U.S. rely less on trade than most other developed nations?   (c) What would happen to its standard of living if the U.S. withdrew completely from international trade?

(a) A rough measure of the degree of interdependence of a nation with the rest of the world is given by the value of its exports as a percentage of its GNP.   For small developed nations such as Switzerland, Belgium and the Netherlands the figure ranges from 35 to 58 percent.   For large developed nations such as Japan, France, Italy, West Germany and the United Kingdom, the figure ranges from 14 to 31 percent.   For the U.S. the figure is 8 percent.   For the Soviet Union it is 4 percent (see Table 1).

(b) The U.S. is a nation of continental size with immense natural and human resources.   As such, it can produce with relative efficiency most of the products it needs.   In contrast a small nation, like Switzerland, can only specialize in the production and export of a small range of commodities and must import all the others.   In general, as the figures in Table 1 indicate, the larger the nation, the smaller its economic interdependence with the rest of the world.

(c) Even though the U.S. relies only to a relatively small extent on foreign trade, *a significant part* of its high standard of living depends on it.   For one thing, the U.S. is incapable of producing such commodities as coffee, tea, cocoa, Scotch whiskey, etc.   In addition, the U.S. has no deposits of such minerals as tin and tungsten, which are important for industrial production.   Though the U.S. is one of the largest petroleum producers in the world, it still needs to import huge quantities of petroleum to keep its economy operating at a high level.   In addition, there are many commodities which the U.S. could produce domestically but only at a relatively higher cost than imported commodities.   Thus, trade is very important to the welfare of the U.S.

THE BASIS AND THE GAINS FROM TRADE: COMPARATIVE ADVANTAGE

23.3. (a) What is a production-possibilities or transformation curve?   What does a straight-line transformation curve indicate?   (b) Plot transformation curves for the U.S. and the U.K. from the data in Table 3.   (c) What is the opportunity cost of food in the U.S. and the U.K.?

Table 3

U.S.		U.K.	
C	F	C	F
40	0	60	0
30	10	45	5
20	20	30	10
10	30	15	15
0	40	0	20

(a) A production-possibilities or transformation curve shows the various alternative combinations of two commodities that a nation can produce by fully employing all of its resources and using the best technology available.   Its slope indicates how much of a commodity the nation must give up in order to release just enough resources to produce more of a second commodity.   A straight-line transformation curve indicates constant opportunity costs. This would occur only if all resources were equally efficient in the production of both commodities. Constant costs are assumed here only to simplify the analysis. (The more realistic increasing cost case is discussed in Problem 23.7.)

(b) See Fig. 23-3.

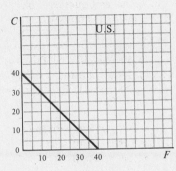

Fig. 23-3

(c) The opportunity cost of F in the U.S. is $1C$. That is, the domestic exchange ratio or cost ratio is $1F = 1C$ and is reflected in the (absolute) slope of 1 of the U.S. transformation curve. This means that for each additional unit of food the U.S. wants to produce, it must give up $1C$. In the U.K., the opportunity cost of $1F$ is $3C$ and equals the (absolute) slope of the U.K. transformation curve. Thus, the opportunity cost of F in the U.K. is three times that of the U.S.

23.4. (a) Explain comparative advantage. In what commodity do the U.S. and the U.K. of Problem 23.3 have a comparative advantage? (b) What combination of cloth and food do the U.S. and the U.K. produce and consume in the absence of trade?

(a) Comparative advantage refers to the commodity that a nation can produce at a *relatively* lower cost or at a lower opportunity cost than the other nation. Since the opportunity cost of $1F = 1C$ in the U.S. and $1F = 3C$ in the U.K., the U.S. has a comparative advantage in food and a comparative disadvantage in cloth with respect to the U.K. In a two-nation, two-commodity world, comparative advantage by one nation (the U.S.) in one commodity (F) necessarily implies that the other nation (the U.K.) has a comparative advantage in the other commodity (C). In Fig. 23-3, the lower absolute slope of the U.S. transformation curve indicates that the opportunity or relative cost of food (the commodity measured along the horizontal axis) is less in the U.S. than in the U.K. Therefore, the U.S. has a comparative advantage in F and the U.K. in C.

(b) The U.S. and the U.K. can produce any combination of C and F indicated on their respective transformation curves. In the absence of trade, the U.S. and the U.K. can only consume what they will produce. Among the various combinations of C and F shown on their respective transformation curves, the U.S. and U.K. will produce that particular combination which, according to national tastes, gives them the greatest satisfaction.

23.5. Suppose that in Fig. 23-3 the U.S. and U.K. produce and consume at A ($30C$ and $10F$) and A' ($15C$ and $15F$) respectively in the absence of trade. (a) Where will the U.S. and the U.K. produce with free trade? By how much does the total output of C and F increase with specialization in production? (b) Draw a figure showing by points E and E', respectively, the combination of C and F consumed by the two countries if the U.S. exchanges $20F$ for $40C$ with the U.K. Explain how points E and E' are reached.

(a) Since the U.S. has a comparative advantage in F, with free trade the U.S. will specialize completely in the production of food and produce $40F$ and $0C$ (see Fig. 23-3). The U.K. will specialize completely in the production of cloth and produce $60C$ and $0F$. Thus, total world output with specialization in production is $40F$ (produced entirely in the U.S.) and $60C$ (produced entirely in the U.K.). This exceeds by $15F$ the combined output of $25F$ ($10F$ in the U.S. and $15F$ in the U.K.) produced in the absence of specialization and trade. Similarly, with specialization in production, the output of $60C$ produced entirely in the U.K. exceeds by $15C$ the output of $45C$ ($30C$ in the U.S. and $15C$ in the U.K.) before specialization and trade.

(b) In the absence of trade, the U.S. produces and consumes at point A (30C and 10F) and the U.K. at point A' (15C and 15F) in Fig. 23-4.   With free trade possible, the U.S. specializes completely in the production of food and produces at B (40F and 0C), while the U.K. specializes completely in the production of cloth and produces at B' (60C and 0F).   The U.S. then exchanges 20F for 40C from the U.K. and reaches point E (40C and 20F) in consumption.   Starting from point B', the U.K. receives from the U.S. 20F in exchange for 40C and reaches point E' (20C and 20F).   The dashed lines are usually referred to as the trade-possibilities curves.

23.6. With regard to Fig. 23-4, (a) indicate how much the U.S. and the U.K. gain from trade. How do these gains arise?   (b) What determines the terms of trade?   How does this affect the distribution of the gains from trade?

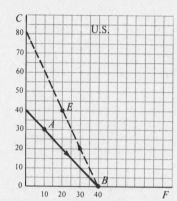 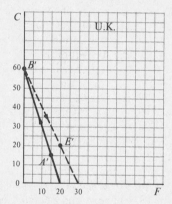

Fig. 23-4

(a) The U.S. produced and consumed at A (30C and 10F) in the absence of trade and at E (40C and 20F) with specialization in trade.   Thus, the U.S. gains from trade are 10C and 10F.   On the other hand, the U.K. produced and consumed at A' (15C and 15F) in the absence of trade and at E' (20C and 20F) with specialization in trade.   Thus, the U.K. gains from trade are 5C and 5F.   The total U.S. and U.K. gains are thus 15C and 15F and equal the increases in the total outputs of food and cloth resulting from specialization in production [see Problem 23.5 (a)].

(b) In order for both the U.S. and the U.K. to gain from trade (and thus be willing to engage in trade), the *trade* exchange ratio or terms of trade must be between the pretrade *domestic* exchange ratios.   Since 20F are exchanged for 40C, the trade exchange ratio is 1F = 2C and lies between the domestic exchange ratio of 1F = 1C in the U.S. and 1F = 3C in the U.K. before trade (see the absolute slope of the solid lines in Fig. 23-4).   The smaller the U.S. demand for U.K. cloth exports and the greater the U.K. demand for U.S. food exports, the closer the *trade* exchange ratio will be to the U.K. *domestic* exchange ratio (in the absence of trade), the greater the relative gains from trade to the U.S. and the lower the gains from trade to the U.K.

23.7. Discuss what happens as nations specialize in the product of their comparative advantage and have increasing opportunity costs.

Since resources are usually not equally efficient in the production of both commodities, for each additional unit of a commodity a nation wants, it must give up more and more of the second commodity.   Thus, nations generally face increasing opportunity costs or a concave or bulging-out transformation curve.   As a result, as each nation specializes in the commodity of its comparative advantage, it has increasing opportunity costs.   Specialization in production then continues only up to the outputs at which the opportunity costs become equal in the two nations.   This occurs before each nation has become completely specialized in production.   More specifically, as the U.S. specializes in the production of food, it incurs increasing opportunity costs in food production.   Similarly, as the U.K. specializes in cloth production, it incurs increasing opportunity costs in cloth production.   This means *decreasing* opportunity costs in the U.K. in food production.   Since the opportunity cost of food was lower in the U.S. than in the U.K. to begin with, and since it rises in the U.S. as the U.S. produces more food, and falls in the U.K. as the U.K. produces less food and more cloth, an output will be reached at which the opportunity costs of F will be the same in the U.S. and the U.K.   At that output, specialization in production and trade will stop expanding.   This is likely to occur before the U.S. has become completely specialized in food production and the U.K. in cloth production.   Thus, even with trade, the U.S. will continue to produce some cloth and the U.K. will produce some of its food. (The diagrammatic exposition for the increasing opportunity cost case is more difficult and left for an international economics course.)

23.8.   How can trade be based upon (a) increasing returns to scale and (b) differences in tastes between two nations?

(a)   Even if two nations are identical in resource endowments and technology (so that they have identical transformation curves) and have identical tastes, there is still a basis for mutually advantageous trade if the two products are subject to increasing returns to scale in production (see Section 16.6).   Then it pays for each nation to specialize completely in the production of either of the two commodities, take advantage of increasing returns to scale, and exchange part of its output for part of the output of the other commodity also produced under increasing returns to scale by the other nation.   By doing so, each nation will end up consuming more of both commodities than it would in the absence of trade.

(b)   Even if two nations are completely identical in resource endowments and technology (so that they have identical transformation curves) and have increasing opportunity costs (rather than increasing returns to scale of decreasing costs in production), there is still a basis for mutually advantageous trade if the two nations have different tastes.   With increasing costs, identical transformation curves but different tastes, each nation would produce a different combination of the two commodities in the absence of trade and thus incur different opportunity costs.   The nation producing and consuming less of a commodity in the absence of trade will have smaller opportunity costs and a comparative advantage in the production of that commodity.   The other nation will then have a comparative advantage in the production of the other commodity.   The process of specialization in production and trade is then the same as described in Problem 23.7.

OBSTACLES TO THE FLOW OF TRADE: TARIFFS AND QUOTAS

23.9.   (a) What is trade protection?   An import tariff?   An import quota?   What are some other forms of import restrictions?   (b) What important U.S. industries seek or have protection?   What are some industries that do not?

(a)   Trade protection refers to restrictions on the imports of goods and services from abroad.   These are advocated by labor and firms in some industries to protect them against foreign competition.   Protection, however, results in a reduced range of commodities and higher prices for society as a whole.   An import tariff is a tax on imports.   This may be imposed to raise revenues (on commodities such as coffee, tea, bananas, etc. not produced in the U.S.) or for protection— usually the latter.   An import quota is a restriction imposed by the government on the quantity of a good that may be imported.   There are other restrictions on imports such as health regulations, safety and pollution standards, labeling and packaging regulations, "buy American" clauses, etc.   These are often disguised methods of protection.

(b)   Some of the most important U.S. industries that already have and seek additional protection are the textile, automobile and steel industries.   These are the industries in which the U.S. has lost or is losing its comparative advantage.   Some of the most important U.S. industries that do not have or need protection are the computer, aircraft, and other high-technology industries.   The same is generally true for agriculture.   These are the areas of U.S. comparative advantage. Tariffs have generally declined since World War II and are now on the average less than 10% on manufactured goods.   Trade in agricultural commodities is still subject to many direct quantitative restrictions and other nontariff trade barriers.

23.10.   (a) Cite some of the specific arguments advanced in favor of protection.   (b) Evaluate these arguments.

(a) Protection is often advocated to protect domestic labor against cheap foreign labor. That is, since wages are generally higher in the U.S. than in other nations, without protection foreign nations (so the argument goes) can undersell the U.S. because of their lower wages, flood the U.S. market with imports, and depress U.S. wages. Another argument often heard in favor of protection is that it reduces domestic unemployment. That is, by restricting imports, domestic production is stimulated and the level of domestic unemployment is reduced. A third argument in favor of protection is the "infant industry" argument. This states that a newly established industry requires protection until it can grow in size and efficiency so as to be able to face foreign competition. Finally, protection is advocated in order to protect such industries as shipyards and the optical industry etc. that are important for national defense.

(b) The argument for protection against cheap foreign labor is generally invalid because it incorrectly implies that higher wages necessarily mean higher labor costs. This is not true if the higher U.S. wages are based on even higher labor productivity. Restrictions on U.S. imports to reduce U.S. unemployment is a beggar-thy-neighbor policy because it leads to higher unemployment in those nations whose exports to the U.S. have been restricted. As a result, these other nations are likely to retaliate and also reduce imports from the U.S. and all nations lose in the end. Domestic unemployment should instead be corrected by appropriate fiscal and monetary policies. The infant-industry argument is generally invalid for the U.S. and other industrial nations but may be valid for poor developing nations. However, the same degree of protection can generally be better achieved by subsidies to the infant industry rather than by tariffs and quotas. Subsidies are also generally preferable to tariffs and quotas as protection to industries important for national defense.

THE BALANCE OF PAYMENTS

23.11. (a) What is a nation's balance of payments? What is its purpose? (b) What are the three main accounts in the balance of payments? What does each measure? (c) How are credits and debits entered into the current and capital accounts?

(a) A nation's balance of payments is a summary record of all the transactions of a nation with the rest of the world during a calendar year. Its main purpose is to inform government authorities of the nation's international position and to help them formulate monetary, fiscal and commercial policies.

(b) The three main accounts of the balance of payments are the current account, the capital account, and the official reserve account. The current account shows the flows of goods, services and government grants between the nation and the rest of the world. The capital account shows the flows of investments and loans between the nation and the rest of the world. The official reserve account shows the change in the nation's official (i.e. government) reserves and liabilities needed to balance the current and capital accounts.

(c) All economic transactions that lead to the U.S. receiving payments from abroad are entered as credits (+) in the current and capital accounts. Thus, exports of goods and services, and investments and loans received from abroad (i.e., capital inflows) are entered as credits. All transactions that lead to payments to foreigners are entered as debits (−). U.S. imports of goods and services, government grants made to foreigners, and investments and loans made to foreigners (i.e. capital outflows) are entered as debits.

23.12. (a) How is a deficit or surplus in a nation's balance of payments measured? How is it settled? What is the function of the statistical "discrepancy"? (b) How did the deficit in the U.S. balance of payments arise in 1977?

(a) If the sum of all the debits in the current and capital accounts exceeds the sum of all the credits in these accounts, the nation has a deficit in its balance of payments equal to the difference. This is settled out of the nation's official (i.e. government) reserves or by foreign surplus nations increasing their holdings of the deficit nation's currency. The latter represent a future claim on the deficit nation. The opposite is true for a surplus. The function of the statistical "discrepancy" is to balance the total credits with the total debits of all three accounts taken together.   For example, if the total credits in the official reserve account fell short of the sum of the total debits in the current and capital accounts (so that the nation had a deficit), a discrepancy equal to the difference is entered at the end of the capital account *as a credit* (representing mostly unreported capital inflows).

(*b*)   During 1977, the U.S. exports of goods and services fell short of its imports of goods and services and net government grants by $15 billion (see Table 2).   On top of this, capital inflows in the form of investments and loans received by the U.S. from abroad fell short of U.S. capital outflows in the form of U.S. investments and loans made abroad by $21 billion.   This together with a (credit) discrepancy of $1 billion, left a deficit of $35 billion ($-15-21+1$) in the U.S. balance of payments for 1977.   This was settled by foreign monetary authorities increasing their holdings of U.S. dollars by $35 billion.   They were willing to accept these dollars because the dollar is accepted as an international currency and is used to settle accounts among almost all nations of the world.

THE FLEXIBLE-EXCHANGE-RATE SYSTEM OF ADJUSTMENT

23.13.   (*a*) What gives rise to a nation's demand for a foreign currency or money?   What is the shape of this demand curve?   Why?   (*b*) What gives rise to a nation's supply of foreign currency?   What is the shape of the supply curve?   Why?   (*c*) How is the rate of exchange between the domestic and foreign currency determined under a flexible-exchange-rate system?

(*a*)   A nation's demand for a foreign currency arises from the nation importing goods and services from abroad, extending economic and military aid, and investing and making loans abroad.   A nation's demand curve for a foreign currency is generally downsloped, indicating that the *lower* the domestic price of the foreign currency or rate of exchange, the *greater* the quantity demanded of the foreign currency.   This is because imports from the foreign nation will be cheaper in terms of the domestic currency and it will be more attractive to invest abroad (see Fig. 23-2).

(*b*)   A nation generates a supply of foreign exchange by exporting goods and services abroad and by receiving grants, investments, and loans from abroad.   A nation's supply of foreign currency is generally upsloped indicating that the *higher* the domestic price of the foreign currency or exchange rate, the *greater* the quantity supplied of the foreign currency.   The reason for this is that the greater the amount of the domestic currency foreigners can exchange for one unit of their currency, the cheaper our exports are to them and the more attractive investments and loans to us are for foreigners (see Fig. 23-2).

(*c*)   Under a freely flexible or floating exchange rate system, the equilibrium rate of exchange and equilibrium quantity of foreign exchange are determined at the intersection of the market demand curve and the market supply curve of the foreign currency (see Fig. 23-2).

23.14.   (*a*) What happens to the equilibrium rate of exchange and to the equilibrium quantity of foreign exchange if the nation's demand for the foreign currency increases?   Why?   (*b*) How is a deficit or a surplus in a nation's balance of payments corrected under a flexible exchange rate system?

(*a*)   Given the nation's supply curve of the foreign currency, an upward shift in the nation's demand curve for the foreign currency will determine a new and higher equilibrium exchange rate and equilibrium quantity (see Fig. 23-2).   An increase in the nation's demand for a foreign currency may result from a change in tastes for more imported goods and services.   It may also occur if the nation increases its investments and loans abroad in the expectation of increased returns.

(*b*)   A deficit in a nation's balance of payments means that at a given rate of exchange, there is a shortage (an excess of quantity demanded over quantity supplied) of the foreign currency.   If the exchange rate is freely flexible or floating, the exchange rate will rise until the quantity demanded of the foreign currency equals the quantity supplied and the deficit is completely eliminated (see Fig. 23-2).   This rise in the exchange rate means that the relative value of the domestic currency is falling or depreciating.   The exact opposite occurs when there is a surplus and the nation's currency appreciates (or increases) in relative value.

CURRENT INTERNATIONAL ECONOMIC PROBLEMS

23.15. (*a*) How is the present international economic system different from a freely flexible exchange rate system?   What are its disadvantages?   (*b*) How can a deficit or surplus in a nation's balance of payments be corrected under a fixed exchange rate system?   (*c*) When was a fixed exchange rate system in operation?   Why did it collapse?

(*a*)   Under the present international economic system, exchange rates are not freely flexible or completely floating because national monetary authorities intervene in foreign exchange markets (managed or dirty floating) to prevent erratic and unwanted fluctuations.   As a result, deficits and surpluses are not completely or automatically eliminated.   A more serious disadvantage is that a nation may attempt to keep its exchange rate artificially high in order to discourage imports and stimulate its exports.   This could lead to retaliation by other nations (whose exports fall) and result in a decline in the volume of and gains from trade and a loss to all nations.   What is needed is to make such a system more formal by devising acceptable rules for intervening in foreign exchange markets.

(*b*)   Under a fixed exchange rate system the rate of exchange is not allowed to vary.   As a result, the elimination of a deficit or surplus can only be accomplished through income and price changes or government controls on trade and payments.   To do this, the deficit nation should deflate the economy (so as to discourage imports) and make sure that domestic prices rise less than in surplus nations (so as to encourage exports).   On the other hand, the surplus nation should stimulate its economy in order to encourage imports and discourage its exports.   If nations are unwilling to do this, a deficit can only be corrected by direct government restrictions on imports of goods and services and loans and investments abroad.

(*c*)   A fixed exchange rate system (the so-called Bretton Woods System) similar to that described above was in operation from the end of World War II until 1971.   The fundamental reason for its collapse was the lack of an adequate adjustment mechanism.   Nations were generally (and justifiably) unwilling to deflate and inflate their economies in order to correct a deficit or surplus in their balance of payments.   On the other hand, direct controls on trade and payments restrict trade and invite retaliation.   Because of the lack of an adequate adjustment mechanism, the U.S. incurred chronic deficits totaling over $50 billion from 1950 to 1971.   Most of these were settled by foreign monetary authorities increasing their holdings of dollars.   But in 1971 they refused to accept more dollars at the fixed exchange rate.   The dollar was then allowed to depreciate and the present system was established in 1973.

23.16. What are the major international economic problems facing the world today?

The major international economic problems facing the world today are:
(1) Worldwide inflation and possibility of a recession.
(2) The more than quadrupling of petroleum prices since the fall of 1973 by OPEC (Organization of Petroleum Exporting Countries) caused huge balance-of-payments deficits in most petroleum-importing nations and created the problem of *recycling* hundreds of billions of "petrodollars."
(3) There is a need to reform the international monetary system or, at least, to formalize present arrangements and devise acceptable rules for intervention in foreign exchange markets.
(4) The huge overhang of foreign-held dollars and the increase in the number and size of multinational corporations reduce the effectiveness of national economic policies and point to the need for more international cooperation and for new arrangements to cope with these problems.
(5) Lagging economic development in the world's poor nations presents a potentially explosive situation.

Nevertheless, we must not exaggerate these problems and paint too bleak a picture.   By the end of the 1970s, current international monetary arrangements were working fairly well, nations were learning to adjust to the higher petroleum prices, and even the recycling problem seemed more manageable.   Perhaps even more important is that the world has been weathering since the early seventies the most serious economic problems since the Great Depression without much strife and without trade wars, but in the spirit of international cooperation and understanding.

Final Examination—
Microeconomics

1. (*a*) Draw a figure showing the best level of output for a monopolist. Include three alternative AC curves, showing that the monopolist (1) makes a profit, (2) breaks even and (3) incurs a loss. (*b*) What happens to this monopolist in the long run if he incurs short-run losses? Short-run profits? (*c*) What are the disadvantages of monopoly? (*d*) How can government regulate a monopolist?

2. (*a*) What is oligopoly? What is the single most important characteristic in oligopolistic markets? (*b*) Draw a figure to rationalize the price rigidity often observed in oligopolistic markets. (*c*) When and how are prices usually changed in oligopolistic markets?

3. With respect to Table 1, (*a*) find the marginal physical product for labor (MPP_L), total revenue (TR), and the marginal revenue product of labor (MRP_L) schedules. (*b*) How many workers should the firm hire if the wage rate is \$40, \$23, \$9, and the firm is a perfect competitor in the labor market? (*c*) Sketch the firm's demand curve for this kind of labor. How is the market demand curve for labor derived? How is the wage rate for this kind of labor determined?

Table 1

(1) Number of Workers	(2) Total Product	(3) Product Price
0	0	—
1	4	\$10
2	7	9
3	9	8
4	10	7

4. (*a*) What are wage differences based on? (*b*) What are equalizing differences? How do these give rise to wage differences? (*c*) What are noncompeting groups? How do they give rise to wage differences? (*d*) What are imperfect labor markets? How do they give rise to wage differences?

5. (*a*) Why is a long-run, perfectly competitive general equilibrium system the most efficient system? (*b*) How do market imperfections, the existence of social goods and divergencies between social and private benefits and costs interfere with the most efficient allocation of resources? (*c*) How does the government seek to overcome these problems? (*d*) Why and how does the government redistribute income from the rich to the poor? How far should this go?

6. (*a*) Why do nations engage in international trade? What major problem may arise from trade? (*b*) Describe how a balance-of-payments disequilibrium (i.e. a deficit or surplus) is adjusted under a freely flexible exchange rate system. How does this differ from the international economic system in operation today? (*c*) What are the most serious current international economic problems?

Answers

1.   (*a*) In Fig. F-1, the best level of output of the monopolist is *OB* given by point *C* where MR = MC. With AC_1, the monopolist makes a per-unit profit of *GF* and a total profit of *GF* times *OB*. With AC_2, *P* = AC and TR = TC and so the monopolist breaks even. With AC_3, the monopolist incurs a per-unit loss of *HG* and a total loss of *HG* times *OB*. Only if *P* exceeds AVC so that TR exceeds TVC will the monopolist stay in business and minimize its short-run total losses by producing *OB*.

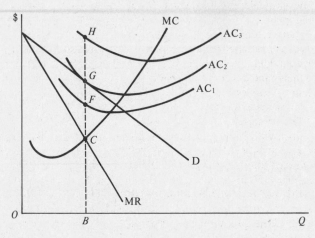

Fig. F-1

      (*b*) If the monopolist is making short-run losses, in the long run, it could build the most appropriate scale of plant to produce the best long-run level of output. It could also advertise in an attempt to cause an upward shift in the D curve it faces (this, however, will also shift its cost curves up). If this monopolist would still incur a loss after having considered all of these long-run possibilities, it will stop producing the commodity in the long run. If the monopolist was already making short-run profits, it will still build the most appropriate plant in the long run and increase its total profits (if entry into the industry continues to be blocked and the monopolist does not fear government action).

      (*c*) The basic disadvantages of monopoly are as follows.

          (1) Since the monopolist produces where MR = MC and *P* exceeds MC (as opposed to *P* = MC in perfect competition), output is restricted and price is higher in the short run. Thus, resources are misallocated (i.e. underallocated).

          (2) Monopoly profits persist in the long run because of blocked or restricted entry. Since corporate stocks are owned mostly by high-income groups, monopoly profits lead to greater income inequality.

          (3) The monopolist may feel so secure as to have little incentive to engage in research and development. On the other hand, in the case of natural monopolies (such as public utilities) a single firm satisfying the entire market demand may be much more efficient than two or more firms.

      (*d*) The government can regulate the price a monopolist, such as a public utility, charges. It can set *P* = AC, and eliminate all of the monopolist's profits. However, *P* would still exceed MC and there would still be some misallocation of resources. The government could set *P* = MC to eliminate the misallocation of resources. However, at *P* = MC, *P* is likely to be smaller than AC so that the public utility would incur a loss and not continue to supply the service in the long run without a government subsidy. This, combined with the fact that it is much more difficult in the real world to estimate MC than AC, often leads the government to set *P* = AC for public utilities.

2.   (*a*) Oligopoly is the form of market organization in which there are few sellers of a commodity. If there are only two sellers, we have a duopoly. If the product is homogeneous (e.g. steel, cement, copper), we have a pure oligopoly. If the product is differentiated (e.g. cars, cigarettes),

we have a differentiated oligopoly.   Oligopoly is the most prevalent form of market organization in the manufacturing sector of modern economies and arises for the same general reasons as monopoly (i.e. economies of scale, control over the source of raw materials, patents and government franchise).

The interdependence among the firms in the industry is the single characteristic that sets oligopoly apart from other market structures.   This interdependence is the natural result of fewness.   That is, since there are few firms in an oligopolistic industry, when one of them lowers its price, undertakes a successful advertising campaign, or introduces a better model, the demand curve faced by other oligopolists will shift down.   This causes the other oligopolists to react. However, the particular solution depends on the reaction pattern.   Thus, there is no general theory of oligopoly.   All we have are specific cases or models.

(b) The price rigidity often observed in oligopolistic markets can be rationalized by the kinked-demand curve model.   In Fig. F-2, the demand curve facing the oligopolist is *CEJ* (with a kink at *E*) and *CFGN* is its MR curve.   The oligopolist produces *OA* units of output at *P* = *OB*.   The demand curve facing the oligopolist is drawn with a kink at the prevailing market price.   It is very elastic above the kink on the assumption that if an oligopolist increases its price, others in the industry will not raise theirs and so it would lose most of its customers.   On the other hand, d is much less elastic below the kink on the assumption that if the oligopolist lowers its price, the others will match the price reduction so that it only retains approximately its share of the market.   The *CF* portion of the MR curve is derived from the *CE* portion of d, and *GN* from *EJ*.   The MR curve is discontinuous directly below (and caused by) the kink at point *E* on d.   MC can vary between *G* and *F* and still give *Q* = *OA* at *P* = *OB*.

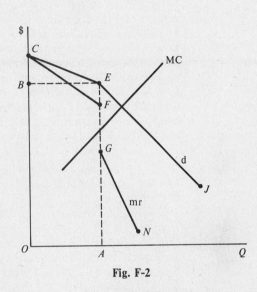

Fig. F-2

(c) When the MC curve shifts up and intersects the MR curve to the left and above the vertical or discontinuous portion of the MR curve (see Fig. F-2), a price change may become inevitable and is usually accomplished by price leadership.   This is a form of tacit and legal price collusion. With price leadership, the dominant or most efficient firm in the industry usually starts a price increase on the tacit understanding that the other firms in the industry will more or less match the price increase within a few days.   This averts the danger of a price war without exposing the oligopolists to possible government antitrust action.

3.   (a) In Table 2, MPP$_L$ declines because of the operation of the law of diminishing returns.   MRP$_L$ declines because MPP$_L$ and the product price decline.   The fact that this firm reduces the product price in order to increase sales indicates that it is an imperfect competitor in the product market.

Table 2

(1) Number of Workers	(2) Total Product	(3) MPP$_L$ or Δ(2)	(4) Product Price	(5) Total Revenue (2) × (4)	(6) MRP$_L$ or Δ(5)
0	0			$ 0	
		4			$40
1	4		$10	40	
		3			23
2	7		9	63	
		2			9
3	9		8	72	
		1			2
4	10		7	70	

(b)   In order to maximize total profits, a perfectly competitive firm in the resource market should hire the resource as long as the resource MRP exceeds the resource price and until they are equal.   Thus, the firm would hire one worker at the wage rate of $40, two at $23, and three at $9.   The firm would not hire the fourth worker even if it were free because the MRP of this fourth worker is negative.   Columns (6) and (1) in Table 2 give the firm's demand schedule for this kind of labor.

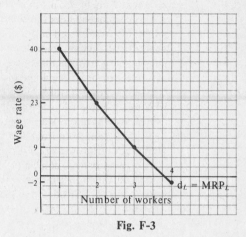

(c)   The firm's demand curve for labor is shown in Fig. F-3.   Broadly speaking, the market demand curve of this kind of labor is obtained by adding each firm's demand for this kind of labor.   The wage rate is then determined at the intersection of the market demand and supply curves.   However, in a mixed economy such as ours, this equilibrium in wage rate is likely to be modified by market imperfections, government regulation (e.g. minimum-wage rate legislation) and union power.

Fig. F-3

4.   (a)   Wages differ among different categories of people and jobs because of (1) equalizing differences, (2) the existence of noncompeting occupational groups, and (3) imperfections of competition in labor markets.

(b)   Equalizing differences are wage differences that serve to compensate for nonmonetary differences among jobs.   That is, jobs requiring equal qualifications may differ in attractiveness so that higher wages must be paid to attract and retain workers in more unpleasant jobs.   For example, garbage collectors receive higher wages than porters.

(c)   Noncompeting occupational groups are human resource categories (occupations) requiring different capacities, skills, training and education and therefore receiving different wages.   That is, labor is not a single productive resource but many different resources, each not in direct competition with others.   Thus, doctors form one group which is not in direct competition with other groups of workers.   Lawyers, accountants, electricians, bus drivers, etc. belong to other noncompeting groups.   There is a particular wage-rate structure for each of these noncompeting groups, depending on the abilities, skills and training required for each occupation.   Note that some job mobility among noncompeting groups may be possible, as for example when an electrician becomes an electronics engineer by going to night school.   However, mobility is limited.

(d)   An imperfect labor market is one in which there is some lack of information on job opportunities and wages, where some workers are unwilling to move to other areas and jobs in order to take advantage of higher wages and where union power, minimum-wage laws and monopsony power exist.   Any of these characteristics will cause wage differences for jobs which are exactly alike and which require equal capacities and skills.

5.   (a)   A long-run, perfectly competitive general equilibrium system is the most efficient system because (1) consumers purchase commodities in such a way as to maximize their total utility in spending their income, and (2) firms produce the goods and services most wanted by consumers with the most efficient allocation of resources.   As a result, there is *economic efficiency* in consumption in the sense that it is impossible to transfer commodities among consumers in a way that would make some better off without at the same time making others worse off.   Similarly, there is *technical efficiency* in production in the sense that it is impossible to reallocate resources to increase the output of some commodities without reducing the output of others (i.e. society is on its production-possibilities curve).

(b)   With imperfect competition in some commodity and factor markets, the output of these commodities and the use of these resources are artificially restricted, thus reducing efficiency.   Even in the absence of imperfect competition, there would be a tendency to underproduce and underconsume social or public goods such as public education, public transportation, etc.   Similarly, there would be a tendency to underinvest in education where the social benefits exceed the private benefits and to overproduce some goods such as cars where the social costs exceed the private costs because of the pollution they create.

(*c*)   The government seeks to overcome the distortions resulting from market imperfections through a system of taxes and controls.   For example, controls and taxes are imposed on monopolists in an attempt to overcome the artificial restrictions that they would otherwise place on production in their effort to maximize total profits.   Governments use most of their tax revenues to provide adequate social or public goods such as education, transportation, law and order, defense, etc.   Similarly, they subsidize private education and basic research and tax and control polluters in an effort to reconcile social and private benefits and costs.

(*d*)   In the name of fairness and equity, the government redistributes income from the rich to the poor (through a system of progressive taxation and subsidies) in order to reduce the income inequality that results from the operation of the market mechanism.   However, since it is impossible to make interpersonal comparisons of utility, governments do not generally know how far this redistribution should be pursued in order to maximize social welfare.   Indeed, it is impossible even to know objectively whether social welfare increases or not once the point is reached whereby in order to make someone better off we must make someone else worse off.

6.   (*a*)   Nations engage in international trade because of the gains that they receive from trade.   That is, with trade each nation can specialize in production of the commodities of comparative advantage, trade part of these for the commodities of comparative disadvantage and end up consuming more of all commodities than without trade.   The gains occur because world output of all commodities increases as each nation specializes in the production of the commodities of its comparative advantage.   The major problem emanating from international trade is the burden placed on individual nations by the necessity to adjust balance-of-payments disequilibria.

(*b*)   A deficit in a nation's balance of payments means that at a given rate of exchange, there is a shortage or an excess of quantity demanded over quantity supplied of the foreign currency. If the exchange rate is freely flexible or floating, the rate of exchange will automatically rise until the quantity demanded of the foreign currency exactly equals the quantity supplied and the deficit is completely eliminated.   This rise in the exchange rate means that the relative value of the domestic currency is falling or depreciating.   The exact opposite occurs with a surplus and the nation's currency appreciates or increases in relative value.   Under the present international economic system, exchange rates are not freely flexible or completely floating because national monetary authorities intervene in foreign exchange markets to prevent erratic and unwanted fluctuations in exchange rates.   As a result, deficits and surpluses are not completely and automatically eliminated.

(*c*)   The major international economic problems facing the world today are: (1) Worldwide inflation and the possibility of recession.   (2) Huge balance-of-payments deficits in most petroleum-importing nations and the related problem of *recycling* hundreds of billions of petrodollars.   These problems were created by the more than quadrupling of petroleum prices since the fall of 1973 by OPEC (Organization of Petroleum Exporting Countries).   (3) An inadequate international monetary system, which needs to be reformed.   In lieu of this, present arrangements should be formalized and acceptable rules devised for intervention in foreign exchange markets.   (4) The reduced effectiveness of national economic policies resulting from the huge amount of foreign-held dollars and the growing number and size of multinational corporations.   International policies are needed to deal with these corporations, which operate outside the jurisdiction of any given nation.   (5) Lagging economic development in the world's poor nations.

Index

The letter *p* following a page number refers to a Problem.